Raspberry Pi®

FOR

DUMMIES®

A Wiley Brand

2nd Edition

Raspberry Pi® FOR DUMMIES®

A Wiley Brand

2nd Edition

by Sean McManus and Mike Cook

Raspberry Pi® For Dummies; 2nd Edition

Published by: **John Wiley & Sons, Inc.,** 111 River Street, Hoboken, NJ 07030-5774, www.wiley.com

Copyright © 2015 by John Wiley & Sons, Inc., Hoboken, New Jersey

Published simultaneously in Canada

For general information on our other products and services, please contact our Customer Care Department within the U.S. at 877-762-2974, outside the U.S. at 317-572-3993, or fax 317-572-4002. For technical support, please visit www.wiley.com/techsupport.

Wiley publishes in a variety of print and electronic formats and by print-on-demand. Some material included with standard print versions of this book may not be included in e-books or in print-on-demand. If this book refers to media such as a CD or DVD that is not included in the version you purchased, you may download this material at http://booksupport.wiley.com. For more information about Wiley products, visit www.wiley.com.

Library of Congress Control Number is available from the publisher.

ISBN 978-1-118-90491-6 (pbk); ISBN 978-1-118-90500-5 (ebk); ISBN 978-1-118-90501-2 (ebk)

Manufactured in the United States of America

10 9 8 7 6 5 4 3 2 1

Contents at a Glance

Table of Contents

Part V: Exploring Electronics with the Raspberry Pi..... 269

Introduction

*I*n recent years, computer education has focused largely on office skills, and not on understanding how computers work, or how you can use them to create new programs and inventions. The Raspberry Pi redresses the balance. It can be used for games, music, photo editing, and word processing, like any computer. But it can do so much more, providing a gateway into programming, electronics, and the mysterious world of Linux, the technically powerful (and free) rival to Windows and Mac OS.

Although the Raspberry Pi presents new opportunities to everyone, it can also be a daunting prospect. It comes as a bare circuit board, so to do anything with it, you'll need to add an operating system on an SD or microSD card and connect it up to a screen, mouse, and keyboard. To get started, you need to learn a few basics of Linux, or at least get acquainted with LXDE, the graphical desktop. You might be a geek who relishes learning new technologies, or you might be someone who wants a new family computer to use with the children. In either case, *Raspberry Pi For Dummies,* 2nd Edition, helps you to get started with your Raspberry Pi and teaches you about some of the many fun and inspiring things you can do with it.

About This Book

Raspberry Pi For Dummies, 2nd Edition, provides a concise and clear introduction to the terminology, technology, and techniques that you need to get the most from your Pi. With the book as your guide, you'll learn how to

- ✔ Connect your Raspberry Pi.
- ✔ Change its settings so it works optimally for you.
- ✔ Discover and install great free software you can use on your Raspberry Pi.
- ✔ Use the desktop environment to run programs, manage your files, surf the web, and view your photos.
- ✔ Use the Linux command line to manage your Raspberry Pi and its files.
- ✔ Use the Raspberry Pi as a productivity tool.
- ✔ Edit photos.
- ✔ Play music and video.
- ✔ Create animations and arcade games with the child-friendly Scratch programming language.

- ✔ Write your own games and other programs using the Python programming language.
- ✔ Compose music by programming with Sonic Pi.
- ✔ Get started with electronics, from an introduction to soldering, to the design and creation of sophisticated electronic games, controlled by the Raspberry Pi.

Incidentally, within this book, you may note that some web addresses break across two lines of text. If you're reading this book in print and want to visit one of these web pages, simply key in the web address exactly as it's noted in the text, pretending as though the line break doesn't exist. If you're reading this as an e-book, you've got it easy — just click or tap the web address to be taken directly to the web page.

Why You Need This Book

After you shake the Raspberry Pi out of the little electrostatic bag it comes in, what next?

This book answers that question. It enables you to get your Raspberry Pi up and running and also introduces you to some of the great things you can do with it, through satisfying practical projects. With this book as your companion, you can write games and other programs and create your own electronic gadgets, all without any prior programming knowledge.

The Raspberry Pi is most likely a bit different compared to other computers you've used, so this book also helps you to do some of the things on your Pi that you expect of every computer, such as playing music and editing documents.

You can learn a lot of this through trial and error, of course, but that can be a frustrating way to spend your time. Using this book as a reference, you can more quickly start using your Raspberry Pi, whatever you plan to do with it.

Foolish Assumptions

Raspberry Pi For Dummies, 2nd Edition, is written for beginners, by which we mean people who have never used a similar computer before. However, we do have to make a few assumptions in writing this book because we wouldn't have enough space for all the cool projects if we had to start by explaining what a mouse is! Here are our assumptions:

- ✔ You are familiar with other computers, such as Windows or Apple computers. In particular, we assume that you're familiar with using windows, icons, and the keyboard and mouse, and that you know the basics of using your computer for things like the Internet, writing letters, or copying files.

✔ The Raspberry Pi is not your only computer. At times, you'll need to have access to another computer — for example, to create your SD or microSD card for the Pi (see Chapter 2). When it comes to networking, we assume you already have a router set up with an Internet connection and a spare port that you can plug the Raspberry Pi into.

✔ The Raspberry Pi is your first Linux-based computer. If you're a Linux ninja, this book still gives you a solid reference on the Raspberry Pi and the version of Linux it uses, but no prior Linux knowledge is required.

✔ You share our excitement at the world of possibilities that the Raspberry Pi can open up to you!

Other than those assumptions, we hope this book is approachable for everyone. The Raspberry Pi is being adopted in classrooms and youth groups, and this book is a useful resource for teachers and students. The Raspberry Pi is also finding its way into many homes, where people of all ages (from children to adult) are using it for education and entertainment.

Icons Used in This Book

If you've read other *For Dummies* books, you know that they use icons in the margin to call attention to particularly important or useful ideas in the text. In this book, we use four such icons:

The Tip icon highlights expert shortcuts or simple ideas that can make life easier for you.

Arguably, the whole book is technical stuff, but this icon highlights something that's particularly technical. We've tried to avoid unnecessary jargon and complexity, but some background information can give you a better understanding of what you're doing, and sometimes we do need to get quite techy, given the sophistication of the projects you're doing. Sections highlighted with this icon might be worth rereading to make sure you understand, or you might decide that you don't need to know that much detail. It's up to you!

Although we'd like to think that reading this book is an unforgettable experience, we've highlighted some points that you might want to particularly commit to memory. They're either important take-aways, or they are fundamental to the project you're working on.

As you would on the road, slow down when you see a warning sign. It highlights an area where things could go wrong.

Beyond the Book

- ✔ **Cheat Sheet:** This book's Cheat Sheet can be found online at www. dummies.com/cheatsheet/raspberrypi. See the Cheat Sheet for tips on installing software and using Scratch.

- ✔ **Dummies.com online articles:** Companion articles to this book's content can be found online at www.dummies.com/extras/raspberrypi. The topics range from handy Linux commands to programming languages available on the Raspberry Pi.

- ✔ **Updates:** If this book has any updates after printing, they will be posted to www.dummies.com/extras/raspberrypi.

- ✔ **Downloadable code and bonus chapter:** Also at www.dummies.com/ extras/raspberrypi, you can download the code listings that appear throughout this book, as well as a bonus chapter on Mathematica, a mathematical program.

Both of us maintain our own personal websites too, which contain some additional information on the Raspberry Pi. Mike's is at www.thebox.myzen.co.uk and Sean's is at www.sean.co.uk.

Where to Go from Here

It's up to you how you read this book. It's been organized to take you on a journey from acquiring and setting up your Raspberry Pi, through learning the software that comes with it, to writing your own programs, and finally creating your own electronics projects. Some chapters build on knowledge gained in earlier chapters, especially the sections on Scratch, Python, and all of Part V.

We understand, though, that some projects or topics might interest you more than others, and you might need help in some areas right now. When a chapter assumes knowledge from elsewhere, we include cross-references to help you quickly find what you might have missed. We also include some signposts to future chapters too, so you can skip ahead to a later chapter if it provides the quickest answer for you.

If you haven't set up your Pi yet, start with Part I. If you have your Pi up and running, Part II shows you how to use the software on it. Part III covers productivity, creativity, and entertainment software. To flex your programming muscles, perhaps for the first time, read Part IV. You can learn Scratch, Python, or Sonic Pi here, and feel free to start with any one of those languages. The Python chapters provide a good foundation for Part V, where you can start building your own electronics projects.

Part I

Getting Started with the Raspberry Pi

In this part . . .

- Get to know the Raspberry Pi, and what other equipment you will need to be able to use it.

- Download the Linux operating system and flash it to an SD card.

- Connect your Raspberry Pi to the power, USB hub, keyboard, mouse, and screen.

- Use Raspi-config to change the settings on your Raspberry Pi.

Chapter 1

Introducing the Raspberry Pi

The Raspberry Pi is perhaps the most inspiring computer available today. Although most of the computing devices we use (including phones, tablets, and games consoles) are designed to stop us from tinkering with them, the Raspberry Pi is exactly the opposite. From the moment you see its shiny green circuit board, it invites you to prod it, play with it, and create with it. It comes with the tools you need to start making your own software (or *programming*), and you can connect your own electronic inventions to it. It's cheap enough that if you break it, it's not going to break the bank, so you can experiment with confidence.

Lots of people are fired up about its potential, and they're discovering exciting new ways to use it together. Dave Akerman (www.daveakerman.com) and friends attached one to a weather balloon and sent it nearly 40 kilometers above the earth to take pictures of earth from near space using a webcam.

Professor Simon Cox and his team at the University of Southampton connected 64 Raspberry Pi boards to build an experimental supercomputer, held together with Lego bricks. In the supercomputer (see Figure 1-1), the Raspberry Pis work together to solve a single problem. The project has been able to cut the cost of a supercomputer from millions of dollars to thousands or even hundreds of dollars, making supercomputing much more accessible to schools and students.

The Pi is also being used to make synthesizers, robots, gaming devices, audiobook players, home automation controls, and much more, as you discover in Chapter 20.

Figure 1-1:
Two of the
Raspberry Pi
boards
used in the
University
of South-
ampton's
supercom-
puter, with
the rest of
the super-
computer
in the
background.

Courtesy of Simon Cox and Glenn Harris, University of Southampton

Although those projects are grabbing headlines, another story is less visible but more important: the thousands of people of all ages who are taking their first steps in computer science thanks to the Raspberry Pi.

Both of the authors of this book used computers in the 1980s, when the notion of a home computer first became a reality. Back then, computers were less friendly than they are today. When you switched them on, you were faced with a flashing cursor and had to type something in to get it to do any-thing. As a result, though, a whole generation grew up knowing at least a little bit about how to give the computer commands, and how to create programs for it. As computers became friendlier, and we started to use mice and win-dows, we didn't need those skills any more, and we lost touch with them.

Eben Upton, designer of the Raspberry Pi, noticed the slide in skill levels when he was working at Cambridge University's Computer Laboratory in 2006. Students applying to study computer science started to have less expe-rience with programming than students of the past did. Upton and his univer-sity colleagues hatched the idea of creating a computer that would come with all the tools needed to program it, and would sell for a target price of $25 (£15). It had to be able to do other interesting things too so that people were drawn to use it, and had to be robust enough to survive being pushed in and out of school bags hundreds of times.

That idea started a six-year journey that led to the Raspberry Pi you probably have on your desk you as you read this book. It was released in February 2012, and sold half a million units by the end of the quarter. By the time the Model B+ launched in July 2014, there were about three million Raspberry Pis in homes, schools, and workplaces.

Getting Familiar with the Raspberry Pi

When your Raspberry Pi arrives, you'll see it's a circuit board, about the size of a credit card, with components and sockets stuck on it, as shown in Figure 1-2. In an age when most computing devices are sleek and shiny boxes, the spiky Pi, with tiny codes printed in white all over it, seems alien. It's a big part of its appeal, though: Most of the cases you can buy for the Raspberry Pi are transparent because people love the look of it.

Figure 1-2:
Up close
with the
Raspberry Pi.

There are several different versions of the Raspberry Pi:

  ✔ **Model B with 256MB memory:** Although it's called Model B, this was the first Raspberry Pi to be released, in February 2012. The Raspberry Pi Model B features an Ethernet connection for the Internet and two

USB ports. This 256MB version is no longer in production. It's called the Model B, incidentally, as a tribute to the BBC Microcomputer that was popular in the UK in the 1980s. It's sobering to think that the BBC Micro cost about ten times the price of a Raspberry Pi, which, thanks to 30 years of progress in computer science, has more than 8,000 times more memory.

✔ **Model B with 512MB memory:** Released from October 2012, the Raspberry Pi Model B had twice the memory capacity. This improved the speed of some software, especially applications that used images heavily. Although the Model B has been superseded by the Model B+, the Raspberry Pi Foundation has said it will keep the Model B in production for as long as there is demand for it.

✔ **Model A:** The Model A, released in February 2013, is a stripped-down version of the Model B. It has just one USB port and doesn't have an Ethernet port for connecting to the Internet. It has 256MB of memory. Because it requires about a third of the power of the Model B, the Model A is ideal for robots and projects in remote locations, where a wired electricity supply isn't viable and batteries must be used instead.

✔ **Model B+:** The Model B+, released in July 2014, has been described by the Raspberry Pi Foundation as "the final evolution of the original Raspberry Pi." It runs all the same software as the previous versions of the Raspberry Pi, but it has four USB ports, more GPIO pins for connecting electronics projects to the Pi, and lower power consumption and better audio than the Model B. In common with the Model B, it has 512MB of memory. Although all previous versions use SD cards for data storage, the Model B+ uses the smaller MicroSD cards.

✔ **Compute Module:** You'll see it in the online stores alongside the Raspberry Pi, but the Raspberry Pi Compute Module is something quite different. It's aimed at engineers creating industrial applications (known as *embedded systems*) or products based on Raspberry Pi technology. At the time of writing, products in development based on it include a media center and a handheld camera. We only mention it here in case you wonder what it is: It's not covered further in this book, and it's almost certainly not what you want to buy for your first Raspberry Pi.

So, which version should you get? Our advice would be to get the Model B+ unless you have a specific application in mind that requires low power, in which case get a Model A. There's one caveat: If you want to use add-on components that connect to your Raspberry Pi, beware of compatibility problems. Because there are more GPIO pins on the Model B+, add-ons designed for the Model A or Model B might not fit the Model B+, and vice versa.

The Raspberry Pi was made possible in part by the advances in mobile computer chips that have happened in recent years. At its heart is a Broadcom BCM2835 chip that contains an ARM central processing unit (CPU) and a

Videocore IV graphics processing unit (GPU). The CPU and GPU share the memory between them. The GPU is powerful enough to be able to handle Blu-ray quality video playback.

Instead of running Windows or Mac OS, the Raspberry Pi uses an operating system called Linux. It's a leading example of open source, a completely different philosophy to the commercial software industry. Instead of being created within the heavily guarded walls of a company, with its design treated as a trade secret, Linux is built by companies and expert volunteers working together. Anyone is free to inspect and modify the source code (a bit like the recipe) that makes it work. You don't have to pay to use Linux, and you're allowed to share it with other people too.

You probably won't be able to run the software you have on your other computers on your Raspberry Pi. It won't run Windows or Mac software, and not all Linux software works on the Raspberry Pi. But a lot of Linux software that is compatible with the Raspberry Pi is available and is free of charge.

Figuring Out What You Can Do with a Raspberry Pi

The Raspberry Pi is a fully featured computer, and you can do almost anything with it that you can do with a desktop computer.

When you switch it on, it has a text prompt (see Chapter 5), but you can use a graphical windows desktop to start and manage programs. You can use it for browsing the Internet (see Chapter 4), word processing and spreadsheets (see Chapter 6), or for editing photos (see Chapter 7). You can use it for playing back music or video (see Chapter 8), or for playing games. You can use the built-in software to write your own music, too (see Chapter 14). It's the perfect tool for homework, but it's also a useful computer for writing letters, managing your accounts, and paying bills online.

The Raspberry Pi is at its best, however, when it's being used to learn how computers work, and how you can create your own programs or electronics projects using them. It comes with Scratch (see Chapter 9), which enables people of all ages to create their own animations and games, while learning some of the core concepts of computer programming along the way.

It also comes with Python (see Chapter 11), a professional programming language used by YouTube, Google, and Industrial Light & Magic (the special effects gurus for the *Star Wars* films), among many others.

It has a General Purpose Input/Output (GPIO) port on it that you can use to connect up your own circuits to the Raspberry Pi, so you can use your Raspberry Pi to control other devices and to receive and interpret signals from them. In Part V, we show you how to build some electronic games controlled by the Raspberry Pi.

Determining Its Limitations

For something that costs so little, the Raspberry Pi is amazingly powerful, but it does have some limitations. Although you probably use it as a desktop computer, its power is closer to a mobile device (like a tablet) than a modern desktop PC.

By way of example, the Raspberry Pi Foundation says the Pi's overall performance is comparable with a PC using a 300 MHz Pentium 2 processor, which you might have bought in the mid to late nineties, except that the Raspberry Pi has much better graphics. The memory of the Raspberry Pi is more limited than you're probably used to, with just 512MB or 256MB available. You can't expand that with extra memory in the way you can a desktop PC.

The graphics capabilities lag behind today's market somewhat too: The Raspberry Pi Foundation says the Pi's graphics are roughly the same as the original Xbox games console, which was released ten years ago.

Both the Pentium 2 PC and the original Xbox were fine machines, of course, for their time. They're just not as snappy as we're used to, and that's where you might experience some problems. You might find that the Pi can't keep up with the demands of some modern software and that some programs don't run fast enough to be useful on it. However, it's easy to find programs, try them, and remove them if they're no good (see Chapter 5), and plenty of programs for work and play run well on the Raspberry Pi (see Chapter 19).

If you already have another computer, the Raspberry Pi is unlikely to usurp it as your main machine. But the Pi gives you the freedom to try lots of things you probably wouldn't dare to try, or wouldn't know how to try, with your main PC.

Getting Your Hands on a Raspberry Pi

The Raspberry Pi was created by the Raspberry Pi Foundation, a charity registered in the UK. The charity's six trustees funded the manufacture of the first large batch themselves, but it sold out rapidly so it quickly became clear that they needed something that would scale better.

The Foundation now licenses the design of the Raspberry Pi to RS Components (www.rs-components.com), Allied Electronics (www.alliedelec.com), and Premier Farnell, which uses the brand name Element 14 (www.element14.com/community/groups/raspberry-pi). In China, you can buy a red-colored Raspberry Pi from Egoman (http://mall.egoman.com.cn). These companies fund and manage the manufacture of the Raspberry Pi, market and sell it, and look after their customers. They accept orders through their websites and are able to offer a number of the accessories you might also need. Some other electrical retailers also stock the Pi now, typically as part of a bundle with a keyboard, mouse, and other accessories. The official Raspberry Pi Swag Store (http://swag.raspberrypi.org/) also sells some Raspberry Pi boards and accessories.

It's possible that more companies will license the design of the Pi in the future, so check the Raspberry Pi Foundation's website at www.raspberrypi.org for current links to stores that sell the Pi.

Secondhand Raspberry Pis can be bought on eBay (www.ebay.com), but we would recommend getting a new one so you benefit from the customer support available, and have the peace of mind that it hasn't been damaged by the previous owner.

Deciding What Else You Need

The creators of Raspberry Pi have stripped costs to the bone to enable you to own a fully featured computer for about $35, so you'll need to scavenge or buy a few other bits and pieces. We say "scavenge" because the things you need are exactly the kind of things many people have lying around their house or garage already, or can easily pick up from friends or neighbors. In particular, if you're using a Raspberry Pi as your second computer, you probably have most of the peripherals you need. That said, you might find they're not fully compatible with the Raspberry Pi and you need to buy replacements to use with the Pi.

Here's a checklist of what else you might need:

✔ **Monitor:** The Raspberry Pi has a high definition video feed and uses an HDMI (high definition multimedia interface) connection for it. If your monitor has an HDMI socket, you can connect the Raspberry Pi directly to it. If your monitor does not support HDMI, it probably has a DVI socket, and you can get a simple and cheap converter that enables you to connect an HDMI cable to it. Older VGA (video graphics array) monitors require a device to convert the HDMI signal into a VGA one. If you're thinking of buying a converter, check online to see whether it works with the Raspberry Pi first. A lot of cheap cables are just cables, when what you need is a device that converts the signal from HDMI format to VGA, not one that just fits into the sockets on the screen and your Raspberry Pi. These converters can be quite expensive, so Gert van Loo has designed a device that uses the Raspberry Pi's GPIO pins to connect to a VGA monitor. He's published the design specs so anyone can build one, and sell it if she wants to too. Take a look at eBay if you need one and you might well find what you need. For more information see www. raspberrypi.org/gert-vga-adapter. (If your monitor is connected using a blue plug, and the connector has three rows of five pins in it, it's probably a VGA monitor.)

✔ **TV:** You can connect your Raspberry Pi to a high definition TV using the HDMI socket and should experience a crisp picture. If you have an old television in the garage, you can also press it into service for your Raspberry Pi. The Pi can send a composite video signal through an RCA cable, so it can use a TV as its display. When we tried this, it worked but the text lacked definition, which made it difficult to read. If a TV is your only option, see Appendix A for advice on tweaking the settings to get the clearest possible picture. It's better to use a computer monitor if you can, though. You'll need to get the a cable with the right connector to fit your Pi: The Model A and Model B have a dedicated RCA video socket, but the Model B+ uses the headphone socket for its video output too.

✔ **USB hub:** The Raspberry Pi has one, two, or four USB sockets (depending on the model you get). It's a good idea to consider using a powered USB hub for two reasons. Firstly, and especially if you have a Model A or B, you're going to want to connect other devices to your Pi at the same time as your keyboard and mouse, which use two sockets. And secondly, a USB hub provides external power to your devices and minimizes the likelihood of experiencing problems using your Raspberry Pi, especially if connecting relatively power-intensive devices such as hard drives. Make sure your USB hub has its own power source independent of the Raspberry Pi.

✔ **USB keyboard and mouse:** The Raspberry Pi only supports USB keyboards and mice, so if you're still using ones with PS/2 connectors (round rather than flat), you need to replace them.

When the Raspberry Pi behaves unpredictably it's often because the keyboard is drawing too much power, so avoid keyboards with too many flashing lights and features.

✔ **MicroSD card or SD card:** The Raspberry Pi doesn't have a hard drive built in to it, so it uses a MicroSD card (Model B+) or SD card (Model A and B) as its main storage. You probably have some SD cards that you use for your digital camera, although you might need to get a higher capacity one. We would recommend an 8GB card as a minimum, but you can use a 4GB card if you use NOOBS Lite (see Chapter 2) or XMBC (see Chapter 8). Even that isn't much space compared to the hard drive on a modern computer, but you can use other storage devices such as external hard drives with your Raspberry Pi too. SD and MicroSD cards have different class numbers that indicate how fast you can copy information to and from them. The Raspberry Pi Foundation recommends using a class 4 card. The easiest way to get started with the Raspberry Pi is to buy a card with the NOOBS software already on it. The official Raspberry Pi Swag Store (`http://swag.raspberrypi.org/`), Element14, and RS Components all sell an 8GB MicroSD card that has the NOOBS software preloaded on it (see Chapter 2). It comes with an SD card adapter, shown in Figure 1-3, so the card fits the Model A and B (with the adapter) and B+ (without it).

Figure 1-3:
A NOOBS card. The MicroSD card fits into the SD card adapter. The MicroSD card works on the B+, and inside the adapter it also fits the Model A and Model B.

✏ **SD or MicroSD card writer for your PC:** Many PCs today have a slot for SD or MicroSD cards so you can easily copy photos from your camera to your computer. If yours doesn't, you might want to consider getting an SD or MicroSD card writer to connect to your computer. You can use it to copy software to an SD card for use with your Raspberry Pi, but you won't be able to use it to copy files from your Raspberry Pi to a Windows computer. Alternatively, as we said previously, you can buy a MicroSD card with an SD adapter that has the Raspberry Pi software already on it.

✏ **USB keys:** *USB keys* (also known as *flash drives* or *memory sticks*) are fairly cheap and high capacity now (a 64GB USB key is readily affordable), which makes them an ideal complement to your Raspberry Pi. You can transfer files between your PC and your Raspberry Pi using a USB key, too.

- **USB Wi-Fi adapter:** The Model A doesn't have an Ethernet socket, so if you want to connect it to the Internet you'll need a USB Wi-Fi adapter. You might already have one of these from a laptop. Some are incompatible with the Raspberry Pi, but companies that sell the Pi usually sell a compatible Wi-Fi adapter too.

- **External hard drive:** If you want lots of storage, perhaps so you can use your music or video collection with the Raspberry Pi, you can connect an external hard drive to it over USB. You'll need to connect your hard drive through a powered USB hub, or use a hard drive that has its own external power source.

- **Raspberry Pi Camera Module:** The Raspberry Pi has stimulated entrepreneurs to create all kinds of add-ons for it, but this is a product that originated at the Raspberry Pi Foundation. This five-megapixel fixed-focus camera can be used to shoot HD video and take still photos.

- **Speakers:** The Raspberry Pi has a standard audio out socket, compatible with headphones and PC speakers that use a 3.5mm audio jack. You can plug your headphones directly into it, or use the audio jack to connect to speakers, a stereo, or a TV. If you're using a TV or stereo for sound, you can get a cable that goes between the 3.5mm audio jack and the audio input(s) on your television or stereo. You won't always need speakers: If you're using an HDMI connection, the audio is sent to the screen with the video signal so you won't need separate speakers, but note that this doesn't work if you use a DVI monitor.

- **Power supply:** The Raspberry Pi uses a Micro USB connector for its power supply, and is theoretically compatible with a lot of mobile phone and tablet chargers. In practice, many of these can't deliver enough current (up to 700 milliamperes), which can make the Raspberry Pi perform unreliably. The resistance in the cables that connect the Pi to the power supply varies greatly too, and this can prevent peripherals like the mouse from working. It's worth checking whether you have a charger that might do the job (it should say how much current it provides on it), but for best results, we recommend buying a compatible charger from the same company you got your Raspberry Pi from. Don't try to power the Pi by connecting its Micro USB port to the USB port on your PC with a cable, because your computer probably can't provide enough power for your Pi. The Raspberry Pi Foundation advises that you should only use batteries to power your Raspberry Pi if you know what you're doing because there's a risk of damaging your Raspberry Pi.

- **Case:** It's safe to operate your Raspberry Pi as-is, but many people prefer to protect it from spills and precariously stacked desk clutter by getting a case for it. You can buy plastic cases on eBay (www.ebay.com), most of which are transparent so you can still admire the circuitry and see the Pi's LED lights. These cases typically come as simple kits for you to assemble. The Pibow (www.pibow.com) is one of the most attractively designed cases, assembled from layers of colored plastic (see Figure 1-4). It's designed by Paul Beech, who designed the Raspberry Pi logo. You don't have to buy a case, though. You can go without or make your own using cardboard or Lego bricks. Whatever case you go with, make sure you can still access the GPIO pins so you can experiment with connecting your Pi to electronic circuits and try the projects in Part V of this book.

Figure 1-4:
The Pibow
Coupe case
for the
Model B+.

✔ **Cables:** You'll need cables to connect it all up, too. In particular, you need an HDMI cable (if you're using an HDMI or DVI monitor), an HDMI to DVI adapter (if you're using a DVI monitor), an RCA cable (if you're connecting to an older television), an audio cable (if connecting the audio jack to your TV or stereo), and an Ethernet cable (for networking on the Model B or B+). You can get these cables from an electrical components retailer and might be able to buy them at the same time as you buy your Raspberry Pi. Any other cables you need (for example, to connect to PC speakers or a USB hub) should come with those devices.

The Raspberry Pi has been designed to be used with whatever accessories you having lying around to minimize the cost of getting started with it but, in practice, not all devices are compatible. In particular, incompatible USB hubs, keyboards, and mice can cause problems that are hard to diagnose. USB hubs that feed power back into your Raspberry Pi through the Pi's USB port (known as *backpowering*) could potentially cause damage to the Raspberry Pi if they feed in too much power.

A list of compatible and incompatible devices is maintained at `http://elinux.org/RPi_VerifiedPeripherals` and you can check online reviews to see whether others have experienced difficulties using a particular device with the Raspberry Pi.

If you're buying new devices, you can minimize the risk by buying recommended devices from Raspberry Pi retailers.

In any case, you should set a little bit of money aside to spend on accessories. The Raspberry Pi is a cheap device, but buying a keyboard, mouse, USB hub, and cables can easily double or triple your costs, and you might have to resort to that if what you have on hand turns out not to be compatible.

Chapter 2

Downloading the Operating System

*B*efore you can do anything with your Raspberry Pi, you need to provide it with an operating system. The operating system software enables you to use the computer's basic functions and looks after activities such as managing files and running applications, like word processors or web browsers. Those applications use the operating system as an intermediary to talk to the hardware and they won't work without it. This concept isn't unique to the Raspberry Pi. On your laptop, the operating system might be Microsoft Windows or Mac OS. On an iPad or iPhone, it's iOS.

In this chapter, we introduce you to Linux, the operating system most frequently used on the Raspberry Pi, and we show you how to create an SD or MicroSD card with an operating system on it. You'll need to use another computer to set up the SD or MicroSD card. It doesn't matter whether you use a Windows, Mac OS, or Linux machine, but you need to have the ability to write to SD or MicroSD cards using it and a connection to the Internet.

Introducing Linux

The operating system used on the Raspberry Pi is GNU/Linux, often called just Linux for short. The Raspberry Pi might be the first Linux computer you've used, but the operating system has a long and honorable history.

Richard Stallman created the GNU Project in 1984 with the goal of building an operating system that users were free to copy, study, and modify. Such software is known as *free software*, and although this software is often given away at no cost, the ideology is about free as in "free speech," rather than free as in "free beer." Thousands of people have joined the GNU Project, creating software packages that include tools, applications, and even games. Stallman aimed to make his operating system compatible with Unix, an operating system that was created by AT&T's Bell Labs and that started to gain popularity in the 1970s. That would make it easy for existing Unix users to switch to using the GNU Project.

In 1991, Linus Torvalds released the central component of Linux, the *kernel*, which acts as a conduit between the applications software and the hardware resources, including the memory and processor. He is still "the ultimate authority on what new code is incorporated in the standard Linux kernel," according to the Linux Foundation, the non-profit consortium that promotes Linux and supports its development. The Linux Foundation reports that 7,800 people from almost 800 different companies have contributed to the kernel since 2005.

GNU/Linux brings the Linux kernel together with the GNU components it needs to be a complete operating system, reflecting the work of thousands of people on both the GNU and Linux projects. That so many people could cooperate to build something as complex as an operating system, and then give it away for anyone to use, is a modern miracle.

Because it can be modified and distributed by anyone, lots of different versions of GNU/Linux exist. They're called *distributions* or *distros*, but not all of them are suitable for the Raspberry Pi. The recommended distribution of Linux for the Raspberry Pi is called Raspbian (see Chapter 3). Software created for one version of Linux usually works on another version, but Linux isn't designed to run Windows or Mac OS software.

Strictly speaking, Linux is just the kernel in the operating system, but as is commonly done, we refer to GNU/Linux as *Linux* in the rest of this book.

Creating a NOOBS Card

The easiest way to get started with the Raspberry Pi is to use the NOOBS software. NOOBS is short for *new-out-of-box software*, although it's also a pun on the term *noob* that is sometimes used to describe beginners in Linux. Don't underestimate the power of this software, though, especially if you're a more experienced user: NOOBS is easy to copy to your SD or MicroSD card, but provides you with a simple menu for installing a number of different operating systems, including different versions of Linux, RISC OS, and XBMC media center software. The options are described in more depth in Chapter 3.

As we say in Chapter 1, you can buy a card with NOOBS already on it, and that might be the quickest way to get started. If you've got one, you can skip ahead to Chapter 3, but maybe have a read-through of this chapter while you're waiting for the OS to install. It's useful to know how to create your own NOOBS cards: It means you can get started with a new card in about 20 minutes, rather than having to wait for the postman to deliver one to you.

You can also download a specific operating system from the Raspberry Pi website and install that on your SD or MicroSD card. In that case, the download is in a special format (an image file) that describes all the different files that need to be created on the SD or MicroSD card. To convert the image file into an SD or MicroSD card that will work on the Raspberry Pi, you need to *flash* the card, and can't just copy the file across. Follow the image installation guidelines on the Raspberry Pi website if you prefer to take this approach (www.raspberrypi.org/documentation/installation/installing-images/README.md).

Downloading NOOBS

In your web browser, visit www.raspberrypi.org/downloads/. There are two versions of NOOBS available. We recommend NOOBS Lite because it offers a wide range of operating systems and media center software (see Chapter 3). It requires a network connection on the Raspberry Pi, so it's not appropriate for the Model A.

The other version is the *offline and network install* version of NOOBS, which includes everything you need for the Raspbian Linux operating system in one file that you can copy to your SD card. It doesn't need an Internet connection on the Raspberry Pi, but it only offers Raspbian. You can follow our instructions here for installing NOOBS Lite and easily adapt them where necessary if you prefer to use the offline and network version of NOOBS.

Formatting your SD card

For best results, you need to format your SD or MicroSD card. You can use a program available from the SD Association called SDFormatter on Mac and Windows, and you can find it at www.sdcard.org/downloads/formatter_4/. At the time of writing, the link to download is in the menu on the left. You need to read and accept the license agreement before you can download.

If you're using Linux, you can use GParted to format your card, as we will show you.

Whichever computer you're using, you need to be extremely careful in doing this. When you format an SD or MicroSD card, its previous contents are completely erased, so make sure you've made copies of any files or photos you might need from the card before you begin. Make sure you have a backup of your hard drive and disconnect any removable disks before you start to minimize the potential damage from accidentally formatting the wrong disk.

Using Windows

The Windows SDFormatter software downloads as a Zip file, so double-click the file to open it, and then click setup.exe to run the SDFormatter installation program. Click Next to work through the steps. The program will suggest where it installs SDFormatter, but you can change this if you want to. Finally, click the Install button. You may receive an alert from Windows that tells you that a program is trying to make changes to your computer, and asks you if this is allowed.

If you are using Windows 8.1, move the mouse to the top-right corner and click the magnifying glass to open the search, type in **SDF**, and then click the program name when it appears. On older versions of Windows, run SDFormatter from the Start menu in the bottom left of the screen.

Figure 2-1 shows the SDFormatter software on Windows. Where it says Drive, select the drive that contains your SD or MicroSD card. If no drive is shown, try clicking Refresh. Check the drive here and double-check it as often as you need to because SDFormatter will erase everything on this drive. It's a sensible precaution to disconnect USB drives and any other removable storage devices to protect them from accidental deletion before you go any further.

Figure 2-1:
SDFormatter, used to format the SD or MicroSD card, on Windows.

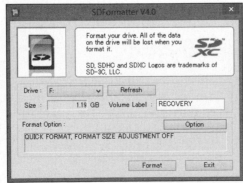

Click the Option button and set the format size adjustment option to ON, and then click the Format button. The Quick Format option is fast but not secure, so you'll receive a warning that data might still be recovered after it. (Don't count on being able to do so, though!) Click OK to start the formatting. On Sean's computer, this took less than a minute.

Using a Mac

The Mac version of SDFormatter downloads as an installation package. Double-click this package to install the software. Note you will need to enter your Mac's password to do this, and also every time you run this utility.

Insert your SD or MicroSD card into your Mac's slot, or into a card reader connected to your Mac and then double-click the SDFormatter icon. The software looks like Figure 2-2.

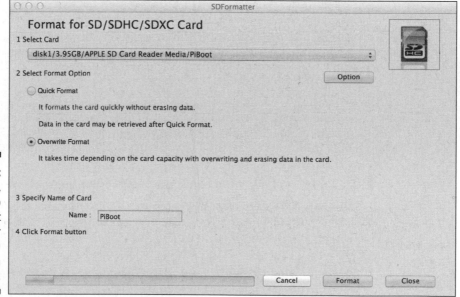

Figure 2-2: SDFormatter, used to format the SD or MicroSD card, on a Mac.

Make sure the Select Card drop-down shows the SD or MicroSD card you want to use. This is the drive that will be wiped, so check this as often as you need to for you to be certain. If the right card isn't shown, use the drop-down menu to choose the right one.

Next, click the Overwrite Format option to select it. Click the Format button and SDFormatter starts to format your card. Note that there is no need to enter anything into the Name box. That will be completed automatically.

This is a great time to have a cup of tea because the card is going to take about half an hour to format. You can still use your Mac while this is running, although it might take a bit longer to format if you do. When the formatter is finished, you will see the icon of the SD or MicroSD card on the desktop.

Using Linux

Our recommended approach for flashing an SD card using a Linux-based computer does not require any additional software. We're using Ubuntu, the most popular desktop distribution, so you might see some variations if you prefer a different distribution. These steps should give you the guidance you need in any case.

Because this process involves completely erasing a disk (your SD card), make sure you have a recent backup of your computer before you proceed, just in case you accidentally wipe the wrong disk.

Follow these steps:

1. **You use a utility called GParted to set up the SD card on Ubuntu. It needs to be run with root permissions, so start it by issuing a command from the terminal. Enter the following:**

```
sudo gparted
```

   You can open a terminal window through Dash Home in Ubuntu, or the applications menu in your distribution, or use a keyboard shortcut (Ctrl+Alt+T in Ubuntu). Figure 2-3 shows GParted running on the desktop.

2. **Click in the top right to choose the correct disk, your SD card.**

   Take particular care here. You can cause serious damage to your hard drive if you choose the wrong disk here. We know this is our SD card because it's showing a capacity of 7.4GB and our hard drive has a capacity of 500GB.

3. **The main window shows the partitions on your card. You want to delete them, so click them in turn and then click the delete icon on the toolbar.**

   The delete icon looks like a No Entry sign, or the international No symbol. This won't take effect yet: You queue up the actions you want to carry out and then trigger them all when you've finished. (If you can't set a partition to delete because it has a key icon beside it, right-click the partition and choose Unmount in the menu that appears.)

4. **Click the unallocated partition and click the Add Partition button.**

   It's on the toolbar and has a picture of a blank page with a plus sign on it.

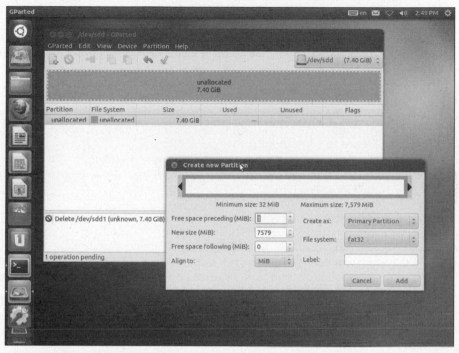

Figure 2-3:
GParted,
running on
the Ubuntu
desktop.

5. **The pop-up window, which you can see in the foreground in Figure 2-3, appears. Click the menu to change the file system to fat32. Click the Add button.**

Again, this doesn't take effect yet.

6. **Click the tick (or check mark) button on the toolbar to carry out the actions you've queued up, which remove the existing partitions and add a single new FAT32 partition.**

Copying NOOBS to your SD or MicroSD card

You should now have a formatted SD or MicroSD card, and the zip file for NOOBS that you downloaded from the Raspberry Pi website. To install NOOBS on your SD or MicroSD card, you simply copy the files inside the zip file to the card.

On a Windows PC, double-click the NOOBS zip file to open it, select all the files in it, and then copy them to your formatted SD card. You can do this by using Ctrl+A to select the files and Ctrl+C to copy them, navigating to your SD card, and then using Ctrl+V to paste them.

On a Mac, double-click the NOOBS zip file and you will see a folder containing all the files you need. From the Edit menu, choose Select All and drag all the files onto the SD card icon on your desktop. It will take about 15 minutes to copy everything across. When it's finished, eject the SD card by dragging it into the Trash can, which has now transformed into an eject icon.

On Linux, you can use the desktop environment (where available) to copy the NOOBS files to your SD card. In Ubuntu, you can simply go to the NOOBS zip file, double-click it to open it, select all the files in it, and drag them to your SD card to copy them across.

Alternatively, you can follow these steps to unzip and copy the files using the Linux command line:

1. **Remove and reinsert your card so it mounts automatically.**

2. **Open a terminal window.**

   You can do this through Dash Home in Ubuntu, or the applications menu in your distribution, or use a keyboard shortcut (Ctrl+Alt+T in Ubuntu).

3. **Enter** sudo fdisk -l, **where the last character is the letter 1.**

   This gives you a list of the disks available, as you can see in Figure 2-4.

Figure 2-4:
A list of the available disks.

4. **Study this list to find your SD or MicroSD card.**

   In Figure 2-4, the screen lists two disks, with the information about each one starting with the word *Disk*. The file size is usually a good indicator of which is your SD card. The first one (Disk /dev/sda) is 500.1GB, which is a large hard drive. The second one (Disk /dev/sdd) is just 7948MB. That's roughly 8GB, so that's your SD card. Take a note of the card's partition name, which in this case is sdd1.

5. **Find out where the card is mounted.**

   Use the `mount` command and search for the directory where your card has been mounted in the file system. In this case, the card's partition name is sdd1, so we enter the following:

   ```
   mount | grep -i sdd1
   ```

   Figure 2-4 shows the output from this, which tells us where the card is mounted. In this case, it's mounted on /media/65E8-9564.

6. **Use `cd` to go to the directory where your card is mounted.**

   ```
   cd /media/65E8-9564
   ```

7. **Unzip your NOOBS download onto your card.**

   This NOOBS download was stored in the folder /home/Ubuntu/ Downloads, so we can unzip it onto our SD card using this command:

   ```
   unzip /home/Ubuntu/Downloads/NOOBS_v1_3_9.zip
   ```

   You can usually type the first couple of characters of each part of the path and then tap the Tab key on the keyboard to have Linux complete it for you, so you don't have to remember the whole filename. It might take five minutes or so to unzip and copy the files across to your card.

Using Your NOOBS Card

Now you have a card with NOOBS on it, you're ready to set up your Raspberry Pi. In the next chapter, we show you how to connect your Raspberry Pi up, insert your SD or MicroSD card, and finish installing the operating system.

Chapter 3

Connecting Your Raspberry Pi

In This Chapter

▶ Inserting the SD or MicroSD card

▶ Connecting a monitor or TV, keyboard, and mouse

▶ Connecting to your router or Wi-Fi

▶ Connecting and testing the Raspberry Pi Camera Module

▶ Using Raspi-config to set up your Raspberry Pi

You might be a bit daunted to be faced with a bare circuit board, but it's easy to connect your Raspberry Pi and get it up and running. You might need to change some of its configuration (see Appendix A), but many people find that their Raspberry Pi works well the moment they connect it all together.

Before we start, make sure you have the Raspberry Pi the right way around, at least as far as these directions are concerned. The top of your Raspberry Pi is the side that has the Raspberry Pi logo printed on the circuit board. Arrange your Raspberry Pi so that the Raspberry Pi logo is the right way up as you look at it, and you should have the spiky GPIO pins in the top left.

Figure 3-1 shows the ports and sockets you will need to use to connect up your Model B Raspberry Pi. The Model A is the same as Figure 3-1 except that it has no Ethernet connection in the bottom right. Figure 3-2 shows the connection points on the Model B+ Raspberry Pi.

Chapter 1 lists everything you might need to use your Raspberry Pi, including the various cables.

Composite video   Audio   USB

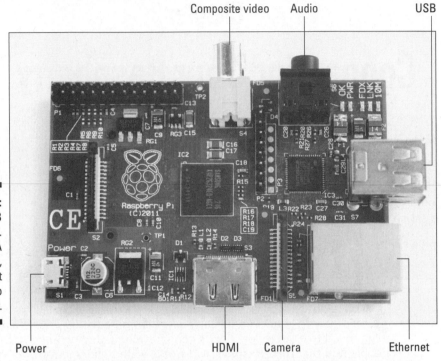

Figure 3-1:
The Model B
Raspberry Pi.
The Model A
is the same,
except that
it has no
Ethernet.

Power   HDMI   Camera   Ethernet

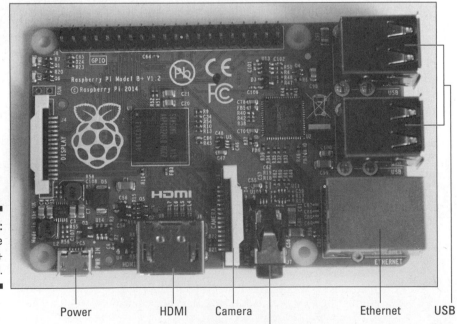

Figure 3-2:
The
Model B+
Raspberry Pi.

Power   HDMI   Camera   Ethernet   USB

Audio and composite video

Inserting the SD Card

The Raspberry Pi requires an SD or MicroSD card with the operating system on it to start up. If you don't have one, see Chapter 2 for advice on download-ing the operating system and copying it to an SD card.

To insert a MicroSD card in a Model B+, turn your Raspberry Pi over as shown in Figure 3-3, so you're looking at its underside. The metal MicroSD card socket is labeled and is at the opposite end of the board to the USB sockets. Slide your MicroSD card into the slot face up (with the notch on the right). It clicks into place, but the card overhangs the board slightly. To remove the card again, press it and the spring will push it back out toward you. You can then pull it out.

Figure 3-3:
The MicroSD card, lined up for inser-tion in a Model B+.

To insert an SD card in a Model A or Model B, flip your Raspberry Pi over (see Figure 3-4). On one of the short sides is a plastic fixture for your SD card. Slide the SD card in with the label side facing you and gently press the card home to make sure it's well connected. The fixture is not big enough to cover your SD card, so most of the card will stick out from the side of the board and will be visible when you turn your Pi back over again. You can remove the card by just pulling it out again.

To avoid data loss, you should only insert and remove SD and MicroSD cards with the power switched off.

Figure 3-4:
The
SD card,
correctly
aligned with
the socket
on the
underside of
the Model A.

Connecting the Raspberry Pi Camera Module

There are lots of accessories and add-ons available for the Raspberry Pi, but the Raspberry Pi Camera Module has the rare status of being an official product from the Raspberry Pi Foundation, so we show you how to connect it. The camera module is a small circuit board, with a strip of flex that plugs directly into the Raspberry Pi board (see Figure 3-5). It's easiest to connect the camera before you plug your Raspberry Pi into any cables.

On the board of your Raspberry Pi is a connector for the camera. You can see it labeled in Figure 3-1 and Figure 3-2. To open it, hold the ends between your finger and thumb and gently lift. The plastic parts don't separate, but they move apart to make a gap. This is where you will insert the camera's flex.

At the end of the camera's flex, there are silver connectors on one side. Hold the flex so that this side faces to the left, away from the side with the USB hub(s). Insert the flex into the connector on the board and press it gently home, and then press the socket back together again.

As you can see in Figure 3-5, the lens has a plastic film over it to protect it. Pull the green plastic tab to remove this.

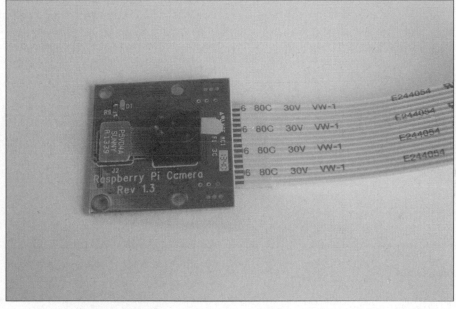

Figure 3-5:
The
Raspberry Pi
Camera
Module.

At the end of this chapter, we show you how you can check to make sure your camera is connected correctly and working.

Connecting a Monitor or TV

You can connect a display device to your Raspberry Pi in one of two ways, depending on the type of screen you have available. This means one of the Raspberry Pi's display sockets will always be unconnected.

There is also a display socket on the surface of the board that accepts a ribbon cable to connect a screen and the Raspberry Pi Foundation intends to enable a screen to connect here. Adafruit (www.adafruit.com) also sells a kit to make a 2.8" touchscreen that connects to your Raspberry Pi using the GPIO pins, and there is a device you can use to connect to a VGA monitor using the GPIO pins (see Chapter 1). We assume here that you are using a monitor or TV.

Connecting an HDMI or DVI display

On the top surface of your board, in the middle of the bottom edge (or slightly to the left of that on the Model B+) is the HDMI connector (see Figure 3-1 or Figure 3-2). Insert your HDMI cable into that, and then insert the other end into your monitor.

If you have a DVI display, rather than a HDMI display, you need to use an adapter on the screen end of the cable. The adapter itself is a simple plug, so you just plug the HDMI cable into the adapter, and then plug the adapter into your monitor and turn the silver screws on the adapter to hold the cable in place. Figure 3-6 shows the HDMI cable lined up for insertion into the DVI adapter.

Figure 3-6:
A photo showing how the HDMI cable is inserted into the DVI converter.

Connecting a television using composite video

If your television has a HDMI socket, use that for optimal results. Alternatively, you can use the composite video socket. On the Model A and B, it's a round yellow and silver socket on the top edge of the board (see Figure 3-1). On the Model B+, it's the same socket as the audio output on the bottom of the board. You'll need to use a special RCA cable for this socket and can't just connect an audio cable.

Connect your RCA cable to the socket, and the other end to the Video In socket on your television, which is likely to be silver and yellow.

TIP

You might need to use your TV's remote control to switch your television over to view the external signal coming from the Raspberry Pi. If you're using HDMI on your TV, you might need to turn the TV on so the Raspberry Pi can detect it when you switch it on.

Connecting a USB Hub

Your Raspberry Pi's USB socket(s) can be found on the right of the circuit board (see Figure 3-1 and Figure 3-2). Your USB hub should have a USB cable that connects snugly into one of these sockets.

It's important to use a USB hub that has its own power source, so plug your USB hub into a wall socket (mains electricity) using the power supply unit that came with it.

Figure 3-7 shows a USB hub that works with the Raspberry Pi. You plug the USB cable coming out of it into your Raspberry Pi's USB socket, and you can then plug your other devices (such as your keyboard and mouse) into the USB hub. There is a tiny round hole on the front of this USB hub where its power supply is connected. USB hubs come in lots of different shapes and sizes: This one has four sockets (two on each long side), but you can get many compatible hubs with seven sockets too.

Figure 3-7:
A USB hub that works with the Raspberry Pi.

Connecting a Keyboard and Mouse

Your keyboard and mouse can be connected directly to the USB socket(s) on your Raspberry Pi, and they should work fine on the Model B+. For earlier models, we recommend connecting the keyboard and mouse to an external-powered USB hub that is connected to the Pi. It reduces the risk of problems caused by the devices drawing too much power from the Pi.

Connecting Audio

If you're using a HDMI television, the sound is routed through the HDMI cable to the screen, so you don't need to connect a separate audio cable.

Otherwise, the audio socket of your Raspberry Pi is a small black or blue box stuck along the top edge of the board on the Model A and B (see Figure 3-1), and on the bottom edge of the board on the Model B+ (see Figure 3-2). If you have earphones or headphones from a portable music player, you can plug them directly into this socket.

Alternatively, you can plug a suitable cable into this socket to feed the audio into a television, stereo, or PC speakers for a more impressive sound. Figure 3-8 shows such a cable with the Pi's 3.5mm audio jack on the right of the picture, and the two stereo plugs that feed audio into many stereos shown on the right. The cable you need might be different, depending on the input sockets on your audio equipment.

Figure 3-8:
A cable for connect-ing your Raspberry Pi to your stereo.

If you're using PC speakers, note that they need to have their own power supply.

Connecting to Your Router

The Raspberry Pi Model A has no network connection on the board. The Model B and Model B+ have an Ethernet socket on the right edge of the board, indicated in Figures 3-1 and 3-2. Use this socket to connect your Raspberry Pi to your Internet router with a standard Ethernet cable.

The Raspberry Pi automatically connects to the Internet when used with a router that supports the Dynamic Host Configuration Protocol (DHCP), which means it works with most domestic routers. For advice on troubleshooting your Internet connection, see Appendix A.

Connecting the Power and Turning on the Raspberry Pi

The last thing you should do is connect the power. The Micro USB power socket can be found in the bottom-left corner of the board (indicated in Figure 3-1 and Figure 3-2).

The Raspberry Pi Foundation warns against using battery power unless you know what you're doing because it's easy to damage your Pi unless you provide a steady 5v of power. Some cellphone emergency battery chargers can be used to provide that steady power, but you should proceed with caution.

The Raspberry Pi has no on/off switch, so when you connect the power, it starts working. To turn it off again, you disconnect the power. To avoid losing data, you should issue a shutdown command first (see Chapter 5) and wait for it to finish. Sean plugs his USB hub and Raspberry Pi into power sockets on an extension lead, so he can switch them both on simultaneously by switching on the power to that extension lead. It's less clumsy than removing or inserting the plug in the wall socket or the power lead in the Raspberry Pi all the time. It can also help to prevent backpowering, where the USB hub feeds power back into the Raspberry Pi.

If you're using the Lite version of NOOBS, you need to plug a network cable into the Ethernet port on the Pi to download the operating systems you want to install.

When you switch on your Raspberry Pi, the screen shows a rainbow of color briefly, and then starts to run the NOOBS software on the SD or MicroSD card, shown in Figure 3-9. The software gives you a choice of operating systems to install. To select one, check the box beside it. The options in NOOBS Lite include

- **Raspbian:** The distribution that the Raspberry Pi Foundation recommends is called Raspbian. It's a version of a Linux distribution called Debian that has been optimized for the Raspberry Pi. It includes graphical desktop software (see Chapter 4), a web browser (see Chapter 4), and various development and programming tools. This is the quickest way to get up and running with your Raspberry Pi, and for most users, this is the one you'll want to use. For the rest of this book, except where noted otherwise, we assume you're using Raspbian. The offline and network version of NOOBS includes Raspbian only.

- **Arch:** The guiding principle in the design of this Linux distribution is that the user should be in full control of the software they install, so it only includes the bare essentials. It has no graphical desktop, for example, although you can choose to install one. This distribution is relatively unfriendly, so although it might suit Linux power users, it's not a good choice for beginners. If you use Arch, the default username and password are both `root`.

- **OpenELEC:** This is software you can use to create an XBMC media center for playing music and video. See Chapter 8 for a guide to using this.

- **Pidora:** This is a version of the Fedora Linux distribution, remixed for the Raspberry Pi. If you're an existing Fedora user, this might be of interest to you.

- **RISC OS:** Most people run Linux on the Raspberry Pi, but you can also use an alternative operating system called RISC OS, which has a graphical user interface. RISC OS dates back to 1987, when Acorn Computers created it for use with the up-market Archimedes home computer. Today, it's maintained and managed by RISC OS Open Limited. See Appendix C for some tips on getting started with RISC OS.

- **RaspBMC:** This is another option for running a media center. We show you how to use this in Chapter 8.

- **Raspbian - boot to Scratch:** This installs the recommended Raspbian operating system, but sets it up so the computer goes straight into the Scratch programming language when you start it up. Scratch is popular with children among others, so this might make it easier for them to switch on the Raspberry Pi themselves and start programming. For more on Scratch, see Chapter 9.

- **Data partition:** This option adds a data partition that you can use for storing data that can be accessed by different distributions — for example by Arch and Raspbian.

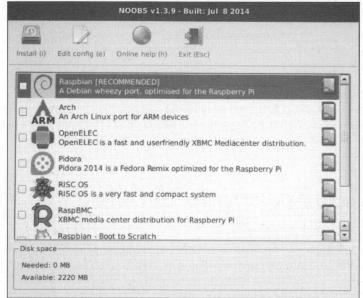

Figure 3-9:
Your operating system choices in NOOBS.

You can install multiple operating systems, and if you do that, the Raspberry Pi will give you a choice of which one you want to use when you switch it on. Keep an eye on the disk space needed and how much is available, shown at the bottom of the window, especially if you're using a 4GB card. When you've chosen the ones you want to use, click the Install button in the top left.

Remember to include Raspbian among your choices so you can follow the rest of this book.

Installing an operating system will delete everything else on that SD or MicroSD card.

If you are using NOOBS Lite, the software downloads from the Internet and is then installed on your SD card. If you're using the offline version of NOOBS, Raspbian is installed using the files you copied to the card.

When the software has finished installing your operating system (be patient!), you'll see a message telling you it's been successful. If you installed just one operating system, your Raspberry Pi will then start that operating system.

If you installed more than one operating system, you'll be given the option of which one you want to start (or "boot"). Double-click it to choose it. Each time you start up your Raspberry Pi, you'll be given a choice of operating systems. If you don't choose something, it'll boot into your previous choice again.

The first time you switch on the Raspberry Pi, you feel a thrill to see it working, followed by nerves that you don't understand all the text shooting up the screen. The text tells you what the Raspberry Pi is doing as it starts up, but you don't need to know or worry about this. It takes a short while for the Raspberry Pi to finish starting up.

To install or reinstall an operating system using NOOBS, you can hold down the Shift key when you start up your Raspberry Pi. Remember that installing or reinstalling operating systems will delete all the files on your SD or MicroSD card.

Using Raspi-config to Set Up Your Raspberry Pi

The first time you use Raspbian, it goes into a program called Raspberry Pi Software Configuration Tool (Raspi-config), which gives you a menu you can use to change some of the settings on your Raspberry Pi.

Note that you can't use the mouse to move through these menus. You use up and down keys to select different options on the screen, and left and right (or Tab, which is usually above the Caps Lock key) to select actions such as OK, Cancel, Select, and Finish. Press Enter to confirm a choice. There is often a short delay between pressing Enter and the next menu appearing.

The options available are

- ✔ **Expand Filesystem:** When you are using NOOBS, you don't need this option, which ensures you can use all the available space on your SD or MicroSD card. If you have downloaded the Raspbian image file and flashed that to an SD or MicroSD card (see Chapter 2), use this option the first time you start your Raspberry Pi.

- ✔ **Change User Password:** This option enables you to change the password for the default user on your Raspberry Pi, which is the user called *pi*. You can leave this setting alone, unless you're particularly security-conscious or are using your Raspberry Pi for particularly sensitive activities. When you use this option, you are asked to enter your new password twice at the bottom of the screen. If you change your password, don't forget it!

- ✔ **Enable Boot to Desktop/Scratch:** When you start your Raspberry Pi, it usually goes into the command line, where you can type in powerful commands to manage your Pi (see Chapter 5). Using this menu option, you can configure your Raspberry Pi to go straight into the graphical desktop (see Chapter 4) or into Scratch (see Chapter 9) instead. Some people might prefer the convenience of this, especially if the Pi is being used by younger children. Part of the fun of the Raspberry Pi is that you get to learn a bit of Linux, however, so we recommend you leave this setting alone.

✔ `Internationalisation Options: Change Locale:` This setting is used to choose your language and its associated character set. You don't need to worry about this option if you're happy using your Raspberry Pi in English. If you go into this setting by accident and want to cancel, press the Tab key on your keyboard to highlight Cancel and then press Enter.

✔ `Internationalisation Options: Change Timezone:` Your Raspberry Pi detects the time from the Internet when you switch it on if you have a network connection, but you'll need to tell it what time zone you're in when you first set it up. When you use this option, you are first asked to choose a region, and then asked to choose the city within it that reflects your time zone.

✔ `Internationalisation Options: Change Keyboard Layout:` When you press Enter, there is a short pause, and then a menu opens for you to select the keyboard you're using. Lots of keyboards are listed by name and model number, but there are also options for generic keyboards if yours isn't. Press Enter to confirm your choice. You are then asked to confirm the layout for your keyboard, in our case, UK. There are additional options to choose an AltGr key if your keyboard doesn't have one (you probably never notice it, but it's usually to the right of the space bar), to choose a Compose key (used to enter characters not on the keyboard: Holding down the Compose key while you type quotation marks and then keeping the Compose key held down while you tap an A enters an A with an umlaut on it, for example), and to enable Ctrl+Alt+Backspace to terminate the X Server (a part of Linux used in networked computer systems). You're unlikely to need any of these additional options. When you finish configuring your keyboard, you are returned to the Raspi-config menu after a short while. We found we didn't need to make any changes in the keyboard configuration: The Raspberry Pi's default option for us was Generic 105-key (Intl) PC keyboard, and this worked perfectly. If you have the wrong symbols coming up onscreen when you type, try changing the keyboard choice.

If you don't know what make and model of keyboard you have, turn it over. Many of them have a sticker underneath with this information.

✔ `Enable Camera:` If you have a Raspberry Pi camera, use this option to enable it or disable it.

✔ `Add to Rastrack:` Rastrack (www.rastrack.co.uk) is a website that maps where Raspberry Pis are being used worldwide. You can use this option to have your Raspberry Pi added to the map. It tries to work out your Raspberry Pi's location from your Internet connection, but you can visit the website to add your precise location. To change your details or remove your Pi, you'll need to visit the website.

✔ **Overclock:** *Overclocking* is making a computer work faster than the manufacturer recommends by changing some of its settings. The menu warns that overclocking may reduce the lifetime of your Raspberry Pi, but the Raspberry Pi Foundation says it is confident you can use these settings without any measurable reduction in your Pi's lifetime. You have five different presets to choose from. The speed of the CPU is measured in MHz, and the highest overclocking setting increases the speed from 700 MHz to 1000 MHz. You won't necessarily be able to use the top setting: It depends on your Pi and your power supply. If your Pi doesn't work with your chosen setting, hold down the Shift key when you switch on the Raspberry Pi and overclocking is disabled. You can then go into Raspi-config to try a different option.

✔ **Advanced option: overscan:** The overscan settings control how much of a border should be used around the screen image and can be used to correct an image that spills off the side of the monitor. In Appendix A, we show you how to change the overscan settings more exactly, but Raspi-config provides an easy way for you to enable or disable them. If your screen display is surrounded by a black border you want to get rid of, disable overscan. If you're happy with your screen image, ignore this setting.

✔ **Advanced option: Hostname:** Use this option to change the name of your Raspberry Pi as it appears to other machines on a network. You probably won't need to change this option from the default of raspberrypi, unless you're using more than one Pi on a network.

✔ **Advanced option: memory_split:** Your Raspberry Pi's memory is shared between the central processing unit (CPU) and the graphics processing unit (GPU). These processors work together to run the programs on your Raspberry Pi, but some programs are more demanding of the CPU and others rely more heavily on the GPU. If you plan to do lots of graphics-intensive work, including playing videos and 3D games, you can improve your Raspberry Pi's performance by giving more of the memory to the GPU. Otherwise, you may be able to improve performance by stealing some memory from the GPU and handing it over to the CPU. Raspbian allocates 64MB to the graphics processor and gives the rest to the CPU. In most cases, this setting will work fine, but if you experience problems, you can change how the memory is shared between the two processors. The Raspi-config program asks how much memory you want to give to the GPU and fills your entry box with the current value as a guide. The rest of the memory is allocated to the CPU. You can safely experiment with the memory split to see which works best for the kind of applications you like to use.

✔ **Advanced Option: SSH:** SSH is a way of setting up a secure connection between computers, usually so you can control one computer from another computer. The settings let you enable or disable this, but unless you know you need to use it, you can ignore this setting.

✔ **Advanced Option: SPI:** The SPI kernel module is software that is used to communicate between the Raspberry Pi and some add-on devices, including the PiFace, which makes it easier to connect sensors and other electronic circuits to your Raspberry Pi. Enable this if you require it for a device you are using with your Raspberry Pi.

✔ **Advanced Option: Audio:** If you can't hear any audio, try using this option to force it to go through either the HDMI or headphone jack.

✔ **Advanced Option: Update:** Use this setting to install an update to Raspi-config if one is available. You need to have a working Internet connection to use this. If you've just created your SD or MicroSD card using the most recent available NOOBS download, you should already be using the latest version of Raspi-config.

When you have finished configuring your Raspberry Pi, press the right arrow key twice to highlight Finish, and then press Enter. Depending on the changes you have made, you might be asked whether you would like to reboot (or restart) your Raspberry Pi. If so, say yes. Some changes only take effect after a reboot.

You can use Raspi-config at any time. To start it, enter the following at the Linux command line:

```
sudo raspi-config
```

Logging In

When you switch on your Raspberry Pi, you might be asked for a username and password. The default username and password differ depending on which version of Linux you are using, but for the Raspbian distribution, the username is **pi** and the password is **raspberry**. Both of these are case-sensitive, so you can't type in **PI**, for example. You receive no feedback on the screen as you enter the password. It not only hides your password, but also doesn't show you that a key press happened, which is a bit unsettling the first time. Press on regardless and you should find your login details are accepted.

After logging in, you are shown the command line prompt followed by a blinking line:

```
pi@raspberrypi ~ $
```

This means your Raspberry Pi is ready for you to use and you can enter Linux commands now to manage your files and programs.

Setting up the data partition

If you use the data partition option, you can have a shared part of your SD card that different operating systems can access. If you plan to use Raspbian and another distribution of Linux, this can be helpful for sharing files between them.

The data partition has the label `data` and you can use this to make a directory point to it. If you want to do this, you are probably already experienced with Linux and can follow the steps below easily. If not, we suggest you come back to this after you've read Chapter 5 and learned how to use the command line.

1. **Boot your Raspberry Pi into Raspbian, log in, and go to the command line.**
2. **Create a directory using the command** `mkdir sharedfolder`.
3. **Point the directory to the shared partition:** `sudo mount -L data sharedfolder`.
4. **Set the permissions so you can write in this folder:** `sudo chown $USER: sharedfolder`.
5. **To go into your shared folder, use** `cd sharedfolder`.

Any files you copy into that folder or create there will be available to other distributions that can access the data partition. To set up the data partition in Arch, follow the same steps as above, but omit the command `sudo` if you've logged in using the default `root` username.

Configuring Your Wi-Fi

To connect a Model A to the Internet, you need to use a USB Wi-Fi adapter because there is no Ethernet port on the Model A.

The Wi-Fi adapter plugs into one of the USB ports on your USB hub.

The easiest way to set it up is to use the Wi-Fi `Config` tool in the desktop environment. To go into the desktop environment, type in this command:

```
startx
```

You learn more about how to use the desktop environment in Chapter 4. For now, double-click the Wi-Fi Config icon on the desktop to open the tool. Click the Scan button to search for available Wi-Fi networks. Double-click the one you'd like to use, and it will prompt you to enter your security information by completing the white (unshaded) boxes (see Figure 3-10). The SSID box is used for the name of the network and will be completed automatically for you. You most likely have a WPA network, so the PSK box is where you type in your Wi-Fi password. You can ignore the optional boxes. Finally, click the Add button to connect to the network.

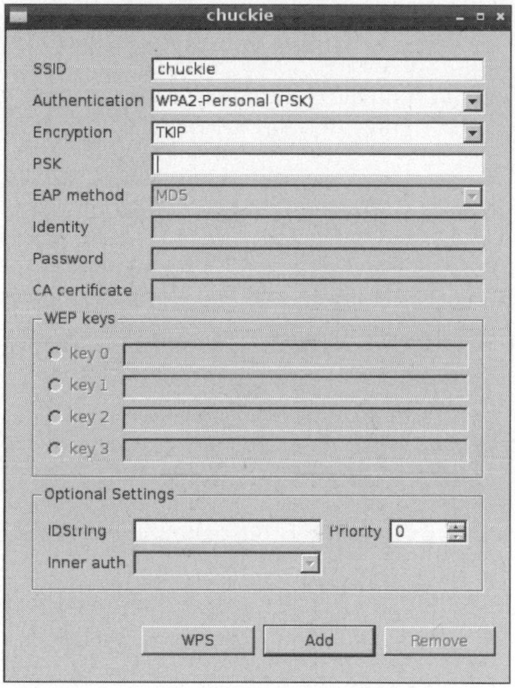

Figure 3-10:
The Wi-Fi
Config tool.

You can test your connection is working by opening the web browser and visiting a web page with it (see Chapter 4).

After you've set up a Wi-Fi network using the tool, your Raspberry Pi will remember it, so it will automatically reconnect when you restart your Raspberry Pi. You can also use the network connection you have set up from the command line.

Testing the Camera Module

If you have a Raspberry Pi Camera Module, you can test it's working now. To take a still photo, type in this command:

```
raspistill -o testshot.jpg
```

You should see what the camera sees onscreen for a moment before it takes the picture. You can check the image was created by looking at the files in your directory with this command:

```
ls
```

You can use lots of different options to take still photos too. This example will take a shot with the pastel filter, and flip the picture horizontally (-hf) and vertically (-vf):

```
raspistill -ifx pastel -hf -vf -o testshot2.jpg
```

All those hyphens and letter combinations might seem a bit random to you now, but after reading Chapter 5, they should make more sense. To see the documentation for raspistill, type

```
raspistill 2>&1 | less
```

Use the down-arrow key to move through the information and press Q to finish.

To shoot video, you use raspivid. Enter this command to shoot a five-second film:

```
raspivid -o testvideo.h264 -t 5000
```

You can get help on using raspivid too with

```
raspivid 2>&1 | less
```

There is also a library you can use in Python to access the camera from your own Python programs. For more information on using the Raspberry Pi Camera Module, see the documentation at www.raspberrypi.org/documentation/usage/camera/.

Taking Your Next Steps with the Raspberry Pi

Now you have your Raspberry Pi working, and you've logged in to it. What next?

Chapter 4 shows you how to get from here to the desktop environment, which uses windows and icons, and how you can use it to browse the web, manage your files, view your images, edit text files, and more.

Chapter 5 shows you how you can use the Linux command line to manage your Raspberry Pi and its files.

Part II
Getting Started with Linux

Visit www.dummies.com/extras/raspberrypi to discover handy Linux commands for your Raspberry Pi.

In this part . . .

- ✔ Use the LXDE desktop environment to manage the files and start the programs on your Raspberry Pi.

- ✔ Use Midori to surf the web and manage bookmarks for your favorite sites.

- ✔ Watch slide shows with the Image Viewer and use it to rotate your photos.

- ✔ Explore your Linux system and get to know the directory tree and file structure.

- ✔ Use the Linux shell to organize, copy, and delete files on your SD card, to manage user accounts, and to discover and download great software.

Chapter 4

Using the Desktop Environment

*T*he quickest way to start playing with your Raspberry Pi is to use the more visual desktop environment, which is called LXDE (short for Lightweight X11 Desktop Environment). LXDE is part of the recommended Raspbian Linux distribution for the Raspberry Pi (see Chapter 3). LXDE is designed to be as efficient as possible in its use of memory and the processor. That makes it perfect for the Raspberry Pi, which is limited in both respects compared to many modern computers.

The desktop environment works in a similar way to the Windows or Mac OS operating systems, which let you use icons and the mouse to find and manage files and operate programs. That makes it relatively intuitive to navigate, and means you can easily find and try out some of the software that comes with your Linux distribution.

In this chapter, we talk you through using the desktop environment and introduce you to some of its programs.

Starting the Desktop Environment

When you switch on your Raspberry Pi, it usually takes you into the command line interface (see Chapter 5), which enables you to control your computer by typing in instructions for it. You might be asked to enter a password first (see Chapter 3), but when you get to the prompt (pi@raspberrypi ~ $), you should type in **startx** to enter the desktop environment. It takes a moment or two to start and the screen might go blank for a short time.

Navigating the Desktop Environment

Figure 4-1 shows the LXDE desktop environment. The giant raspberry logo in the middle of the screen is just a wallpaper (a decorative background image on the screen), so don't worry if you see a different image there.

The strip along the bottom of the screen is called the *taskbar,* and this is usually visible whatever program you're using.

Figure 4-1:
The desktop environment, LXDE.

LXDE Foundation e.V.

Using the icons on the desktop

Down the left of the screen you can find icons that provide rapid access to essential programs, including your web browser, programming tools, and some reference guides and tutorials. These programs are

✔ **Sonic Pi:** This is a programming language for creating music. See Chapter 14 for a guide to making your own tunes with it.

- **Scratch:** This is a simple programming language, approachable for people of all ages, which can be used to create games and animations. Chapters 9 and 10 introduce you to Scratch and show you how to make your own game.

- **Wolfram:** This is a programming language that aims to incorporate knowledge into it, so programmers can get results more quickly. You can find out more about it at `www.wolfram.com/language/`.

- **Mathematica:** Used for scientific and technical computing, Mathematica is based on Wolfram. See the bonus chapter online for more information on Mathematica. This book's Introduction explains how to access the online materials on the companion website. There's also a short introduction to Mathematica in Chapter 19.

- **IDLE and IDLE 3:** These programs are used for programming in the Python programming language. See Chapters 11 and 12 for advice on using these and getting started with Python.

- **Minecraft Pi:** The Raspberry Pi version of world-building game Minecraft, which you can program using Python, as you see in Chapter 13.

- **WiFi Config:** The WiFi Config tool is used to set up a wireless Internet connection. You use it together with a Wi-Fi dongle that you can plug in to a spare USB socket on your Raspberry Pi's USB hub. You can buy a compatible Wi-Fi dongle from `www.thepihut.com`, among other places. See Chapter 3 for a guide to setting up Wi-Fi.

- **Epiphany:** This is a web browser. We cover it in greater depth later in this chapter.

- **LXTerminal:** This opens a window you can use to issue instructions through a command line (see Chapter 5) without leaving the desktop environment. This is handy if you want to do something quickly using the command line, but you don't want to exit your desktop session to do it.

- **OCR Resources**: OCR is an exam board. Double-clicking this link takes you to its website, where it has published some teaching resources and recipes for simple electronics projects.

- **Debian Reference:** The Raspbian version of Linux is a Pi-specific version of the Debian distribution, so this icon gives you a guide to using Linux on your Pi. The documentation is stored on your SD card, but appears in a web browser like a website. To get started, double-click the icon and then click the HTML (Multi-Files) link at the top of the screen. You probably won't need to use this resource often, but it's good to know it's there if you get stuck.

- **Pi Store:** This store is used to discover and download free and paid software for your Raspberry Pi. Click the Explore button to start searching the store. It includes only a fraction of the packages available to install from the shell (see Chapter 5), but the store makes it easier to discover and install tutorials, applications, and games. Chapter 19 includes a couple of recommendations from the store and tips on using it.

✔ **Python games:** These games, created by Al Sweigart, are demonstrations of Python, but they also provide entertainment. Games include Reversi, Four in a Row, a sliding puzzle game, and a snake game. You can choose any of 13 games to play from a simple menu.

✔ **Shutdown:** Double-clicking this icon shuts down your Raspberry Pi. It asks you to confirm before it shuts down. When you've finished using the Raspberry Pi, use this icon to switch it off. If you just want to exit LXDE and go back to the command line, use the power button on the right of the taskbar.

To start a program using one of the icons on the desktop, just double-click it as you would in Microsoft Windows or Mac OS.

Note that it might take a moment for a program to open: The Raspberry Pi probably isn't as powerful as the computers you are used to using, and so it can feel a bit less responsive.

Using the Programs menu

For all the other programs you might want to run, you use the Programs menu. At the bottom left of the screen is an icon that looks like a bird in flight. Click it and you'll see the menu appear, similar to Figure 4-2.

The menu works in the same way as the Windows Start menu. As you move your mouse over the categories of programs, a submenu appears on the right, showing you the programs in that category. Click one of these once to start it.

You can access the programs on your desktop through the Programs menu, but you can also access some additional programs in the menu too. Most of these are covered later in this chapter. You can also find Squeak, which is the programming language Scratch is built on, Xarchiver, which is used for creating and opening compressed collections of files, and VLC Media Player (see Chapter 8). If you right-click a program in the menu, you can add its icon to the desktop, so you can start it more quickly in future.

The bottom-left corner of the screen also includes some buttons (see Figure 4-2) that you can use to gain quick access to File Manager and the web browser.

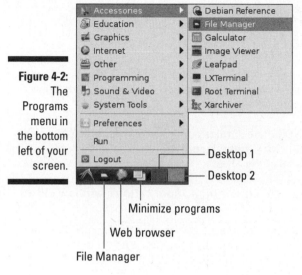

Figure 4-2:
The
Programs
menu in
the bottom
left of your
screen.

— Desktop 1
— Desktop 2

Minimize programs

Web browser

File Manager

LXDE Foundation e.V.

Using multiple desktops

LXDE enables you to use two desktops on your monitor, which is particularly helpful if you're using a small screen. It means you can double the amount of space you have for using and arranging your programs. You can use two buttons at the bottom left of the screen to switch between the desktops (see Figure 4-2).

Even if you have no plans to use multiple desktops, it's worth knowing about them because it can make it look like your programs have disappeared with all your work if you click one of the buttons by accident. That's never a good feeling!

The two desktops work independently of each other, so if you start a program on one desktop, you can't see it when you switch to the other, but the program is still there. You can switch desktops to go back to it again.

You can move a program from one desktop to the other by clicking the icon in the top-left corner of its window, hovering over Send to Desktop in the menu that opens, and then choosing which desktop you would like it to go to. You can also send a program to all desktops this way, so you can see the program no matter which desktop you're using. Another way to move a program to another desktop is to click the title bar at the top of its window, drag the window to the side of the screen, and hold it there (with the mouse button still held down) until the desktop switches.

You can run different programs in each desktop, but in practice, you shouldn't run too many programs at the same time.

Resizing and closing your program windows

You'll probably want to use more than one program in an LXDE session, so you need to know how to close programs when you've finished with them, and how to rearrange programs on the screen.

The program windows in LXDE have similar controls to Microsoft Windows that enable you to resize and close them. Figure 4-3 shows the Task Manager application, with these controls indicated:

✔ The X button in the top-right corner of the application's window closes the application.

✔ The Maximize button is used to enlarge the application so it fills your screen. After you've used it, you can click the new button in its place to return the window to its original size, just like in Windows.

✔ The Minimize button hides your program from view but doesn't stop it from running. You can get back to the program again by clicking its name on the taskbar at the bottom of the screen.

Close application
Maximize application
Minimize application

Task Manager								
<u>F</u>ile <u>V</u>iew <u>H</u>elp								
CPU usage: 4 %			Memory: 73 MB of 183 MB used					
Command	User	CPU% ▼	RSS	VM-Size	PID	State	Prio	PPID
bash	pi	-1%	1.8 MB	5.3 MB	1545	S	0	1453
startx	pi	-1%	532.0 KB	1.7 MB	1556	S	0	1545
xinit	pi	-1%	788.0 KB	2.9 MB	1573	S	0	1556
ck-launch-session	pi	-1%	1.3 MB	5.5 MB	1581	S	0	1573
lxsession	pi	-1%	1.5 MB	12.5 MB	1605	S	0	1581
dbus-launch	pi	-1%	688.0 KB	3.3 MB	1608	S	0	1
dbus-daemon	pi	-1%	1.1 MB	3.6 MB	1609	S	0	1
openbox	pi	-1%	6.8 MB	15.8 MB	1615	S	0	1605
more details							🔘 Quit	

Figure 4-3:
The Task Manager for LXDE.

LXDE Task Manager written by Hong Jen Yee, Jan Dlabal, derived from Xfce4 Task Manager by Johannes Zellner

TIP

If you want to get back to an empty desktop quickly, click the button on the taskbar to minimize all your programs (refer to Figure 4-2).

It's easy to change the size of windows so you can see more than one at a time, for example. Move your mouse cursor to one of the edges until the mouse icon changes, and you can click and drag it inward or outward to reshape the window. You can also click and drag a corner to change the window's height and width at the same time. To arrange the windows side by side, you can move them around by clicking and dragging the title bars at the top of them.

Using the Task Manager

If your Raspberry Pi doesn't seem to be responding, it might just be very busy. At the bottom right of the taskbar is the CPU Usage Monitor, which tells you how heavily the Raspberry Pi's processor is being used. It's a bar chart that scrolls from right to left, so the right-most edge shows the latest information. A green bar that fills the height of the graph indicates that your Raspberry Pi is working flat out, so it might take a moment or two to respond to you, especially when starting programs. In our experience, the Raspberry Pi doesn't crash often, but it can sometimes be overwhelmed to the extent that it looks like it has. It's usually worth being patient.

You can see which programs are running on your Raspberry Pi by running the Task Manager (see Figure 4-3). You can find it in the Programs menu among your system tools, but you can also go straight to it by holding down the Ctrl and Alt keys and pressing Delete.

If you have a program that is not responding, you can stop it using the Task Manager. Right-click it in the task list and choose Term to terminate it. This sends a request to the program and gives it a chance to shut down safely, closing any files or other programs it uses. Alternatively, you can choose Kill. That terminates the program immediately, with the possible loss of data.

You should only use the Task Manager to close programs as a last resort. Most of the tasks you see in the Task Manager are system tasks, which need to be running for LXDE to work properly. Avoid closing programs you don't recognize — that might crash LXDE and result in you losing data in any open applications.

Using External Storage Devices in the Desktop Environment

When you're using the desktop environment, you can plug in external USB storage devices, such as external hard drives or USB keys (also known as flash drives), and the Raspberry Pi automatically recognizes them. Figure 4-4 shows you the window that appears when you connect a device. You can then view the device in File Manager to access its files.

Flipping ahead to Figure 4-5, the USB key is shown in the list of places on the left as *66 MB Filesystem*. Click its name to see its files.

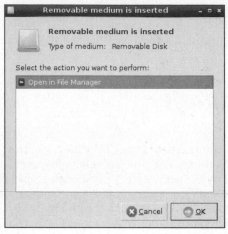

Figure 4-4:
Removable storage attached to your Raspberry Pi is automatically detected.

LXDE Foundation e.V.

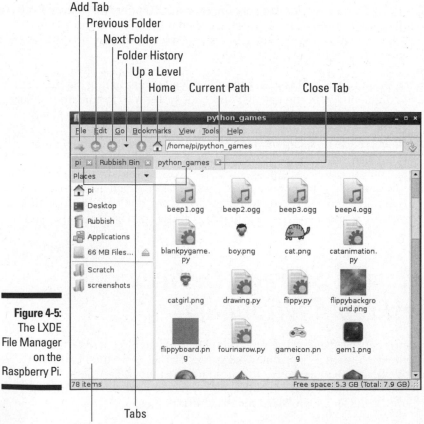

Add Tab
Previous Folder
Next Folder
Folder History
Up a Level
Home   Current Path   Close Tab

Figure 4-5:
The LXDE File Manager on the Raspberry Pi.

Tabs
Bookmarks pane

LXDE File Manager written by Hong Jen Yee

Using File Manager

You can manage your files using the command line (see Chapter 5), but it's often easier to do it in LXDE. File Manager (see Figure 4-5) is used to browse, copy, delete, rename, and otherwise manage the files on your Raspberry Pi or connected storage devices.

You start File Manager by clicking its button at the bottom left of the screen (indicated on Figure 4-2), or by using the Programs menu, where it is among the System Tools.

In Linux, people usually talk of storing files in directories, but LXDE uses the term *folders* instead, which is probably familiar to you from other computers you've used. A folder is just a way of grouping a collection of files or programs and giving that collection a name. You can put folders inside other folders too.

Navigating File Manager

On the right of File Manager, you can see the files (and any folders) that are inside the folder you're currently looking at. Each file has an icon indicating what type of file it is, except for image files, which have a small representation of the picture itself. In Figure 4-5, you can see the different files that make up the Python games that come with your Raspberry Pi in your pi folder, including pictures of game characters and backgrounds, and sound effects that are shown with a musical note on the icon.

You can double-click a folder in this area to open it, and you can double-click a file to open it with the default program for that file type. An image file opens using the Image Viewer, for example, and a Scratch file opens in Scratch. If you want to choose which program to open a file in instead, you can right-click the file's icon to bring up an option called Open With. Select it to bring up a menu of all the programs available on your Raspberry Pi, and then make your choice.

On the left is a list of your places, which are special types of folders. There are four main folders here:

✔ The pi folder is where you are expected to store most of your files, such as your documents and photos. It is the only place you have permission to write and edit files as an ordinary user. In the next chapter, we look at Linux and its directory structure in more detail, but for now, the key thing is to only try to store files and folders in your pi folder, or in any folder inside that.

✔ The Desktop folder shows you the programs and files that are on the desktop. If you're always editing a document and you want it to be on the desktop for easy access, simply move it into the Desktop folder.

✔ The Rubbish Bin is used as a temporary place to put any folders or files you plan to remove. You can empty the Rubbish Bin, and delete any files or folders in it, by right-clicking on its name in File Manager. If you put something in the Rubbish Bin that you change your mind about, right-click its icon in the Rubbish Bin and choose to Restore it to where it was before. You can also cut or copy it, so you can paste it wherever you want (especially useful if you've forgotten where it used to be!). You can send files to the Rubbish Bin by right-clicking on them in File Manager or selecting them (see the section on "Copying and moving files and folders" later in this chapter) and then pressing the Delete key on your keyboard (usually marked Del or Delete, and not to be confused with the Backspace key).

✔ The Applications folder gives you access to the same programs as the Programs menu at the bottom of the screen.

You might also see other places here, depending on how your Raspberry Pi is set up. Figure 4-5 shows an entry beneath Applications for a 64MB USB key Sean plugged in.

If there are folders you use particularly often, you can bookmark them — an idea borrowed from web browsers, and from (in the dim distant past) print books before that. A bookmark makes it easy for you to go straight back to where you were. To add a bookmark to the folder you are viewing, click Bookmarks on the menu at the top of File Manager, and then choose Add to Bookmarks. Your bookmarks are shown in the Bookmarks pane, under your Places list. In Figure 4-5, you can see we've bookmarked the Scratch and screenshots folders. Click one of these bookmarks to go straight to its folder. To remove or rename a bookmark, right-click its entry in the Bookmarks pane and select the appropriate option from the menu that opens.

Across the top of File Manager is a menu bar, including File, Edit, Go, Bookmarks, View, Tools, and Help menus. Most of the options here you can also do in other ways with File Manager, as we show you, but if you get stuck, this menu is a good way to quickly get back on track.

Underneath the menu bar is an icon bar that includes a number of useful shortcuts. They're indicated in Figure 4-5:

✔ **Add Tab:** Tabs are particularly useful if you're carrying out work that involves more than one folder. You might want to quickly switch between the source and destination folders if you're copying files, for example. The tab metaphor comes from paper filing cabinets, with cardboard tabs sticking out of the folders at the top so you can easily find the one you're looking for. In web browsers today, it's common to find tabs that you use to switch between different web pages open in the browser. It's similar in File Manager. The tabs enable you to have two different folders open at the same time. You simply click the tabs to switch between them. Within each tab, you can use File Manager as usual, navigating between the different folders. In Figure 4-5, you can see we have three tabs open: the pi folder, the Rubbish Bin, and the python_games folder. To close a tab and its associated folder, click on the orange X icon in the tab (see Figure 4-5).

✔ **Previous Folder:** File Manager keeps a history of the folders you navigate through, and the Previous Folder button works a bit like a web browser's Back button. It takes you back to the last folder you accessed in that tab. You can click it repeatedly to keep going back.

✔ **Next Folder:** After you've used the Previous Folder button, you can use the Next Folder button to go forward through your history again, taking you back to a folder you visited after the one you're looking at now. If you click the Previous Folder button and then the Next Folder button, you'll end up where you started.

✔ **Folder History:** Click the Folder History button to open a menu showing you a list of the folder in the history. You can go straight to one of them by clicking it. That saves you wearing out your clicking finger by repeatedly clicking the Previous Folder or Next Folder button!

✔ **Up a Level:** A folder might be inside another folder, known as a *parent folder*. Your Desktop folder is inside your pi folder, for example, so pi is the parent folder for Desktop. Click the Up a Level button to go to the parent folder. Pressing the Backspace key (usually used when typing to delete a single character to the left of the cursor) has the same effect as clicking this button.

✔ **Home:** This button takes you back to your pi folder so you have quick access to your work.

✔ **Path:** The path is a text description of the location of the folder you are looking at, including a list of the folders above it. Chapter 5 covers paths in depth, but if you know a path, you can type it in here, and then press the Enter key to go straight to it in File Manager.

Copying and moving files and folders

File Manager makes it easy to copy and move your files and folders, without the need for any text commands.

When you right-click on a file or folder in File Manager, a menu opens that enables you to rename the file, delete the file or folder (which sends it to the Rubbish Bin), and to cut or copy it.

If you cut a file, it is *moved* to wherever you choose to paste it. If you copy the file, a *duplicate* copy of it is placed where you paste it. You paste by going to the folder where you would like the file to be stored and then right-clicking on an empty space inside a folder and choosing Paste from the menu that appears. (If you copy or cut a file without pasting it, nothing happens to it.)

You can also drag files onto a folder's icon to move them into it.

Selecting multiple files and folders

There are several ways to select more than one file at a time, so you can delete, copy, or move them all at the same time:

- ✔ The first way is to hold down the Ctrl key and click each of the files in turn to select them.

- ✔ You can also select a group of consecutive icons (read from left to right, top to bottom) by clicking the first icon, holding down the Shift key, and then clicking the last icon.

- ✔ Finally, you can click the mouse on the background of File Manager and hold the button down while you lasso the files you want to select.

After you've selected a group of files, you can drag them all into a different folder by clicking one of the selected files and dragging it into the folder. You can also right-click on one of your selected files and choose to cut or copy the whole group, as shown in Figure 4-6. If you delete one of the selected files, they will all be moved to the Rubbish Bin.

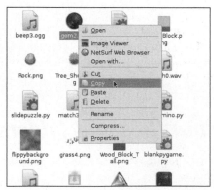

Figure 4-6: Right-clicking a file in the File Manager brings up a menu of options.

LXDE File Manager written by Hong Jen Yee

LXDE supports some keyboard shortcuts that might be familiar to you from Microsoft Windows. You can use Ctrl+A to select all files and folders, Ctrl+C to copy, Ctrl+V to paste, and Ctrl+X to cut selected files and folders in LXDE.

It's worth remembering, however, that Ctrl+C is used to cancel an operation in the Linux command line (see Chapter 5), so the Copy shortcut isn't universal on your Raspberry Pi the way it is in Windows.

If you're selecting almost all the files, it's probably easiest to use Ctrl+A to select all, and then hold down the Ctrl key and click to deselect the files you don't want. There's also an option on the Edit menu to invert your selection, so you can select the files you don't want and then use this option to flip your choice so everything else is selected instead.

Creating new folders and blank files

Organizing your files in folders makes it easier to manage them. You can more easily see what files you have where, go straight to a file when you need it, and back up a group of files by copying the folder to an external storage device.

It's easy to make a new folder. First go to the location where you would like your new folder to be stored. Typically, this will be in your pi folder, or one of its subfolders, such as your Desktop. Right-click a blank space in the right pane of File Manager and hover the mouse over Create New. Click Folder in the fly-out menu that appears and you'll be prompted to enter a name and click OK to confirm. If you change your mind, click Cancel instead.

You can also click the File menu at the top left of File Manager, find Create New, and then click Folder.

Both options also enable you to create a blank file. If you want to practice creating folders and moving files around, you can create a few blank files so you can do this safely without worrying about moving anything you didn't intend to.

Changing how files are displayed

When you right-click on an empty space in the right pane in File Manager, a menu opens with an option to change how the files there are sorted. You can sort files by name, modification time, size, or file type, in either ascending or reverse order.

You can change how files and folders are shown in File Manager, so you can strike a balance between how many you can see at once, and how easy they are to see. The View menu in the menu bar at the top of File Manager gives you the choice of four different ways to display the files and folders. By default, File Manager uses the icon view, which strikes a good balance between the number of files you can see at a time and how large each icon is. The thumbnail view is particularly useful in a folder of images because it enlarges the preview that takes the place of a generic icon for picture files. To see as many files as possible at once, use the Compact view, which lists the files and folders in columns with a small icon and the filename.

The detailed list view (see Figure 4-7) reveals more information about each file, showing a short description, its size, and when it was last modified. You can click the column headings to sort the view by the filename, description (which groups similar files), size, or modification date. If you click the column heading again, the sort order is reversed.

Figure 4-7: The detailed list view in File Manager.

LXDE File Manager written by Hong Jen Yee

Sometimes you might need to refresh the view of File Manager to reflect your latest changes. To do that, tap the F5 key on the keyboard or choose Reload Folder from the View menu.

The View menu also enables you to change the side pane in File Manager so it shows you the directory tree instead of the places. You'll learn more about the directory tree in Chapter 5, but it's worth knowing there's an option to navigate using it in File Manager too.

Opening a folder as root or in the terminal

Linux has a rigorous permissions structure that governs who can access all its files, and whether they have permission to modify them or run them. It's a good thing because it means it's relatively difficult for you to do any real harm to your Raspberry Pi's operating system accidentally. You're free to use File Manager to explore all the files your operating system uses, but if you try to delete an essential file, you'll be told you don't have permission (see Figure 4-8).

If you want to explore your system, go to your pi folder, click the Up a Level button twice (see Figure 4-5), and then take a look in the folders there. Chapter 5 covers some of these in more depth.

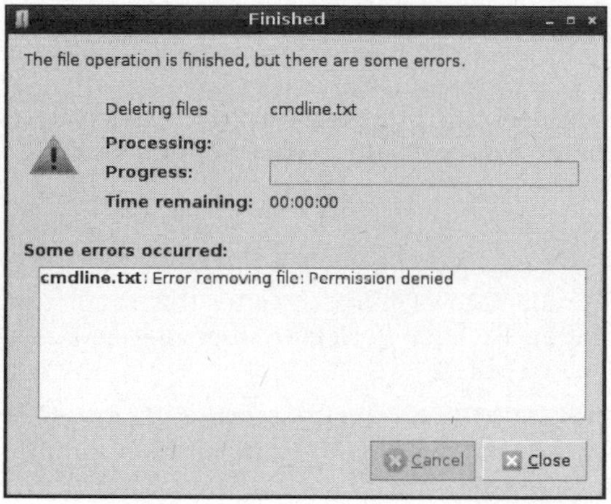

LXDE Foundation e.V.

Figure 4-8: Whoops! Denied permission to delete a file from the Raspberry Pi's boot folder.

If you find you need to do something you don't have permission to do, you can brush away all the restrictions by opening the current folder as the root user, one of the options in the Tools menu. As a root user, you can do anything on the computer, including deleting things you shouldn't, so it's good practice to only use this option if you really need to. When you've finished working as the root user (also called the Super User in File Manager), close File Manager window to protect yourself against accidentally making further changes you shouldn't.

The Tools menu also has an option to open the current folder in the terminal. This enables you to use Linux commands (see Chapter 5) to make changes to the folder. Often this is the quickest way to accomplish something, especially after you've mastered the finer points of Linux. While you're using File Manager, you can also use the keyboard shortcut F4 to access the terminal.

Browsing the Web

When it comes to browsing the web on your Raspberry Pi, you really are spoiled for choice, with three browsers to choose from. Epiphany is the recommended browser for most websites, although it's good to be aware of the others because they can be faster (albeit they achieve speed by stripping out some of the web page's features). Open the Programs menu, and you'll see the browsers in the Internet category:

✔ **Dillo:** This browser is fast, but web pages look different than intended on it because it can't handle sophisticated layout instructions or JavaScript, the language used for creating interactive web pages. Several websites we tried were rendered as a single deep column because Dillo couldn't understand where the header box, sidebars, the main page content, and the bottom box should go. You can switch off images in the Tools menu, which can greatly speed up downloads of complex pages. If you're accessing mainly text information or have a particularly slow web connection, this browser might be a good choice, but you won't benefit from much of the work website owners put into creating web page designs that are easy to use.

✔ **Netsurf:** This is capable of handling more sophisticated layouts than Dillo, but it also lacks support for JavaScript. Many websites look as they do on a PC or Mac browser, but any sites that require JavaScript won't work (including Facebook). Netsurf offers a friendlier experience than Dillo for most websites.

✔ **Epiphany:** This browser has been optimized for the Raspberry Pi, including hardware decoding of video. Epiphany supports JavaScript, and is most able to re-create the richer experience you have with websites using other devices. This is the default browser on your Raspberry Pi. Sites like Facebook and Google Maps work, but might be noticeably slower than you're used to.

At present, the Raspberry Pi does not support Flash. Flash is used for online games and videos, so often these won't work on your Raspberry Pi. On the upside, Flash is also used for annoying blinking advertisements, so surfing the web with the Raspberry Pi might be more serene than you are used to!

Using Epiphany to browse the web

Figure 4-9 shows the Epiphany browser in use. Its layout is similar to other browsers you might have used in the past, with a thin toolbar at the top, and most of the screen given over to the web page you're viewing. To get started with it, either run it from the Programs menu or double-click its icon on the desktop.

If you know the address of the website you want to visit, you can type it into the address bar (see Figure 4-9). When you start to type an address, a menu under the address bar suggests pages you've previously visited that might match what you want. Click one of these to go straight to it or carry on typing. When you've finished typing the address, press the Enter key.

You can scroll your page using the scrollbar on the right of the browser, or the scrollwheel on your mouse.

New tab

Back   Forward   Address bar   Reload   Menu

Figure 4-9:
The
Epiphany
browser.

When your mouse pointer is over a link, the pointer changes to a small hand. You can then click the left mouse button to follow that link to another web page. The browser keeps a list of the web pages you visit (called your *history*), so you can click the Back button (indicated in Figure 4-9) to retrace your steps and revisit the pages you browsed before the current one. The Forward button beside it takes you forward through your history again.

Some web pages update frequently with new information, so you can click the Reload button to download the current page again and see any updates since you first opened it. While a page is downloading, this button becomes a Stop button. Click it to halt the download.

Searching within web pages

To find a word or phrase within a web page, press Ctrl+F after the page has loaded. The Find bar opens at the top of the screen, with a box for you to type into. The first occurrence of the text you're looking for is highlighted on the page in yellow, and you can press the Enter key or click the Down button in the Find bar to move to the next one. You can close the Find bar again by clicking the Close button (an X) on the far right of the Find bar.

Using tabbed browsing

Like many other browsers today, Epiphany uses tabs to enable you to switch between several websites you have open at the same time. Click the button in the top right (refer to Figure 4-9) to add a new tab, which opens to show your most visited websites. You can click to visit one of these or type an address in the address bar.

To switch to a page, just click its tab above the main web page area. In Figure 4-9, Facebook and Sean's website are open, and we can click the tabs to flick between those pages instantly. To close a tab, click the Close button to the right of its name.

If you hold down the Ctrl key while you click a link, the link opens in a new tab.

Adding and using bookmarks

Bookmarks make it easy to revisit your favorite web pages. You can add a bookmark by going through the menu in the top right, or by using Ctrl+D.

The New Bookmark window looks like Figure 4-10. The default name for a bookmark is the web page's title, but you can edit it, and choose a topic to file it under. You can click to show the existing topics, or type a new topic into the Topics box. When you browse your bookmarks, the topics are like folders, organizing your bookmarks. To add the bookmark, you click the Add button.

"Malaysia | Travel Photos" Properties _ □ ×	
Title:	Malaysia | Travel Photos
Address:	http://www.sean.co.uk/photography/stock/Ma
Topics:	
	▸ Show all topics
Help	1 Similar	Cancel	Add

Figure 4-10: Adding a bookmark in Epiphany.

To access your bookmarks while you're browsing, click the menu in the top-right (its icon is indicated in Figure 4-9), and choose Bookmarks.

Protecting your privacy

As you know, your browser stores the history of web pages you visit. If you want to make a visit to a website without any traces being left in the browser, perhaps to plan your Christmas shopping without the risk of other family members coming across the websites you've visited, open a new incognito window first. You do this through the menu in the top right. When you close the private browsing window, your secret session stops.

When information has already been stored in the browser, you can delete it by viewing your Personal Data and History from the menu in the top right.

Using the Image Viewer

It's easy to look at your digital photos and other images using LXDE. Among the accessories in the Programs menu is the Image Viewer. You can start it through the menu, or by right-clicking an image file.

The Image Viewer displays your picture, with a toolbar along the bottom underneath it, as you can see in Figure 4-11. From left to right, this is what the buttons do:

- ✔ **Previous:** Goes to the previous photo in the folder. Note that any unsaved changes (such as rotation) are lost. You can also use the left-arrow key on the keyboard.

- ✔ **Next:** Goes to the next photo in the folder. As with the Previous button, clicking this discards any unsaved changes you've made to the current photo. You can also use the right-arrow key on the keyboard.

- ✔ **Start Slide show:** Click this button to begin a slide show of all the photos in the folder. The interval between photos is set at five seconds, but you can change that in the preferences. You can also use the W key to start a slide show.

- ✔ **Zoom Out:** Click this to reduce the magnification of the image. The keyboard shortcut is the minus key.

- ✔ **Zoom In:** Increase the magnification of the image. Scrollbars appear if the image becomes too big to fit in the Image Viewer, and you can use these to see different parts of the picture. The keyboard shortcut is the + (plus sign) key, with no need to use Shift.

IMG_1572.JPG (5184x3456) 12%

Figure 4-11:
Sean in
China,
as seen
through
the Image
Viewer.

- **Fit Image to Window:** This shrinks a large image to make it fit the Image Viewer snugly. If an image is smaller than the Image Viewer window, it won't be blown up to fill it, though. This button (or its keyboard shortcut F) is a good way to recover if you get lost zooming in or out.

- **Go to Original Size:** This resets any zooming by showing the image at its full original size. This might be bigger than the Image Viewer window, in which case scrollbars appear to enable you to move around the image. The keyboard shortcut is G.

- **Full Screen:** The image fills the monitor, and you lose your Image Viewer controls. Right-click the image to open a menu with all the same options. To revert to using the Image Viewer in a window, chose Full Screen from the menu. You can also use the F11 key to switch the full screen view on and off.

- **Rotate Left:** This rotates the image 90 degrees counterclockwise. The keyboard shortcut is L.

- **Rotate Right:** This rotates the image 90 degrees clockwise. The keyboard shortcut is R.

- **Flip Horizontally:** This mirrors the image horizontally and can also be done with the H key.

- **Flip Vertically:** This turns the image upside down. The V key does the same.

- ✔ **Open File:** Click the folder icon to open a new image file. You can also drag and drop an image on the Image Viewer from a folder in File Manager. This doesn't move the file, just opens it.

- ✔ **Save File:** This saves your image (including any rotations or mirroring you have done) and replaces the original image. You get a warning before it happens. Keyboard shortcut: S.

- ✔ **Save File As:** Use this button (or press the A key) to save your image with a new filename so it doesn't overwrite your original image.

- ✔ **Delete:** Click the bin icon or use the Delete key to delete an image from your storage device. If you delete an image, it's not sent to the Rubbish Bin: It's deleted and cannot be recovered. You get one warning, but then it's toast!

- ✔ **Preferences:** This is where you change the settings for Image Viewer, so you can customize it for your needs. You can turn off the warnings you get before overwriting or deleting an image, set Image Viewer to automatically save rotated images, change the background colors of Image Viewer, and change the slide show interval here. There's also an option to rotate images by changing their orientation value in the EXIF tag, which changes some of the information stored with the image to say which way up the camera was, instead of actually rotating the image content itself. It's okay to keep this selected, but this is where you disable it if you prefer.

- ✔ **Exit Image Viewer:** Click the far-right icon in Image Viewer to close it. Confusingly, the same icon design is used to exit the Image Viewer as is used to log out of LXDE itself and shut down the Raspberry Pi. It doesn't matter if you click the wrong one because LXDE makes you confirm before it exits.

Using the Leafpad Text Editor

Among the accessories in the Programs menu is Leafpad, which is a simple text editor (see Figure 4-12). You can use it for writing and word processing, but it's not ideal for creating print-ready documents. It's most useful for editing documents intended to be read by computers, such as web pages and configuration files.

The menus are logically organized, and if you've ever used a text editor on another computer, you'll find your way around in Leafpad easily.

The File menu is used to start new documents and open, save, and print files. There's also an option to Quit here, although you can just close the Leafpad window.

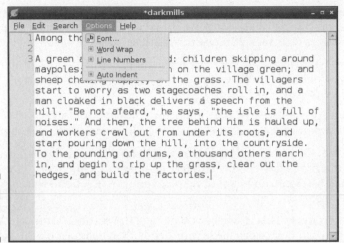

Figure 4-12:
The Leafpad
text editor.

Leafpad written by Tarot Osuji with artwork by Lapo Calamandrei

The Edit menu gives you tools for undoing and redoing your work, cutting, copying, pasting, and deleting, and selecting all your text. Leafpad uses Windows shortcuts too, so you can use Ctrl+C to copy, Ctrl+V to paste, Ctrl+X to cut, and Ctrl+A to select all the text.

The Search menu has options to find a particular word or phrase, jump to a particular line in the document, or replace a chosen word or phrase with an alternative. You can click the box to replace all in one go, or step through them individually. The search and replace features highlight all the occurrences in yellow, and the one that it's currently focused on in blue. You can use the Search menu to move forward or backward through the list of results.

The Options menu (shown in Figure 4-12) has options to change the font (although the choices available are more limited than you're probably used to), switch on Word Wrap (which means text goes on to a new line when it reaches the edge of the window, instead of a horizontal scrollbar appearing), and switch on Line Numbers (shown in the upper left in Figure 4-12). The auto indent feature means that any indentation used on one line is automatically applied to the next line when you press Enter.

Customizing Your Desktop

You can do quite a few things to stamp your identity on LXDE and make it easier to use. Just like other desktop computers you might have used, you can change the look and feel of it. To find the options for this, click Customise Look and Feel in the Preferences section of the Programs menu. You can choose the default font and pick from different colors and styles used for the content of windows in the Widget tab, including a style named Redmond for the location of Microsoft's HQ, which might be a suitable look for Windows users suffering from homesickness on their Raspberry Pi. In the Colour tab, you can choose your own color scheme. The Icon Theme tab gives you a choice of different icon sets, and you can change the layout of toolbars in the Other tab.

To adjust the sensitivity of the keyboard and mouse, use the keyboard and mouse settings in the Programs menu. For left-handers, you can swap the left and right mouse buttons too.

Two other entries in the Programs menu are available to tailor your desktop environment. The Openbox Configuration Manager gives you control over the look of menus and title bars at the top of your windows, where new windows appear, and how many desktops you have.

The Preferred Applications settings let you choose your default web browser and e-mail program, which is opened when you click on links to web pages or e-mail addresses. There is no e-mail program in LXDE, but you can add one of your own choice. Claws Mail is an e-mail program that works on the Raspberry Pi. The Raspberry Pi isn't the ideal machine for this kind of application. Usually, you'd run something like this in the background while you do other things, but with the Pi's limited memory, it can be a bit slow even when it's focused exclusively on these activities. E-mail is one of the most popular computer activities today, however, so if you'd like to try it on the Raspberry Pi, give Claws a go. You can install using the following command line instruction (see Chapter 5):

```
sudo apt-get install claws-mail
```

It appears among Other applications in the Programs menu.

The taskbar at the bottom of the screen can be customized by right-clicking it and then selecting Panel Settings. You can move it to the top or one of the sides of the screen, change its height and the size of icons, change its background picture and colors, and change the tools you have on there (Panel Applets). Not all of these are useful on the Raspberry Pi, but you can add a volume control, which is useful. If you would rather not see the taskbar, you can set it to hide (minimize) when you're not using it by going to Advanced options.

Any settings you change in the Panel Preferences change immediately without you having a chance to save or confirm them. Don't go too wild experimenting because you'll have to manually reset everything again if you don't like the results.

If you want to change your desktop wallpaper (the image behind the windows and icons), right-click the background and click Desktop Preferences. Click the filename of the wallpaper to choose a new one using a file browser that is a bit like File Manager. Click the pi icon in the Places list on the left to find your own photos to use as a background. You can set the wallpaper to be centered onscreen, repeated to cover it, or stretched to fill it.

Logging Out from LXDE

To log out from LXDE and get back to the command prompt, click the red power off icon in the bottom right of the screen, or open the Programs menu and click Logout. You are prompted to confirm you want to log out, and LXDE then closes and returns you to the command line prompt. When you've finished with the command line, issue a command to shut down, as described in Chapter 5.

If you have set up your Raspberry Pi to go straight into LXDE when you switch it on, it works a bit differently. When you log out, you are prompted to log on again. When you click the icon in the taskbar, you also see options to reboot (which means restart) or shut down your Raspberry Pi.

Remember that you don't have to log out to use the Linux command line. You can double-click the LXTerminal icon on the desktop to open the terminal in a window, or use File Manager to find the folder you want to use and then choose to open the current folder in the terminal, using the Tools menu. When you are using File Manager, the F4 key on your keyboard also opens the terminal for you.

To switch off your Raspberry Pi without logging out, use the Shutdown icon on the desktop. After it's shut down, you can disconnect the power. When you reconnect it, your Pi will start up again.

Chapter 5

Using the Linux Shell

You've already had a glimpse of the Linux shell: It's the text-based way of issuing instructions to your Raspberry Pi. When you switch on your Raspberry Pi, the shell is the first thing you see, and it's where you type startx if you want to enter the desktop environment. The shell on the Raspberry Pi is called Bash, which is used in most other Linux distributions too. Its name is short for Bourne Again Shell, a pun because it was created to replace the Bourne shell.

In this chapter, you learn how to use the shell to manage your Raspberry Pi. There are several reasons why it's a good idea to learn how to use the shell. Most importantly, it's a faster solution for certain tasks than the desktop environment is. Learning Linux is also a useful skill in itself: Linux is a powerful and popular operating system, and the Raspberry Pi can provide an accessible introduction to the basics. It also gives you some understanding of what's going on behind the scenes on your Raspberry Pi.

To get ready for this chapter, log in to your Raspberry Pi, but don't type startx to go into the desktop environment. Alternatively, if you're already in the desktop environment, double-click the LXTerminal icon to open a shell session in a window there.

If the screen goes blank while you're using the shell, don't worry. You can get it back again by pressing any key on the keyboard.

Understanding the Prompt

When you log in to your Raspberry Pi, you see a prompt that looks like this, with a cursor beside it ready for you to enter your command:

```
pi@raspberrypi ~ $
```

At first glance, that prompt can look quite foreign and unnecessarily complicated (why doesn't it just say *OK* or *Ready?*), but it actually contains a lot of information. This is what the different bits mean:

✓ **pi:** This is the name of the user who is logged in. Later in this chapter, we show you how to add different users to your Raspberry Pi, and if you log in as a different user, you see that user's name here instead.

✓ **raspberrypi:** This is the hostname of the machine, which is the name other computers might use to identify the machine when connecting to it.

✓ **~ :** In Linux, people talk about organizing files in *directories* rather than *folders*, but it means the same thing. This part of the prompt tells you which directory you are looking at (the current working directory). The tilde symbol (a horizontal wiggly line) is shorthand for what is known as your *home directory*, and its presence in the prompt here shows that you're currently working in that directory. As explained in Chapter 4, this is where you should store your work and other files. An ordinary user doesn't have permission to put files anywhere except for his or her home directory or any directories inside that home directory.

✓ **$:** The dollar sign means that you are a humble ordinary user, and not an all-powerful superuser. If you were a superuser, you would see a # symbol instead. Later in this chapter, we go into more detail about user permissions.

Exploring Your Linux System

It's perfectly safe to take a look at any of the files and directories on your SD card. As an ordinary user, you're blocked from deleting or damaging any important files in any case, so you can explore the files on your SD card without fear of deleting anything important.

Listing files and directories

The command for listing files and directories is ls. Because you start in your home directory, if you enter it now, you see the folders and files (if any) in your home directory. Here's what the output looks like on Sean's Raspberry Pi. In this chapter, we use bold text for the bits you type, and normal text for the computer's output.

```
pi@raspberrypi ~ $ ls
Desktop   ocr_pi.png   python_games
```

Linux is case-sensitive, which means LS, ls, Ls, and lS are completely differ-ent instructions. Linux doesn't see that uppercase and lowercase letters are related to each other, so an S and an s look like completely different symbols to the computer, in the same way that an A and a Z look different to us. If you get the capitalization wrong in your command, it won't work, and that applies to everything in the shell. If you misplace a capital letter in a filename, Linux thinks the file you want doesn't exist. When you come to use more advanced command options later, you might find that some commands use upper- and lowercase options to mean different things.

Changing directories

Desktop and python_games are both blue, which means they are directories, so we can go into them to take a look at the files they have inside. The com-mand to change a directory is cd, and you use it together with the name of the directory you would like to go into, like this:

```
pi@raspberrypi ~ $ cd python_games
```

Your prompt changes to show the directory you have changed to after the tilde character, and you can double-check that the current directory has changed by using ls to view the files there.

Checking file types

If you want to find out more about a particular file, you can use the file command. After the command name, put the name of the file you'd like more information on. You can list several files in one command by separating them with spaces, like this:

```
pi@raspberrypi ~/python_games $ file boy.png match0.wav
        wormy.py
boy.png:    PNG image data, 50 x 85, 8-bit/color RGBA,
        non-interlaced
match0.wav: RIFF (little-endian) data, WAVE audio,
        Microsoft PCM, 16 bit, mono 44100 Hz
wormy.py:   Python script, ASCII text executable
```

The file command can tell you quite a lot about a file. You not only learn what kind of data is in the first two files (an image and an audio recording), but also how big the image is (50×85 pixels) and that the audio is mono.

If you're an experienced computer user, you might have been able to guess what kind of files those were from the file extensions (the .png, .wav, and .py on the end of the filenames). Linux doesn't require files to have extensions like that, however, so the `file` command can sometimes be a huge help. (In practice, a lot of applications choose to use file extensions, and users often prefer to do so because it's more user-friendly than having filenames without any context for the file type.)

You can also use the `file` command on a directory. For example, when you're in your `pi` directory, you can find out about Desktop and python_games like this:

```
pi@raspberrypi ~ $ file Desktop python_games
Desktop:       directory
python_games:  directory
```

That confirms to us that both of these are directories. It might seem counterintuitive to use a command called `file` to find out about a directory, but it illustrates an important feature of Linux: Linux considers everything to be a file, including hard drives and network connections. It's all just a bunch of files according to Linux.

Changing to the parent directory

In this chapter so far, we've used `cd` to change into a directory that's inside the current working directory. However, you will often want to change into the directory *above* your current working directory, which is known as its *parent* directory. The python_games directory is inside your pi directory, for example, so the pi directory is the parent directory for it.

To change to the parent directory, you use `cd` with two dots. You can use that command while in python_games to change your home directory (indicated by a ~ symbol in the command prompt).

```
pi@raspberrypi ~/python_games $ cd ..
pi@raspberrypi ~ $
```

The ~ symbol is really just a shorthand for your home directory. Its real name is the same as your username, which means it will usually be *pi*, the default username. The parent directory of your home directory is, rather confusingly, called *home* and it's used to store the home directories of all users of the computer.

When you're in your home directory, try using `cd  ..` to go into the directory called *home*. If you use it again, you will find yourself at the highest directory of your operating system, known as the *root* and indicated with a / in your command prompt. Try navigating through the parent directories to get to the root and then listing what's there, like this:

```
pi@raspberrypi ~ $ cd ..
pi@raspberrypi /home $ cd ..
pi@raspberrypi / $ ls
bin  boot  dev  etc  home  lib  lost+found  media  mnt
          opt  proc  root  run  sbin  selinux  srv
          sys  tmp  usr  var
```

Feel free to use the cd command to nose around these directories. You can use ls to see what's in the directory, cd to change into a directory you come across, and file to investigate any files you find.

Understanding the directory tree

When people think about how the directories are organized on a computer, they often use the metaphor of a tree. A tree has a single trunk with many branches that come off it, secondary branches that sprout from those branches, and so on until you get down to twigs.

Your Raspberry Pi has a single root directory, with directories that come off it, and subdirectories inside those, and maybe subdirectories inside those too.

Figure 5-1 is a partial picture of the directory tree on your Raspberry Pi. It doesn't show all the subdirectories in the root, and it doesn't show all their subdirectories either, but it does show you where your home directory is, relative to other directories and the root. You can think of it as a map. If you are at the root and you want to get to the python_games directory, the tree shows you need to go through the home and pi directories to get there.

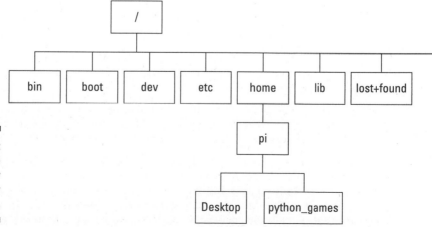

Figure 5-1:
Part of the directory tree on your Raspberry Pi.

When you get to the root, there are 20 directories there. All the programs, files, and operating system data on your Raspberry Pi are stored in these directories, or in their subdirectories. It's safe to go into the various directories and have a look around, and to use file to investigate any files you find.

You will rarely need to use any of these directories, but in case you're curious, here's what some of them are used for:

✔ **bin:** This is short for *binaries*, and contains small programs that behave like commands in the shell, including ls and mkdir, which you will use to make directories later.

✔ **boot:** This contains the Linux kernel, the heart of the operating system, and also contains configuration files that store various technical settings for the Raspberry Pi. Appendix A shows you how you can edit the config.txt file here to change some of your computer's settings.

✔ **dev:** This stores a list of devices (such as disks and network connections) the operating system understands.

✔ **etc:** This is used for various configuration files that apply to all users on the computer.

✔ **home:** As already discussed, this directory contains a directory for each user and that is the only place a user is allowed to store or write files by default.

✔ **lib:** This directory contains libraries (shared programs) that are used by different operating system programs.

✔ **lost+found:** The name looks intriguing, but hopefully you'll never have to deal with this directory. It's used if the file system gets corrupted and recovers partially.

✔ **media:** When you connect a removable storage device like a USB key and it is automatically recognized in the desktop environment, its details are stored here in the media directory.

✔ **mnt:** This directory is used to store the details of removable storage devices that you mount yourself (see "Mounting External Storage Devices" in Appendix A).

✔ **opt:** This directory is used for optional software on your Raspberry Pi. Usually in Linux, this directory is used for software you install yourself, but on the Raspberry Pi, many programs install into /usr/bin instead.

✔ **proc:** This directory is used by the Linux kernel to give you information about its view of the system. Most of this information requires specialist knowledge to interpret, but it's fun to take a peek anyway. Try entering less /proc/cpuinfo to see how the kernel views the Raspberry Pi's processors, or less /proc/meminfo to see how much memory your

Raspberry Pi has and how it's being used. (You'll learn how to use `less` fully later, but for now, you just need to know that you press Q to quit.) If you use the `file` command to look at these files, they appear to be empty, which is a peculiarity that arises because they're being constantly updated.

✔ **root:** You don't have permission to change into this directory as an ordinary user. It's reserved for the use of the root user, which in Linux is the all-powerful user account that can do anything on the computer. The Raspberry Pi discourages the use of the root account and instead encourages you to use `sudo` to issue specific commands with the authority of the root user (sometimes called the superuser). Later in this chapter, we show you how this is used to install software (see "Installing software").

✔ **run:** This directory is a relatively recent addition to Linux and provides a place where programs can store data they need and have confidence it will be available when the operating system starts up. Data in the tmp folder is vulnerable to being removed by disk cleanup programs, and the usr directory might not always be available at startup on all Linux systems (it can be on a different file system).

✔ **sbin:** This directory contains software that is typically reserved for the use of the root user.

✔ **selinux:** This directory is used by Security-Enhanced Linux, a security enhancement to Linux. The directory is empty by default.

✔ **srv:** This is another empty directory, which is sometimes used in Linux for storing data directories for services such as FTP, which is used to copy files over the Internet.

✔ **sys:** This directory is used for Linux operating system files.

✔ **tmp:** This directory is used for temporary files.

✔ **usr:** This directory is used for the programs and files that ordinary users can access and run.

✔ **var:** This directory stores files that fluctuate in size (or are variable), such as databases and log files. You can see the system message log with the command `less /var/log/messages` (use the arrow key to move down and press Q to quit).

Using relative and absolute paths

We've been discussing how to move between directories that are immediately above or below each other on the directory tree, a bit like the way you might work in a desktop environment. You click to open one folder, click to open the folder inside it, and click to open the folder inside that. It's easy (which is why it's popular), but if you've got a complex directory structure, it soon gets tedious.

If you know where you're going, the shell enables you to go straight there by specifying a path, which is a description of a file's location. There are two types of paths: relative and absolute. A relative path is a bit like giving directions to the directory from where you are now (go up a directory, down through the Desktop directory, and there it is!). An absolute path is more like a street address: It's exactly the same wherever you are.

Absolute paths are usually measured from the root, so they start with a / and then they list the directories you go through to find the one you want. For example, the absolute path to the pi directory is /home/pi. Whichever directory you are in, you can go straight to the pi directory using

```
cd /home/pi
```

If you wanted to go straight to the Desktop directory, you would use

```
cd /home/pi/Desktop
```

To go straight to the root, just use a slash by itself, like this:

```
cd /
```

Besides using the root as a reference point for an absolute path, you can also use your home directory, which you represent with a tilde (~). You can use it by itself to jump back to your home directory:

```
cd ~
```

Alternatively, you can use it as the start of an absolute path to another directory that's inside your home directory, like this:

```
cd ~/Desktop
```

Relative paths use your current working directory as the starting point. It's shown in the command prompt, but you can also check it by entering the command

```
pwd
```

Whereas your command prompt uses the tilde (~) character if you're in your home directory, pwd tells you where that actually is on the directory tree and reports it as /home/pi.

A relative path that refers to a subdirectory below the current one just lists the path through the subdirectories in order, separating them with a slash. For example, on Figure 5-1, you can see that there is a directory called home, with a directory called pi inside it, and a directory called Desktop inside that. When you're in the directory with the name home, you can change into the Desktop directory by specifying a path of pi/Desktop, like this:

```
pi@raspberrypi /home $ cd pi/Desktop
pi@raspberrypi ~/Desktop $
```

You can change into any directory below the current one in this way. You can also have a relative path that goes up the directory tree by using .. to represent the parent directory. Referring to Figure 5-1 again, imagine you want to go from the Desktop directory into the python_games directory. You can do that by going through the pi directory using this command:

```
pi@raspberrypi ~/Desktop $ cd ../python_games
pi@raspberrypi ~/python_games $
```

As the prompt shows, you've moved from the Desktop directory into the python_games directory. You started in Desktop, went into its parent directory (pi), and then changed into the python_games directory there. You can go through multiple parent directories to navigate the tree. If you wanted to go from the pi directory to the boot directory, you could use

```
pi@raspberrypi ~ $ cd ../../boot
pi@raspberrypi /boot $
```

That takes you into the parent directory of pi (the directory called home), takes you up one more level to the root, and then changes into the boot directory.

You can choose to use an absolute or relative path depending on which is most convenient. If the file or directory you're referring to is relatively close to your current directory, it might be simplest to use a relative path. Otherwise, it might be less confusing to use an absolute path. It's up to you. Paths like this aren't just used for changing directories. You can also use them with other commands and to refer to a specific file by adding the filename at the end of the path. For example, you can use the `file` command like this:

```
file /boot/config.txt
```

As you discover more commands in this chapter that work with files, you'll be able to use your knowledge of paths to refer to files that aren't in the same directory as your current working directory.

Be careful not to confuse absolute and relative paths. In particular, pay attention to where you use a slash. You should only use a / at the start of your path if you intend to use an absolute path starting at the root.

If you want to change into a directory for a quick look around and then go back again, you can use a shortcut to change back to your previous directory:

```
cd -
```

If you enter this, the shell shows you the previous directory you were in and then changes your current working directory to that.

You can also change to your home directory quickly by using the cd command alone, like this:

```
pi@raspberrypi /boot $ cd
pi@raspberrypi ~ $
```

Investigating more advanced listing options

You can use ls to look inside any directory outside the current working directory by specifying its path, like this:

```
pi@raspberrypi ~ $ ls /boot
```

Although you're in your home directory, that command gives you a listing from the /boot directory.

When we provide information for a command to process like this, such as a filename or a path, it's called an *argument*. Many Linux commands can accept arguments in this way (including the cd and file commands). Some commands can also accept options. Options tell the command how to do its work, and they have the format of a hyphen followed by a code that tells the command which option(s) to use.

There are several options you can use with ls to change its results, shown in Table 5-1. For example, change into your home directory and use

```
pi@raspberrypi ~ $ ls -R
```

This lists all the contents in your home directory, and then all the contents in the Desktop and python_games folders, which are both inside your home directory.

When you are using options and arguments together, the options come before the arguments, so the format of the typical Linux command is

```
command -options arguments
```

For example, try using the -X option to list the contents of the python_games folder. All the .png, .py, and .wav files will be grouped together, so it's easier to see what's there. The command to use is

```
pi@raspberrypi ~ $ ls -X ~/python_games
```

You can use several options together by adding all the option codes after a single hyphen. For example, if you want to look in all your directories under your current directory (option R), and you want to group the results by file type (option X), and use symbols to indicate directories and executables beside their filenames (option F), you would use

```
pi@raspberrypi ~ $ ls -RXF
```

Figure 5-2 shows the resulting output. One thing you might notice here is that a single period (full stop) is used to refer to the current directory in the pathnames, so the path for the first set of results is simply a period. This short code for the current directory is similar to the two periods used to refer to the parent directory.

Figure 5-2: A listing including all subdirectories, sorted by file type, with symbols used to indicate folders and executables by their filenames.

When you're experimenting with ls (or at any other time, come to that), use the command clear to empty the screen if it gets messy and hard to follow.

Table 5-1	Options for ls Command
Option	**Description**
-1	Adding a number 1 outputs the results in a single column instead of a row.
-a	Displays all files, including hidden files. The names of hidden files start with a period (full stop). Hidden files are usually put there (and required) by the operating system, so they're best left alone. You can create your own hidden files by using filenames that start with a period.
-F	This option puts a symbol beside a filename to indicate its type. When you use this option, directories have a / after their names, and executables have a * after their name.
-h	In the long format, this option expresses file sizes using kilobytes, megabytes, and gigabytes to save you the mental arithmetic of working them out. It's short for human-readable.
-l	This displays results in the long format, which shows information about the permissions of files, when they were last modified and how big they are. Note that this option uses a letter l, short for *long*.
-m	Lists the results as a list separated by commas.
-R	This is the recursive option. As well as listing files and directories in the current working directory, it opens any subdirectories and lists their results too, and keeps opening subdirectories and listing their results, working its way down the directory tree. You can look at all the files on your Raspberry Pi using ls -R from the root. Be warned: It'll take a while. To cancel when you get bored, use Ctrl+C.
-r	This is the reverse option, and it displays results in reverse order. By default, results are in alphabetical order, so this will show them in reverse alphabetical order. Note that -r and -R are completely different options.
-S	This sorts the results by their size.
-t	This sorts the results according to the date and time they were last modified.
-X	This sorts the results according to the file extension.

Understanding the Long Listing Format and Permissions

One of the most useful ls options is long format, which provides more information on a file. You trigger it using the option –l (a letter l) after the ls command, like this:

```
pi@raspberrypi ~/ $ ls -l
total 40
-rw-r--r-- 1 pi pi    256 Nov 18 13:53 booknotes.txt
drwxr-xr-x 2 pi pi   4096 Oct 28 22:54 Desktop
drwxrwxr-x 2 pi pi   4096 Nov 17 13:40 python_games
drwxr-xr-x 2 pi pi   4096 Nov  3 17:43 seanwork
-rw-r--r-- 1 pi pi  20855 Nov 12  2010 spacegame.sb
```

This listing includes some of Sean's work files on the Raspberry Pi (book-notes.txt, spacegame.sb and the directory seanwork), which we can use to see how different files are described.

This layout might look a bit eccentric, but it's easier to follow if you read it from right to left. Each line relates to one file or directory, with its name on the right and the time and date it was last modified next to that. For older files, the date's year appears in place of the modification time, as you can see for the file spacegame.sb in the preceding list.

The number in the middle of the line is the size of the file. Three of the entries (Desktop, python_games, and seanwork) are directories that have the same file size (4096 bytes), although they have vastly different contents. That's because directories are files too, and the number here is telling you how big the file is that describes the directory, and not how big the directory's contents are. The file size is measured in bytes, but you can add the -h option to give you more meaningful numbers, translating 4096 bytes into 4K, for example.

The rest of the information concerns *permissions,* which refer to who is allowed to use the file and what they are allowed to do with it. Linux was designed from the start to offer a secure way for multiple users to share the same system, and so permissions are an essential part of how Linux works.

Many people find they can use their Raspberry Pi without needing to know too much about permissions, but permissions tell you a lot about how Linux works, and you might find the knowledge useful if you want to be a bit more adventurous.

The permissions on a file are divided into three categories: things the file's *owner* can do (who is usually the person who created the file), things that *group owners* can do (people who belong to a group that has permission to use the file), and things that *everyone* can do (known as the world permissions).

In the long listing, you can see the word pi is shown twice for each file. These two columns represent the owner of the file or directory (the left of the two columns), and the group that owns the file. These both have the same name here because Linux creates a group for each user with just that user in it, and with the same name as the user. In theory, the group could be called something like *students,* and include all the students who have usernames for the computer.

The far left column contains a code that explains what type of file each file is, and what the permissions are on that file. To make sense of the code, you need to break it down into four chunks, like Table 5-2, which represents the code shared by booknotes.txt and spacegame.sb in our long listing.

Table 5-2	Understanding Permissions		
File type	*Owner*	*Group*	*World*
-	rw-	r--	r--

The two main file types you're likely to come across are regular files and directories. Regular files have a hyphen (-) for their file type at the start of their code, and directories have a d. You can see both of these symbols used in our long directory listing.

Next come the permissions for the owner, group and world. These are the three different types of permission someone can have:

- **Read permission:** The ability to open and look at the contents of a file, or to list a directory
- **Write permission:** The ability to change a file's contents, or to create or delete files in a directory
- **Execute permission:** The ability to treat a file as a program and run it, or to enter a directory using the cd command

That probably seems logical and intuitive, but there are two potential catches: Firstly, you can only read or write in a directory if you also have execute permission for that directory; and, secondly, you can only rename or delete a file if the permissions of its *directory* allow you to do so, even if you have write permission for the file.

The permissions are expressed using the letters r (for read), w (for write), and x (for execute), and these make up a three-letter code in that order. Where permission has not been granted, the letter is replaced with a hyphen. So in Table 5-2, you can see that the owner can read and write the file, but the group owner and world (everyone else) can only read it.

The code for the Desktop folder in our long listing is drwxr-xr-x. The first letter tells you it's a directory. The next three letters (rwx) tell you that the owner can read, write to it, and execute it, which means they have freedom to list its contents (read), add or delete files (write), and enter the directory in the first place to carry out those actions (execute). The next three characters (r-x) tell you group owners may enter the directory (execute) and list its contents (read), but may not create or delete files. The final three characters (r-x) tell you everyone else (the world) has been granted those same read-only permissions.

Several commands are used to change the permissions of a file (including chmod to change the permissions, chown to change a file's owner, and chgrp to change the file's group owner). We don't have space to go into detail here, but see "Learning More about Linux Commands" in this chapter for guidance on how to get help with them. The easiest way to change permissions, in any case, is through the desktop environment. Right-click a file in File Manager (see Chapter 4) and open its properties. The Permissions tab of the File Properties window, shown in Figure 5-3, enables you to change all the permissions associated with a file.

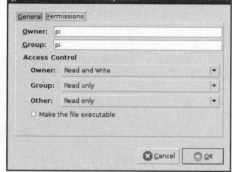

Figure 5-3:
Changing file permissions using File Manager.

LXDE Foundation e.V.

Slowing Down the Listing and Reading Files with the Less Command

The problem with ls is that it can deluge you with information that flies past your eyes faster than you can see it. If you use the LXTerminal from the desktop environment, you can use a scrollbar to review information that has scrolled off the screen.

The more usual solution, however, is to use a command called less, which takes your listing and enables you to page through it, one screen at a time. To send the listing to the less command, you use a pipe character after your listing command, like this:

```
ls | less
```

When you're using `less`, you can move through the listing one line at a time using the up and down arrow keys, or one page at a time using the Page Up (or b) and Page Down (or space) keys. You can search by pressing / and then typing what you'd like to search for and pressing Enter. When you've finished, press the Q key (upper- or lowercase) to quit.

You can cancel a Linux command, including an overwhelming listing, by pressing Ctrl+C.

You can also use `less` to view the contents of a text file by giving it the file-name as an argument, like this:

```
less /boot/config.txt
```

This is a great way to read files you find as you explore Linux. The `less` command warns you if the file you want to read might be a binary file, which means it's computer code and likely to be unintelligible, so you can try using the `less` command on anything and bow out gracefully if you get the warning. Displaying binary code on screen can result in some strange results, including distorting the character set in the shell.

If you want to see the first ten lines of a file, perhaps just to check what version it is, you can use the command `head` followed by the filename.

Now you have all the tools you need to explore your Linux operating system!

Speeding Up Entering Commands

Now you've learned a few basic commands, we can teach you a few tricks to speed up your use of the shell.

First of all, the shell keeps a record of the commands you enter called your history, so you can save retyping if you want to reuse a command. If you want to reuse the last command, just type in two exclamation marks and press Enter. If you want to use an earlier command, tapping the up arrow brings back your previous commands in order (most recent first) and puts them after your prompt. The down arrow moves through your history in the other direction if you overshoot the command you want. You can edit the command before pressing Enter to issue it.

The shell also tries to guess what you want to type and automatically completes it for you if you tap the Tab key. You can use it for commands and files. For example, type

```
cd /bo
```

and then press the Tab key, and the path is completed as /boot/.

This technique is particularly helpful if you're dealing with long and complicated filenames. If it doesn't work, you haven't given the shell enough of a hint, so you need to give it some more letters to be sure what you mean.

Using Redirection to Create Files in Linux

Before you look at how you delete files and copy them, you should prepare some files to play with.

It's possible to send the results from a command to a file instead of the screen; in other words, to redirect them. You could keep some listing results in a file, for example, so you have a permanent record of them or so you can analyze them using a text editor. You turn screen output into a file by using a greater-than sign and the filename you'd like to send the output to, like this:

```
ls > ~/listing.txt
```

You don't need to have the file extension of .txt for it to work in Linux, but it's a useful reminder for yourself, and it helps if you ever copy the file back to a Windows machine.

Try using this command twice from two different directories and then looking at the contents of listing.txt with the `less` command. You'll see just how unforgiving Linux is. The first time you run the command, the file listing.txt is created. The second time you do it, it's replaced without warning. Linux trusts you to know what you're doing, so you need to be careful not to overwrite files.

If you want a bit of variety, you can use some other commands to display content on screen:

✔ `echo`: This displays whatever you write after it on screen. You can use it to solve mathematics problems if you put them between two pairs of brackets (parentheses) and put a dollar sign in front, for example:

```
echo $((5*5)).
```

✔ `date`: This shows the current time and date.

✔ `cal`: This shows the current month's calendar, with today highlighted. You can see the whole year's calendar using the option -y.

If you want to add something to the end of an existing file, you use two greater-than signs, as you can see in this example:

```
pi@raspberrypi ~ $ echo I made this file on > testfile.txt
pi@raspberrypi ~ $ date >> testfile.txt
pi@raspberrypi ~ $ cal >> testfile.txt
pi@raspberrypi ~ $ echo $((6+31+31+28+31+7)) Days until
        my birthday! >> testfile.txt
pi@raspberrypi ~ $ less testfile.txt
I made this file on
Sat Nov 24 14:40:43 GMT 2012
    November 2012
Su Mo Tu We Th Fr Sa
             1  2  3
 4  5  6  7  8  9 10
11 12 13 14 15 16 17
18 19 20 21 22 23 24
25 26 27 28 29 30

134 Days until my birthday!
```

You can use redirection like this to create some files you can practice copying and deleting. If you don't want to spend time creating the file contents, you can make some empty files by redirecting nothing, like this:

```
> testfile1.txt
```

Top Tips for Naming Your Files in Linux

If you plan to use the shell, you can follow a few guidelines when creating files that will make your Linux life much easier. These tips apply even if you're creating files using the desktop environment, but it only really matters when you start working with files in the shell.

Here's our advice:

- ✔ Only use lowercase so you don't have to remember where the capital letters are in a filename.

- ✔ Don't use filenames with spaces. They have to be treated differently in the shell (put inside single or double quote marks); otherwise, Linux thinks each of the words in the filename is a different file. An underscore is a good substitute.

- ✔ Don't use filenames that start with a hyphen. They're liable to get confused with command options.

🗸 Don't use the / character anywhere in a filename.

🗸 Avoid using an apostrophe ('), question mark (?), asterisk (*), quotation (speech) marks ("), slash (\), square brackets ([]), or curved braces ({}). If they appear in a filename in the shell, you'll need to either put a \ character before each one or put the whole filename in speech marks (assuming it doesn't already have any).

Creating Directories

As you may know from other computers you've used, it's a lot easier to manage the files on your computer if they're organized into directories (or folders). You can easily create a directory in your home directory using the command `mkdir`:

```
mkdir work
```

To save time, use one command to create several directories, like this:

```
pi@raspberrypi ~ $ mkdir work college games
pi@raspberrypi ~ $ ls
college  Desktop  games  ocr_pi.png  python_games  work
```

You might see additional files here, especially if you followed the earlier examples to make some text files, but the important thing is that one command made three new directories for you.

The `mkdir` command's ability to make several directories at the same time isn't unusual: Many other commands can also take several arguments and process them in order. You can see the listing of two different directories like this, for example:

```
ls ~ /boot
```

The `mkdir` command doesn't give you a lot of insight into what it's doing by default, but you can add the `-v` option (short for *verbose*), which gives you a running commentary as each directory is created. You can see what it looks like in the next code snippet.

If you want to make some directories with subdirectories inside them, it would be a nuisance to have to create a directory, go inside it, create another directory, go inside that, and so on. Instead, use the `-p` option, like this:

```
pi@raspberrypi ~ $ mkdir -vp work/writing/books
mkdir : created directory 'work'
mkdir : created directory 'work/writing'
mkdir : created directory 'work/writing/books'
```

The command keeps you informed of any changes it makes, but if the work directory already exists, you won't see the first line of output above.

Deleting Files in Linux

After experimenting with creating files and directories, you probably have odd bits of file and meaningless directories all over the place, so it's time to tidy up.

To delete files in Linux, you use the rm command, short for *remove*. Use it *very* carefully. There's no trash can or recycle bin to recover your file from again, so when it's gone, it's gone. Actually, expert Linux users *might* be able to get it back using specialized software and huge amounts of time and patience, so it's not a secure deletion. But for an average user without access to such software and expertise, when you tell Linux to remove a file, it acts fast and decisively.

The rm command has this format:

```
rm options filename
```

As with mkdir, the command doesn't tell you what it's doing unless you use the verbose option (-v). As an example, you could remove a file called letter. txt using

```
pi@raspberrypi ~ $ rm -v letter.txt
removed 'letter.txt'
```

Like mkdir, running the rm command can take several arguments, which means it can remove several files at once if you list all their names, for example:

```
pi@raspberrypi ~ $ rm -v letter.txt letter2.txt
removed 'letter.txt'
removed 'letter2.txt'
```

This is where you need to be extremely careful. Imagine you have two files called *old index.html* and *index.html*. The latter is your new website home-page, which you've toiled over all weekend (you can see where this is going, can't you?). You want to clear out the old development file, so you issue this command:

```
pi@raspberrypi ~ $ rm -v old index.html
rm : cannot remove 'old': No such file or directory
removed 'index.html'
```

Arrrggh! Because of that space in the *old index.html* filename, the `rm` command thinks that you wanted to remove two files, one called *old* and the other called *index.html*. It tells you it can't find the file called *old*, but goes right ahead and wipes out *index.html*. Nasty!

To pin up a safety net, use the `-i` option (for interactive), which tells you which file(s) will be deleted, and prompts you to confirm each deletion. Using that would have avoided this mistake, as shown here:

```
pi@raspberrypi ~ $ rm -vi old index.html
rm : cannot remove 'old': No such file or directory
rm : remove regular file 'index.html'?
```

No, no, no! When prompted, you enter **Y** to confirm the deletion or **N** to keep the file and move on to the next one (if any).

The risk of deleting the wrong file is one reason why you should avoid files with spaces in their names. For the record, the correct way to remove a file whose name contains a space would be to enclose it in quotes:

```
pi@raspberrypi ~ $ rm -vi 'old index.html'
```

Using Wildcards to Select Multiple Files in Linux

Often, a directory contains lots of files that have similar filenames. Sean's digital camera, for example, creates files with names like these:

```
img_8474.jpg
img_8475.jpg
img_8476.jpg
img_8477.jpg
img_8478.jpg
```

If you want to delete a group of them, or to copy them or do anything else with them, you don't want to repeat the command typing out each filename in turn. Computers are good at repetition, so it's better to leave the donkey work to the shell.

Wildcards enable you to do that. Instead of giving a specific filename to a command, you can give it a pattern to match, such as all the files that begin with img, or all the files that have the extension .jpg. The asterisk wildcard replaces any number of any character, so *.jpg returns any filenames that end with .jpg, no matter how long they are, and no matter how many of them there are. The question mark asterisk replaces just one character, so img?.jpg would select img1.jpg, img2.jpg, and imgb.jpg, but ignore img11.jpg or any other longer filenames.

If you want to choose files that begin with a particular letter, you can use the square brackets wildcard. To choose any files beginning with the letters a, b, or c, you would use [abc]*. To narrow that down to just those that end with .jpg, you would use [abc]*.jpg.

Table 5-3 provides a quick reference to the wildcards you can use, with some examples.

Table 5-3	Raspberry Pi Wildcards		
Wildcard	*What It Means*	*Example Usage*	*What the Example Selects*
?	Any single character	photo?.jpg	Any files that start with photo and have exactly one character after it before the .jpg extension. For example, photo1.jpg or photox.jpg, but not photo10.jpg.
*	Any number of characters (including no characters)	*photo*	Any files that have the word photo in their filenames.
[. . .]	Matches any one of the characters in brackets	[abc]*	All files that start with a letter a, b, or c.
[^. . .]	Matches any single character that isn't between the brackets	[^abc]*	Any files that do not start with a letter a, b, or c.
[a-z]	Matches any single character in the range specified	[a-c]*.jpg	Any files that start with a letter a, b, or c and end with the .jpg extension.
[0-9]	Matches any single character in the range specified	photo[2-5].jpg	Matches photo2.jpg, photo3.jpg, photo 4.jpg, and photo5.jpg.

You can use wildcards anywhere you would usually use a filename. For example, you can delete all your files starting with the letters img, like this:

```
rm -vi img*
```

To delete all the files ending with the extension .txt, use

```
rm -vi *.txt
```

Be especially careful about where you put your spaces when you're using wildcards. Imagine you add a sneaky space in the previous example, like this:

```
rm -vi * .txt
```

Doh! The shell thinks you want it to delete *, which is a wildcard for every file, and then to delete a file called .txt. Luckily, you've used the -i option, so you'll be prompted before deleting each file, but people often omit that when they're deleting a lot of files because otherwise they spend a long time confirming each deletion, which is almost as tedious as not using wildcards in the first place.

One way you can test which files match a wildcard is to use the file command with it before you delete using it. For example

```
file *.txt | less
```

Take care that you don't introduce any spaces between testing with file and removing with rm!

Another thing to be careful about is using wildcards with hidden files. Hidden files begin with a full stop, so you might think that .* would match all the hidden files. It does, but it also matches the current directory (.) and its parent directory (..), so .* matches everything in the current directory and the directory above it.

Removing Directories

You can use two commands for removing directories. The first one, rmdir, is the safer of the two, because it refuses to remove directories that still have files or directories inside them. Use it with the name of the directory you want to remove, for example books, like this:

```
rmdir books
```

If you want to prune a whole branch of your directory tree, you can use the rm command to remove a directory and delete anything inside it and its subdirectories. Used with the recursive option (-R), it works its way down the directory tree, and with the force option (-f), it deletes any files in its way. It's a rampaging beast of a command. Here's an example:

```
rm -Rf books
```

It acts silently and swiftly, deleting the books directory and anything in it.

You can add the interactive option to cut the risk, which prompts you for confirmation of each deletion, as you can see in this example where we've left a file in the folder work/writing/books:

```
pi@raspberrypi ~ $ rm -Rfi work
rm: descend into directory 'work'? Y
rm: descend into directory 'work/writing'? Y
rm: descend into directory 'work/writing/books'? Y
rm: remove regular file
        'work/writing/books/rapidplan.txt'? Y
rm: remove directory 'work/writing/books'? Y
rm: remove directory 'work/writing'? Y
rm: remove directory 'work'? Y
```

You can use wildcards when removing directories, but take special care with them, and make sure you don't introduce any unwanted spaces that result in you removing * (everything). If you use rm -Rf .* to try to remove hidden directories, you also match the current directory (.) and the parent directory (..). That means it deletes every file in the current directory (hidden or not), all its subdirectories and their contents (hidden or not), and everything in the parent directory, including its subdirectories (again, whether or not they are hidden).

Our own experience of the Linux community has been that it's friendly and supportive, and people welcome newcomers who want to join. But occasionally, you might come across some joker online advising inexperienced users that the solution to their problems is to issue the command rm -Rf /* as root, which attempts to delete everything, starting at the root.

Copying and Renaming Files

One of the fundamental things you'll want to do with your files is copy them, so let's take a look at how to do that. The command you need to use is cp, and it takes this form:

```
cp [options] copy_from copy_to
```

Replace `copy_from` with the file you want to copy, and `copy_to` for where you want to copy it to.

For example, if you wanted to copy the file config.txt from the /boot directory to your home directory (~) so you can safely play with it, you would use

```
cp /boot/config.txt ~
```

If you wanted to copy the file into your current working directory, wherever that is, you could use

```
cp /boot/config.txt .
```

You can also specify a path to an existing folder to send the file to

```
cp /boot/config.txt ~/files/
```

Your original file and the copy don't have to have the same name. If you specify a different filename, the copy takes that name. For example:

```
cp /boot/config.txt ~/oldconfig.txt
```

That copies config.txt from the /boot directory to your home directory and renames it as oldconfig.txt. This same technique enables you to keep a safe copy of a file you're working on, in case you want to revert to an old version later. The paths are optional, so if you were in your home directory, you could create a backup copy of the file timeplan.txt there using

```
cp timeplan.txt timeplan.bak
```

You can use several options with `cp`, some of them familiar from the `rm` command. The `cp` command overwrites any files in its way without asking you, so use the `-i` option to force it to ask you before it overwrites any existing files with the new copies. The `-v` option gives you an insight into what the command has done, as it does with `rm`.

You can use wildcards, so you can quickly copy all your files, or all your files that match a particular pattern. If you want it to copy subdirectories too, however, you need to use the recursive option, like this:

```
cp -R ~/Scratch/* ~/homebak
```

That command copies everything in your Scratch directory (including any subdirectories) into a folder called homebak in your home directory. The homebak directory must exist before you run the command for it to work. For advice on using the shell to copy to external storage devices, see Appendix A.

If you don't want to make a copy of a file, but instead want to move it from one place to another, use the mv command. For example, if you misfiled one of your images and wanted to move it from the *australia* directory to the *japan* one, both in your home directory, you would use

```
mv ~/australia/itinerary.txt ~/japan
```

That works as long as the destination directory exists. If it doesn't, the command assumes you want the file to have the new filename of japan, and so the file stops being itinerary.txt in the *australia* directory, and becomes a file called *japan* in the home directory. It's confusing if you do it by mistake, but this quirk is how you rename files in Linux. You move them from being the old name, into being the new name, usually in the same folder, like this:

```
mv oldname newname
```

There's no recursive option with the mv command because it moves directories as easily as it moves files by default.

Installing and Managing Software on Your Raspberry Pi

After you've got the hang of it, the Raspberry Pi makes it incredibly easy to discover, download, and install new software. Linux distributions come with thousands of packages, which are software programs that are ready to download from the Internet and install on your computer.

Some packages require other packages to work successfully, but luckily a program called a *package manager* untangles all these dependencies and takes responsibility for downloading and installing the software you want, together with any other software it needs to work correctly. On the Raspberry Pi, the package manager is called apt.

Installing software requires the authority of the root user or superuser of the computer. The Raspberry Pi doesn't come with a root account enabled, in common with some other Linux distributions. One school of thought says that a root account is a security threat because people are inclined to use it all the time rather than log in and out of it when they need it. That leaves the whole system and its files vulnerable, including to any malicious software that might get in. Instead of using a root account, you use the word sudo before a command on the Raspberry Pi to indicate that you want to carry it out with the authority of the root user. You can't use it before all commands, but it's essential for installing software.

If you ever get an error message that tells you something can only be done with the authority of the root, try repeating the command but putting sudo in front of it.

Updating the cache

The first step in installing software is to update the repository, which is the list of packages the package manager knows about. You do that by entering the following command:

```
sudo apt-get update
```

You need to have a working Internet connection for this to work, and it's likely to take some time. Consider leaving the Raspberry Pi to get on with it while you have a cup of tea, or a slice of raspberry pie, perhaps.

Finding the package name

The apt cache contains an index of all the software packages available, and you can search it to find the software you want. For example, you can find all the games by using

```
sudo apt-cache search game
```

The list is huge, so you might want to use less to browse it, like this:

```
sudo apt-cache search game | less
```

The screen output looks like this:

```
pi@raspberrypi ~ $ sudo apt-cache search game
0ad-data - Real-time strategy game of ancient warfare
          (data)
3dchess - Play chess across 3 boards!
4digits - guess-the-number game, aka Bulls and Cows
7kaa-data - Seven Kingdoms Ancient Adversaries - game data
a7xpg - chase action game
a7xpg-data - chase action game - game data
abe - Side-scrolling game named "Abe's Amazing Adventure"
abe-data - Side-scrolling game named "Abe's Amazing
           Adventure"
[list continues. . .]
```

The bit before the hyphen tells you the name of the package, which is what you need to be able to install it. That might not be the same as the game's title or its popular name. For example, there are lots of solitaire card games you can install, but none of them have the package name `solitaire`. To find the package name for a solitaire game, you would use

```
sudo apt-cache search solitaire
```

This search returns 20 results, and the first one is

```
ace-of-penguins - penguin-themed solitaire games
```

Installing software

If you know the name of the package you would like to install, the following command downloads it from the Internet and installs it, together with any other packages it needs to work correctly (known as *dependencies*):

```
sudo apt-get install ace-of-penguins
```

The last bit is the name of the package we found by searching the cache.

Note that when you're searching the cache, you use `apt-cache` in the command and when you're installing software you use `apt-get`. It's easy to get these mixed up, so if it doesn't work, double-check you're using the right one.

Running software

Some programs can be run directly from the command line by just typing in their names, such as

```
penguinspuzzle
```

which runs the Penguins Puzzle game (see Chapter 19). This game doesn't show up in the menus in the desktop environment, and needs to be run from the command line using this command.

Most end-user applications require the X server, which means you need to be in the desktop environment to run them. After installing them, you can find them in your Programs menu.

Whether a program should be run from the command line or in the desktop environment depends on the program, so consult its instructions if you can't work out how to start it.

Upgrading the software on your Raspberry Pi

The package manager's responsibility doesn't end once it has installed software. It can also be used to keep that software up to date, installing the latest enhancements and security improvements. You can issue a single command to update all the software on your Raspberry Pi:

```
sudo apt-get upgrade
```

It's a good idea to update the cache first to make sure apt installs the latest updates to your installed packages. You can combine both commands into a single line, like this:

```
sudo apt-get update && sudo apt-get upgrade
```

The && means that the second command should be carried out only if the first one succeeds. If the update to the cache doesn't work, it won't attempt to upgrade all the software.

The upgrading process ties up your Raspberry Pi for some time.

If you want to update just one application, you do that by issuing its install command again. Imagine you've already installed Ace of Penguins and you enter

```
sudo apt-get install ace-of-penguins
```

That prompts apt to check for any updates to that package and install them. If there are none, it tells you that you're already running the latest version.

Removing software and freeing up space

The package manager can also be used to remove software from your Raspberry Pi. For example:

```
sudo apt-get remove ace-of-penguins
```

This leaves traces of the applications, which might include user files and any files of settings. If you're sure you won't need any of this information, you can completely remove and clean up after an application using

```
sudo apt-get purge ace-of-penguins
```

You can do two other things to free up some precious space on your SD card and clean up your system. First, you can automatically remove packages that are no longer required. When a package is installed, other packages it requires are usually installed alongside it. These packages can remain after the original program has been removed, so there's a command to automatically remove packages that are no longer required. It is

```
sudo apt-get autoremove
```

It lists the packages that will be removed and tells you how much space it will free up before prompting you to enter a **Y** to confirm you want to continue.

When you install a package, the first step is to download its installation file to your Raspberry Pi. After the package has been installed, its installation file remains in the directory /var/cache/apt/archives. Over time, as you try out more and more packages, this can amount to quite a lot of space on your SD card. Take a look in that directory to see what's built up there. These files aren't doing much. If you reinstall a program, you can always download the installation file again.

The second thing you can do to clean up your SD card is remove these files using

```
sudo apt-get clean
```

Finding out what's installed on your Raspberry Pi

To find out what software is installed on your Raspberry Pi, you can use

```
dpkg --list
```

This command doesn't need root authority to run, so it doesn't require you to put sudo at the start.

If you want to find out whether a specific package is installed, use

```
dpkg --status packagename
```

For applications that are installed, this also provides a longer description than the short apt cache description, which might include a web link for further documentation.

The Raspberry Pi includes many packages that come with the Linux operating system and are required for its operation. If you didn't deliberately install a package, exercise caution before removing it.

Managing User Accounts on Your Raspberry Pi

If you want to share the Raspberry Pi with different family members, you could create a user account for each one, so they all have their own home directory. The robust permissions in Linux help to ensure that people can't accidentally delete each other's files too.

When we looked at the long listing format, we discussed permissions. You might remember that users can be members of groups. On the Raspberry Pi, groups control access to resources like the audio and video hardware, so before you can create a new user account, you need to understand which groups that user should belong to. To find out, use the groups command to see which groups the default pi user is a member of:

```
pi@raspberrypi ~ $ groups pi
pi : pi adm dialout cdrom sudo audio video plugdev
        games users netdev input spi gpio
```

When you create a new user, you want to make him a member of most of these groups, except for the group pi (which is the group for the user pi). Be warned that if you give users membership of the sudo group, they will be able to install software, change passwords, and do pretty much anything on the machine (if they know how). In a home or family setting, that should be fine, however. The permissions system still protects users from accidentally deleting data they shouldn't, as long as they steer clear of the sudo command.

To add a user, you use the useradd command with the -m option to create a home directory for him and the -G option to list the groups the user should be a member of, like this:

```
sudo useradd -m -G [list of groups] [username]
```

For example:

```
sudo useradd -m -G
            adm,dialout,cdrom,sudo,audio,video,plugdev,game
            s,users,netdev,input,spi,gpio karen
```

Make sure the list of groups is separated with a comma and there are no spaces in there.

You can do a quick check to confirm that a new home directory has been created with the user's name in the directory /home, alongside the home directory for the pi user:

```
ls /home
```

You also need to set a password for the account, like this:

```
sudo passwd [username]
```

For example,

```
sudo passwd karen
```

You are prompted to enter the password twice, to make sure you don't mistype it, and you can use this command to change the password for any user. There is no output on the screen as you type the password, which can be a bit off-putting, but keep typing and it should work fine.

You can test whether it's worked and log in as the new user without restarting your Pi by logging out from your current user account:

```
logout
```

If you use the `passwd` command to set a password for the username root, you will be able to log on as the superuser, who has the power to do anything on the machine. As a last resort, this might enable you to get some types of software working, but we advise you against using it. It's safer to take on the mantle of the superuser only when you need it, by using `sudo`.

Don't forget how cheap SD cards are. If you want to share the Raspberry Pi with different family members, you could just give each user his own SD card to insert when he's using the machine, and let him log on with the pi username and password.

Learning More about Linux Commands

Lots of information about Linux is available on the Internet, but plenty of documentation is also hidden inside the operating system itself. If you want to dig further into what Linux can do, this documentation can point you in the right direction, although some of it is phrased in quite a technical way.

Commands in Linux can take several different forms. They might be built in to the shell itself, they might be separate programs in the /bin directory, or they could be aliases (which are explained in the next section). If you want to look up the documentation for a command, first find out what kind of command it is, using the `type` command, like this:

```
pi@raspberrypi ~ $ type cd
cd is a shell builtin
pi@raspberrypi ~ $ type mkdir
mkdir is /bin/mkdir
pi@raspberrypi ~ $ type ls
ls is aliased to 'ls --color=auto'
```

If you want to find out where a particular program in installed, use the `which` command together with the program name:

```
which mkdir
```

To get documentation for shell built-ins, you can use the shell's `help` facility. Just enter **help** followed by the filename you're looking for help with:

```
help cd
```

The `help` command's documentation uses square brackets for different options (which you may omit), and uses a pipe (|) character between items that are mutually exclusive, such as options that mean the opposite of each other.

For commands that are programs, such as `mkdir`, you can try using the command with `--help` after it. Many programs are designed of accept this and display help information when it's used. Example usage is

```
mkdir --help
```

When we used this approach on `apt-get`, the `help` page told us that "APT has Super Cow Powers." Try `apt-get moo` to see what it means!

There is also a more comprehensive manual (or `man` page) for most programs, including program-based Linux commands and some applications such as LibreOffice (see Chapter 6). To view the manual for a program, use

```
man program_name
```

For example,

```
man ls
```

The manual is displayed using `less`, so you can use the controls you're familiar with to page through it. This documentation can have a technical bent, so it's not as approachable to beginners as the `help` pages.

If you don't know which command you need to use, you can search across all the manual pages using the `apropos` command, like this:

```
pi@raspberrypi ~ $ apropos delete
argz_delete (3)         - functions to handle an argz list
delete_module (2)       - delete a loadable module entry
dphys-swapfile (8)      - set up, mount/unmount, and delete
                          an swap file
groupdel (8)            - delete a group
rmdir (2)               - delete a directory
shred (1)               - overwrite a file to hide its
                          contents, and optionally delete it
tdelete (3)             - manage a binary tree
timer_delete (2)        - delete a POSIX per-process timer
tr (1)                  - translate or delete characters
unlink (2)              - delete a name and possibly the file
                          it refers to
userdel (8)             - delete a user account and related
                          files
```

You can then investigate any of these programs further by looking at their man pages, or checking whether they can accept a `--help` request. The number in brackets (parentheses) tells you which section of the man page contains the word you searched for.

For a one-line summary of a program, taken from its man page, use `whatis`:

```
pi@raspberrypi ~ $ whatis ls
ls (1)                  - list directory contents
```

If you're not yet drowning in documentation, there's an alternative to the man page, which is the `info` page. Info pages are structured a bit like a website, with a directory of all the pages at the top, and links between the various pages. You use `info` like this:

```
info ls
```

The controls used to move around an `info` document are a bit different to those in a man page. To call up the list of keys, tap ? (pressing the Shift key) when the info page opens.

Customizing Your Shell with Your Own Linux Commands

If you want to stamp your identity on your Raspberry Pi, you can make up your own Linux commands for it. You can have fun inventing a command that shows a special message if someone enters your name (use the `echo` command for this), but it's genuinely useful for making more memorable shortcuts so you don't have to remember all the different options you might want to use. We show you how to make a command for deleting files that uses the recommended options to confirm each file that will be deleted, and to report on what's been removed. We'll call it `pidel`, a mashup of *Pi* and *delete*.

The first step is to test whether your preferred command name is already in use. If the `type` command tells you anything other than *not found*, you need to think up another command name, or risk upsetting an existing command. Here's our test:

```
pi@raspberrypi ~ $ type pidel
-bash: type: pidel: not found
```

Now that you know that the command `pidel` is not yet taken, you can create your command. To do that, make an alias, like this:

```
alias pidel='rm -vi'
```

Between the quote marks, put the Linux command you want to execute when you enter the `pidel` command. As you can see from this alias instruction, when you use `pidel`, it behaves like `rm -vi`, but you won't have to remember the letters for those options any more. For example:

```
pi@raspberrypi ~ $ pidel *.txt
rm: remove regular file 'fm.txt'? y
removed 'fm.txt'
rm: remove regular file 'toc.txt'? n
pi@raspberrypi ~ $
```

You can combine lists of commands in your alias definition by separating them with semicolons, for example:

```
alias pidel='clear;echo This command removes files with
            the interactive and verbose options on.;rm -vi'
```

Your alias only lasts until the computer is rebooted, but you can make it permanent by putting the alias instruction into the file .bashrc in your home directory. To edit that file, use

```
nano ~/.bashrc
```

Nano is a simple text editor that is covered in more detail in Appendix A, but in brief, you can edit your file, use Ctrl+O to save, and Ctrl+X to exit.

Your alias can go anywhere in the .bashrc file. For convenience, and to avoid the risk of disturbing important information there, we suggest you add your aliases at the top. Each one should be on its own line.

Any commands added in .bashrc take effect when you next start up your Raspberry Pi (see the next section, "Shutting Down and Rebooting Your Raspberry Pi").

Sometimes you might want to replace an existing command with an alias, so that your chosen options are enforced whenever you use it. If you look at the type for ls, for example, it's aliased so it always uses the color option to classify files.

Shutting Down and Rebooting Your Raspberry Pi

You can just remove the power on your Raspberry Pi to switch it off, but there is a risk that this might corrupt the SD card. To minimize that risk, use the following Linux command to turn off your Raspberry Pi safely:

```
sudo halt
```

To switch on your Raspberry Pi again, disconnect and reconnect the power. This is easiest to achieve, with minimal wear on your power supply or Raspberry Pi, if you plug your power supply into a power socket that has a switch on it. You can then use that switch to first remove and then, after a few seconds, restore the power to your Raspberry Pi.

You can reboot (or restart) your Raspberry Pi without disconnecting and reconnecting the power, like this:

```
sudo reboot
```

Part III

Using the Raspberry Pi for Both Work and Play

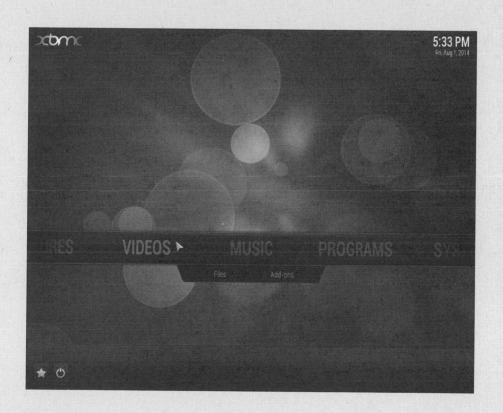

In this part . . .

- ✔ Use LibreOffice to write letters, manage your budget in a spreadsheet, create presentations, and design a party invitation.

- ✔ Use GIMP to edit your photos, including rotating and resizing them, retouching imperfections, and cropping out unnecessary detail.

- ✔ Watch high-definition movies and play music on your Raspberry Pi using Raspbmc or OpenELEC, which turn your Raspberry Pi into a media center.

Chapter 6

Being Productive with the Raspberry Pi

*T*here comes a time in everyone's life when she has to get down to work, and when you do, the Raspberry Pi can help. Whether you need to do your homework or work from home, you can use LibreOffice, a fully featured office suite compatible with the Raspberry Pi.

If you haven't heard of LibreOffice, you might have heard of its more famous ancestor, OpenOffice. A team of developers took OpenOffice as a starting point and developed LibreOffice using its source code.

There are a lot of similarities between LibreOffice and Microsoft Office for Windows, so LibreOffice will probably feel familiar to you. You can copy files between the two programs too, although you might lose some of the layout features when you do that.

In this chapter, I'll show you how to use four of the programs in LibreOffice for common household activities. You'll learn how to write a letter, how to use a spreadsheet to plan a budget, how to create a presentation, and how to design a simple party invitation.

LibreOffice doesn't cost anything and is free to download and distribute. If you're feeling generous, the charitable foundation that drives its development, The Document Foundation, invites donations through its website at www.libreoffice.org.

Installing LibreOffice on Your Raspberry Pi

To download and install LibreOffice, issue the following two commands in the Linux shell:

```
sudo apt-get update
sudo apt-get install libreoffice
```

For further guidance on installing software, and an explanation of how these commands work, see Chapter 5.

Starting LibreOffice on the Raspberry Pi

When you enter the desktop environment using `startx` (see Chapter 4), you should find LibreOffice in your Programs menu, in the Office category. There are separate entries for LibreOffice Base (databases), LibreOffice Calc (spreadsheets), LibreOffice Draw (page layouts and drawings), LibreOffice Impress (presentations), and LibreOffice Writer (word processing).

Another option simply says LibreOffice. This opens a menu (shown in Figure 6-1) from which you can choose to create a text document, spreadsheet, presentation, drawing, database, or formula. If you can't remember which LibreOffice application you need, use this menu. Otherwise, it's probably quicker to go straight to the appropriate application.

You can start a new LibreOffice file of any type from the File menu, irrespective of which application you're using. For example, you can create a new spreadsheet from the word processor's File menu. When you do this, the correct application opens (Calc, in this case) with a blank file ready for you to use.

In this chapter, we show you how to get started with Writer, Calc, Impress, and Draw.

You can also start LibreOffice and open a file in it by double-clicking a LibreOffice or Microsoft Office file in the desktop environment.

If you're a student or academic and have to write scientific or mathematical formulae, the suite also includes LibreOffice Math, which is used to lay out them out (but won't generate the answers for you, we're afraid). To use it, go to the LibreOffice menu and choose Formula.

Figure 6-1:
The
LibreOffice
menu.

Saving Your Work

In all the LibreOffice applications, you save your work through the File menu. You have a choice of formats. The ODF formats are the default, and can be read by other applications, including Microsoft Office. You can also save in the normal file formats of Microsoft Office.

The applications save automatically from time to time and have some capabilities built in to recover files if the computer crashes, but it's better to catch the trapeze than to test the safety net. Save frequently.

Writing Letters in LibreOffice Writer

LibreOffice Writer is a word processor, similar to Microsoft Word on Windows, which makes it the perfect application to use to write a letter.

It can open Microsoft Word files, in fact, and its default file format, the ODF Text Document (a .odt file), can be opened and saved by Word too. For anything but the most basic files, you're likely to experience some corruption of the document's appearance when you open a Word document in LibreOffice, however. You probably won't have the same fonts on your Raspberry Pi, for example, and more advanced layouts tend to get distorted.

Figure 6-2 shows LibreOffice Writer in action. If you've used other word processing packages, it won't take you long to find your feet here. The icons are similar to those used in Microsoft Office, and if you hover over an icon, a tooltip appears to tell you what it does.

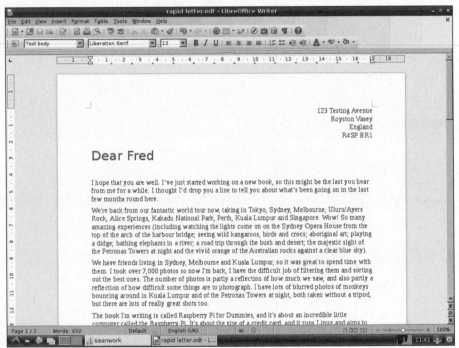

Figure 6-2: Writing a letter with LibreOffice.

You can change the text appearance and the style using the icons and options in the menu bars above your document, and then type onto the page using your chosen formatting in the document. Alternatively, you can click and drag to highlight text in your document and then click the menu bar to apply different formatting to your selected text.

The pull-down menus at the top of the screen provide access to all of LibreOffice Writer's features. Browsing them is a good way to see what the application is capable of.

The Insert menu enables you to add special characters, manual breaks (including page breaks and line breaks), formatting marks (including non-breaking hyphens), document headers and footers, footnotes, bookmarks (they don't appear onscreen, but can help you to navigate the document), comments (useful if you are collaborating on documents), frames (boxes for text that you can arrange where you want on the page), and tables.

The Format menu includes options for character formatting (which includes font and font effects, underlining, superscript, rotation, links, and background colors), paragraph formatting (which includes indents and spacing, alignment, text flow, and borders), bullets and numbering, page formatting (including paper size, background colors and images, headers, and footers), columns (for multicolumn layouts), and alignment.

Using those two menus, you can achieve most of what you need. The most common options are also replicated with icons on the menu bars at the top of the screen.

If you use styles to structure your document (using Heading 1 for the most important headings, and Heading 2 for subheadings, for example), you can use the Navigator to jump to different parts of your document easily. Tap F5 to open it. It also enables you to jump to tables, links, and bookmarks.

Using the File menu, you can save your document as a PDF (.pdf) format file (or *export* it). The great thing about this is that it preserves the formatting of the file, so you can share your document with people who might not have the same fonts or software as you, and guarantee they will see exactly what you see. Most people have software for reading PDF files, but the drawback is that very few people have software for editing them. For that reason, this format is really only suitable for circulating final copies of documents you want people to read but not edit.

Managing Your Budget in LibreOffice Calc

LibreOffice Calc is a spreadsheet application, similar to Microsoft Excel. A good way to try it out is to open one of your Excel spreadsheets using it. Your formulae should work fine and the cell formats should carry over. The interface is similar to LibreOffice Writer, with icons you can roll the mouse pointer over to find out what they do. Figure 6-3 shows Sean's holiday budget in LibreOffice Calc. We've used the slider at the bottom of the screen to magnify the content so it's easy for you to read.

More advanced Microsoft Excel spreadsheets that use macros might not be compatible with LibreOffice.

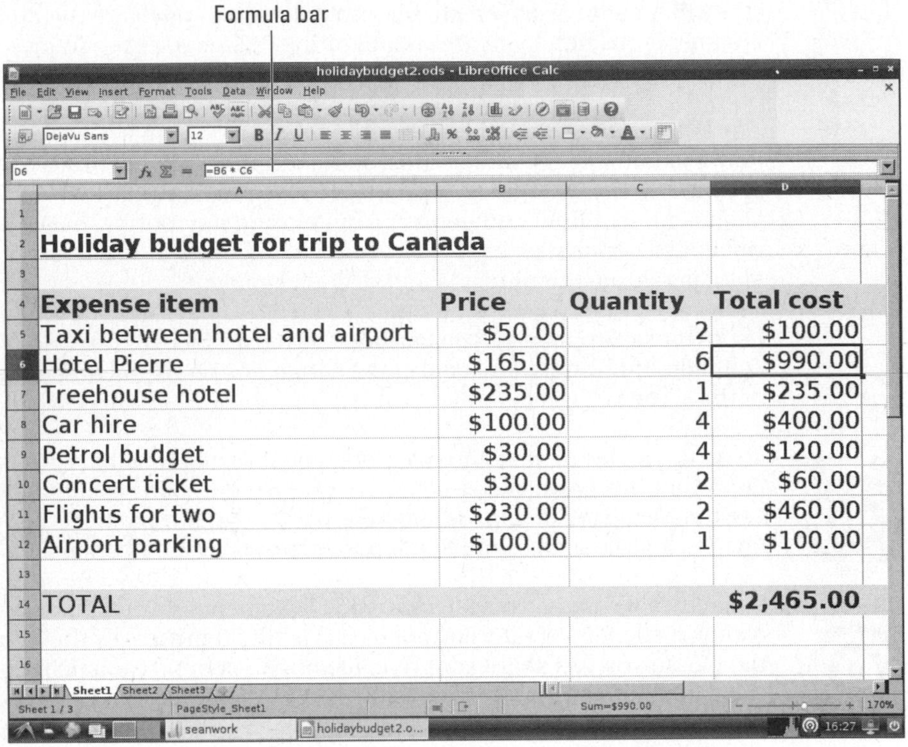

Formula bar

Figure 6-3:
How much?!
Planning
a holiday
budget in
LibreOffice
Calc.

We don't have room to provide an in-depth guide to spreadsheets here, but we can show you how to work out a simple holiday budget.

A spreadsheet is basically a grid of information, but it's powerful because you can use it to perform calculations using that information. The boxes on the spreadsheet are called *cells*. To enter information into a cell, you just click it and then type what you want to enter. Alternatively, you can click a cell and then type into (or edit the contents of) the formula bar at the top of the screen, which is indicated in Figure 6-3.

Each cell has a grid reference, taken from the letter at the top of its column and the number on the left of its row. The top-left cell is A1, and the next cell to the right is B1, and the one below that is B2, as you can see in Figure 6-3.

To start with, enter a list of the different expenses you'll incur, working your way down the screen in column A. Beside each item, in column B, enter how much it costs. In column C, enter how many of that item you will need. For example, one row of our example shows the name of the hotel in column A, how much it costs per night (in column B on the same row), and then a 6 for the number of nights Sean will stay there in column C on that row. In Figure 6-3, you can see we've also written titles in the cells at the top of the columns of data so we can easily see what is in each column.

You can make a column wider so you can more easily enter the descriptions of your budget items. Click and drag the line between the letter at the top of the column and the letter at the top of the column to its right.

To show a currency sign in a cell, click the Format menu, choose Cells, and then change the category to Currency and the format to the layout and currency symbol you would like to use. You can select a group of cells and format them at the same time by clicking and dragging the cells before you go into the Format menu.

You can enter formulae (or calculations) into cells, and the answers will appear in the spreadsheet. If you want to enter a formula into a cell, you type the equals sign (=), followed by the formula. You use an asterisk (*) for multiplication and a slash (/) for division. For example, click any empty cell and enter

```
=7*5
```

The result (35) appears in the cell on the spreadsheet where you entered the formula. You can view or edit the formula itself by clicking the cell and then clicking the formula bar above the spreadsheet, or by double-clicking the cell.

The magic happens when you start using the numbers in one cell to work out what should go in another one. You do that by using the grid reference of a cell in your formula. For the holiday budget, we want to multiply the cost of an item (such as a night in a hotel) by how many of them we buy (six nights' worth). The first of those values is stored in column B, and the second one is beside it in column C, both on the same row. After the titles and spacing at the top of the spreadsheet, the first expense is on row 5. In column D5, we enter

```
=B5*C5
```

This multiplies the values in cell B5 (the price) and cell C5 (the quantity) and puts the result (the total amount spent on that particular item) into cell D5. You can click cell D5, and then copy its contents and paste them into the cells below. There are options for copying and pasting in the Edit menu, but LibreOffice also supports Windows shortcuts, including Ctrl+C to copy and Ctrl+V to paste.

You might think the same number would go into those cells, but it actually copies the formula and not the result, and it updates it for the correct row number as it goes. If you copy the formula from cell D5 into cell D6 and then click D6 and look in the formula bar, you'll see it says

```
=B6*C6
```

After you've copied the formula down the column, you will have a column of results that shows the total cost of each expense item. The final step is to calculate the grand total, totting up the values in those cells. To do that, you use a special type of formula, called SUM, which adds up the values in a set of cells. To use that, follow these steps:

1. **Click a cell at the bottom of the cost column and type** =sum(. **Don't press Enter when you've finished.**

2. **Click the top cell in your column of expenses (D5) and hold down the mouse button.**

3. **Drag the mouse down the screen until the red box encloses all your cost entries.**

4. **Type a closing bracket**) **(parenthesis) and press Enter.**

The grand total appears in that cell, and your budget is complete. A spreadsheet is more than a glorified calculator because you can use it for planning and asking "What if?" For example, you can see what happens if you use a more expensive hotel. Just change the price of the hotel per night, and all the other cells calculated from that update automatically, including your total cost at the bottom. Similarly, you can double the length of your stay at the hotel by changing the number of nights in column B to see how that affects your budget total.

Creating Presentations in LibreOffice Impress

If you're called upon to deliver a presentation, or if you want to force your holiday photos slide show on your friends, you can use LibreOffice Impress to create your slides and play them back. You're probably realizing that most LibreOffice programs have a counterpart in the Microsoft Office suite, and Impress is a bit like Microsoft PowerPoint. You can open PowerPoint presentations using it, and although some of the nifty slide transitions are missing, we found that quite sophisticated layouts can be carried across without a problem. Each picture has some placeholder text on it, however, which is hidden by the pictures in PowerPoint but appears onscreen in Impress.

Figure 6-4 shows Sean's holiday photo slide show in Impress. To create a presentation, simply follow these steps:

1. **Start Impress, or choose to create a new presentation through the File menu in any of the LibreOffice applications.**

2. **In the Tasks panel on the right, click the Layouts heading.**

   This opens a panel that gives you 12 different slide layouts to choose from.

3. **Click the slide layout you would like to use.**

4. **Click in the title box and type the title you'd like to use for the slide.**

5. **Your slide has up to six boxes for content. Click one of these and start typing to add text in the box.**

   Alternatively, in the center of the content box are four buttons you can click to add different types of content, including a table, a chart, an image, or a video. If you want to add a picture, click the bottom-left button and then choose the picture you'd like to use. Note that if you click a different slide layout on the right, it is applied to the slide you're already working on.

6. **To add a new slide, click the Slide button on the menu bar (indicated in Figure 6-4), or use the Insert menu.**

   Repeat Steps 3 to 5 to fill in the slide.

7. **To edit a previous slide, click it in the Slides panel on the left.**

Slide

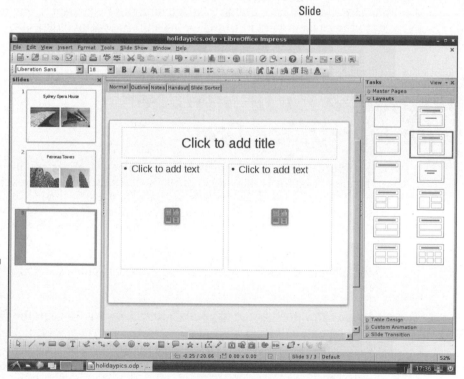

Figure 6-4: Creating a photo slide show using LibreOffice Impress.

You change the formatting of a title, piece of text, or picture by clicking it in the main slide area and then clicking the options on the menu bar at the top of the screen. The menu bar changes depending on whether the content is an image or text.

For best results, avoid using image files that are much bigger than you need: They slow down the computer and can crash the software if you use too many. See Chapter 7 for guidance on resizing your digital photos and other images.

When you put your mouse pointer over one of the slides in the panel on the left, three buttons appear that you can click to start the slide show, hide the slide (which stops it showing in the slide show, but doesn't delete it), or duplicate the slide. You can also start the slide show from the Slide Show menu at the top of the screen or by pressing F5. To start from the first slide, click it in the Slides panel before you begin the slide show.

When the slide show is playing, you can use the left and right cursor keys to advance through the slide show and the Escape key to exit.

Impress has lots of additional features to explore, including colorful templates (click Master Pages in the Tasks panel on the right), transitions that animate the display of a slide (also found in the Tasks panel), and tools (similar to those in LibreOffice Draw) for making shapes, including speech bubbles and stars (see the menu at the bottom of the screen).

Creating a Party Invitation with LibreOffice Draw

LibreOffice Draw is used for designing simple page layouts and illustrations and can be used for making posters and invitations. Despite the application's arty name, the drawing tools are basic and are best suited to creating flowcharts and simple business graphics, although children might enjoy the ease with which they can add stars, smiley faces, and speech bubbles to their pictures.

Refer to Figure 6-5 as you work through this quick guide to making an invitation using LibreOffice Draw:

1. **Start Draw or choose to create a new drawing through the File menu in any of the LibreOffice applications.**

2. **Use the toolbar at the bottom of the screen to select your drawing tool. As you move your cursor over the buttons, a short description appears.**

   Click the smiley face in the symbol shapes to select it.

3. **Move your mouse cursor to the page. Click the mouse button and hold it as you drag the mouse down and to the right.**

   As you move the mouse, you see the face fill the space you're making between where you clicked the button and where your cursor is. When you release the mouse button, the face is dropped in place. You might find it easier to just place the face anywhere onscreen and then reposition and resize it afterwards.

4. **After you have placed the face onscreen, you can reposition it by clicking and dragging it. To resize it, click it and then click and drag one of the blue boxes that appears on its edges.**

5. **Use a similar process to add a speech bubble from the group of items called Callouts on the menu bar. (Click the bubble in the menu to select it, and then click and drag the page to place it.)**

   When it's on the page, you can resize and reposition the speech bubble in the same way you arranged the face. To move the tail of the speech bubble, click and drag the yellow point at the end of it. Arrange it so it points to the smiley face.

6. **Click your speech bubble and type your text.**

   The text spills out of the bubble if there is too much of it, so press the Enter key to start a new line when necessary, and resize the bubble to fit.

7. **Some of the buttons have pop-up menus you can open by clicking the small down arrow to the right of the icon. Click the pop-up menu beside the Stars button to find the Vertical Scroll and position it on the page. Add text to it in the same way you added text to the speech bubble.**

8. **To change the color of your scroll, face, or bubble, click it on the page and then change the colors in the style menu bar at the top of the screen.**

   Two colors are shown. The one on the left is the color of the outline, and the one on the right is the color of the background. Click the menu item that says Color in it and you can select a gradient, hatching pattern, or bitmap (colored pattern) instead of a solid color.

9. **To change the color of the text in your speech bubble or scroll, click it, press Ctrl+A to select it all, and then use the Font Color option on the far right of the style menu bar at the top of the screen.**

10. **You can also change the font and size of the text using the style menu bar.**

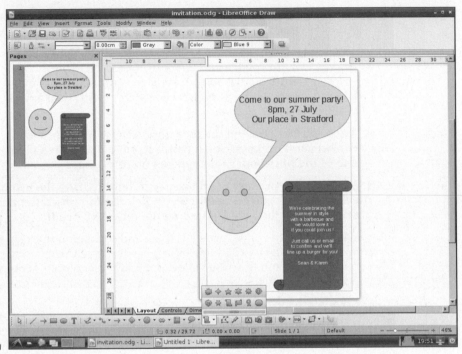

Figure 6-5:
Making
a party
invitation
using
LibreOffice
Draw.

As you might expect, you can do lots more with Draw. The Text option (the T icon on the menu bar at the bottom of the screen) enables you to place text boxes anywhere, so you can create posterlike layouts. The Curve option enables you to draw freehand by clicking and dragging on the page, and it smoothes your lines for you. The Fontwork Gallery gives you a choice of different bulging, curved, bent, and circular text styles to choose from. After you've placed the Fontwork item, click its default *Fontwork* text and type your words to have them inserted in the eccentric style of your choice. If you want to use your own pictures or photos, the From File button on the menu at the bottom enables you to choose your image file. When it loads, you can resize and reposition it to fit your design.

Chapter 7

Editing Photos on the Raspberry Pi with GIMP

*W*e live in probably the best documented era in our history. Not only do we write about our daily lives in blogs and Facebook, but many people also carry a camera everywhere they go, built in to their phone or tablet device. More serious photographers might have a dedicated digital camera. Whatever you use, and whatever you do with your day, photography is a great way to record your life and express yourself creatively.

The Raspberry Pi can play a part in this hobby, enabling you to edit your photos to improve the composition and quality. The photos generated by digital cameras are quite large files, however, so a Raspberry Pi with just 256MB of memory struggles to process them, and often became impractically slow or crashed when we tried it. The 512MB edition of the Pi, which you have if you bought a Model B after October 15, 2012, delivers much better performance, although you still need to be patient at times.

In this chapter, we introduce you to GIMP, one of the most popular image editing packages and give you some tips for editing your photos with it. You learn how to resize, crop, rotate, and flip your photos. We also tell you how to change colors and fix any imperfections, such as dust or unwanted details, in your shots.

Some of the skills here are valuable for other projects in this book. In particular, resizing images so they're smaller cuts the amount of memory they require and makes it easier to use them in other programs including LibreOffice (see Chapter 6) and Scratch (see Chapter 10).

Installing and Starting GIMP

The program we're going to use is the GNU Image Manipulation Program, known as GIMP for short. It's a highly sophisticated tool, and it's available for free download not just on Linux, but for Windows and Mac computers as well.

To install GIMP on your Raspberry Pi, enter the following at the shell:

```
sudo apt-get install gimp
```

If you experience any difficulties, consult Chapter 5 for advice on installing software.

After installation is complete, you can start GIMP from the Graphics category in your Programs menu in the desktop environment (see Chapter 4).

Understanding the GIMP Screen Layout

Figure 7-1 shows the screen layout of GIMP. When it first opens, the large area in the middle is empty, with a picture of Wilber, the GIMP mascot, in the background. We've used the File menu in the top left to open a photo for editing, which you can see in the center pane.

GIMP can be used in such a way that each pane of tools or content is a separate window onscreen, but we find it easier to arrange everything in a single window, especially when we're using a smaller screen. If your layout looks different from the one shown in Figure 7-1, click to open the Windows menu at the top of the screen and select Single Window Mode.

Across the top of the screen is a bar with menus for File, Edit, Select, View, Image, Layer, Colours, Tools, Filters, Windows, and Help. You can browse these menus to get an idea of what the program can do, and to find options quickly if you don't know what icons they use on the toolbar.

On the left is a pane that contains icons for the different tools at the top and the tool options at the bottom. When you roll the cursor over a tool's icon, a tooltip pops up to tell you what it does. When you click a tool to select it, the options at the bottom of the pane change depending on the tool you're using. For example, if you're using the paintbrush, the options cover properties such as opacity and the brush type.

The pane on the right is also divided into two halves. The top half has tabs for Layers, Channels, Paths, and History. Of these, the Layers and History tabs (indicated in Figure 7-1) are most important for new users because they enable you to edit your photos safely.

History pane

Layers pane

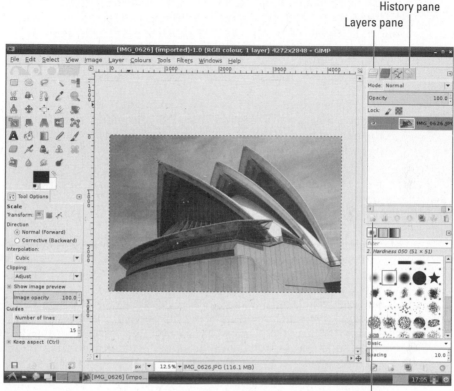

New layer

Figure 7-1:
GIMP
enables
you to edit
photos
on your
Raspberry Pi.

The History tab enables you to retrace your steps if you make changes you don't like.

Layers are used for adding new elements to an image without disturbing whatever is underneath. For example, if you wanted to add text to an image, you would do that in a new layer on top of the old one. If you change your mind, you can just remove the layer and the picture underneath is unchanged. The text tool (which has an A as its icon) automatically adds text in a new layer when you use it. If you intend to use the drawing tools, add a layer for each part of the drawing by clicking the New Layer button under this pane (indicated in Figure 7-1). New layers appear on top of older layers, but you can change the order of layers by dragging them in the pane on the right. Those near the top of the screen in this pane appear nearer the foreground in the image. To hide a layer temporarily, click the eye next to it in the pane.

The bottom half of the right pane is for brushes, patterns, and gradients. The brushes are used when you're drawing or painting on the image. The patterns and gradients are used for the Fill tool, which fills in a part of the image with a particular color or pattern. In this chapter, we won't cover the drawing tools because there's a significant lag when using them on the Raspberry Pi, which makes it hard to draw intuitively or precisely.

You can change the width of the left and right panes, as we have in Figure 7-1, to make it easier to see all the tabs. Put your mouse cursor at the edge of the pane adjoining the central image area. When the cursor turns into a two-headed arrow, click and drag left or right to resize the pane.

Resizing an Image in GIMP

One of the most useful things you can do on your Raspberry Pi is to resize an image. All computer images are made up of pixels, which are tiny colored dots. Sean's camera produces images that are 4,272 pixels wide and 2,848 pixels high. High-quality images like that are great for printing photos, but if you just want to use pictures onscreen, quality comes at a price. That level of detail requires a large file size, and big files can significantly slow down your Raspberry Pi. Often, you can use a lower quality image without noticeably affecting the end result, assuming your finished result will only be displayed on the screen.

Here's how you can resize an image using GIMP:

1. **Click to open the Image menu at the top of the screen and click Scale Image.**

   A window like Figure 7-2 opens.

2. **In the Width box, enter the width you would like your final image to be in pixels. Press Enter when you've finished entering your width.**

   If you wanted to put a holiday snap on your website, you probably wouldn't want it to be more than 500 pixels wide. If you want to use a photo as a Scratch background (see Chapter 10), the ideal size is 480 by 360 pixels.

   When you enter a new value for the Width, the Height is updated automatically, so the image stays in proportion and doesn't become stretched. You can also enter a value for the Height and have the Width calculated automatically. If you want to be able to adjust the Width and Height independently, click the chain to the right of their boxes to break it.

3. **Alternatively, instead of using absolute values for the width and height, you can resize your image to a certain percentage. Click the Units drop-down list box (it says px) and choose Percent.**

   The values in the Width and Height box will then be percentages. For example, you would enter 50% to shrink the image by half. The size of the image in pixels is shown under the Height box.

4. **When you've set your size, click the Scale button.**

At the bottom of the screen, underneath the image pane, you can see some information about the file, including the current zoom level, which is how much the image has been magnified or reduced for you to view it. If you set this to 100%, you can get an idea of how much detail is in the image now, and it's easier to edit too.

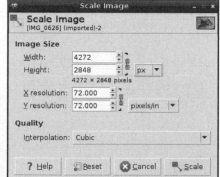

Figure 7-2:
The scale
options in
GIMP.

©1995–2012 Spencer Kimball, Peter Mattis, and the GIMP
Development Team

Resizing an image reduces its quality. This would be noticeable if you tried to create a high-quality print of it later. Don't overwrite your existing image with a resized version. Instead, save your resized image by choosing Save As from the File menu at the top of the screen and giving it a different filename.

Cropping Your Photo

If your photo has excessive space around an edge, or you'd like to change the composition of the picture, you can cut off the sides, or *crop* it. To do that, follow these steps:

1. **Click the icon that looks like an art knife or press Shift+C to choose the crop tool.**

2. **Click your image in the top left of the area you'd like to keep, hold down the mouse button, and drag your mouse down and to the right.**

   When you release the mouse button, a box appears on the image, as you can see in Figure 7-3.

   The inside of the box shows which bits of your image will be kept. Anything outside the box is cut off when you crop the image. You don't have to get the position or size of the box right first time because it's easy to adjust.

3. **Click one of the corners and drag the mouse to change the size and shape of the box. You can also click and drag along one of the edges inside the box to adjust the width or height.**

4. **To reposition the box, click and drag in its center.**

5. **To crop the image, click inside the box or press the Enter key.**

If you make a mistake, you can use Ctrl+Z to undo, or use the History pane (see Figure 7-1) to go back to a previous version of the image.

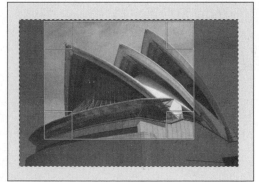

Figure 7-3:
Cropping a photo in GIMP.

©1995–2012 Spencer Kimball, Peter Mattis, and the GIMP Development Team

Rotating and Flipping Your Photo

If you rotate your camera sideways to take a picture, you might need to rotate the resulting image too. The easiest way to do this is to click the Image menu, and then use the rotation options in the Transform submenu there. You can rotate clockwise or anticlockwise (counterclockwise) after anticlockwise by 90 degrees, rotate the image by 180 degrees, and flip it horizontally or vertically.

For a simple rotation like this, it's quicker to rotate a photo using the LXDE Image Viewer (see Chapter 4).

If you have a photo that's slightly wonky, you can manually adjust it in GIMP. Click the Rotate tool (or use Shift+R) and you can enter an angle for rotation, or click and drag the image to rotate it. To change the pivot point about which the picture rotates, click the circle in the middle of the image and drag it.

Adjusting the Colors

In common with other image editing programs, GIMP has options for adjusting the colors in a photo. You can find all these options in the Colours menu at the top of the screen. If your picture has a tint of color you don't want, or if you would like to add a tint, use the Colour Balance settings to alter the amount of red, green, and blue in the image. The Brightness and Contrast settings can help to bring out detail in shadows, or to give the image more impact.

There are also options in this menu (further down, under Auto) to automatically adjust the colors using six different methods. These can give strange and undesirable results, but you can always undo them with Ctrl+Z if you don't like them. The Normalize option can be a quick fix for images that look a bit wishy-washy, and the White Balance option can fix pictures that don't already have strong black and white areas.

Fixing Imperfections

On Sean's holiday to Australia, he found a beautiful unspoiled beach in Darwin. He took a picture of it: a lone tree in the foreground, the shimmering sea, and wisps of cloud in a light blue sky. When he got home, he noticed that some idiot had left a crushed beer can in the foreground.

Thankfully, in GIMP, you can use a handy tool called the Clone tool to make little details like this vanish. It enables you to use part of the image as a pattern that you spray over another part of the image. In Sean's case, he can use a clean piece of beach as the pattern and spray it on top of the litter. Hey, presto! The rubbish vanishes.

Here's how you use the Clone tool:

1. **Zoom in to your image using the menu underneath it. Use the scrollbars at the side of the image pane to position your image so you have a clear view of the imperfection.**

2. **Click the Clone tool, which looks like a rubber stamp, or press the C key.**

3. **Move your cursor to an unspoiled part of the image you would like to use as the pattern, or** *clone source.* **This needs to be somewhere as plain as possible, more of a texture than a shape, with no obvious prominent details or lines. Sky, grass, or sand is perfect. Hold down the Ctrl key and click the mouse button.**

   A crosshair icon appears on your image at that spot.

4. **In the tool options, at the bottom of the left pane, check the brush that is being used. Click the shape (a circle by default) if you want to change it.**

   For best results, use a brush with a fading edge, rather than a solid edge. You can change the size of the brush in this pane too by clicking the Size box and typing your preferred value. The bigger the brush you use, the bigger your pattern will be.

5. **Move your cursor to the imperfection in the image and click the mouse button. This copies an area the size of your brush from your clone source to the place where you clicked.**

   If you've done it right, the imperfection should appear to vanish. If you see unwanted picture details included in the pattern, either reduce the size of your brush, or move your clone source. Repeat this step until the imperfection is gone.

6. **Adjust the magnification at the bottom of the image pane to view your image at 100%.**

   Check whether you can see any evidence of your handiwork. If so, you might need to try another clone source or brush size. Otherwise, it's worked!

Converting Images between Different Formats

There are several different file formats that can be used for images, but not all programs can open all files. If you want to use a picture as a background in Scratch (see Chapter 10), for example, you need to use .jpg files, which usually deliver the best quality for photos, or .png or .gif files, which are optimal for illustrations.

The default format used by GIMP is .xcf, which stores additional information about your editing session along with your picture, but this format isn't widely used in other programs.

You can use GIMP to save your picture in a more widely used format, or to convert a picture between different file formats. First, open the image through the File menu, and then use the File menu to Export. The Export window looks similar to the Save window, but you can click Select File Type (By Extension) at the bottom and choose the file format you'd like to convert the image into.

The conversion is quite memory-intensive, so you might need to resize (shrink) a digital photo before you can convert it.

Finding Out More about GIMP

There's much more you can do with GIMP, and you can find detailed documentation on its website. To access it, click Help at the top of the screen, open the GIMP Online menu and click User Manual Web Site. Alternatively, in any browser, go to http://docs.gimp.org/2.8/en/.

Chapter 8

Playing Audio and Video on the Raspberry Pi

*I*n this chapter, we show you how you can turn your Raspberry Pi into a media center, capable of playing high definition video files and music.

To do that, we use dedicated media player software based on the XBMC software that powers some set-top boxes and smart TVs. You can use it to play music and video you have on storage devices connected to your Raspberry Pi, or to play back media from other devices on your home network. To a more limited degree, you can also use it to play back streaming TV shows and radio stations from the Internet.

At the end of this chapter, we also show you how to play music on your Raspberry Pi in the desktop environment.

Setting Up Your Media Center

The Raspberry Pi can play back full HD 1080p video, which makes it ideal as the heart of a cheap and low-powered media center. The NOOBS software includes two Linux distributions, both based on XBMC, that turn your Raspberry Pi into a media center. The choices are Raspbmc, created by Sam Nazarko, and OpenELEC. Because they're both based on the XBMC core, they mostly look and work the same. Raspbmc offers additional add-on features and is the one we use here, but you should be able to set up either while reading this chapter.

To start, create an SD or MicroSD card with NOOBS Lite on it (see Chapter 2), and then use that card to install Raspbmc or OpenELEC (see Chapter 3).

When you are using RaspBMC, your Raspberry Pi boots straight into it without you needing to enter a password. There's a slightly uncomfortable period when the screen is blank for a while, so you need to be patient and resist the urge to interrupt it.

Navigating the Media Center

The Home screen looks like Figure 8-1. Both Raspbmc and OpenELEC have inherited XBMC's simple interface, which is designed to work with only a remote control. In this chapter, we assume you're using a mouse, but we give you some pointers on using remote controls in the section "Using a Remote Control" later in this chapter.

Figure 8-1:
The Home
screen
and menu
options.

The menu bar across the middle of the screen scrolls left and right as you roll your cursor over it. It has the following options: Pictures, Videos, Music, Programs, and System. When you hover your mouse pointer over one of these items, a submenu of related shortcuts appears underneath the main menu bar. In Figure 8-1, the submenu has options for Files and Add-ons. The Music submenu enables you to jump straight to artists, albums, or songs. To select an item in the main menu or the submenu, simply click it.

At the bottom right of the screen is a button to take you back to the Home screen, with a picture of a house on it, and a Back button to return to the previous screen.

If a button isn't working, check that you don't have an unclosed window open onscreen somewhere. You have to close any windows that pop up before you can use the Home button, for example.

Adding Media

Before you can play music or video on your Raspberry Pi, or even look at photos, you need to connect some content to your Pi. You can do this by plugging a USB storage device into the Raspberry Pi or connecting to a storage device on your home network. There is also an option to connect to a streaming media source over the Internet.

Adding a USB device

If your media files are on a USB device, plug it into a spare slot on the Raspberry Pi's powered USB hub. A message appears in the bottom right, confirming that the USB device is being mounted, which just means it's being prepared so you can use it. After it's been mounted, you can find the device in the Music, Video, and Pictures menus.

Adding networked media

If you have a media server on your home network, you can also connect your Raspberry Pi to that. For example, you might have a computer running media server software to make its music files accessible to other devices over the network, or you might have a router with a built-in media server so it can share any files on USB devices you connect to it. These networked devices most likely use the UPnP (Universal Plug and Play) standard.

You need to add the connected media device separately in each of Music, Videos, and Photos, assuming you wish to use all three content types with it. However, you only have to do this once for each content type, as Raspbmc then remembers the device's location, even after the Raspberry Pi reboots.

To add a new connected media source for music, click Music on the Home screen, and then click Add Music. Click Browse, choose the type of device, and then select your connected device. For best results, navigate to the folder with music in and add that. Pictures are added in the same way by going through Pictures on the Home screen first.

To add a connected media source for video, it's a bit different. Click Videos on the Home screen, click Files, click Add Videos, and then click Browse and choose your device type and then your device.

Using streaming media

You can also connect Raspbmc to streaming media sources, which means the content flows into your Raspberry Pi over the Internet as you watch it or listen to it. As a result, they only work when you have a good Internet connection.

To do this, you use *add-ons*, which are third-party applications that access sources of content online. Music add-ons, for example, enable you to listen to Internet radio stations and access music sharing sites such as SoundCloud. You can use Picture add-ons to directly access Internet picture libraries on your Raspberry Pi from the Picasa and Flickr photo websites, or to browse photos from the 500px photography showcase.

Some add-ons come pre-installed in Raspbmc, whereas others need to be installed. Like all software, the availability of add-ons varies over time as new services come online and older services disappear. The music and video add-ons can be particularly short-lived and unreliable, and OpenELEC doesn't currently support them, perhaps as a result of this.

There are different add-ons available for Music, Videos, and Pictures, but you install them in a similar way. From the Home screen, hover over Music, Videos, or Pictures and then click Add-Ons in the shortcuts menu. Click Get More and you can scroll through a list of those available. Click one for more information about it and to find the Install button. When you're browsing the list of add-ons, any already installed on your Pi will have *Installed* or *Enabled* written next to them. Steer clear of add-ons that say *Broken*. These have been flagged as not working and need to be fixed by their authors.

Playing Music

To get started with playing music, click Music on the Home screen. You can use the panel on your left to browse your various music sources, and you can then find individual albums and songs by working through the directory structure. As in Linux, the two dots represent a folder's parent folder, which moves you up a level in the directory structure. You can see the two dots at the top of the panel on the left except when you're already at the root.

Figure 8-2 shows the music player in action. When music is playing, click the Play button in the bottom left to open options to pause, rewind, fast forward, skip track, shuffle, or repeat. Halfway down the screen on the left is a tab, a visual hint that there's a menu offscreen. When you move your mouse pointer to the left of the screen (not necessarily over the tab), the View Options menu slides out, which also includes playback controls.

Figure 8-2:
Playing music in Raspbmc.

You can continue to browse your music while it is playing, and queue songs or albums to play next by right-clicking them and choosing Queue Item.

If you leave the player for a while, it switches into full-screen mode. To return to the Home screen, click the Close button in the top right of the screen.

For more advanced features, including the ability to create playlists, you can enable Library mode in the View Options menu on the left. This works a bit like iTunes on the PC and Mac and stores information about your music separately from the music itself. In Raspbmc, you can use the library to make smart playlists, which are automatically generated from information about the music, such as a playlist containing all your pop songs from the 1960s. Library features, including the smart playlists, only work on music that has been added to the library.

You'll need to add an entry in the library before you can activate Library mode for the first time. To add a song, album, artist, or entire storage device to the library, right-click it and then choose Scan Item to Library. Note that this doesn't actually copy the music itself into the library, just some information about it. To turn off Library mode, so you can browse music that isn't in it yet, use the View Options menu again.

When you're in Library mode, you can only browse and play music that's been added to the library.

To create static playlists (of specific songs or albums), go into your library, click Playlists in the pane on the left, and then New Playlist. The playlist window opens so you can browse to the songs you want, and right-click to add them. When you're finished, click Save Playlist and follow the instructions to name it and save it. To close the playlist window, right-click when the mouse pointer is not over a file.

Smart playlists can only contain songs that have been added to the music library, but standard playlists can contain songs from any of your connected media devices.

Playing Videos

Use the Videos option to view movies and other video media. The XBMC software supports the H.264 video format to 1080p, which means you'll be able to watch most .mp4, .m4v, and .avi files in high definition.

If you want to watch other formats, you might be able to buy a license from the official Raspberry Pi website at www.raspberrypi.org. Licenses to watch MPEG2 and VC1 format videos are available now and cost a couple of pounds or dollars each. Each license is valid for one Raspberry Pi. To enter your license number, go to the Home screen, click Programs, double-click Raspbmc settings, click System Configuration, and scroll down to find the option for the license key you've bought. Note that OpenELEC does not currently have a menu to add your license key: You'll need to edit the configuration file directly. See http://wiki.OpenELEC.tv/index.php?title=Raspberry_Pi_Codec_Licences.

To play videos, click Files to display USB or other connected devices, browse through the folders, and find the video you want. Right-click the video's name for options like Resume Play, or to add to a queue or a favorites list. Click the video name to start playing it. While the video is playing, it fills the screen, so move the mouse to bring up the playback controls.

From the View Options menu, accessed by moving the mouse to the left of the screen, you can search for a specific file, or hide videos you've already watched.

Viewing Photos

Click Pictures on the Home screen and you'll see a simple file browser that you can use to access your pictures. The media center software supports standard image formats, including JPEG, bitmap, and TIFF, and generates thumbnails of your photos and folders. Navigate to a photo and click it. You use the left and right keys to move through your photos and the Escape key (or right-click the mouse) to return to the menu.

When you're in a folder, open the View Options menu to choose the sort order and viewing mode, which includes various arrangements of thumbnails. You can also run a slide show from here, but if you want to remove the zany animation, you'll need to go to the Home screen, click System, click Settings, click Pictures, and click Slideshow. Here you can switch off the pan and zoom effect, which is a very good idea.

Changing the Settings

On the Home screen are two options that enable you to change the settings: Programs and System.

These two options enable you to manage hardware and software settings, change the look and feel of the media player, and configure additional media player options. It's not always clear whether you'll find what you're looking for in Programs or System, but a good rule of thumb is that standard media player options (like volume levels) are found in System, whereas additional external software is in Programs.

In the System menu, you can find configuration options related to the XMBC media player, like playback options for the different media. It's worth taking a moment to look through the options so you're aware of the possibilities.

By default, the sound is set to pass through your HDMI cable. If you want to use your Raspberry Pi's audio output (and speakers) but you're using HDMI for your screen, you'll need to change the audio setting from HDMI to Analog. You'll find this option in the System menu. When you're in the settings menu, click the System tab on the left and click Audio Output.

Using a Remote Control

With all of the functionality we've covered in this chapter, you're not that far away from running a low-power home media center. To complete it, you can use a remote control.

There are many ways to remotely control your Raspberry Pi media center. You can use a USB device, a cheap infrared remote, a keyboard remote, or even your Xbox controller, if you have one. Or you can use the existing XBMC remote app (available for iOS and Android operating systems) to talk to your Raspberry Pi over your home network via Wi-Fi.

The Raspbmc page at `www.raspbmc.com/wiki/user/` includes a list of compatible remote controls.

You can find the remote control settings in the System menu, the System tab, and then under Input devices.

If you have a television that supports the HDMI CEC (Consumer Electronics Council) standard, a neat option is to enable your existing television remote to control your Pi. To do this, connect your networked Pi to your television's HDMI socket. XMBC appears as a new input. Use the TV's remote control to change to this input, and your Home screen appears on the television. You can find a demonstration video, together with a link to some Raspberry Pi media center software that has been modified to support CEC, at `www.youtube.com/watch?v=XPyOyJsnB1o`.

Turning Off Your Media Center

To turn off your media center, click the shutdown button in the bottom left of the Home screen. You can just power off, but you minimize the risk of corrupting your SD card or MicroSD card by shutting down properly.

Playing Music in the Desktop Environment

Looking for musical inspiration while you program? The good news is that you can also play music and video from the Raspbian desktop environment (see Chapter 4). If you're still using Raspbmc or OpenELEC, shut down your

Raspberry Pi using the Shutdown icon in the bottom left of Raspbmc, and then reboot into Raspbian. You will either need to swap SD or MicroSD cards, or, if you're using NOOBS, choose to use Raspbian when you reboot. Go into the desktop environment (see Chapter 4).

VLC Media Player is a music and video player that is provided with Raspbian. You can find it in the Sound and Video category of your Programs menu, and click its name there to start it.

In the Media menu of VLC, there are options to open a file or a directory. Usually, you'll want to open a directory, so you can play a whole album. By default, VLC shows you the album artwork (where available), but you can open the View menu and click Playlist to see a list of songs so you can pick another to play (as shown in Figure 8-3). In the box on the left, you can pick a device to play from, including several Internet services for streaming music. Click Playlist in the View menu again to revert to the full-window artwork.

Figure 8-3:
Playing music in VLC Media Player.

Written by Hong Jen Yee and Juergen Hoetzel. Icon by Arnaud Didry.

The playback controls to pause, play, skip, shuffle, and repeat songs are at the bottom left of the window. The volume control is at the bottom right.

For an alternative to VLC, try LXMusic (Figure 8-4), a minimalist music player. We found it performed better than VLC and was easier to use. To install or update LXMusic, use the following command:

```
sudo apt-get install lxmusic
```

Your music collection is listed as a scrolling list of songs that you can filter by typing an artist, album, or song name into the filter box at the bottom. To add music into LXMusic, click the Add button (a green plus sign) in the bottom left. Double-click a song to play it. When you close LXMusic, it continues to play in the background, so to stop the music, bring LXMusic back by clicking its icon on the right of the taskbar.

Figure 8-4:
Playing
music in
LXMusic.

Part IV
Programming the Raspberry Pi

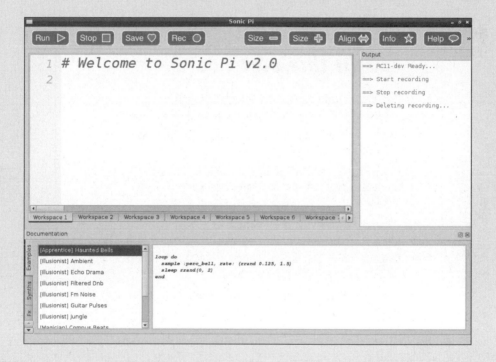

In this part . . .

- Get familiar with the Scratch interface, and how you can use it to create your own simple animations or games programs.

- Use Scratch to build an arcade game, which you can customize with your own artwork.

- Learn how to use Python to create a times table calculator and Chatbot, a program that simulates basic artificial intelligence.

- Use Pygame with Python to create an arcade game that you can customize with your own level of designs and artwork.

- Discover how you can use Python to build worlds in Minecraft, including a maze you can explore.

- Use Sonic Pi to compose your own computer music on your Raspberry Pi.

Chapter 9

Introducing Programming with Scratch

. . . .

In This Chapter

▶ Starting Scratch

▶ Understanding the Scratch screen layout

▶ Positioning and resizing your sprite

▶ Making your sprite move

▶ Changing your sprite's appearance

▶ Adding sounds and music

. . . .

*T*he Raspberry Pi was created partly to inspire the next generation of pro-grammers, and Scratch is the perfect place to start. With it, you can make your own cartoons and games and discover some of the concepts that pro-fessional programmers use every day.

Scratch is designed to be approachable for people of all ages. The visual interface makes it easy to see what you can do at any time without having to remember any strange codes, and you can rapidly achieve great results. Scratch comes with a library of images and sounds, so it only takes a few minutes to write your first Scratch program.

In this chapter, we introduce you to Scratch so you can start to experiment with it. In Chapter 10, we show you how to use Scratch to make a simple arcade game.

Understanding What Programming Is

Before we dip into Scratch, we should clear up some of the jargon surrounding it. A *program* is a repeatable set of instructions to make a computer do some-thing, such as play a game. Those instructions can be extremely complicated because they have to describe what the computer should do in detail. Even a simple bouncing-ball game requires instructions for drawing the ball, moving it in different directions, detecting when it hits something, and then changing its direction to make it bounce.

Programming is the art and science of creating programs. You can create programs in lots of different ways, and Scratch is just one of them. In Chapter 11, you read about Python, another one.

Scratch and Python are both *programming languages*, different ways of writing instructions for the computer. Different programming languages are best suited for different tasks. Scratch is ideal for making games, for example, but it's not much use if you want to create a word processor. Using Python to create games takes longer, but it is more powerful than Scratch and gives you much more flexibility in the type of things you can get the computer to do.

Starting Scratch

You access Scratch from the desktop environment, so switch on your Raspberry Pi and then use `startx` to access it (see Chapter 4 for a guide to using the desktop environment).

To start Scratch, either double-click its icon on the desktop (which shows the head of a smiley orange cat), or select it from your Programs menu in the bottom left of the screen. You can find Scratch in the Programming folder.

Understanding the Scratch Screen Layout

Scratch divides the screen into four main areas, as you can see in Figure 9-1. In the top right is the Stage, where you can see your game or animation take shape. There's a cat on it already, so you can get started straightaway by making him do things, as you see in a minute.

The bottom-right area is your Sprite List. You can think of sprites as the characters in your game. They're images that you can make do things, such as move around or change their appearance. For now, there's just the cat, which has the name Sprite1.

You create a Scratch program by snapping together *blocks*, which are short instructions. On the left, you can see the Blocks Palette, which currently shows the Motion blocks, which include instructions to move ten steps, rotate, go to a particular grid reference, and point in a particular direction.

Enlarge Sprite

Shrink Sprite

Maximize window

Full Stage

Small Stage

Figure 9-1:
The screen
layout
when you
first start
Scratch.

Blocks Palette   Scripts Area   Sprite List   Stage

Scratch is developed by the Lifelong Kindergarten Group at the MIT Media Lab. See http://scratch.mit.edu.

The tall middle panel is the Scripts Area. This is where the magic happens! You assemble your program in this space, by dragging blocks into it from the left.

You can use two buttons in the top right (indicated in Figure 9-1) to toggle the size of the Stage between full and small. When the Stage is small, the Scripts Area is bigger, so you might find that useful when you're writing scripts later in this chapter.

You'll find it easier to use Scratch if you maximize it so it fills the screen. Click the button in the top right of its window, as indicated on Figure 9-1.

Positioning and Resizing Your Sprite

You can drag and drop your sprite (the cat) around the Stage to position it where you would like it to be at the start of your program.

You can also resize it. Two buttons above the Stage (indicated in Figure 9-1) are used to enlarge or shrink a sprite. Click one of them, and your mouse pointer changes to arrows pointing outward (for enlarging) or inward (for shrinking). Click your sprite on the Stage repeatedly to change its size to what you want.

When you've finished resizing, click something that isn't a sprite to return the mouse pointer to normal and stop resizing.

Making Your Sprite Move

Experimenting with Scratch is easy. To try out different blocks, just click them in the Blocks Palette. For example, try clicking the block to move 10 steps, and you should see your cat move to the right. You can also turn it 15 degrees in either direction by clicking the appropriate blocks.

If your cat goes somewhere you don't want it to (don't they always?), you can click it on the Stage and drag it back to where you want it. You can fix rotation too by clicking the tiny cat at the top of the Scripts Area, holding down the mouse button, and rolling your mouse in a circle pattern on the desk.

Not all the blocks will work at the moment. Some of them need to be combined with other blocks, or only make sense at certain times. There's no harm in experimenting, however. If you click something that doesn't work, you might get an error message, but you won't cause any harm to Scratch or your Raspberry Pi.

Next, we talk you through the different Motion blocks you can use.

Using directions to move your sprite

You can use two different methods to position and move your sprites. The first is to make your sprite "walk," and to change its direction when you want it to walk the other way.

Here are the five blocks you use to move your sprite in this way (see Figure 9-2):

✔ **Move 10 Steps:** This makes your sprite walk in the direction it is facing. If your sprite has been rotated, the steps taken could move your sprite in a diagonal line across the Stage. You can click the number in this block and then type another number to increase or decrease the number of steps taken, but bigger numbers spoil the illusion of movement.

Figure 9-2:
The directional movement blocks.

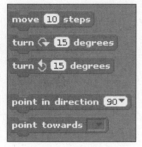

Scratch is developed by the Lifelong Kindergarten Group at the MIT Media Lab. See http://scratch.mit.edu.

✔ **Turn Right or Left 15 Degrees:** This block rotates your sprite. As with the number of steps, you can edit the number to change the degree by which your sprite is rotated. Your sprite walks in the direction it is facing when you use the Move 10 Steps block.

✔ **Point in Direction 90:** Whatever direction your sprite is facing, this block points it in the direction you want it to face. Use this block as-is to reset your sprite to face right. You can change the number in this block to change the direction you want your sprite to face and the numbers are measured in degrees from the position of facing up (see Figure 9-3). It helps to think of it like the hands of a clock: When the hand is pointing right, it's 90 degrees from the 12 o'clock position; when it's pointing down, it's 180 degrees from the top. To point left, you use −90. When you click the arrow in the right of the number box, it gives you a menu from which you can select the four main directions, but you can enter any number. You might be wondering whether you can enter 270 to point left, and the answer is that it works, but it can cause errors in your programs. If you turn your cat to direction 270 and then ask Scratch which way your cat is facing, it tells you −90. To avoid any inconsistencies like this, keep your direction numbers in the range −179 to 180.

✔ **Point Towards:** You can also tell the sprite to point toward the mouse pointer or another sprite. Use the menu in this block to choose what you would like your sprite to point toward.

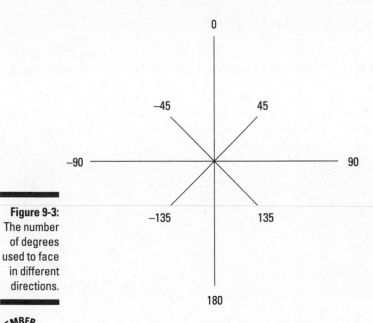

Figure 9-3:
The number
of degrees
used to face
in different
directions.

If you're changing the number value in a block, you still need to click the block to run it.

Using grid coordinates to move and position your sprite

You can also move and position your sprite using grid coordinates. That makes it easy to position your sprite at an exact place on the screen, irrespective of where it currently is.

Every point on the Stage has two coordinates, an X position (for where it is horizontally) and a Y position (indicating where it is vertically). The X positions are numbered from -240 at the far left, to 240 at the far right. The Y positions are numbered from -180 at the bottom edge of the Stage, to 180 at the top edge. That means the Stage is a total of 480 units wide and 360 units tall. The center point of the screen, where your cat begins his day, is where X equals 0 and Y equals 0. Figure 9-4 provides a quick visual reference of how the coordinates work.

When you move your mouse over the Stage, the grid reference of your mouse pointer is shown just underneath the Stage on the right.

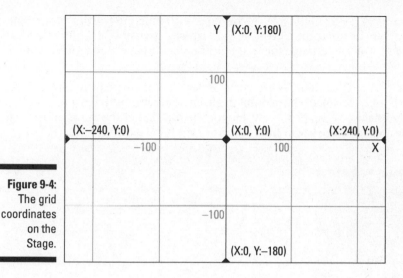

Six Motion blocks use the X and Y coordinates (see Figure 9-5):

✔ **Go to x:0 y:0:** You can use this block to position your sprite at a specific point on the Stage. By default, it returns a sprite to the center of the screen (x=0, y=0). Edit the numbers for X and Y to position your sprite somewhere else.

✔ **Go to:** Use this block to move your sprite to the mouse pointer's location, or to the location of another sprite if you have more than one.

✔ **Glide 1 secs to x:0 y:0:** When you use the Go To block, your sprite just jumps to its new position. The Glide block makes your sprite float there smoothly instead. You can change the number of seconds the glide takes, including using decimals for part of a second (for example, 0.5 for half a second).

✔ **Change X by 10:** This moves your sprite 10 units right. You can change the number of units and use a negative number if you want to move left instead. Note that this doesn't affect your sprite's vertical position and is independent of which way around your sprite is facing.

✔ **Set X to 0:** This changes the horizontal position of your sprite on the Stage, without affecting its vertical position. The value 0 returns it to the center of the screen horizontally, and you can edit the number to position it left or right of that. Use a negative number for the left half of the screen and a positive number for the right half.

✔ **Change Y by** 10: This moves your sprite 10 units up the Stage, without affecting its horizontal position, and irrespective of which direction it is facing. You can change the number of units and use a negative number to move the sprite down the screen instead.

✔ **Set Y to** 0: This changes the vertical position of your sprite on the Stage without affecting its horizontal position, and without regard to which way it faces. Use a positive value for the top half of the Stage and a negative value for the lower half.

Figure 9-5:
The blocks used for moving sprites using grid coordinates.

Scratch is developed by the Lifelong Kindergarten Group at the MIT Media Lab. See http://scratch.mit.edu.

Don't forget that you need to run a block to actually see its effect on your sprite. Do this by clicking it.

Showing sprite information on the Stage

It can be hard to keep track of where your sprite has got to and which direction it's facing, but you can show the values for its X position, Y position, and direction on the Stage. Select the boxes at the bottom of the Blocks Palette to do this (see Figure 9-6). They clutter up the screen a bit, but they can be essential tools for testing when you're creating a game.

Figure 9-6:
The blocks used to show sprite information on the Stage.

Scratch is developed by the Lifelong Kindergarten Group at the MIT Media Lab. See http://scratch.mit.edu.

Changing Your Sprite's Appearance

As well as moving your sprite around the screen, you can change what it looks like.

Using costumes

One way to think of sprites is like the characters in a game (although they can be used for lots of other objects too, such as obstacles). Each sprite can have a number of *costumes*, which are different pictures of it. If the costumes look fairly similar, you can create the illusion of animation by switching between them. Your cat sprite comes with two costumes, and when you switch between them, it looks like the cat is running.

You can see the costumes for your sprite by clicking the Costumes tab at the top of the Scripts Area, as shown in Figure 9-7. If you want to modify the cat's appearance, you can click the button to edit one of the costumes, or if you want to create a new animation frame, you can click the Copy button beside a costume and then edit the bits you want to change.

Costume name
Costumes tab

Figure 9-7:
You can
change
a sprite's
appearance
by giving
it a new
costume.

*Scratch is developed by the
Lifelong Kindergarten Group at
the MIT Media Lab.
See http://scratch.mit.edu.*

It doesn't matter so much when you're experimenting with sprites, but when you make your own games and animations, you can save yourself a lot of brain ache by giving your sprites meaningful names. It's much easier to remember that the costume with the name *gameover* should be shown when the player is defeated than it is to remember it's called *costume7*. To rename a costume, click the Costumes tab to show the costumes, and then click the costume's current name (see Figure 9-7) and type its new name.

In the Blocks Palette, there are two blocks you can use to switch between costumes (see Figure 9-8). Click the Looks button above the Blocks Palette to show them:

- **Switch to Costume:** If you want to switch to a particular costume, choose its name from the menu in this block and then click the block.

- **Next Costume:** Each time you use this block, the sprite changes to its next costume. When it runs out, it goes back to the first one again.

Looks button

Figure 9-8: Some of the Looks blocks you can use to change your sprite's appearance.

Scratch is developed by the Lifelong Kindergarten Group at the MIT Media Lab. See http://scratch.mit.edu.

You can show a sprite's costume number on the Stage too so it's easier for you to work out what's going on. Just check the box next to Costume # in the Blocks Palette.

Using speech and thought bubbles

Scratch includes four blocks you can use to show a speech bubble or a thought bubble onscreen, as you can see in Figure 9-8. To see them, and the other blocks that change a sprite's appearance, click the Looks button above the Blocks Palette. The speech and thought bubbles are great for giving a message to the player or viewer. You can edit the word in the block (Hello or Hmm...) to change the text in the bubble. Figure 9-9 shows the speech bubbles (top row) and thought bubbles (bottom row) in action.

If you use one of the options with a length of time in it, the sprite pauses for that length of time and the bubble disappears when it's elapsed.

If you use a block without a length of time, you can make the bubble disappear again by using the Say or Think block again, but editing the text so the text box in the block is empty.

Using graphic effects

You can apply several graphic effects to your sprite using Looks blocks. In Figure 9-9, we've used eight sprites to demonstrate them on the Stage. The Color effect changes the sprite's color palette, turning orange to green in the case of the cat. The Fisheye effect works like a fish-eye lens, making the central parts of the sprite appear bigger. Whirl distorts the sprite by twisting its features around its middle. Pixelate makes the sprite blocky. Mosaic shrinks the sprite and repeats it within the space it usually occupies. The Brightness and Ghost effects can sometimes look similar, but the Brightness effect increases the intensity of the colors (turning the cat's black outline silver while softening the orange) and the Ghost effect fades all the colors out evenly.

Figure 9-9:
The different graphic effects you can apply to your sprite.

Scratch is developed by the Lifelong Kindergarten Group at the MIT Media Lab. See http://scratch.mit.edu.

Here are the three blocks you use to control graphic effects:

- **Change Color Effect by** 25: You can select which effect you want to change (by default, it's the color effect), and enter the amount of it you want to add. You can use negative numbers to reduce the extent to which the effect is applied to your sprite. The color effect has 200 different levels (from 0 to 200), and the other effects typically look best with levels in the range -100 to 100. Experiment!

- **Set Color Effect to** 0: Use this block to set a chosen effect to a specific level. Choosing 0 turns the effect off again. You can use any of the seven effects with this block.

✔ **Clear Graphic Effects:** This block removes all the graphic effects you've applied to a particular sprite, so it looks normal again.

The graphic effects look great, but they are quite slow. They're best used in moderation for special moments in your animation or game; otherwise, they make it appear unresponsive.

Resizing your sprite

Earlier in this chapter, we show you how to change the starting size of your sprite on the Stage. You can use blocks to issue instructions to change its size too, so you could make it get larger as the game progresses, for example.

There are two blocks you can use to resize your sprite:

✔ **Change Size by 10:** This block enables you to change the size of your sprite by a certain number of units, relative to its current size. As usual, you can edit the number. If you want to decrease the sprite's size, use a negative number.

✔ **Set Size to 100%:** This block sets your size to a percentage of its original size, so with the default value of 100 percent, it effectively resets any resizing you've done.

You can also select the check box beside the Size block to show the sprite's size on the Stage, in the same way you displayed other sprite information (see "Showing sprite information on the Stage" earlier in this chapter) there. This can be useful for testing purposes.

Changing your sprite's visibility

Sometimes you might not want your sprite to be seen on the Stage. If a space-ship is blown up in your game, for example, you want it to disappear from view. These two blocks give you control over whether a sprite is visible:

✔ **Hide:** Use this block to make your sprite invisible on the Stage. If a sprite is hidden, Scratch won't detect when it touches other sprites, but you can still move a hidden sprite's position on the Stage, so it's in a different place when you show it again.

✔ **Show:** By default, your sprite is visible, but you can use this block to reveal it again after you have hidden it.

Sometimes sprites might get on top of each other. You can use the Go to Front block to make a sprite appear on top of all the others. To push a sprite backward and allow others to appear on top of it, use the Go Back 1 Layers block.

Adding Sounds and Music

As well as changing a sprite's appearance, you can give it some sound effects. Scratch comes with sounds including slurps, sneezes, and screams; ducks, geese, and owls; and pops, whoops, and zoops. There are effects there for most occasions, and many of them are a natural partner for one of the sprites that Scratch provides.

1. **Import the sound to your sprite. To do this, click the Sounds tab above the Scripts Area, as shown in Figure 9-10, and then click the Import button. Browse the provided sounds. You can click a file once to hear a preview of it, and click it twice to bring it into your sprite.**

   After you've imported a sound, click the speaker beside it to preview it, or click the X button to delete it from your project. If you a delete a sound in this way, it remains on your SD card so you can import it again later.

2. **Use one of the blocks to play a sound. To see the Sound blocks, click the Sound button at the top of the Blocks Palette first.**

   The Play Sound block enables you to choose which sound you'd like to play from those you have imported. The Play Sound Until Done block stops any movement or other blocks on the same sprite until the sound has finished playing.

In Chapter 10, we cover how to use multiple sprites in a project. The sound is imported to a particular sprite, so if you can't see it as one of the choices in the Play Sound block, be sure you've imported it to the correct sprite.

There are also blocks you can use to create music using Scratch, using drums and pitched instruments. Notes are numbered, with C being 60, C# being 61, D being 62, and so on. There's a block called Play Note 60 For 0.5 Beats that plays a note with a particular number for a certain duration. When you click the menu in this block to specify which note to play, a piano opens that you can use to select the note. If you're new to music, you can generally get a good result by starting with C, sticking to the white notes, and making sure no two consecutive notes are too far apart on the piano. There is also a block called Set Instrument to 1 that you can use to change the instrument, although at the time of writing, this doesn't work on the Raspberry Pi.

The note numbers used in Scratch are the same as those used in Sonic Pi (see Table 14-1 in Chapter 14).

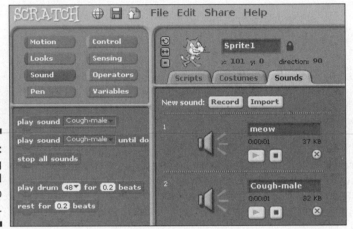

Figure 9-10:
Adding
sound
effects to
your sprite.

Scratch is developed by the Lifelong Kindergarten Group at the MIT Media Lab. See http://scratch.mit.edu.

Creating Scripts

Clicking blocks in the Blocks Palette is one way to issue commands to Scratch, but you're not really programming. If you have to click each block every time you want to run it, you're doing all the hard work of remembering the instructions, and the computer can only work as fast as you can click the blocks.

A program is a reusable set of instructions that can be carried out (or *run*) whenever you want. To start to create a program, you drag blocks from the Blocks Palette and drop them in the Scripts Area in the middle of the screen. Most blocks mentioned so far have a notch on the top of them and a lug on the bottom of them, so they fit together like jigsaw pieces. You don't have to align them perfectly: Scratch snaps them together for you if they're close enough when you release the mouse button.

You put your blocks in the order you want Scratch to run them, starting at the top and working your way down. It's a bit like making a to-do list for the computer.

A group of blocks in the Scripts Area is called a script, and you can run it by clicking anywhere on it. Its border flashes white, and you'll see the cat move around the Stage as you've instructed it to.

You can have multiple different scripts in the Scripts Area, so you could have one to make the cat walk left and another to make it walk right, for example.

When you add multiple sprites (see Chapter 10), each sprite has its own Scripts Area and scripts there to control it.

If you want to tidy up the Scripts Area, you can move a script by dragging its top block. If you drag a block lower down in the script, it is separated from the blocks above it and carries all the blocks below it with it. If you want to delete a block or set of blocks, drag it back to the Blocks Palette on the left.

The moonwalk is the dance popularized by Michael Jackson where the dancer looks like he's walking forward, but actually moves backward. Figure 9-11 shows an example script to make your cat moonwalk across the Stage. The first two lines in the script reset the cat to the middle of the screen, facing right. The cat tells you it loves to moonwalk and then lets out a little whoop like Michael Jackson, which it keeps up for the duration of the dance. The costume switch changes the position of the cat's legs, and it then glides 150 units to the left. Close the speech bubble by using the Say block with nothing in it, and then switch back to the other costume, which makes the cat's legs move back to their default position. Give it a go!

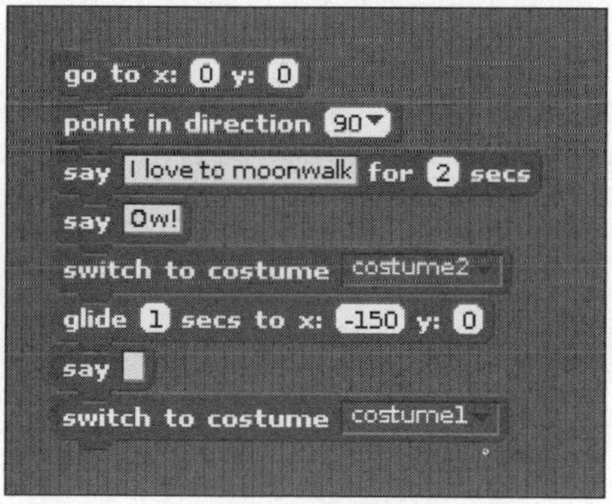

Figure 9-11:
This is how
you make a
cat moon-
walk. Ow!

```
go to x: 0 y: 0
point in direction 90▾
say I love to moonwalk for 2 secs
say Ow!
switch to costume costume2 ▾
glide 1 secs to x: -150 y: 0
say █
switch to costume costume1 ▾
```

*Scratch is developed by the Lifelong Kindergarten Group at the MIT
Media Lab. See http://scratch.mit.edu.*

Using the Wait Block to Slow Down Your Sprite

As you put your script together, you might find that some of the movements happen so fast you can hardly see what's going on.

If you click the Control button at the top of the Blocks Palette, you can find a set of yellow blocks that are used to govern when particular things happen. You read more about these in Chapter 10, but for now, it's worth knowing that there is a block here that enables you to wait for a certain number of seconds. Drag this into your script where necessary to introduce a delay so you can see each of your blocks in action. The length of the delay is 1 second by default, but you can change it to whatever you want, including parts of a second (for example, 0.5 for half a second).

The Say Hello! for 2 Secs block can be also be used to force the sprite to pause before running any more blocks.

Saving Your Work

Remember to save your work so you can come back to it again later. You can find the option to save in the File menu at the top of the screen, or you can click the floppy disk icon in the top left.

When the Save dialog box opens (see Figure 9-12), you'll see buttons on the left to choose from various places you could save your file, although you might not have permission to use all of them (see Chapter 5 for more on permissions). We recommend you use the Scratch folder inside your pi directory.

On the right, you can add your name and some project notes to remind you what the project was about later. You can see and edit the project notes associated with a file by going through the File menu when you're working on a program.

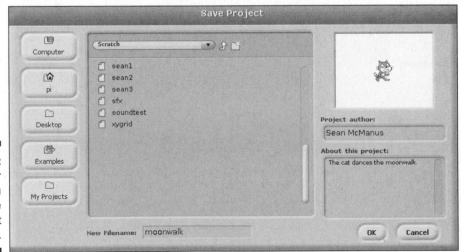

Figure 9-12: Saving your work so you can come back to it later.

Scratch is developed by the Lifelong Kindergarten Group at the MIT Media Lab. See http://scratch.mit.edu.

Chapter 10

Programming an Arcade Game Using Scratch

*I*n this chapter, we show you how to use Scratch to create and play an arcade game. You can customize the game with your own graphics, but more importantly, you learn how to put a game project together so you can invent your own games.

In this sample game, you control a flying saucer as it defends its planet from invasion. Grumpy-looking aliens zoom in from above, but you can stop them by hurling fireballs at them. If they get to you, it's game over. Not just for you, but for your entire planet . . .

This chapter explains the Control blocks that enable you to coordinate the actions of different sprites with each other and with the player. It assumes a basic understanding of the Scratch interface and how you use blocks to build a script, so refer to Chapter 9 for a refresher if you need it.

You can download the Scratch file for this game from this book's companion website. (See the Introduction for more on how to access the book's online content.) You might find it helpful to look at the color-coded script onscreen while you read this chapter. You can use the File menu at the top of the Scratch window to open the project when you download it, or you can double-click the file's icon.

Starting a New Scratch Project and Deleting Sprites

If you've been playing with Scratch and have blocks and scripts scattered all over the screen, you can start a new project by clicking File on the menu at the top of the screen and then choosing New.

All projects start with the Cat sprite in them, so the first thing you need to do is delete it. Here are the three ways you can delete a sprite:

- ✔ Right-click the sprite on the Stage, and then choose Delete from the menu.

- ✔ Right-click the sprite in the Sprite List in the bottom right of the screen, and then choose Delete from the menu you see in Figure 10-1.

- ✔ Click the scissors icon above the Stage and then click the sprite on the Stage or in the Sprite List.

Paint New Sprite
Choose New Sprite from File
Get Surprise Sprite

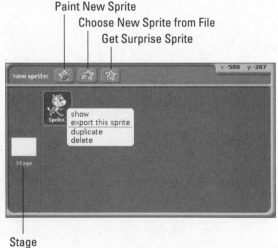

Figure 10-1:
The Sprite List, with the right-click menu open on the cat sprite.

Stage

Scratch is developed by the Lifelong Kindergarten Group at the MIT Media Lab.
See http://scratch.mit.edu.

Take care with the scissors icon: In most art packages, it means Cut, and you can use Paste to replace what you've removed. In Scratch, it means Delete, so you lose your sprite completely. If you delete a sprite accidentally, go straight to the Edit menu at the top of the Scratch window and use Undelete to bring it back.

Deleting a sprite is not the same as hiding it. If you hide a sprite, it's still part of your project, but it's not visible. You can bring it back later by showing it. If you delete a sprite, its scripts, costumes, and sounds are removed from your project altogether.

Changing the Background

So far, you've been working with a plain white Stage, but you can change the background to something more inspiring. The Sprite List contains an entry for the Stage (see Figure 10-1). The Stage can have scripts and different images, just like a sprite can. The Stage's images are called *backgrounds* rather than costumes. Click the Stage's icon in the Sprite List, and then click the Backgrounds tab at the top of the Scripts Area.

You can choose to paint a new background, using the built-in art package (see the section "Drawing Sprites in Scratch," later in this chapter). Alternatively, you can use an existing image file (or *import* it in Scratch-speak). Scratch comes with a number of backgrounds you can choose from, or you can use your own photo. Scratch can open images in .jpg, .gif, or .png format.

For this background, we've used a photo Sean took of Lanzarote's barren land-scape, which looks almost like it could have been beamed back from Mars.

Adding Sprites to Your Game

There wouldn't be much demand for a programming language that could only be used to create games about cats. (Actually, given the popularity of cat videos online, maybe there would.) In any case, Scratch gives you three ways to bring new sprites in to your game. You can find the buttons for all three at the top of the Sprite List, indicated in Figure 10-1.

- ✔ **Paint New Sprite:** This opens the Paint Editor so you can draw your sprite in Scratch.

- ✔ **Choose New Sprite from File:** You can use this button to bring one of the preset sprites into your project or to bring in a graphic you've created using a different art package. Scratch comes with a wide range of sprites, including dancing people, flying hippos, and fire-breathing dragons (our kind of party!).

- ✔ **Get Surprise Sprite:** Looking for some inspiration? This button fires up your creativity by bringing in a randomly chosen sprite from those that Scratch comes with. It's also a quick way to get started if you want to experiment with scripting. If you don't like the sprite you get, you can always delete it and try another surprise.

Drawing Sprites in Scratch

One of the most distinctive ways to put your fingerprint on your game is to draw your own sprites for it. Even if it plays the same as a well-known game, it'll look unique if you hand-craft your images. Figure 10-2 shows the Paint Editor in Scratch.

Undo   Drawing and editing tools

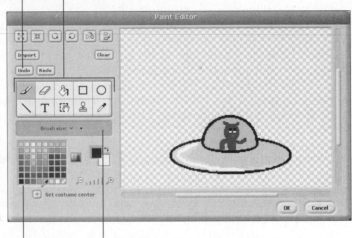

Figure 10-2:
The Paint
Editor in
Scratch.

Color Palette   Options area

Scratch is developed by the Lifelong Kindergarten Group at the MIT Media Lab. See http://scratch.mit.edu.

The checkered area on the right is the Canvas. The checkered pattern has a special meaning and is used to indicate parts of the image that are transparent, where the background will show through. Usually, you want everything outside the outline of your sprite to be transparent and everything inside it to be another color. Choose the color you want to use, or the checkered transparent "ink," by using the Color Palette at the bottom left of the Paint Editor (indicated in Figure 10-2).

Above the Color Palette, you can see your drawing and editing tools. Click one to select it, and you can then use it on the Canvas. The icon for your chosen tool is tinted blue so you can easily see which tool you are using. Underneath the tool icons is the Options area (indicated in Figure 10-2). This is where you can choose how to use a particular tool. The main tools are (from left to right, top row first):

🖊 **Paintbrush:** Hold down the mouse button as you move over the Canvas to leave a line. In the Options area, you can select how big your brush is.

✔ **Eraser:** Click the mouse button to delete part of your image. You can hold down the button and move the mouse if you want to delete large parts of the image, or want to delete small sections but have a steady hand. In the Options area, you can choose how big the eraser is.

✔ **Fill:** Click inside a shape on your image to fill it with your chosen color. In the Options area, you can choose a graduated pattern to use with your chosen color. To choose a different color to fade into, right-click the Color Palette.

✔ **Rectangle:** Click and hold the mouse button to mark one corner of the rectangle and then drag your mouse to the opposite corner and release the button. In the Options area, choose whether you want a filled rectangle or an empty one.

✔ **Ellipse:** This is similar to the rectangle tool. Click to indicate the point where lines from the top and left of the ellipse would meet, and then drag the mouse to the opposite side before releasing the button. Again, you have options to draw a filled or empty shape. You can create a perfect curved line by drawing an ellipse and then deleting some of it.

✔ **Line:** Click and hold the mouse button at the start of the line, move the mouse to the end of the line, and then release the mouse button. Your options let you choose the brush size, or line thickness.

✔ **Text:** You can't control where text is placed (although you can start a new line by pressing Enter), but you can choose different fonts and sizes in the options.

✔ **Select:** Use this to select a rectangular area of your image you would like to modify or remove. Click and hold the mouse button in one corner and drag to the opposite corner and then release the mouse button. You can drag your selected area to move it to a different part of the image or use the buttons at the top of the Paint Editor to enlarge or shrink, rotate anti-clockwise (counterclockwise) or clockwise, flip horizontally, or flip vertically. You can also press Delete on your keyboard to delete the selected area.

✔ **Stamp:** Use this tool to copy and paste part of your image. Click and hold the mouse button to mark one corner of the area and then drag your mouse to the opposite corner and release the button. A copy of that area follows your mouse cursor. Click the mouse button to stamp it (or paste it) at that position on the Canvas.

✔ **Eyedropper:** Use this tool to choose a color that's already on your Canvas. If you want to amend part of your sprite and need to use the same ink you used earlier, this tool saves you from having to remember which ink that was.

The Clear button clears the Canvas (except for text), irrespective of what you've selected. If you make a mistake, click Undo, shown in Figure 10-2.

When you've finished drawing your image, click Set Costume Center at the bottom left of your Paint Editor and then click in the middle of your image. This is important because it controls the point around which your sprite rotates if you use rotation in your game.

Don't forget to save your game frequently. It's a good idea to save a new copy of your game with a new filename as you reach each significant point in its development. It means you can go back if you introduce an unexpected error, and also protects you against losing too much of your work if a file gets corrupted (as happened to Sean once while creating this game!).

If you want to edit your picture later, click your sprite's Costumes tab (see Figure 10-3) and then click Edit beside the costume you want to change. If you want to create additional costumes for a sprite, you can also do that in your sprite's Costumes tab.

Costumes tab
Sprite name

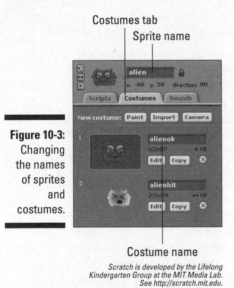

Figure 10-3:
Changing
the names
of sprites
and
costumes.

Costume name

*Scratch is developed by the Lifelong
Kindergarten Group at the MIT Media Lab.
See http://scratch.mit.edu.*

Naming Your Sprites

Whenever you're programming, you should give things meaningful names so that you (and others) can easily understand what your program does. Scratch gives your sprites names like *Sprite1* and *Sprite2*, but you can rename them. To rename a sprite, click its name above the Scripts Area (see Figure 10-3) and then type its new name. Your sprite's costumes are called *costume1*, *costume2*, and so on. If you've created different costumes for your sprite, you should also give them sensible names so you can easily tell which is which. Go to your sprite's Costumes tab, click the name beside a costume (see Figure 10-3), and type the new name.

For the space game, you need to create a flying saucer sprite named *ship* and a sprite named *fireball* to represent the ship's weapon. The baddie is a sprite called *alien*, and should have two costumes: *alienok,* which shows him looking menacing, and *alienhit,* which shows him after he's been hit by the fireball.

To make it easier to see what you're doing, we recommend you drag your ship to the bottom of the screen, the alien to the top, and put the fireball somewhere in the middle. That roughly reflects where they will be in the finished game.

Controlling When Scripts Run

In Chapter 9, we show you how to start scripts by clicking them in the Scripts Area. Most of the time, you'll want your scripts to run automatically when certain things happen, such as a player pressing the Fire key.

This is where the Control blocks come in: They allow you to trigger scripts to run when a particular event happens, such as a sprite hitting another sprite or a key being pressed. You use the Control blocks to craft the rules and instructions that govern how your game works.

Using the green flag to start scripts

One of the Control blocks is particularly useful for starting your game and synchronizing your scripts across all your sprites. Above the Stage are two buttons: a green flag and a red stop button. The green flag is used to start scripts running, and you can use a Control block to detect when it's clicked. This Control block has a curved top on it because no other block can go above it, but it has a notch underneath so you can join motion, looks, sound, or other blocks to it. You can put scripts that are triggered by the green flag being clicked into all your sprites, so clicking the flag makes it easy to start scripts on different sprites at the same time.

At the end of a game, aliens and the ship could be anywhere, so at the start of the game, you need to reset each sprite to its starting position. For the player's ship, you need to reset the X position to the center of the screen, set the Y position near the bottom of the screen, reset the ship's direction, and bring the ship to the front, so that any other sprites will be behind it. Later on, this makes the fireball come from behind the ship, so it looks like it's being fired from inside, rather than just appearing on top of it.

Figure 10-4 shows the script you should assemble to reset your ship when the green flag is clicked. If you're making your own graphics, your Y position might need to be higher up, depending on the size of your sprite.

When you have multiple sprites in your project, make sure you're adding blocks to the right one (the ship, in this case). Each sprite has its own Scripts Area. To choose a sprite, click it in the bottom right.

Figure 10-4:
Using a green flag Control block to reset your sprite.

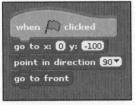

Scratch is developed by the Lifelong Kindergarten Group at the MIT Media Lab. See http://scratch.mit.edu.

Using the Forever Control block

Computers are great at repetitive tasks, and a game program often requires the computer to do the same things over and over again until the game is finished.

Repeated bits of program like this are called *loops*.

You can use two main Control blocks to make the computer repeat a set of blocks. The Repeat block enables you to specify how many times you want a block or set of blocks to be run. The Forever block runs a block or set of blocks repeatedly until the program is stopped.

Both of them are shaped like a bracket, so they can enclose the blocks you want to repeat inside them. The Forever block doesn't have a notch on the bottom because it doesn't make sense to put any other blocks after it: They would never be run because forever never comes to an end.

For the ship in this space game, you need to make sure you keep checking for key presses until the game is finished. Without the Forever loop, the script would check once for a key press, and then finish.

You can find the Forever block by clicking the Control button at the top of the Blocks Palette. Drag it into the script for your ship at the end of your green flag script. The first time you use it, we recommend you test it how it works by dragging a Motion block into its bracket. Figure 10-5 shows a script that makes the ship sprite rotate for as long as the program runs. Click the green flag to start it, but don't forget to take that rotation block out again when you've finished testing.

Figure 10-5:
The Forever block used to make the ship rotate all the time the program runs.

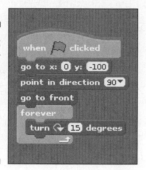

Scratch is developed by the Lifelong Kindergarten Group at the MIT Media Lab. See http://scratch.mit.edu.

Enabling keyboard control of a sprite

For our space game, the player needs to be able to move the ship sprite left and right using the arrow keys. In plain English, we need to use a set of blocks that says "If the player presses the left-arrow key, move the ship left." And we need to put those blocks inside a Forever block, so Scratch keeps checking and moving the sprite all the way through the game. We need a similar set of blocks that move the sprite right too.

The If block is a Control block that enables a set of blocks to be run only under certain conditions. For that reason, it's often called a *conditional statement* in programming. Like the Forever block, it's shaped like a bracket, so you can put other blocks inside it. In the case of the If block, the blocks inside are ones you want to run only in certain circumstances. Drag your If block into the Scripts Area.

Scratch is designed like a jigsaw puzzle, so it gives you visual hints about what blocks can go where if the program is to make sense. The If block has a diamond-shaped hole in it, which is where you describe the circumstances under which you want its blocks to run. There are diamond-shaped Operator and Sensing blocks as well, and we use both in this program.

The block we need for keyboard control is a Sensing block called Key Space Pressed?. It detects a tap on the spacebar. If you want it to detect the pressing of a key other than the spacebar, use its menu to set that. In this case, we want it to detect the left-arrow key. You can drag and drop this Sensing block into the diamond-shaped hole in the If block in the Scripts Area.

Figure 10-6 shows the piece of script you need to move the ship left. We've used a Motion block to change its X position by -10 units, and we've also adjusted its direction, which makes it tilt toward the direction it's moving. You could change its costume so it looks different when it's moving left or right, or add any other visual effects or sounds here.

Figure 10-6:
The If block is used to enable keyboard movement of the sprite.

Scratch is developed by the Lifelong Kindergarten Group at the MIT Media Lab. See http://scratch.mit.edu.

Enabling a sprite to control another sprite

In programming, you can often choose between several ways to achieve the same effect. The game's firing mechanism is one such example. You could sense the spacebar (the Fire key) being pressed using a script on the fireball, for example, and use that to trigger the fireball's ascent.

We're going to use the firing mechanism as an opportunity to show you how you can make one sprite control another sprite, however. You can't actually make the ship move the fireball, but you can send a message from the ship to tell the fireball you want it to move itself.

There are two parts to this. The first is that you need to use the Broadcast block on the ship to send a message to all the other sprites. You only want to do this when the spacebar (the Fire button in our game) is pressed, so you need to drag an If block to the Scripts Area of your ship, add a diamond Sensing block to check whether the spacebar is pressed, and finally put the Broadcast block inside the If block's bracket.

The Broadcast block is one of the Control blocks and it has a menu built into it. Click the menu and click New to create a new message. We've called our message `fire`.

This approach has a couple of advantages. First, you can keep all your game control scripts on one sprite (the ship), which makes the program easier to manage. Second, it's an efficient way to coordinate multiple sprites. We could, for example, make our alien look terrified when the Fire button is pressed by just changing its costume, and that only requires two blocks: a Control block for when the message `fire` is received, and the block to change to a new costume where it looks scared. It's much more efficient than having to look out for the Fire button on the alien too.

Figure 10-7 shows the script for the ship. When the green flag is clicked, it resets the ship's position and then enters a loop where it moves the ship left if the left-arrow key is pressed, moves the ship right if the right-arrow key is pressed, sends the `fire` message if the spacebar is pressed, and then keeps checking for those keys forever. You can run this script to test that the ship moves as expected.

If your script doesn't behave as expected, check your brackets. You're allowed to put an If block inside another If block, but that doesn't make sense here, and it will stop the game's controls from working properly. If you put the bracket for detecting the Fire key inside the bracket for detecting the right-arrow key, the game will only check for the Fire key when the right-arrow key is pressed.

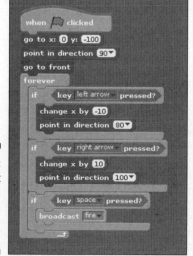

Figure 10-7:
The script
for resetting
and then
controlling
the ship.

Click the fireball sprite in the Sprite List. You can now add scripts to that sprite. A Control block called When I Receive `fire` is used to trigger a script when the `fire` message is broadcast. This script is quite simple: We move the fireball sprite to where the ship is, show the fireball sprite (although it will be behind our ship), play a suitably sci-fi sound from the effects included with Scratch, glide the sprite to the top of the screen, and then hide it again.

In the Glide block, we can drop a block called X Position in place of entering a number for the X position. That means we can keep the X position the same as it already is, while changing the Y position with a gliding movement. The result is that the fireball moves vertically.

The other script we need on the Fireball is one to hide it when the green flag is clicked, just in case it's onscreen from the previous game when a new one starts.

Remember to make sure you're adding scripts to the correct sprite.

Figure 10-8 shows the scripts for the fireball sprite. Remember to add the Laser1 sound effect using the sprite's Sounds tab before creating this script. It's in the Electronic folder.

Figure 10-8:
The scripts
for the fire-
ball sprite.

Scratch is developed by the Lifelong Kindergarten Group at the
MIT Media Lab. See http://scratch.mit.edu.

Using Random Numbers

Games wouldn't be much fun if they were always exactly the same, so Scratch enables you to use random numbers in your scripts. To keep players on their toes, we can make the alien appear at a random X position at the top of the screen.

Click your alien in the Sprite List, and then drag in the Green Flag Control block. As with the other sprites, we need to create a script that resets the alien to its starting position. In the case of the alien, the sprite switches to a different costume when it's hit, so we should make sure it is using its normal costume at the start of a new game and that it is visible onscreen.

For its screen position, the alien needs to have a Y coordinate of 150, which is near the top of the screen. We don't want to use the full width of the Stage because it looks odd when half the alien is off the edge of the Stage. From experimentation, we found that the ideal starting X position for our alien is between -180 and 180, but yours might vary depending on its size.

Drag in the Motion block you used previously to go to a particular X and Y position. If you click Operators at the top of the Blocks Palette, you can find a block to pick a random number from 1 to 10. Drag this block into the hole where you would normally type the X position, and then change the numbers in the random number block to -180 and 180.

Figure 10-9 shows your initial script for the alien. You can use the green flag to test whether it works and positions the alien at a random point at the top of the screen each time.

Figure 10-9:
The script to reset the alien at the start of the game.

Scratch is developed by the Lifelong Kindergarten Group at the MIT Media Lab. See http://scratch.mit.edu.

Detecting When a Sprite Hits Another Sprite

There's no point throwing flaming fireballs at an alien if it's not even going to raise an eyebrow. To make this game fun, we need to make the alien sprite react when it's hit. Most games involve sprites hitting each other (bats and balls, targets and weapons, chasing and catching), so *collision detection*, as it is often called, is a staple of game design.

You can detect whether the fireball is touching the alien sprite from the fireball, but it is the alien that must react, so that's where we need to put our script.

You can use a Sensing block to check whether a sprite is touching another sprite, and we combine that with an If block to trigger a reaction when the alien and fireball touch each other.

Like the key press detection for the ship, we want to keep checking for the alien being hit throughout the game, so we put the If block inside a Forever block (see Figure 10-10). Inside the first If block are the instructions for what to do when the alien is touching the fireball: Change the alien's costume to what it looks like when it's been hit, make it say "Arggh!" in a speech bubble, play a sound effect, and then hide the alien. After a random delay of a few seconds, the alien is repositioned at the top of the screen, switched back to its normal costume and shown, so the horrible cycle of invasion and destruction can begin again.

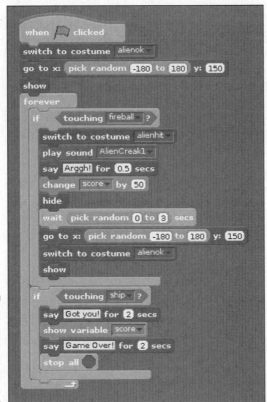

Figure 10-10: Setting up the alien and detecting when it's hit.

Scratch is developed by the Lifelong Kindergarten Group at the MIT Media Lab. See http://scratch.mit.edu.

Introducing Variables

Variables are a way of storing information in a program so you can refer back to it later or reuse it. You give that piece of information a name, and then you can refer to it by that name in your script. For example, we want to keep a running tally of the score, and we use a variable to do that. They're called *variables* because their value can change over time. The score is zero at the start of the game, for example, but it goes up each time the player zaps an alien out of the sky.

We can tell our script to reset the score to zero, increase it when an alien is hit, and display the score at the end. Each time, we just refer to it as score, and the program works out what number that refers to.

To create a variable, click the Variables button above the Blocks Palette. In the Blocks Palette itself is a button called Make a Variable. Click that, and you will be asked for the variable's name, which is score in this case.

You're also asked whether this variable should be for all sprites or just for the sprite you're working on now. It's important to get this right. For our score, we want to make a variable that all our sprites can see. If you have a variable that's only used by one sprite, it's better to create a variable that's only for that sprite because it stops other sprites from being able to interfere with it. When you duplicate a sprite, all its scripts and variables are duplicated with it too, so you might find you have sprites that use variables that share the same name, but that you want to use independently of each other. You see an example of this later in this chapter when we add extra aliens.

When you create a variable, new blocks appear in the Blocks Palette that you can use to change the variable's value and show or hide it on the Stage. We want the score to go up by 50 each time the alien is hit (be generous — it's not an easy game!), so drag the Change score by 1 block into your script and edit the number in it to 50. This block needs to go inside the If bracket that detects whether the alien touches the fireball, as you can see in Figure 10-10.

In Chapter 9, you see how you can display a sprite's position and direction on the Stage. By default, the values of variables are shown on the Stage too. They appear in the top left, but you can drag them wherever you want them. This can be useful for tracing and fixing problems, but it can get in the way of the game. We recommend you deselect the check box beside your new score variable in the Blocks Palette to remove it from the Stage again.

In the finished game, the alien comes down the screen toward the ship, and the game ends when the alien catches the player's flying saucer. At this point, we want to show the score variable on the Stage and use a special Control block that stops all scripts so the program comes to an end. Figure 10-10 also includes the blocks that do this, which use a similar pattern to the blocks used for detecting when the alien is hit.

Making Sprites Move Automatically

If you're wondering why we left the alien's movement to the end, it's because it makes it easier to test the game. We've now got a spaceship that the player can move, a working firing mechanism, and an alien that dies and then regenerates when shot. We can test all that at our leisure and fix any problems without worrying about having to keep up with the alien.

Our alien moves from left to right and then from right to left, and then back again. Each time it changes direction, it moves down the screen a little bit. This is quite sophisticated behavior, but you can create most of it using the blocks you've already used this chapter. The art of programming is partly about working out how you use the different blocks or commands at your disposal to achieve what you want to.

To start, we need to make a new variable, which we'll call `leapsize`. When you create the `leapsize` variable, you are asked whether this variable should apply to all sprites or to this sprite only (the alien). Make sure you click the button to make it apply only to this sprite.

Each time Scratch goes around the alien's Forever loop, it moves the sprite and then checks whether it's touching a fireball or the spaceship. The `leapsize` variable is used to store how much the alien's X position should change by each time. If the alien is going right, the `leapsize` variable is `20`, and if it's going left, it's `-20`.

If you don't make the `leapsize` variable for this sprite only, you'll have problems when you duplicate the sprite later because the aliens will use the same `leapsize` variable. The `leapsize` variable is personal to each sprite and its correct value depends partly on where a sprite is on the screen. If you have sprites stuck at the edge of the screen, they are probably interfering with each other's variables.

When the alien reaches the edge of the screen, the `leapsize` variable is changed so that the alien goes back in the other direction, and the alien is moved down the screen by `20` units.

Figure 10-11 shows the movement script you need to insert into your alien's Forever loop as its first blocks.

The green Operators blocks enable you to build more sophisticated instructions. They include the capability to do sums, check how one value compares to another value, and combine different conditions in an If block. They can be hard to understand because you can often put other blocks inside them.

Figure 10-11: The alien's movement script.

Scratch is developed by the Lifelong Kindergarten Group at the MIT Media Lab. See http://scratch.mit.edu.

The If blocks in our alien's movement script use Operator blocks to compare the X position with a number so that they can detect when the alien reaches the edge of the screen. We found that -200 and 200 represented the minimum and maximum desirable X positions if you want to avoid the alien slipping partly off the Stage. The comparison blocks are diamond-shaped, so they slot into the hole in the If block. You can use one to check whether the X position is more than (>) 200 and another to check whether it is less than (<) -200. (We shouldn't check for an exact match with 200 or -200 because the alien starts at a random position, and its steps increase by 20 units. If it started at X position 170, for example, it would go to 190 and 210 but never 200.)

You also need to insert a block to set the starting value of leapsize to 20; otherwise, it will be zero and your alien won't move. In the Blocks Palette, drag the block for setting a variable's value to the start of your script, and edit it to set leapsize to 20. This block must go inside your alien's green flag script but outside your Forever loop.

Fixing the Final Bug

In many commercial software development projects, most of the time and money is spent testing programs to make sure they work as expected, and then fixing them when they don't. Errors in programs are often called *bugs*, and even in our simple game here, we have one that would enable the player to cheat.

If the fireball is moving up the screen and the player presses the Fire key again, the firing sequence starts over. That means the fireball that was traveling through the air disappears, and a new one is sent up from the ship. That doesn't make any logical sense, and it means players suffer no consequences if they misfire: They can just fire again and it's as if the misfired shot never happened.

We can use a variable to keep note of when the fireball is moving up the screen so that we can stop the ship from allowing a fireball to be fired again at that time. Variables like this, which are just used to keep track of whether something is happening, are called *flags*. Our firing flag needs to be able to say whether the fireball is in play or not, so it has two values. While the fireball is onscreen, we give the firing flag a value of 1. When it isn't, the firing flag has a value of 0.

Click the Variables button at the top of the Blocks Palette, and click the option to make a variable. Give it the name firingflag and make sure the button is selected so it is available for all sprites.

After you've created the variable, you can drag a block in from the Variables section of the Blocks Palette to set its value to 1 at the start of the fireball's firing sequence, and to 0 at the end again. You should also update the fireball's green flag script so that it resets the firing flag to 0 at the start of a game in case a game ended while the fireball was onscreen. Figure 10-12 shows the final scripts for the fireball.

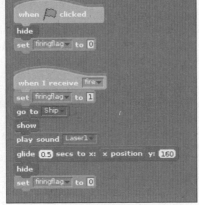

Figure 10-12:
The final scripts for the fireball, including the firing flag.

Scratch is developed by the Lifelong Kindergarten Group at the MIT Media Lab. See http://scratch.mit.edu.

We also need to modify the script for the ship so that it only fires if the firingflag variable is 0 at the time the spacebar is pressed. This is a little bit complicated because we need to lock together lots of different blocks to express this idea.

Go back to the ship's script. You'll need to modify the If block that checks whether the spacebar is pressed. Figure 10-13, read from top to bottom, shows how you build up your blocks. For simplicity's sake, we've emptied the instructions from inside the If block and separated it out from the rest of the script.

Start by dragging the Sensing block for the spacebar out of the If block's diamond-shaped hole. In its place, drag the And operator block. This means the blocks inside the If block's bracket are run only if two things are true. The first is that the spacebar must be pressed, so drag your Sensing block for the spacebar into the diamond-shaped hole inside the And statement. The second is that we need to make sure the firingflag is 0. Drag the '=0' Operator block into the And operator block on the right, and then drag the firingflag variable into the other side of the And operator.

That should ensure the ship can only fire one fireball at a time. They might be aliens, but they still deserve a fair fight!

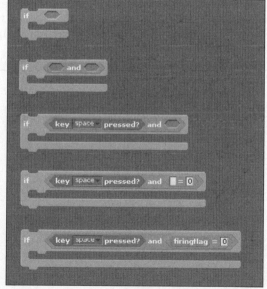

Figure 10-13:
How to build the If block that checks whether the ship should fire.

Scratch is developed by the Lifelong Kindergarten Group at the MIT Media Lab.
See http://scratch.mit.edu.

Adding Scripts to the Stage

As well as sprites, you can add scripts to the Stage. Click the Stage in the Sprite List, and you'll find it has its own Scripts Area. It's a real pain to have to hunt through your sprites to find where you put a particular block so you can change it, so this is a good place to put scripts that affect the whole game and that aren't associated with a particular sprite.

For this game, we should add a block to the Stage to set the score to 0 when the green flag is clicked. Otherwise, the score will rise ever higher with each successive game and will never be set back to zero when a new game starts.

Duplicating Sprites

Because of the way we've created our alien, with the leapsize variable only applying to that one sprite, we can add more aliens by simply duplicating the first one. Right-click it in the Sprite List and choose Duplicate. Having two aliens makes the game more nail-biting.

Playing Your Game

To play your game without the distraction of your scripts and other clutter on the screen, click the Easel icon near the top right of the screen that says Switch to Presentation Mode when you hover over it. The Stage enlarges to fill the screen. You can use the green flag to play as usual. To close the full-screen view again, click the arrow in the top left. Figure 10-14 shows our final game, but yours might look quite different with your own art in it.

Figure 10-14: Got him! The final game.

Adapting the Game's Speed

This game runs at a challenging but playable speed on my Raspberry Pi, and runs faster now than it did when the first edition of this book was written. That's because a lot of work has been done to improve the speed of Scratch over the last couple of years. If the game is unplayable on your Raspberry Pi with the latest software, you can slow down the aliens by reducing the magnitude of the `leapsize` variable (including after the alien changes direction), or changing the amount by which the alien's Y position decreases when the sprite changes direction. You can also put a small wait into the alien's loop, although that might mean the collision detection is less accurate. The game also slows down if you add more aliens or other sprites to it, which would be a creative way to adjust the gameplay to take advantage of the increased speed.

Taking It Further with Scratch

In this chapter, we've covered many fundamental concepts that are used in programming, including loops, operators, and variables. You've seen how you can use Scratch to design your own games, where sprites interact with each other and respond to the player's control. You can do lots of things to customize this game. Draw your own sprites. Change the speed of the aliens each time they're shot, or the way they move. But your next real adventure is to use Scratch and the skills learned in this chapter, perhaps with some of the other blocks we haven't had room for, to make your very own game.

To find out more about Scratch, and find games and animations others have made, visit the website at `http://scratch.mit.edu`. You can also share your own work there and get feedback from other Scratch fans.

To dig deeper into Scratch and find more example programs, see Sean's book *Scratch Programming in Easy Steps*.

Chapter 11

Writing Programs in Python

In This Chapter

▶ Accepting user input and printing to the screen

▶ Using variables, strings, lists, and dictionaries

▶ Using `for` and `while` loops

▶ Using conditional statements for decision-making

▶ Creating and using your own functions

*I*n this chapter, we introduce you to Python, a powerful programming language that's widely used commercially.

One of the best ways to learn programming is to study other people's programs, so in this chapter, we talk you through two different programs. One is a simple calculator for multiplication tables. The other is an artificial intelligence simulation that enables you to chat with your Raspberry Pi.

You'll probably find it easiest to learn if you try creating the examples with us, but you can also download the finished programs from the book's website. For more information on accessing this book's website, see the Introduction.

In a book of this size, it's not possible to cover everything you can do with Python, but this chapter gets you started with your first programs. As you work through these examples, you'll learn about some of the fundamental principles in Python and programming generally, and you'll gain an understanding of how Python programs are put together.

You'll be able to draw upon this knowledge when exploring the electronics programs in Part V of this book, and when creating an arcade game with Pygame in Chapter 13.

Some lines of code are too wide for the page. We use a curving arrow at the end of a line of code to indicate a line continues. When you see one, just carry on typing and ignore the indent on the next line.

Starting Python

The Raspberry Pi has two versions of Python installed on it: Python 2.7 and Python 3. Usually when software or programming languages are updated, the new version is compatible with the old version. Python 3 was intentionally designed not to be compatible, however, so programs written for Python 2.7 might not work with Python 3, and vice versa. In this book, we use Python 2.7, because it makes it easier to install some of the software required for the projects in Part V of the book. You can find out more about what's different about Python 3 at `http://docs.python.org/3.0/whatsnew/3.0.html`.

Programmers often use something called an *integrated development environment* (IDE), which is a set of tools for creating and testing programs. The Python IDE is called IDLE, and there are two versions of it on your desktop: IDLE (which is for Python 2.7) and IDLE 3 (which is for Python 3). Double-click the IDLE icon to get started.

Entering Your First Python Commands

When you start IDLE, a window opens with text at the top that looks something like Figure 11-1.

This is the Python shell, and the three arrows are your prompt, which means Python is ready for you to enter a command. You can test this by entering the `license()` command, which shows you a history of Python before displaying the terms and conditions of using it. If you don't want to get bogged down in legalese, abort by pressing q and then pressing Enter when prompted.

One of the most basic commands in any programming language is the one that tells the computer to put some text on the screen. In Python (and some other languages too), this command is `print`, and you use it like this:

```
>>> print "hello"
hello
>>>
```

Whatever you type in the quotes after the `print` command is "printed" on the screen, and Python then returns you to the prompt so you can enter another command.

Like the Linux shell, Python is case-sensitive, which means it won't work if you use capital letters where you shouldn't. The command `print` must be entered in lowercase; otherwise, Python tells you you've made a syntax error, which means you're using a command incorrectly. You can mess around with the word in quotes as much as you like, however: This is the text that you want to appear onscreen. Take a look at these examples:

Figure 11-1:
The Python shell, just after it opens.

```
>>> PRINT "Hello Karen!"
SyntaxError: invalid syntax
>>> Print "Hello Karen!"
SyntaxError: invalid syntax
>>> print "Hello Karen!"
           Hello Karen!
```

Using the Shell to Calculate Sums

You can also use the shell to carry out simple calculations. Table 11-1 shows you the different mathematical operators you can use in your sums. Just put the sum after the print command, like this:

```
>>> print 5 + 5
10
>>> print 9 - 4
5
>>> print 7 * 7
49
>>> print 10 / 2
5
```

Table 11-1	Mathematical Operators in Python
Operator	*Description*
+	Addition
–	Subtraction
*	Multiplication
/	Division
//	Division, discarding any decimal portion
%	Modulo, which shows the remainder after a division

Note that you don't use quotes around the sum in your `print` command. What would happen if you did? Python would put on the screen literally what you asked it to, like this:

```
>>> print "5 + 5"
5 + 5
```

There are a few surprises in how division is carried out in Python. If you cast your mind back to your mathematics lessons, you might remember that whole numbers, which have no decimal portion, are called *integers*. In Python 2.7, if you divide an integer by an integer, you get an integer as a result, which means the answer can be less accurate than you might expect from a computer. For example, what's 7 divided by 2?

```
>>> print 7 / 2
3
```

Close, but not close enough. To force Python to give you an answer that would pass a teacher's scrutiny, add a decimal portion to one of the values in your sum, like this:

```
>>> print 7 / 2.0
3.5
>>> print 7.0 / 2
3.5
```

If you want to force the rounding effect to remove any decimal portion from your answer, you can use the // (floor division) operator, like this:

```
>>> print 10.0 / 3
3.33333333333
>>> print 10.0 // 3
3.0
```

An operator you might not have come across before is *modulo*. It uses the % sign and tells you the remainder after a division. Here are some examples:

```
>>> print 10 % 3
1
>>> print 10 % 2
0
```

You can use that operator to tell whether one number is divisible by another (the modulo is 0 if so).

These sums are quite basic, but you can enter more advanced sums by stringing together numbers and operators. As in algebra, you use parentheses to surround the bits of the sum that belong together and should be carried out first. For example:

```
>>> print (10.0/3) * 2
6.66666666667
>>> print 10.0 / (3*2)
1.66666666667
```

You can also do mathematics in the shell by just entering the sums without a `print` command, but it's essential to use it when you're creating programs, as you see shortly.

The spaces we've used around the mathematical operators are optional. They help with readability, and in that last example, help to show which parts of the sum belong together.

Creating the Times Tables Program

Now we're going to show you how to make a program that generates multiplication tables. For example, if the user requests a multiplication table for the number 7, it outputs the sequence 7, 14, 21, and so on. The program is only a few lines long, but it teaches you how to create programs, how to use variables to store numbers, how to ask the user for information, and how to create sections of program that repeat (*loops*). You build on your understanding of the `print` command to do all this, and if you've read Chapters 10 and 11 on Scratch, some of the ideas should be familiar to you.

Creating and running your first Python program

The problem with entering instructions in the shell is that you have to enter them each time you want to use them. The commands are carried out straightaway, too, which limits the sophistication of the kinds of things you can do. You can solve these problems by creating a *program*, a set of repeatable instructions that you can save as a file and use again.

To create a program, you use script mode, which is a blank window when you open it, but otherwise looks like Figure 11-2. To open the script mode window, click the File menu at the top of the Python shell, and then click New Window.

When you enter commands in script mode, they're not carried out straightaway. The window acts like a simple text editor, and enables you to enter your list of commands (or program), and gives you control over when those commands are carried out.

Enter the following commands in the script mode:

```
# simple times table program
print "This program calculates times tables"
print "It is from Raspberry Pi For Dummies"
```

The window should look like Figure 11-2. The two print commands should look familiar to you, but the first line is new. In Python, anything after a # (hash mark) is ignored by the computer. The hash mark indicates a comment, used to add notes to programs so you can understand them later. The very best programs are written in such a way that you can understand them easily anyway, but it's a good idea to leave little messages to your future self (or other people) so you can quickly understand important aspects of the program. We've put a one-line summary at the start of the program here, so if we open it later, we can immediately see what it does.

To save your program, click the File menu at the top of the script mode window and choose Save. You use this same menu to reopen previously saved programs too.

The term used for starting a program is *running* it, so click the Run menu and then click Run Module to see your program in action. Alternatively, the keyboard shortcut to run the program is F5. When you run the program, Python switches back to the shell and you see those two lines of text printed out on the screen.

Congratulations! You've just written your first Python program!

Before you can run your program, you must save it. If you made changes since the last time it was saved, you are prompted to save the program when you try to run it. This overwrites the previous version of the program. On the File menu of the script mode window is an option to save a copy of the program or to save it using a different filename (Save As), which can be useful if you might want to revert to an earlier version.

Figure 11-2:
The script
mode
window.

Using variables

The next step in our program is to ask the user which multiplication table
he would like us to generate. We'll store this number in a variable. As you
learned when you were using Scratch, a variable is a way of storing a number
or a piece of text so you can refer back to it later.

For example, you might have a variable that stores your bank balance. It
might go up (ker-ching!) or it might go down (sadly, more often), but you can
always refer to it as your bank balance. Variables are one of the basic building blocks of programming, and not just in Python.

Taking the example of a bank balance, you can create a variable in Python for
your bank balance called `balance` by just giving it a value, like this:

```
balance = 500
```

You can vary the value later (which is why it's called a variable), by just giving
it a new value:

```
balance = 250
```

More often, you'll want to do sums with the balance, such as taking some money off the total when money is withdrawn, or adding money to it when a deposit is received. To do that, you change the variable's value to a number that's calculated from its current value. Here's an example:

```
balance = balance - 250
```

That takes the value of the balance variable, knocks 250 off it, and then puts the answer back into the variable balance. You can display the value of a variable onscreen using the print command with the variable name:

```
print balance
```

TIP

Programmers often use a shorthand form when they're adding numbers to or subtracting them from a variable. The shorthand is += for addition and -= for subtraction. Here's an example:

```
balance = 500
balance += 20
print balance
```

If you run that tiny program, it prints 520 on the screen.

```
balance = 500
balance- = 70
print balance
```

That program subtracts 70 from the initial balance of 500, so it shows 430 onscreen. This shorthand is an elegant way and concise way to express the idea of changing a variable's value, and you'll see it used widely in Python.

Accepting user input

Before we go any further, we should clarify one piece of jargon: function. A *function* is a set of commands that do a particular job, and there are lots of them built in to Python. Later on, you'll learn how to make your own too (see "Creating your own functions"). To use a function, enter its name, followed by parentheses. If you want to send it any information to work with, you put that inside the parentheses.

When our program runs, we want to ask the user which multiplication table she would like to generate, and then store that number in a variable which we'll call tablenum. To do that, we set up the tablenum variable using a built-in function called input(), which asks the question, waits for the user to type something in, and then puts whatever is typed in into the variable.

Here's how the input() function works:

```
tablenum = input("Which multiplication table shall→ I
                  generate for you? ")
```

We've put a space after the question mark and before the quote mark closes the question because otherwise the cursor appears right next to the question mark. It looks much clearer and more professional with a space between the question and the user's answer.

Add that line into your program and run it, and you'll see that the program displays the question and then gives you a cursor and waits for you to enter your number. Enter any number to try it out. The program won't do anything else yet, however, because you haven't told it to do anything with the number you enter.

Printing words, variables, and numbers together

Start by printing a title for the multiplication table the user has requested. This requires something we haven't had before: the capability to print text and variables in the same line of text. The print command can be used to print more than one thing in a line, if they're separated by commas, so we can combine text and our variable tablenum, like this:

```
print "\nHere is your", tablenum, "times table:"
```

The first two characters here, \n, have a special meaning. They're known as an *escape code*, and they're used to start a new line. Here they create a bit of space between the question asking for input and the resulting heading.

Don't forget that anything between the quotes is actually printed onscreen. If you put the variable name tablenum between quotes, you'll see the word "tablenum" onscreen, instead of the number the user typed in.

Now you need to print a line for each entry in the times table, from 1 to 12. As you know, you can use variables in sums, and you can print sums, so you could display the times table like this:

```
print "1 times", tablenum, "is", tablenum
print "2 times", tablenum, "is", tablenum*2
print "3 times", tablenum, "is", tablenum*3
print "4 times", tablenum, "is", tablenum*4
```

It works, as you can see in Figure 11-3. But it's not really a good solution. For each line of output, we're entering a new line in the program and adding a new sum at the end of it. Even using the copy and paste in the script mode (in the Edit menu), we ran out of patience at line four. What if we wanted to create a times table that goes up to 50? Or 500? Or 5,000? Clearly, we need a more scalable solution.

Figure 11-3:
The times table program, in development.

Using for loops to repeat

To save the slog of entering all those print commands, and to make our program more flexible, we can use a `for` loop. This enables you to repeat a section of program a set number of times, and to increase a variable each time the code repeats. That's exactly what we need for our times table program: We want to display one line for each number from 1 to 12, showing the result of multiplying that number by the figure the user entered.

Here's how the code looks that makes that happen:

```
for i in range(1, 13):
    print i, "times", tablenum, "is", i*tablenum
```

This tiny program snippet introduces several new programming concepts. First, take a look at the `range()` function. This is used to create a list of numbers, and you give it a number to start at (1) and the end point (13). The end point is never included in the list, so we had to use a 13 to make our multiplication tables go up to 12.

You can use `range()` outside a `for` command too. Try the following in the shell:

```
>>> print range(5, 15)
[5, 6, 7, 8, 9, 10, 11, 12, 13, 14]
```

If you add a third number between the brackets (parentheses), it's used to specify how big you want the gap to be between the numbers. We don't need that here, but for completeness, this is how it works:

```
>>> print range(5, 15, 2)
[5, 7, 9, 11, 13]
```

Our `range()` function, then, creates a list of numbers from 1 to 12. The rest of the line it's on sets up the start of the bit we want to repeat, and says that we should give the variable i the next value from our number list each time we repeat. The first time around, i has a value of 1, the first number in our list. The second time around, i has a value of 2, which is the second number in our list. This goes all the way up to the last repetition, when i has a value of 12.

We tell Python which commands should be repeated by indenting them. The `print` command we've used has four spaces before it, and in Python, these spaces are meaningful. Many languages let you space your programs out however you want, but in Python, the spacing is often part of how the computer understands your intentions. By enforcing the use of indentations like this, Python makes it easier to read programs because you can see which bits belong together at a glance. They're all indented to the same depth.

We can repeat multiple commands by just indenting them all:

```
for i in range(1, 13):
    print i, "times", tablenum, "is", i*tablenum
    print "-------------------"
print "Hope you found that useful!"
```

If you can't get your loop to work, make sure you have remembered the colon at the end of the `for` line.

The previous snippet works its way through numbers 1 to 12 and prints the times table line for each one, followed by a line of dashes to space it out. When it's finished all 12 lines, it prints "Hope you found that useful!" just once because that command isn't indented with the others in the loop.

Pulling it all together, the final program looks like this:

```
# simple times table program

print "This program calculates times tables"
print "It is from Raspberry Pi For Dummies"

tablenum = input("\nWhich multiplication table shall I ↵
    generate for you? ")

print "\nHere is your", tablenum, "times table:\n"

for i in range(1, 13):
    print i, "times", tablenum, "is", i*tablenum
    print "------------------"

print "\nHope you found that useful!"
```

Although indentations at the start of lines have special meaning, you can use blank lines to help lay out your program however you want. We've used some blank lines here to make it easier to see which bits of program go together. We've also added in some extra \n escape codes in the print and input commands to put blank lines into the screen output.

Many people find they learn best from actually typing in programs, but you can download this program from the book's website if you can't get it working, or want to save time.

Figure 11-4 shows what the screen looks like when the program runs. If you want to experiment with the program, there are a few things you can try. How about making it go up to 20, or making it show only the odd lines in the times table (1, 3, 5)? You can make both those changes by playing with the `range()` function used in the loop. You can customize the screen output too, to provide more in-depth instructions, or to strip them out entirely. Perhaps you can use keyboard characters such as dashes and bars to put your multiplication table into a box.

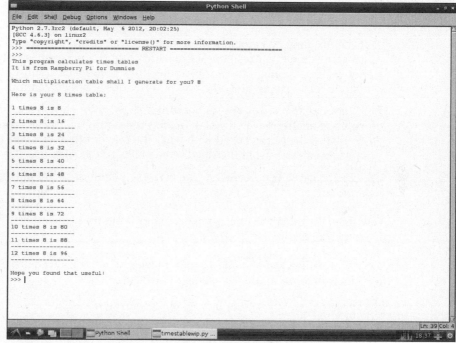

```
                                    Python Shell                                    _ ō x
File Edit Shell Debug Options Windows Help
Python 2.7.3rc2 (default, May  6 2012, 20:02:25)
[GCC 4.6.3] on linux2
Type "copyright", "credits" or "license()" for more information.
>>> =============================== RESTART ===============================
>>>
This program calculates times tables
It is from Raspberry Pi for Dummies

Which multiplication table shall I generate for you? 8

Here is your 8 times table:

1 times 8 is 8
--------------------
2 times 8 is 16
--------------------
3 times 8 is 24
--------------------
4 times 8 is 32
--------------------
5 times 8 is 40
--------------------
6 times 8 is 48
--------------------
7 times 8 is 56
--------------------
8 times 8 is 64
--------------------
9 times 8 is 72
--------------------
10 times 8 is 80
--------------------
11 times 8 is 88
--------------------
12 times 8 is 96
--------------------

Hope you found that useful!
>>> |
                                                                        Ln: 39 Col: 4
 Python Shell        timestablewip.py ...                                18:57
```

Figure 11-4:
The finished multiplica-tion table. Now, what was 7 times 8 again?

Creating the Chatbot Program

Do you ever find yourself talking to your computer? Wouldn't it be great if it could chat back? The next program enables you to have a conversation with your computer onscreen. Using a few tricks, we'll make the program appear to be intelligent, and able to learn from what you type in. It's not actual artificial intelligence, of course: That discipline of computer science is highly evolved, and this is a simple demo program. Chatbot can throw up some surprises, however, and you can expand its vocabulary to make it smarter. For a sneak preview of what it can do, see Figure 11-5 at the end of the chapter.

As you build this program, you'll deepen your understanding of Python. In particular, you'll learn about conditional statements, lists, dictionaries, and random choices.

The program works like this:

1. It introduces itself and then invites the player to respond.

2. The player types something in.

3. If the player types in **bye**, the computer replies with a message to say thanks for chatting, and then finishes the program.

4. The program has stock responses for certain words, so it checks whether it recognizes any of the words that the player has entered. If it does, it uses one of the appropriate stock responses. If more than one stock response applies, the computer chooses one at random.

5. If none of the words are recognized, the program chooses a random phrase and replies with that. To stop the random phrases repeating, it replaces the phrase used with what the player typed in. Over time, the program learns from the player and starts to talk like her.

6. The program keeps on chatting with the player until the player types in **bye**.

Now that you know the final goal, take your first steps toward it by setting up the random responses.

You can download the finished program from this book's website. See the Introduction for more on accessing the website.

Introducing lists

There are several different ways you can organize information in Python, and one of the most fundamental is called a *list*. You came across a list already when we used the range() function to create a list of numbers for our for loop. You can also create your own lists.

The following code shows you how to create a list that has the name shoppinglist. You can enter this in the shell, or create a program so you can more easily edit and refine it. If you create a program, make sure you run it, so that the shopping list is set up.

```
shoppinglist = ["eggs",
                "bacon",
                "tomatoes",
                "bread",
                "tin of beans",
                "milk"]
```

It's similar to the way you create a variable. After the list name comes an equals sign, and then we have square brackets that contain the list. Each item in the list is separated by a comma. Because each item is a piece of text (known as a *string* in programming circles), we put quotes around it, so Python knows where it starts and ends.

Python doesn't mind whether you use double quotes or single quotes around the strings in your list, but we recommend you use double quotes. That's because strings often include apostrophes. If you're using a single quote mark (the same symbol as an apostrophe) to close the string, Python thinks it's reached the end of the string when it hits the apostrophe. If you do need to use an apostrophe inside a string that's marked at each end with a single quote, put a \ (slash) before the apostrophe (for example, `'Mum\'s custard'`). It's easier to just use double quotes for your strings.

You can put all your list items on one line, but it's easier to read if you put each item on a new line. Using IDLE, if you press Return at the end of a list item, it starts the next line indented to the same depth as the item above, so your list looks neat, as in the previous example. When you're using IDLE, your program is color-coded too, so the black commas stand out against the green list items.

When you're entering lists, pay particular attention to the commas. There should be one after every list item, except for the last one. This is another reason it's a good idea to put list items on separate lines: It makes it easier to see at a glance if a comma is missing.

You can print a list to screen in the same way you print a variable to the screen. Try this in the shell:

```
>>> print shoppinglist
['eggs', 'bacon', 'tomatoes', 'bread', 'tin of beans', ↵
        'milk']
```

Python uses single quotes around the strings in your list, irrespective of what kind of quotes you used to set it up. To find out how many items are in a list, use the `len()` function, like this:

```
>>> print len(shoppinglist)
6
```

What if you've forgotten something? You can easily add items to the end of the list using the `append()` function. Here's an example:

```
>>> print shoppinglist
['eggs', 'bacon', 'tomatoes', 'bread', 'tin of beans', ↵
        'milk']
>>> shoppinglist.append("fish")
>>> print shoppinglist
['eggs', 'bacon', 'tomatoes', 'bread', 'tin of beans', ↵
        'milk', 'fish']
```

Each item in the list has a number, starting at zero, which means the second item is number 1 and the third item is number 2 and so on. You can refer to a particular item by putting the item number (known as the item's index) in square brackets:

```
>>> print shoppinglist[3]
bread
```

That gives us the fourth item in the list, remember, because the first item has the index 0. You can also change items in the list by using their index number. For example, if we wanted to change the fourth item from bread to a baguette, we would use

```
>>> shoppinglist[3] = "baguette"
```

For Chatbot, that's everything you need to know about lists, but they're an incredibly flexible way of organizing information and there's much more you can do with them. Table 11-2 provides a cheat sheet for some of the other functions, if you want to experiment.

Table 11-2	Additional List Operations	
Action	**Code to Use**	**Notes**
Sorting a list	`shoppinglist.sort()`	Sorts alphabetically, or from low to high in number lists.
Sorting a list in reverse order	`shoppinglist.sort ↩ (reverse=True)`	Sorts in reverse alpha- betical order, or from high to low in number lists.
Deleting a list item	`del shoppinglist[2]`	Deletes the list item with the index number specified. List items after it move up the list, so no gap is left.
Removing an item from the list	`if "eggs" in ↩ shoppinglist:` `shoppinglist.↩ remove("eggs")`	Deletes the list item that matches the item given. Results in an error if the item isn't in the list, so use the `if` command to avoid this.

For other projects you work on, it's worth knowing that lists can include num- bers as well as strings, and can even include a combination. For example, here's a list of answers to quiz questions:

```
Myquizanswers = ["Isambard Kingdom Brunel", ↩
                 1945, 2012, "Suffragettes", ↩
                 7500, "Danny Boyle"]
```

A list can have any items in any order. Python doesn't understand what the list contents mean or how they're organized. To make sense of it, you need to write a program that interprets the list.

Using lists to make a random chat program

After you've mastered the list structure, you can create a simple chat program. For this first version, you take some input from the player, display a random response, and then replace that random response with whatever the player types in.

Here's the program that does that. It introduces a few new ideas, but we talk you through them all shortly:

```
# Chatbot - random-only version
# Example program from Raspberry Pi For Dummies

import random

randomreplies = ["Oh really?",
        "Are you sure about that?",
        "Hmmmmm.",
        "Interesting...",
        "I'm not sure I agree with that...",
        "Definitely!",
        "Maybe!",
        "So what are you saying, exactly?",
        "Meaning what?",
        "You're probably right.",
        "Rubbish! Absolute nonsense!",
        "Anyway, what are your plans for tomorrow?",
        "I was just thinking exactly the same.",
        "That seems to be a popular viewpoint.",
        "A lot of people have been telling me that.",
        "Wonderful!",
        "That could be a bit embarrassing!",
        "Do you really think so?",
        "Indeed...",
        "My point exactly!",
        "Perhaps..."]

print "What's on your mind?"
playersays = raw_input("Talk to me: ")
replychosen = random.randint(1, len(randomreplies)) - 1
print randomreplies[replychosen]
randomreplies[replychosen] = playersays
```

The first two lines are comments, a quick reminder of what the program does.

Python has been designed to be easily extended, and so the next line, `import random`, tells Python you want to use the extension for generating random numbers. Extensions like this one are called *modules*, and you use several different modules as you play with the projects in this book. The modules provide pre-written functions you can reuse in your programs, so they simplify and accelerate your own programming. The random module includes functions for generating random numbers, and will be essential when you want to pick a random response for the computer to display.

The next part of the program creates a list called `randomreplies`, which contains statements the computer can say in response to whatever the player enters. You can personalize this by changing the responses, or adding more in. The more there are, the more effective the illusion of intelligence is, but for this demo, we've kept the list fairly short. It doesn't matter what order the responses are in, but keep an eye on those commas at the end of each line.

After printing a short line that invites the player to share what's on their mind with the computer, we request input from them. Instead of using the `input()` function, we use a function called `raw_input()`. That's because we are asking the player to enter a string and not a number this time. In Python 2.7, you have to use `raw_input()` for strings. Whatever the player enters is stored in a variable called `playersays`.

The next line picks an index number for the random response. In order to understand how this works, it helps to break it down. First, you need to know how to generate random numbers. You give the `random.randint()` function two integer numbers to work with (or *arguments*). The two numbers specify how big you want your random number to be, with the first figure being the lowest possible value and the second figure being the highest possible number. For example, if you wanted to display a random number between 1 and 10, you would use

```
print random.randint(1, 10)
```

You can try this multiple times to check whether it works. Sometimes the numbers repeat, but that's the nature of random numbers. It's like rolling the dice in Monopoly. Sometimes you're stuck in jail, but sometimes you throw doubles.

The range of numbers we want to use for our random number is the size of our `randomreplies` list. As you know, we can use the `len()` function to check what this is, so you can add things to your list or remove them without having to worry about updating this part of your program. In our random statement, we replace the second number with the length of the list:

```
print random.randint(1, len(randomreplies))
```

We don't want to just print the result onscreen, however, so we store the number chosen in a variable called `replychosen`. There's one final twist: Because list indexes start counting at 0, we need to subtract one from the random number. Otherwise, the program would never choose our first list item, and would try to choose one at the end of the list that isn't there. Here's the final command we use:

```
replychosen = random.randint(1, len(randomreplies)) - 1
```

The final two lines print the randomly selected list item, and then replace that list item with whatever the player entered:

```
print randomreplies[replychosen]
randomreplies[replychosen] = playersays
```

You can run the program to test it, but there's one thing missing. At the moment, it just gives you one turn before finishing. To fix that, you need to learn about the `while` loop.

Adding a while loop

Previously, we used the `for` loop to repeat a piece of code a set number of times. For this program, we want to keep the conversation going until the player types in **bye**, so we need to use something called a `while` loop.

The section we want to repeat begins with the line that requests the player's input, and finishes where the program currently ends, with the player's entry going into the list of random replies.

To repeat this section, we add two lines at the top of the section, and then indent it, so that Python knows which commands to repeat:

```
playersays = ""
while playersays != "bye":
    playersays = raw_input("Talk to me: ")
    replychosen = random.randint(1, len(randomreplies)) - 1
    print randomreplies[replychosen]
    randomreplies[replychosen] = playersays
```

IDLE makes it easy to indent an existing chunk of your program: Click and drag the mouse to highlight it, and then click to open the Format menu at the top of the script mode window and click Indent Region. You can use the Dedent Region option to take indentation out of a highlighted section.

The while command tells Python to repeat the indented block below as long as the second half of the while command is true. The != operator means *not equal to*. In our program, the second half of the while command is playersays != "bye", which means the block below should keep repeating as long as the contents of the variable playersays are not equal to bye.

In order to use the playersays variable in the while command, you have to set it up first because it triggers an error if you try to use a variable that doesn't exist yet in a while command. Immediately before the while command, you create the variable and give it a blank value, just to get the program past the while command and into the loop. Almost immediately it changes when the player types something in, but that doesn't matter.

If you run the program now, you should find the conversation rambles on until you type in **bye**. Remember you can improve the quality of the experience by adding more random sayings in the program's random replies list.

Using a loop to force a reply from the player

Another trick we can perform with the while loop is to make sure that the player doesn't just press Enter without typing anything in, either accidentally or deliberately. That protects the extremely high quality of our random replies list (ahem!) by preventing empty entries from going into it. In more complex programs, a quality control check like this can be essential for preventing errors.

You can put loops inside loops, which is called *nesting* them. In this case, we'll have a small loop that keeps asking for input until it gets it, running inside the bigger loop that repeats the whole process of the conversation until the player enters **bye**.

To check whether something is equal to something else, we use two equal signs (=) together. This can be confusing to new programmers, but a single equal sign is only used to assign a value to something, such as when you're putting a value into a variable. When you want to compare the value of two things to see if they're the same, you use two equal signs together. In English, we use the same word, but they're completely different ideas when you think about it, and Python certainly considers them as being separate and unique concepts.

The code below puts a while loop around the input, so that it repeats as long as the playersays variable is empty. If the player doesn't type anything in and just presses Enter, he is prompted to enter something again. And again, and again if necessary.

```
playersays = ""
while playersays != "bye":

    playersays = ""
    while playersays == "":
        playersays = raw_input("Talk to me: ")
    replychosen = random.randint(1, len(randomreplies)) - 1
    print randomreplies[replychosen]
    randomreplies[replychosen] = playersays
```

Notice how we indented the input command, so that Python knows what should be repeated while the playersays string is empty.

You might read this and wonder why we've set up playersays as an empty variable twice. The first time is necessary because the while command can't reference a variable that doesn't exist yet. The second time is a special case: If we don't reset the value to nothing, the second time around the loop, playersays still contains what the player typed in the first time. The way a while loop works means that the block underneath, the input() function, isn't run because playersays already has something in it. That code only runs if playersays is empty. This is a nice example of a logic error. The program works in that Python doesn't complain or crash. The program chatters away to itself, however, not letting you get a word in, so it doesn't work as intended.

Using dictionaries

Besides lists, there is another data structure that we're going to use in our program, called a *dictionary*. To access an item in a list, you use an *index number*, which represents its position in the list. Dictionaries are different because to access an item, you use its key, which is a string or a number that uniquely identifies it. The idea is used a lot in computing. Your bank account number, for example, belongs to you and only you, so it's a unique key for your data. Unlike with a list, you don't need to know where that item is in the dictionary to be able to use it — you just need to know the key that identifies it.

Dictionaries use curly braces, and contain pairs of items, which are the keys and the values for those keys. If that sounds confusing, here's an example that won't seem too different from the paper dictionary on your bookshelf:

```
chatdictry = {"happy": "I'm happy today too!",
              "sad": "Cheer up, mate!",
              "raspberry": "Oh yum! I love raspberries!",
```

```
            "computer": "Computers will take over the ↵
                world! You're already talking to one", ↵
            "music": "Have you heard the new Lana Del Rey ↵
                album?",
            "art": "But what is art really, anyway?",
            "joke": "I only know this joke: How do you ↵
                kill a circus? Go for the juggler.",
            "python": "I hate snakes!",
            "stupid": "Who are you calling stupid, jelly ↵
                brain?",
            "weather": "I wonder if the sun will shine on ↵
                Saturday?",
            "you": "Leave me out of this!",
            "certain": "How can you be so confident?",
            "talk": "You're all talk! Do something!",
            "think": "You can overthink these things, ↵
                though.",
            "hello": "Why, hello to you too, buddy!",
            "wearing": "I don't wear clothes. I don't even ↵
                come with a case."}
```

In this example, we've given the dictionary the name *chatdictry*, but you can call it anything. You can have more than one dictionary in your program too, if you give them different names.

In this dictionary, we look up a word to see what the reply to it should be. For example, if someone uses the word *happy*, the computer should reply "I'm happy too." If we look up the word *hello*, we can see the computer's response should be "Why, hello to you too, buddy!" Each dictionary entry is made up of the key and its value, separated by a colon, for example, the key `happy` and its value, which is the computer's response to that word. The entries are separated from each other with a comma.

The punctuation here is quite fiddly, so take care. The strings have quotes around them, but the colon between the keys and their values must be outside the quotes. Each pair needs to end with a comma except the last one, and we're using curly braces (usually found on the same key as the square brackets).

Dictionaries only work if every key is unique. You can't have two entries in there for the word *happy,* for example; otherwise, Python wouldn't know which one to choose.

Dictionaries only work one way around: You can't use the value to look up the key. One way to remember this is to think of a real paper dictionary. It would be almost impossible to trace a particular definition back to a word because you wouldn't know what page you could find the definition on. Finding definitions from the words is simple, though.

Here's how you print a value from the dictionary:

```
>>> print chatdictry["hello"]
Why, hello to you too, buddy!
>>> print chatdictry["weather"]
I wonder if the sun will shine on Saturday?
```

If you try to use a key that doesn't exist in the dictionary, you trigger an error. Later in this chapter (see "Creating the dictionary look-up function"), we show you how to test whether a key is in the dictionary.

In the real program, we've extended the vocabulary to cover some other words too, and this is where you can stamp your identity on the program most clearly. The words you put into the vocabulary, and the responses you give to go with them, are what really gives the chat character its intelligence and personality, so after you've got the demo working, it's worth spending time refining the language here. When you try playing with the finished program, take a note of the kinds of words you type in, and the kinds of things you want to chat about, and use that understanding to shape your Chatbot's vocabulary.

You can use the responses you give here to steer the conversation. We've included a joke for when players ask the computer to tell them one (as they inevitably do). Our full definition list also recognizes the word *funny* because that is reasonably likely to come up in the player's response to the joke. (Possibly in the context of "not very," but heigh-ho!)

Creating your own functions

One of the things you can do in Python, and many other programming languages, is parcel up a set of instructions into a function. A *function* can receive some information from the rest of the program (one or more *arguments*), work on it, and then send back a result. In our Chatbot program, we'll use a function to look up whether any words entered are in the dictionary of known words and responses.

Before we can use a function, we have to define it, which we do using a def statement. To tell Python which instructions belong in the function, we indent them underneath the def statement. Here's an example program to familiarize you with the idea of functions, and how we'll be using it:

```
# Example of functions

def dictionarycheck(message):
    print "I will look in the dictionary for", message
    return "hello"
```

```
dictionarycheck("test message")

result = dictionarycheck("test message2")
print "Reply is:", result
```

We talk you through that program in a moment, but here's a glimpse of what is shown onscreen when you run it:

```
I will look in the dictionary for test message
I will look in the dictionary for test message2
Reply is: hello
```

This is a short but powerful program because it tells you nearly everything you need to know about functions. As you can see, we defined our function at the start of the program, with this line:

```
def dictionarycheck(message):
```

This sets up a function with the name `dictionarycheck()`, but also sets it up to receive a piece of information from the rest of the program and to put it into the variable we've called `message`. The next line prints out a statement saying "I will look in the dictionary for" followed by the contents of the variable `message`. That means it prints out whatever information is sent to the function. The next line starting with `return` exits the function and sends a message back, which in our example is `hello`.

Functions are self-contained units so the variable `message` can't be used by the rest of the program (it's what's known as a *local variable*). When you're writing your own functions, you should give them a job to do, and then use `return` to send the result back to the rest of the program.

Functions aren't run until you specifically tell the program to run them, so when Python sees the function definition, it just remembers it for when it needs it later. That time comes shortly afterward, when we issue the command:

```
dictionarycheck("test message")
```

This runs our `dictionarycheck()` function, and sends it the text "`test message`" to work with. When the function starts, Python puts "`test message`" into the function's variable called `message`, and then prints the text onscreen that contains it. The text "`hello`" is sent back by the function, but we don't have a way to pick up that message.

The next code snippet shows you how you can pick up information coming back from a function. Instead of just running the function, you set a variable to be equal to its output, like this:

```
result = dictionarycheck("test message2")
print "Reply is:", result
```

When the text "hello" is sent back by the function, it goes into the variable result, and the main program can then print it on the screen.

This simple example illustrates a few reasons why functions are a brilliant idea, and have become fundamental building blocks in many programming languages:

- Functions enable you to reuse parts of your program. For example, we've used our function to display two different messages here, just by sending the function a different argument each time. When you use more sophisticated programs, being able to reuse parts of your program makes your program shorter, simpler, and faster to write.

- Functions make understanding the program easier because they give a name and a structure to a set of instructions. Whenever someone sees `dictionarycheck()` in our program, she can make a good guess at what's going on. So far, our programs haven't been particularly complex, but as you work on bigger projects, you'll find readability becomes increasingly important.

- It makes it easier to maintain and update your program. You can easily find which bits of the program to change, and all the changes you need to make will be in the same part of the program. If we think of a better way to do a dictionary look-up later, we can just modify the function, without disturbing the rest of the program.

- Functions make prototyping easier. That's what we've done here: We've built an experimental program that takes some text and sends back a message. That's what our finished `dictionarycheck()` function will do, except that this one just sends the same message back every time and the finished one will send different messages back depending on what the player said. We could build the rest of the program around this prototype to check it works, and then go back and finish the `dictionarycheck()` function.

Creating the dictionary look-up function

Now that we know how to create a function, we're going to build a function that takes the player's text and checks for any relevant responses. To do this, we'll use what we've learned so far about dictionaries and functions, and we'll add in some new ideas relating to loops, strings, and decision-making.

The function is only 12 lines long, but it's quite sophisticated. It needs to take what the player entered, and check each word in it to see whether the dictionary has a response for that word. The player might use more than one word that's in the dictionary. For example, if the player says "I love pop music," the words *love* and *music* might both be in the dictionary. We'll deal with that eventuality by showing one of the possible responses, chosen at random. Alternatively, the player might use no words the program recognizes, so we need to design our function to cope with that situation too.

Before we start to break it down, here's the function in its entirety, so you can see how all the bits fit together:

```
def dictionarycheck(message):
    message = message.lower()
    playerwords = message.split()
    smartreplies = []
    for eachword in playerwords:
        if eachword in chatdictry:
            answer = chatdictry[eachword]
            smartreplies.append(answer)
    if smartreplies:
        replychosen = random.randint ↵
                      (1, len(smartreplies)) - 1
        return smartreplies[replychosen]
    else:
        return ""
```

The function definition is the same as we used in our example function previously. When we use it, we send it what the player has typed in, so this goes into the variable called message.

The next two lines introduce something new: *string methods*. These are like built-in functions that are attached to a string and transform it in some way. The lower() method converts a string into lowercase. This is important because if a player uses capital letters or mixed case, they won't match the lowercase words we've used in our dictionary keys. As far as Python is concerned, hello and Hello aren't the same thing. The split() method takes a string and splits it into a list of its constituent words. The first two lines in our function, then, turn the contents of the message variable into a lowercase version of itself, and then create a new list of the words the player entered, called playerwords.

We're going to store possible replies to the player in a list called smartreplies, so we create that as an empty list.

The next step is to set up a loop that goes through the list of words that the player entered in turn. When we used a for loop previously, we worked our way through a sequence of numbers. This time, we're going to work our way through a list of words. Each time around the loop, the variable eachword contains the next item from the list of words the player entered.

The next line introduces a new idea, the *conditional statement*, which starts with if. A conditional statement is used to enable the computer to make a decision about whether it should carry out certain instructions, and you'll come across it in almost every program you write. Here, it's being used to avoid the program stopping and reporting an error if we try to use a key that isn't in the dictionary:

```
if eachword in chatdictry:
    answer = chatdictry[eachword]
    smartreplies.append(answer)
```

The `eachword` variable contains one of the words the player entered, so the `if` statement checks whether that word is in the dictionary and only carries out the next two instructions if they are. Notice how indenting is used here to show which commands belong together — in this case, which commands are controlled by the `if` statement. If the word is in the dictionary, the program looks it up and adds the resulting response to the `smartreplies` list, using `append()`.

This process is repeated for every word the player entered, but that's all that happens in the loop. The next line is not indented below the `for` statement, so it's not controlled by it.

When we come out of the loop, we check whether the list `smartreplies` has anything in it, by using simply

```
if smartreplies:
```

In English, this means "if `smartreplies` has content in it." The commands indented underneath are carried out only if some entries were added to the `smartreplies` list, which only happens if one or more of the words the player entered were found in our dictionary. In that event, we want to return one of the items in the `smartreplies` list to the main program, so we pick one at random from the list and use `return` to send it back to the main program and exit the function.

After that, we use the `else` command. In plain English, this means *otherwise*, and it's joined to the `if` command. So if `smartreplies` has content in it, the commands are carried out to send back an appropriate reply, chosen at random. If none of the player's words were found in the dictionary and so `smartreplies` is empty, the instructions indented underneath the `else` command are carried out instead. The function sends an empty message (`" "`) back to the main program and exits the function.

Creating the main conversation loop

We previously created a version of Chatbot that could only provide random responses. Now we need to change the main conversation loop so it checks for words in the dictionary and shows an intelligent response if they're found, and if not, shows a random response and replaces it with what the player entered. This final version brings together all the ideas we've explored as we've built this program.

After the command that accepts the player's input, we put the following:

```
smartresponse = dictionarycheck(playersays)
if smartresponse:
    print smartresponse
else:
    replychosen = random.randint ↵
                  (1,len(randomreplies)) - 1
    print randomreplies[replychosen]
    randomreplies[replychosen] = playersays
```

This starts by using the `dictionarycheck()` function (or *calling* it, to use the jargon), sending it whatever the player typed in, and putting the response from the function into the variable `smartresponse`.

The next line checks whether `smartresponse` has any content in it (or is not empty), and if so, it prints it onscreen. After that, we use the `else` command. If `smartresponse` has content in it (or is not empty), it is printed onscreen. Otherwise, the instructions under the `else` command are used to show a random response from our list of random replies, and to replace it with what the player entered.

Final thoughts on Chatbot

That completes the Chatbot program. Along the way, you've learned how to use variables, lists, loops, random choices, dictionaries, conditional statements (`if` and `else`), and functions. You've learned how to take input from the user and print responses onscreen, and you've created the skeleton of a chat program you can flesh out with your own personality.

Figure 11-5 shows a sample run of the program. There are a few bits where the computer clearly hasn't understood, but this can be improved by extending the vocabulary. As you expand the vocabulary in the dictionary and include more random replies in the list, you'll find the program can often surprise you with its apparent intelligence. You're never alone with a Raspberry Pi!

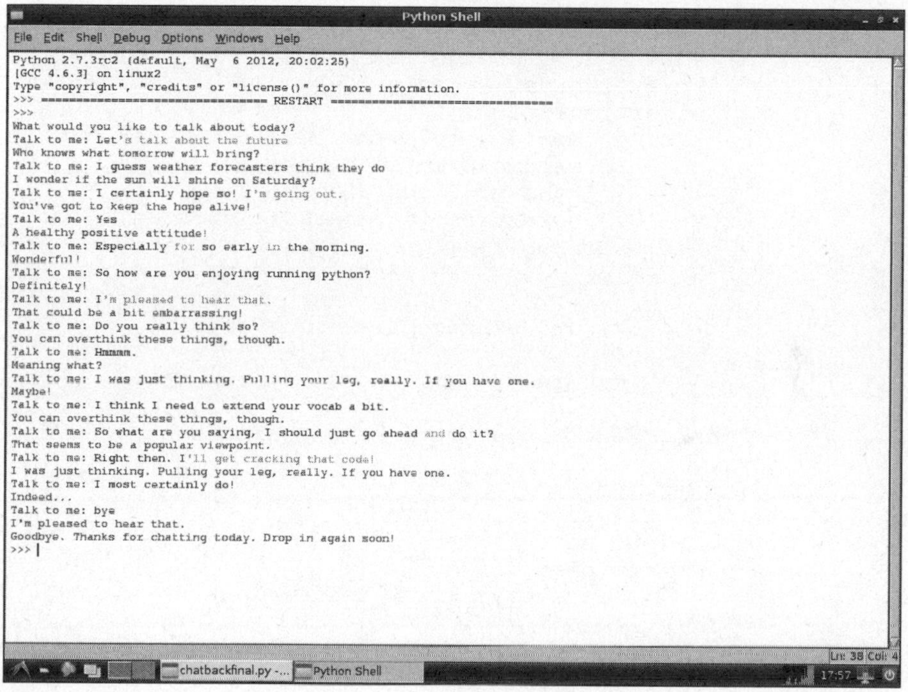

Figure 11-5:
Having a conversation with Chatbot.

The final Chatbot program

For your reference, here's a final listing of the Chatbot program, ready for you to customize with your own responses.

```
# Chatbot
# Example program from Raspberry Pi For Dummies
import random

# Following list is heavily abbreviated
# to save space in the book. Should be 20+ entries.
randomreplies = ["Oh really?",
                 "Are you sure about that?",
                 "Perhaps..."]

# Following dictionary is also heavily abbreviated
chatdictry = {"happy": "I'm happy today too!",
              "sad": "Cheer up, mate!",
              "computer": "Computers will take over the ↵
              world! You're already talking to one"}
```

```
def dictionarycheck(message):
    message = message.lower()
    playerwords = message.split()
    smartreplies = []
    for eachword in playerwords:
        if eachword in chatdictry:
            answer = chatdictry[eachword]
            smartreplies.append(answer)
    if smartreplies:
        replychosen = random.randint ↵
                      (1, len(smartreplies)) - 1
        return smartreplies[replychosen]
    else:
        return ""

print "What would you like to talk about today?"

playersays = ""
while playersays != "bye":
    playersays = ""
    while playersays == "":
        playersays = raw_input("Talk to me: ")

    smartresponse = dictionarycheck(playersays)
    if smartresponse:
        print smartresponse
    else:
        replychosen = random.randint ↵
                      (1, len(randomreplies)) - 1
        print randomreplies[replychosen]
        randomreplies[replychosen] = playersays
print "Goodbye. Thanks for chatting today. Drop in again ↵
                    soon!"
```

Chapter 12

Creating a Game with Python and Pygame

In this chapter, you build on your Python skills to create a simple arcade game called PiBuster (see Figure 12-1). It's a variation on the classic format where you have to keep a ball in play using your bat, and your goal is to knock out all the blocks.

Our version has a fruity twist: The wall of bricks is replaced with a giant Raspberry for you to chip away at. The program is written in such a way that you can easily design your own levels. We talk you through how the game works and show you how to build it up step by step.

To help you to create games like this, we introduce you to Pygame, a free library of Python modules that makes it easier to create graphics and other game features. You learn how to draw colorful text, circles, and rectangles with it.

In this chapter, you also learn how to store a simple two-dimensional map of the screen using a list, and how to enable an onscreen character to be moved using the cursor keys.

This program is too long to print here in full, so we talk you through it chunk by chunk. You can download it from the book's website if you have any difficulties putting it together. For more on accessing the book's website, see the Introduction.

Figure 12-1:
The
PiBuster
game at the
start.

Installing and Updating Pygame

Pygame should be installed in your Linux distribution already, but if it isn't, or if you want to make sure you're using the latest version, enter the following command at the shell (see Chapter 5):

```
sudo apt-get install python-pygame
```

Importing Pygame

Before you can use Pygame, you need to import it, in the same way you imported the random module in Chapter 11. We'll also be using the sys, time, and random modules for this game, so we need to import them too.

One of the modules in Pygame is called *locals*, and we'll use its rect function for drawing rectangles, as well as some of its other features. So we don't have to tell Python each time that the functionality we need is inside the locals module. We can import it in the second line of our program. It'll save us time typing and make the program easier to read.

Here are the first two lines of our program:

```
# PiBuster from Raspberry Pi For Dummies
import pygame, sys, time, random
from pygame.locals import *
```

Setting Up the Game Window

Before you can use Pygame in a program, you need to set it up, or *initialize* it, by calling the pygame.init() function:

```
pygame.init()
```

After you've done that, you can use Pygame to open a new window. Here are the instructions to open a window with a width of 440 pixels and a height of 480 pixels, and with *PiBuster* in the window's title bar:

```
gameSurface = pygame.display.set_mode((440, 480))
pygame.display.set_caption("PiBuster")
pygame.mouse.set_visible(0)
```

 Take care with the number of parentheses in the first line: You need two opening and closing parentheses around the window width and height. That's because they are a *tuple* — a type of list that you can't change the values in — and they're inside the parentheses for a function. Tuples always use parentheses and you'll come across them lots in this chapter. As long as you get the parentheses in the right place, they won't cause you any trouble!

 Because you can't change the items in a tuple, it's much less flexible than a list. At times it's the ideal solution, however. You might want to ensure data can't be changed, and a tuple not only enforces permanence but also helps to communicate it when someone looks at your program code. To use a tuple instead of a list, you use parentheses instead of square brackets for it.

The preceding code also gives our canvas the name gameSurface. In Pygame jargon, a *surface object* is used to represent an image. We use the surface object called gameSurface to represent the whole screen.

You can run this program in order to test that it creates an empty black window. We haven't told the program how to check whether you have clicked the Close button, so the window can't be closed, but we come to that later. If you run the program again, the previous window closes before the new one opens.

Using Colors in Pygame

In Pygame, colors are expressed according to how much red, green, and blue they have in them, hence the term *RGB color code*. You provide three values in parentheses, one for each color (red, green, and blue), ranging from 0 for none at all, up to 255 for the maximum. Pure red would be (255, 0, 0), which is the maximum amount of red and no green or blue. Black is (0, 0, 0), a complete absence of color.

Using these numbers can get quite clumsy, and it makes the program hard to understand, so instead, it's a good idea to create variables to store the color numbers. Variables that don't change their values while the program is running are known as *constants*, and it's a good idea to write them with capital letters so you can immediately see they're constants, wherever they are in the program. Here are our color constants:

```
SHADOW = (192, 192, 192)
WHITE = (255, 255, 255)
LIGHTGREEN = (0, 255, 0)
GREEN = (0, 200, 0)
BLUE = (0, 0, 128)
LIGHTBLUE = (0, 0, 255)
RED = (200, 0, 0)
LIGHTRED = (255, 100, 100)
PURPLE = (102, 0, 102)
LIGHTPURPLE = (153, 0, 153)
```

We've chosen these colors especially for PiBuster. The SHADOW color is a light gray, but we've given it a more meaningful name because it will be used to create the impression of shade.

Drawing with Pygame

Drawing on the screen has two stages. The first is that you draw onto the canvas (or surface object), and the second is that you update the screen with those changes. To make the window background white, use

```
gameSurface.fill(WHITE)
pygame.display.update()
```

You don't need to update the display for every drawing instruction. Your program runs more quickly (and often looks more professional) if you wait until you've finished all your drawing instructions and then update the screen just the once.

In our game, we're going to use two shapes. The first is a rectangle. To draw a rectangle, you need to specify the surface object you are drawing on, which will be our canvas gameSurface; the color; the X coordinate of the rectangle's top-left corner; the Y coordinate of the rectangle's top-left corner; and its width and height. The coordinates are measured from the top-left corner of the window, so X values get higher as you cross the screen from left to right, and Y values get higher as you go down the screen.

The command to draw a rectangle looks like this:

```
pygame.draw.rect(object, color, (x, y, width, height))
```

Imagine you wanted to draw a green rectangle that was 150 pixels wide by 75 pixels high, and you wanted to put it at the coordinate X=30, Y=90. Here's how you'd do that:

```
pygame.draw.rect(gameSurface, GREEN, (30, 90, 150, 75))
```

The frame around our game arena (see Figure 12-1) is made of three thin rectangles, two down each side, and one across the top. Here is the code to draw first the top one, and then the left side, and then the right side.

```
pygame.draw.rect(gameSurface, PURPLE, (16, 16, 406, 2))
pygame.draw.rect(gameSurface, PURPLE, (16, 16, 2, 440))
pygame.draw.rect(gameSurface, PURPLE, (422, 16, 2, 440))
```

We also use rectangles for the bricks in our game, as you see later (see "Drawing the Bricks"). The other shape we use in our game is, obviously, a circle for the ball. We need to tell Pygame to use our canvas gameSurface; which color we want; the X and Y coordinates of the center of the circle; and its radius.

The command to draw a circle looks like this:

```
pygame.draw.circle(object, color, (x, y), radius)
```

Here's how to draw a blue circle at X=100 and Y=170 with a radius of 40 pixels:

```
pygame.draw.circle(gameSurface, BLUE, (100, 170), 40)
```

We don't need the blue circle or the green rectangle for this game, so you can take them out again if you tried them out.

Creating the Game Map

In Chapter 11, you learn how to use lists to store lists of information. In this chapter, we're going to use a list to store a map that shows where the bricks are. This is quite a bit more complex. The lists we've used so far are just like a single column of information. Each list item was just a number or a piece of text. A map is two-dimensional, so we'll use a nested list, or a list in which each list item is also a list. To put it another way, we're going to make a list of rows, and each list item will itself be a list containing the information for each column in that row.

It's easier to understand if you look at an example, so this is how we create our map list:

```
map = [
#-----0 1 2 3 4 5 6 7 8 9 0 1 2 3 4 5 6 7 8 9--
      [0,0,0,0,1,1,0,0,0,0,0,0,0,0,1,1,0,0,0,0,0],
      [0,0,0,1,1,1,1,0,0,0,0,0,0,1,1,1,1,0,0,0,0],
      [0,0,0,0,1,1,1,1,0,0,0,0,1,1,1,1,0,0,0,0,0],
      [0,0,0,0,0,1,1,1,1,0,0,1,1,1,1,0,0,0,0,0,0],
      [0,0,0,0,0,0,1,1,0,0,0,0,0,1,1,0,0,0,0,0,0],

      [0,0,0,0,0,0,0,0,0,0,2,2,0,0,0,0,0,0,0,0,0],
      [0,0,0,0,0,0,2,2,2,2,2,2,2,2,0,0,0,0,0,0,0],
      [0,0,0,0,0,2,2,2,2,2,2,2,2,2,2,0,0,0,0,0,0],
      [0,0,0,0,0,2,2,2,2,2,2,2,2,2,2,0,0,0,0,0,0],
      [0,0,0,0,2,2,2,2,2,2,2,2,2,2,2,2,0,0,0,0,0],

      [0,0,0,0,2,2,2,2,2,2,2,2,2,2,2,2,0,0,0,0,0],
      [0,0,0,0,0,2,2,2,2,2,2,2,2,2,2,0,0,0,0,0,0],
      [0,0,0,0,0,2,2,2,2,2,2,2,2,2,2,0,0,0,0,0,0],
      [0,0,0,0,0,0,2,2,2,2,2,2,2,2,0,0,0,0,0,0,0],
      [0,0,0,0,0,0,0,0,0,2,2,0,0,0,0,0,0,0,0,0,0],

      [0,0,0,0,0,0,0,0,0,0,0,0,0,0,0,0,0,0,0,0,0],
      [0,0,0,0,0,0,0,0,0,0,0,0,0,0,0,0,0,0,0,0,0],
      [0,0,0,0,0,0,0,0,0,0,0,0,0,0,0,0,0,0,0,0,0],
      [0,0,0,0,0,0,0,0,0,0,0,0,0,0,0,0,0,0,0,0,0],
      [0,0,0,0,0,0,0,0,0,0,0,0,0,0,0,0,0,0,0,0,0],
      ]
```

The first line in the list is a comment to number the columns so you can more easily navigate the map. The map list starts and ends with a square bracket. Notice how each list item (or row) is surrounded by square brackets too because it's also a list.

If you squint, you might be able to make out the shape of a raspberry in there. A 1 represents a green brick (for the leaves at the top), and a 2 represents a red brick (for the juicy berry). A 0 represents no brick. To create your own level designs, just edit this list. We recommend keeping the bottom few rows almost empty; otherwise, the game gets too hard. The bottom line must always be empty because that's where the bat lives.

The size of the map is 20 rows of 20 columns. The index of each list starts at zero, so when we look up a location in the map, we have to subtract 1 from the X and Y coordinate we want. To find out what's in the second row and the fifth column (Y=2, X=5), use

```
print[1][4]
```

Note that we reference the Y coordinate first (the row number), and then the X coordinate (the column in that row).

Run the program to set up the map and use the shell to try printing different values from the map. It's a good way to familiarize yourself with how it works.

Drawing the Bricks

Now that we have a map, and we know how to make rectangles, we can draw the start screen showing the brickwork raspberry.

Our game map is 20 rows of 20 columns, and each position on the map can have a brick in it, have nothing in it, or have the ball or half of the bat in it (because the bat occupies two spaces).

To draw a brick onscreen, we need to take a brick's position on the map and use it to calculate the brick's position onscreen. Each position on the map is a square with sides of 20 pixels, so a brick's real coordinate on the screen (in pixels) is 20 times its coordinate in the game (measured in our map rows and columns). For example, the brick that's in the fifth row and the fourth column of our map is 100 pixels from the left of the window edge, and 80 pixels from the top. To calculate these pixel positions for Pygame, we're going to create two functions called `realx()` and `realy()`:

```
def realx(x):
    x = x * 20
    return x

def realy(y):
    y = y * 20
    return y
```

Remember that all your functions need to go at the start of your program, so Python knows about them before you try to use them.

The next step is to create a function to draw a brick. In the last chapter, you learned how to pass arguments to a function. In this chapter, we extend the idea and pass several values at once. Our function `drawbrick()` receives the X map coordinate, Y map coordinate, and the color value of the brick to be drawn (1 for green and 2 for red).

Each brick comprises five rectangles. As well as the square box, there are two thin lighter-colored rectangles across the top and down the left of the box, and there are two gray rectangles along the bottom and down the right edge. This makes the bricks look like they're 3D, or at least look a bit more interesting than a flat block of color. On red squares, the highlight color is a lighter red, and on green ones, it's a lighter green. The drawbrick() function first checks the color argument passed to it and then sets the variables boxcolor and highlightcolor to be the right red or green values.

The function can then draw the brick using those colors and use the realx() and realy() functions to work out where to place the box onscreen in pixel coordinates.

```
def drawbrick(xcoord, ycoord, col):

    if col == 1:
        boxcolor = GREEN
        highlightcolor = LIGHTGREEN
    else:
        boxcolor = RED
        highlightcolor = LIGHTRED
    pygame.draw.rect(gameSurface, boxcolor, ↵
            (realx(xcoord), realy(ycoord), 20, 20))
    pygame.draw.rect(gameSurface, highlightcolor, ↵
            (realx(xcoord), realy(ycoord), 2, 20))
    pygame.draw.rect(gameSurface, highlightcolor, ↵
            (realx(xcoord), realy(ycoord), 20, 2))
    pygame.draw.rect(gameSurface, SHADOW, ↵
            (realx(xcoord)+18, realy(ycoord), 2, 20))
    pygame.draw.rect(gameSurface, SHADOW, ↵
            (realx(xcoord), realy(ycoord)+18, 20, 2))
```

Now that we have those functions in place, we can use nested loops to go through the rows and columns, check whether there is a brick in the map at each point, and draw the brick if so. Each time we draw a brick, we add one to the variable brickcount, so it represents the total number of bricks onscreen. We use this later to check when the player's won.

This code goes into the body of your program, after all the functions:

```
brickcount = 0
for x in range(1, 21):
    for y in range(1, 20):
        if map[y-1][x-1] != 0:
            drawbrick(x, y, map[y-1][x-1])
            brickcount += 1
pygame.display.update()
```

Remember that the end point used by `range()` isn't in the list, so we have to go up to `21` in X, for example. We want to stop at row `19` in Y because the bat is in row `20`.

When you run the program, you should see the brick raspberry and frame onscreen.

Positioning the Bat

The game uses the variable `batx` to refer to the X coordinate of the bat in the game map. The player can't move the bat up and down, so we've used a constant called `BATY` to represent the bat's row. The variable `batx` is assigned a random value at the start, so the bat starts in a random position. When setting up the bat, we also set the player's score to zero:

```
#initialize bat and score
batx = random.randint(1, 19)
BATY = 20
drawbat(batx)
score = 0
```

The function `drawbat()` does exactly what it says on the function name. It takes the bat's X position as an argument and draws the bat there. Like the bricks, we've compiled the bat from several rectangles so it looks a bit more interesting. One thing to notice here is that the bat is 40 pixels wide, which means it's two bricks wide. Here's the routine to draw the bat, which goes at the start of your program with your other functions:

```
def drawbat(x):
    pygame.draw.rect(gameSurface, LIGHTPURPLE, (realx(x), ↵
        realy(BATY), 40, 4))
    pygame.draw.rect(gameSurface, PURPLE, (realx(x), ↵
        realy(BATY)+4, 40, 6))
    pygame.draw.rect(gameSurface, SHADOW, (realx(x), ↵
        realy(BATY)+10, 40, 2))
    pygame.draw.rect(gameSurface, SHADOW, (realx(x)+38, ↵
        realy(BATY), 2, 12))
```

Animation is just an illusion. To make the bat look as though it's moved, you delete it and then redraw it nearby. It happens so fast that our eyes think it's jumped, but from a programming point of view, it's important to know what's really going on. As well as drawing the bat, you need to be able to clear it again. We use two functions for that. The `blank()` function clears a point onscreen by drawing a white box on top of it. It's used to make bricks disappear and to make the ball move too. The `clearbat()` function removes the bat. Remember the bat occupies two squares on the map, so we have to use the `blank()` function twice.

```
def blank(x, y):
    pygame.draw.rect(gameSurface, WHITE, (realx(x), ↵
        realy(y), 20, 20))

def clearbat(x):
    blank(x, BATY)
    blank(x+1, BATY)
```

When you run the program now, it should draw the frame, the raspberry, and the bat. The bat is in a randomly chosen position each time.

If something's missing onscreen, don't forget you need to update the display after drawing on the canvas. Add this line at the end:

```
pygame.display.update()
```

Positioning the Ball

Now, please welcome, the star of our show: the ball! To keep track of it, we use four variables, as detailed in Table 12-1.

Table 12-1	Variables for the Ball
Variable	**Meaning**
ballx	X position (from 1 to 20)
bally	Y position (from 1 to 20)
ballxdir	Direction of travel horizontally. 1 for right or –1 for left.
ballydir	Direction of travel vertically. 1 for down or –1 for up.

The drawball() function accepts two arguments for the ball's position and draws the ball there. Because you draw a circle by giving Pygame its center instead of its top-left corner, we had to add 10 to the pixel coordinates given by realx() and realy(). To give the ball some depth, we've added a second circle to it in a color and position that looks like a reflected light. Actually, that might be overselling it, but it does make the ball look less flat.

```
def drawball(x, y):
    pygame.draw.circle(gameSurface, BLUE, ↵
        (realx(x)+10, realy(y)+10), 10, 0)
    pygame.draw.circle(gameSurface, LIGHTBLUE, ↵
        (realx(x)+6, realy(y)+6), 2, 0)
```

That function goes with the rest at the top of your program listing. Back in the main part of the program, when a game begins, we want to position the ball in a random location in the top seven rows of the screen where we know there isn't a brick. To do that, we use a `while` loop that keeps picking random coordinates until it finds an empty square. We also check for `ballx` being zero to get us over the `while` statement first time around and pick our first random numbers. Here are the commands to set up the ball:

```
#initialize ball
ballx = 0
bally = 0
while map[bally-1][ballx-1] != 0 or ballx == 0:
    ballx = random.randint(1, 20)
    bally = random.randint(1, 7)
ballxdir = 1
ballydir = -1
drawball(ballx, bally)
```

Run the program now, and you should have a frame, a giant raspberry, a bat, and a ball placed in an empty space near the top of the screen.

Displaying the End Game Messages

Whether the player wins or loses, we need to let him or her know with a message onscreen. The `showtext()` function takes a string as its argument and then uses Pygame to show it.

You don't necessarily need to know this, but this function draws (or *renders*) text onto a surface object using your choice of font and font size. It then creates a rectangle from that surface object, repositions it in the center of the screen, and copies (or *blits*) the text onto the rectangle.

You can reuse this function in your own programs. To adapt it, the things you need to know are that freesansbold.ttf is the name of the font, 64 is the font size in points, PURPLE is the text color, WHITE is the background color for the text, and the center of the text is at pixel position X=220 and Y=200.

The values we've used position the text across the middle of the giant raspberry. The text is huge. We have room for only about nine characters in the game window, but that's perfect for this game.

```
def showtext(text):
    fontObj = pygame.font.Font('freesansbold.ttf', 64)
    textsurface = fontObj.render(text, True, PURPLE, ↵
        WHITE)
    textRectObj = textsurface.get_rect()
    textRectObj.center = (220, 200)
    gameSurface.blit(textsurface, textRectObj)
    pygame.display.update()
```

Now that you know how to display text, you can create functions called `gameover()` for when the player loses and `gamewon()` for when the player wins. They look like this:

```
def gameover():
    showtext('GAME OVER')
    time.sleep(8)
    endgame()

def gamewon():
    showtext('GAME WON!')
    time.sleep(8)
    endgame()
```

The `time.sleep()` function pauses the computer for the specified number of seconds, so there's an eight-second pause to view the message before the `endgame()` function is called. This quits Pygame (freeing up any resources it was using) and closes the PiBuster window. Here's what it looks like:

```
def endgame():
    pygame.quit()
    sys.exit()
```

Checking for a Win

Before we create the main game loop, we need one final function. Each time the player knocks out a brick, the score variable is increased by 1. When the score variable is equal to the `brickcount` variable (which holds the number of bricks at the start of the game), the player has won. This short function checks and returns the value `True` if the player has won, and returns the value `False` if not. `True` and `False` don't have quotation marks (or speech marks) around them because they're not text strings. They're special values you can use in Python.

```
def havetheywon():
    if score == brickcount:
        return True
    else:
        return False
```

Setting Up the Timings

Before we go into our main game loop, we need to add some instructions for timing. We're going to use the clock in Pygame to control how fast our game runs. Using this, we can specify the maximum speed we want the game to run at, measured in frames per second. We store that value in a constant called FPS. For a reasonably challenging game of PiBuster, 20 is a good value. Higher values are faster and lower values are slower. During testing, we set it as low as 4 so we could closely watch how the ball was bouncing, and set it as high as 50 to speed up the computer playing itself when we were confirming that gamewon() worked.

By default, keys on the keyboard are set to not repeat, which means if you hold down a key, it only triggers one movement in the game. That's really annoying because you would have to hammer a key for each step you want to move the bat. We set the keys to repeat so that if you hold down the key, the bat glides for as long as you hold the key down. The two numbers in the pygame.key.set_repeat() command specify the delay before the key starts repeating, and then how often it repeats, so 1,1 is the fastest setting. (If you use 0,0, it turns off the repeat.)

Add these instructions at the end of your program so far:

```
FPS = 20
fpsClock = pygame.time.Clock()
pygame.key.set_repeat(1, 1)
```

Before we enter the game loop, we should make sure we have updated the screen with everything we've drawn on it, and give the player a short time to see where the bat and ball are before the game starts:

```
#update screen and short pause
pygame.display.update()
time.sleep(2.5)
```

Making the Bat Move

Now we have all our functions in place, our starting screen drawn, and all our variables set up. It's time to make the game loop, which repeats until the game is won, lost, or abandoned by the player closing the window.

Each run through the loop checks for key presses, moves the bat if required, moves the ball (including changing its direction if it should bounce), knocks out bricks if necessary, updates the screen, checks if the player has won, and then pauses briefly to match your desired game speed.

Here's the shell of the main loop, with all the bat controls included, but with a gap left for the ball movement instructions to be added later:

```
#main game loop
while True:
    for event in pygame.event.get():
        oldbat = batx
        if event.type == QUIT:
            endgame()
        if event.type == KEYDOWN:
            if event.key == K_RIGHT:
                batx = batx + 1
            elif event.key == K_LEFT:
                batx = batx - 1
        if batx == 0 or batx == 20:
            batx = oldbat
        clearbat(oldbat)
        drawbat(batx)

    # ball movement goes here

    pygame.display.update()
    if havetheywon() == True:
        gamewon()
    fpsClock.tick(FPS)
```

The instruction while True sets the loop up to run forever and is a construct that's often used for loops you want to repeat indefinitely. The first thing that happens inside the while loop is that there is a for loop that works through Pygame's list of *events*, which are things that happened like key presses or clicks on the window's Close button. Each time around the for loop, the program checks the next event in the list.

First, we store the position of the bat in a variable called oldbat. This will be important later.

Then we check whether the event type is QUIT, which means the player clicked the Close Window button. If it is, we end the game.

If the event type is a key press, we check whether it was the right-cursor key (K_RIGHT) and add 1 to batx if so. If not, we check whether it was the left-cursor key (K_LEFT), and subtract 1 from batx in that case.

We have to stop the player from moving the bat out of the play area, so we check whether batx is now 0 (too far left) or 20 (too far right, because the bat is two squares wide). If it is either of those, we reset batx to oldbat, its value at the start of this loop. That stops the bat from being able to go off the screen.

All we've done so far is change the bat's variables, so now we need to actually move it on the screen. To update the canvas, we simply call `clearbat()` with the old bat position, and then draw the bat in the `batx` position. Sometimes, these will be the same, but it doesn't matter. There won't be any flicker because nothing changes visibly until you update the display.

The `while` loop finishes by doing that update, checks whether the player has won, and then performs the timing synchronization.

Add that in to your program, and you can move the bat. We're ready to introduce the bouncing ball.

Making the Ball Move

The instructions that make the ball move also go inside the `while` loop, so they are all indented by four spaces, except where they need to be indented further. You need to insert them where indicated by a comment in the previous chunk of code.

We start by storing the current position of the ball in the variables `oldballx` and `oldbally`. Then we check for whether we need to bounce off the left, right, or top wall. If the ball's X position is 1, for example, it can't go any further left, so we change its horizontal direction to be to the right by giving `ballxdir` a value of 1. If the ball is in the top row, its Y direction is changed to downward.

```
oldballx = ballx
oldbally = bally
if ballx == 1:
    ballxdir = 1
if ballx == 20:
    ballxdir =- 1
if bally == 1:
    ballydir = 1
# uncomment below for cheat mode
# if bally == BATY - 1:
#     ballydir = -1
```

We've included a cheat mode in the preceding code, which stops the ball from falling out of the bottom of the game. It's useful for testing purposes. To use it, uncomment the two extra lines by removing the # (hash mark) at the start, and make sure they are still indented to line up with the statements above.

The next thing we need to do is check whether the ball has hit the bat, or fallen out of play. First we check whether the ball is on the row above the ball, which is BATY-1. If it is, we check whether it's hit the bat. There are two ways the ball can hit the bat, shown in Figure 12-2.

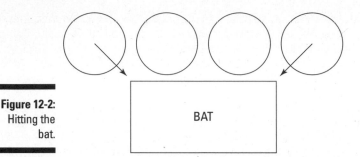

Figure 12-2:
Hitting the
bat.

The most obvious way that the ball can hit the bat is when the ball is directly above the bat, so it looks like it's sitting on top of it. Through experimentation, we've found that it also feels natural (and fair to the player) if you can hit the ball with the corner of the bat. That means the ball bounces off the bat if the ball is one square to the right of the bat and traveling to the left, or if the ball is one square to the left of the bat and traveling right.

If you remember, `ballxdir` stores the direction the ball is moving horizontally, and it does this by having a value of 1 or –1. If the ball is moving right, the value is 1; if it's moving left, it's –1. Each time around the loop, we just add the value of `ballxdir` to the ball's X position stored in `ballx`.

To check whether the ball is on a course to hit the corner of the bat, we check whether the ball's current position plus the value of `ballxdir` matches the position of the left or right half of the bat.

If the ball hits the bat in either of those ways, we change the ball's vertical direction to –1, so it will move back up the screen.

So far we've only tested whether values are the same or not. We can also check whether numbers are greater or smaller than each other. We use `>=` to check whether one value is greater than or equal to another value, and `<=` to check whether one value is less than or equal to another.

Here's the code for bouncing the ball off the bat:

```
if bally == BATY - 1:
    batleft = batx
    batright = batx + 1
    if ballx >= batleft and ballx <= batright:
        ballydir = -1
    if ballx + ballxdir >= batleft and ballx + ↵
      ballxdir <= batright:
        ballydir = -1
if bally == BATY:
    gameover()
```

If the ball reaches the same row as the bat, the player has failed to catch it, and the `gameover()` function is called.

So far, we've just changed the direction the ball is traveling in, but we haven't actually moved it. To move it, we use these commands:

```
ballx += ballxdir
if map[bally-1][ballx-1] == 0:
    bally += ballydir
```

First we move the ball horizontally. Then, we check whether the ball has landed on an empty space. If so, we move the ball vertically. Changing the X and Y position at the same time makes the ball move diagonally, but we need to make sure the ball isn't on a brick before we move it up or down. Otherwise, it appears to jump over bricks and smash through them diagonally, which looks wrong.

Next, we need to check whether the ball is on a brick, remembering that its vertical position might have changed since we checked a moment ago. If it is, we clear that space, clear that entry in the map, reset the ball to its previous position, and reverse its Y direction so it bounces back. We reverse the `ballydir` variable by making it negative, which involves putting a minus sign in front of it. This has the effect of turning 1 into –1, and –1 into 1 (because negative –1 equals 1).

To add a random element, we reverse the X direction back again half the time, but only if the map position would be empty if we did that. We check that by looking at the map value at the next Y position (`bally + ballydir`), and at the next X position if `ballxdir` were reversed (`ballx - ballxdir`). Note that we use a minus sign instead of a plus sign here because we need a minus sign to reverse the direction variable, and the plus sign is then redundant. The code `ballx - ballxdir` means the same as `ballx += ballxdir`.

As a final step, we increase the score variable, which is used to check when the player has hit all the bricks.

```
    if map[bally-1][ballx-1] != 0:
        blank(ballx, bally)
        map[bally-1][ballx-1] = 0
        bally = oldbally
        ballx = oldballx
        ballydir = -ballydir
        if random.randint(1, 10) > 5 and map[bally ↵
            +ballydir-1][ballx-ballxdir-1] == 0:
            ballxdir = -ballxdir
        score += 1
```

So far everything we've done has just been changing the ball's variables, so we need to finish the ball movements by deleting the old ball and drawing the ball in its new position.

```
blank(oldballx, oldbally)
drawball(ballx, bally)
```

Plug those lines in and you should have a fully functioning game!

If you can't work out where something belongs or if you get your indentations in a twist, remember you can download the full game at the book's website. See this book's Introduction for more on the website.

Adapting the Game

You can do plenty of things to customize or adapt this game. We've kept the logic simple for demonstration purposes, but you could make the game randomly decide whether the ball bounces left or right when it hits the bat, so it feels more chaotic and realistic. You can add in Pygame sound effects, using pygame.mixer, which is demonstrated in Chapter 17. You can make your own map, change the colors used, and add in new colored bricks. Perhaps you could modify it to display the score total during the game, and to incorporate multiple levels of gameplay. Remixing existing programs like this is a good way to study how they work, and to generate ideas for your own original games. If you come up with improvements, we'd love to see them!

You can find in-depth Pygame documentation (and information about features we don't have room for here) at www.pygame.org. You can find comprehensive documentation for Python online at www.python.org.

Chapter 13

Programming Minecraft with Python

Minecraft appeals to the Lego fan in everyone. It enables you to build immersive 3D worlds from blocks of materials, and it's fired up imaginations to the extent that an estimated 20 million copies have been sold across platforms, including the PC and Xbox.

An early development version of Minecraft is available for the Raspberry Pi. It features only the creative mode, where you can build things peacefully without the threat of monster attacks or starvation, but it has one neat twist: You can program it using multiple languages, including Python. This means that you can build a grand palace without having to manually place every block, and can write programs that can invent original new structures for you to roam around and explore, as you see in this chapter.

This project uses a Python program to build a maze in Minecraft. Each time you run the program, it will build a new maze for you, and you can control how big you want it to be and which materials you want it to be made of. During the course of this project, you'll learn how to place and remove blocks in Minecraft using Python, so you'll have the skills to write your own programs that supercharge your construction work.

At the time of writing, Minecraft: Pi Edition is alpha software, which means that it's a very early test version (less well developed than a beta version). We had only a couple of minor issues with it: The window and its content were strangely aligned using a screen resolution of 1024 x 768 (so we switched to 1280 x 1024), and the cursor misbehaved when we maximized the window.

You can download the code for this chapter from Sean's website at `www.sean.co.uk`.

Playing Minecraft

Minecraft is preinstalled in Raspbian. You start it by double-clicking its icon on the desktop, or by clicking it in the Programs menu at the bottom left of the screen, where Minecraft is filed under Games. When you start Minecraft on the Raspberry Pi, the title screen gives you two options:

- ✔ **Start Game:** This is the option you'll be using in this chapter to generate your own game world to explore. You can also use this option to choose a previously generated world to revisit, when you replay Minecraft later. To choose between the different worlds, click and drag them left and right to position your chosen one in the middle, and then click it to open it.

- ✔ **Join Game:** This option is used if you want to join other players in a game on a local network. It's outside the scope of this chapter, but can enable collaborative or competitive play in a Minecraft world.

Click Start Game, and then click Create New, and Minecraft will generate a new world for you, with its own distinctive terrain of mountains, forests, and oceans. When it's finished, you'll see a first-person view of it (see Figure 13-1).

You can change your perspective to show the player's character in the game. Press the Esc key to open the game menu, and then click the icon beside the speaker icon in the top left to change the perspective.

When you've finished playing, you can quit the game by pressing the Esc key to open the game menu.

Moving around

Minecraft is easiest to play using two hands, one on the mouse and one on the keyboard. Use the mouse to look around you and change your direction, sliding it left and right to turn sideways, and forward and backward on the desk to look up and down. To move, you use the keys W and S for forward and backward, and A and D to take a sidestep left and right. Those keys form a cluster on the keyboard, which makes it easy to switch between them.

Figure 13-1:
Minecraft
on the Pi.

You character will automatically jump onto low blocks if you walk into them, but you can deliberately jump by pressing the spacebar.

For the best view of your world, take to the skies by double-tapping the spacebar. When you're flying, hold the spacebar to go higher, and the left Shift key to go lower. Double-tap the spacebar to stop flying and drop to the ground. There's no health or danger in this edition of Minecraft, so you can freefall as far as you like.

Making and breaking things

To break blocks in your world, use your mouse to aim your crosshair at the block you want to destroy and click and hold the left mouse button. Some blocks are easier to break than others. There's a limit as to how far away you can be, so move closer if you can't see chips flying off the blocks as you attempt to smash them.

The panel at the bottom of the window shows the blocks you can place in the world (refer to Figure 13-1). You choose between them using the scroll wheel on your mouse, or by pressing a number between 1 and 8 to pick one (from left to right). Press E to open your full inventory, and you can use the movement keys (W, A, S, D) to navigate around it and Enter to choose a block, or simply click your chosen block with the mouse.

To position a block, right-click where you would like to place it. You can put a block on top of another one only if you can see the top of it, so you might need to fly to make tall structures.

You can build towers and rise into the air on them by looking down and repeatedly jumping and placing a block under you.

Although Python makes it much easier to build things, we recommend that you spend some time familiarizing yourself with how players experience the world. In particular, it's worth experimenting with how blocks interact with each other. Stone blocks will float in the air unsupported, but sand blocks will fall to the ground. Cacti can't be planted in grass, but can be placed on top of sand. If you chip away at the banks of a lake, the water will flow to fill the space you made. You can't place water and lava source blocks within the game, although you can program them using Python and they can cascade down and cover a wide area. When they come into contact with each other, water sometimes cools lava into stone.

Preparing for Python

One of the peculiarities of Minecraft is that it takes control of your mouse, so you have to press Tab to stop it doing that if you want to use any other programs on your desktop. To start using the mouse in Minecraft again, click the Minecraft window. You'll soon become used to pressing Tab before you try to do any programming. Press Tab now to leave Minecraft running, but bring the mouse cursor back into the desktop. To make your Minecraft programs, you're going to use IDLE, so double-click its icon on the desktop to start it. You might have to click the top of the Minecraft window and drag it out of the way first.

Note that the Minecraft API doesn't work in Python 3, the latest version of Python. Make sure you use IDLE and not the IDLE 3 icon to start Python.

One of the first things you'll notice is that Minecraft sits on top of other windows, and your IDLE window might well be underneath it, so a certain amount of reorganization is necessary. To move a window, you click and drag the title bar at the top of it, and you click and drag the edges or corners of a window to resize it. We recommend that you arrange your windows so that you can see them all at once. On a reasonably standard size monitor, we found we have room for Minecraft in the top left, a small box for the Python shell in the top right, and the window we're writing the program in is in the bottom half of the screen. We don't recommend resizing the Minecraft window: In the version we're running, the mouse controls became unresponsive when we did that. You can ignore (but not close) the LXTerminal window.

Using the Minecraft Module

You're now ready to write your first Python program for Minecraft, which will send a message to the chat feature in the game.

From the Python shell, click the File menu and choose New to open your programming window. Enter the following in the window, use the File menu to save it in your pi directory and press F5 to run it. You must have a Minecraft game session running for this to work.

```
import sys, random
from mcpi import minecraft
mc = minecraft.Minecraft.create()
mc.postToChat("Welcome to Minecraft Maze!")
```

The first line imports the `sys` and `random` modules. The `random` module you'll need later to build a random maze as you develop this program.

To issue Python commands to Minecraft, you use `minecraft.Minecraft.create()` and then add the command at the end. For example, to put a greeting in the chat window, you might use the following:

```
minecraft.Minecraft.create().postToChat("Welcome to ↵
Minecraft Maze!")
```

That soon gets hard to read, so in the program above, you set up `mc` so that you can use it as an abbreviation for `minecraft.Minecraft.create()`. As a result, you can use the shorter line that you see in the program to post a message.

If your code isn't working, pay particular attention to the case. Python is case-sensitive, so you have to use upper- and lowercase exactly as shown here. Look out for the mixed upper- and lowercase in `postToChat`, and the capital `M` in `minecraft.Minecraft.create()`.

Understanding coordinates in Minecraft

As you might expect, everything in the Minecraft world has a map coordinate. Three axes are required to describe a position in the game world:

- **x:** This axis runs parallel to the ground. The values run from -127.7 to 127.7.

- **y:** This axis runs vertically and could be described as the height. You can fly at least as high as 500, but you can't see the ground from higher than about 70, so there's not much point. Sea level is 0. You can break blocks to tunnel under the sea too. We made it down to about -70 before we fell out of the world and died. This is the only way we've seen that you can die in Minecraft on the Pi.

✔ **z:** This is the other axis parallel to the ground. The values run from -127.7 to 127.7.

We put them in that order deliberately because that's the order that Minecraft uses. If, like us, you often use x and y to refer to positions in 2D (as you do in Scratch), it takes a short while to get your head around the fact that y represents height. Most of the time in this chapter, you'll be using the x and z coordinates to describe a wall's position (which differs depending on the wall), and the y coordinate to describe its height (which doesn't).

As you move in the game, you can see the player's coordinates in the top left of the Minecraft window change. If you try to move outside the game world, you hit a wall of sky that you can't penetrate, like in the *Truman Show* (except that he had a door).

Repositioning the player

You can move your character to any position in the Minecraft world, using this command:

```
mc.player.setTilePos(x, y, z)
```

For example, to parachute into the middle of the world, use

```
mc.player.setTilePos(0, 100, 0)
```

You don't have to put this command into a program and run it. If you've already run the program to set up the Minecraft module, you can type commands to move the player and add blocks in the Python shell.

Assuming that you are not in flying mode, you'll drop from the sky into the middle of the world. If you are in flying mode, click the Minecraft window and double-tap the spacebar to turn it off and start your descent.

You can put the player anywhere in the game world, and sometimes that means she'll appear in the middle of a mountain or another structure, where she can't move. If that happens, reposition the player using code. Putting her somewhere high is usually a reasonably safe bet because she can fall to the highest ground from there.

Adding blocks

To add a block to the world, you use this command:

```
mc.setBlock(x, y, z, blockTypeId)
```

blockTypeId is a number that represents the material of the block you're adding. You can find a full list of materials at www.minecraftwiki.net/wiki/Data_values_(Pocket_Edition). (Take the number from the Dec column in the table on that page. You want the decimal number, rather than the hexadecimal one.) Any number from 0 to 108 is valid, and a few higher numbers are as well. Table 13-1 shows some of the materials you might find most useful for this project and for experimentation.

Table 13-1	Materials in Minecraft: Pi Edition
blockTypeId	**Block type**
0	Air
1	Stone
2	Grass
3	Dirt
5	Wooden plank
8	Water
10	Lava
12	Sand
20	Glass brick
24	Sandstone
41	Gold brick
45	Brick
47	Bookshelf
53	Wooden stairs
57	Diamond block
64	Wooden door
81	Cactus

If you use the water and lava blocks, you could flood your world, so create a new world to experiment with.

There is another command you can use to create a large cuboid shape built of blocks of the same material. To use it, you provide the coordinates of two opposite corners, and the material you'd like to fill the space with, like this:

```
mc.setBlocks(x1, y1, z1, x2, y2, z2, blockTypeId)
```

You can quickly build a brick shelter by making a large cuboid of brick, and then putting a cuboid of air inside it. Air replaces any other block, effectively deleting it from the world. Here's an example:

```
mc.setBlocks(0, 0, 0, 10, 5, 7, 45) #brick
mc.setBlocks(1, 0, 1, 9, 5, 6, 0) #air
```

These lines build a shelter that is 10 × 7 blocks in floor space, and 5 blocks high, starting at coordinate 0, 0, 0. The walls have a thickness of 1 block because you fill the space from 1 to 9 on the x axis, 1 to 6 on the z axis, and 0 to 5 on the vertical axis with air, leaving 1 block of brick from the original cuboid intact on four sides, and the roof open.

The # symbol represents a comment that's just there as a reminder for you. The computer ignores anything on the same line after the #.

Although players can have coordinate positions with decimal portions (such as 1.7), when you place a block, its position is rounded down to the nearest whole number.

Stopping the player from changing the world

We know you wouldn't cheat, but there's no fun in a maze that you might *accidentally* just hack your way through, is there? To stop players from being able to destroy or place blocks in the world, use the following:

```
mc.setting("world.immutable", True)
```

The word *immutable* is often used in programming, and just means "unchangeable."

Setting the maze parameters

Now that you know how to place blocks in the world and use the air block to remove them again, you're ready to start making the maze program. In this program, you'll use a number of constants to keep track of important information about the maze. Constants are just variables which you *decide* not to change the values of as the program is running, so their values are always the same. As you saw in Chapter 12, it's conventional to use uppercase for the names of constants to signal your intent to others reading the program, and to remind yourself that you're not supposed to be letting the program change these values. Replacing numbers in your program with constants makes it easier to customize your program later, but also makes it much easier to read your program and understand what different numbers represent.

Variable names are case sensitive, so Python would think SIZE and size were two different variables. You'd be mad to use both in the same program, though!

The program starts by setting up these constants:

```
SIZE = 10
HEIGHT = 2
MAZE_X = 0
GROUND = 0
MAZE_Z = 0
MAZE_MATERIAL = 1 #stone
GROUND_MATERIAL = 2 #grass
CEILING = False
```

To build the maze, you will start with a grid of walls with one-block spaces (or cells) between them, which looks a bit like a potato waffle (see Figure 13-2). Each cell starts with four walls, and the program knocks walls down to create paths between them and build the maze. The maze is square, and its SIZE is measured in cells. A maze with a SIZE of 10 will have 10 cells in the x and z dimensions, but will occupy double that space in the Minecraft world (that is, 20 blocks by 20 blocks) because there is a one-block wall between each cell. This will become clearer as you start to build the maze. We've tried mazes as big as 40, but they take some time to build and ages to explore. Ten is big enough for now. The program will stop with an error if there isn't enough room for all of the maze in your world.

The HEIGHT is how many blocks tall the maze walls are. We chose 2 because a value of 1 means that the player can just walk over the maze. (The player automatically steps up onto blocks 1 unit high.) Higher values obscure any mountains in the distance that can otherwise give a nice visual hint to the player.

The constants MAZE_X, GROUND and MAZE_Z are used for the starting coordinates of the maze. The MAZE_MATERIAL is stone (1), and the GROUND_MATERIAL is grass (2). We've added an option for a ceiling, to stop players from just flying out of the top of the maze, but we've turned it off for now so that you can freely explore the maze as you're building it.

A maze of bookshelves (MAZE_MATERIAL=47) looks great!

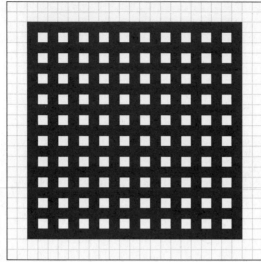

Figure 13-2:
The starter
grid.

Laying the foundations

One of the first things you need to do is make sure that you're building on solid land. Because Minecraft worlds are dynamically generated, you might find that you're building a maze inside a mountain or in the sea, otherwise.

As well as the area the maze will occupy, you'll clear an area of 10 blocks all the way around it, so the players can approach it easily and walk around the outside of it. First you clear the area by filling it with air blocks, which will wipe out anything else in that space.

The maze occupies a ground space measured in blocks from MAZE_X to MAZE_X+(SIZE*2), and from MAZE_Z to MAZE_Z+(SIZE*2). The number of blocks is twice the number of cells (SIZE) because each cell has a wall on its right and below it. The middle of the maze in the Minecraft world is MAZE_X+SIZE, MAZE_Z+SIZE.

You need to clear 10 blocks further in each direction. The following code clears everything as high as 150 above the ground level of the maze to stop the risk of any remaining mountain blocks falling from the sky into the maze:

```
mc.setBlocks(MAZE_X-10, GROUND, MAZE_Z-10, ↩
MAZE_X+(SIZE*2)+10, GROUND+150, MAZE_Z+(SIZE*2)+10, 0)
mc.setBlocks(MAZE_X-10, GROUND, MAZE_Z-10, ↩
MAZE_X+(SIZE*2)+10, GROUND, MAZE_Z+(SIZE*2)+10, ↩
GROUND_MATERIAL)
```

We recommend adding a block to indicate the starting corner of the maze (where MAZE_X and MAZE_Z are). You will find it useful when writing and debugging the program because it will enable you to tell which way around the maze is as you fly around it. To do so, use the following:

```
mc.setBlock(MAZE_X, GROUND+HEIGHT+1, MAZE_Z, ↵
    MAZE_MATERIAL)
```

Put your player character above the middle of the maze, too, so you can watch it being built by looking down, as follows. If you're not flying, you'll fall onto the maze wall, but you can just fly up again.

```
mc.player.setTilePos(MAZE_X+SIZE, GROUND+25, MAZE_Z+SIZE)
```

Placing the maze walls

To make the potato waffle-like grid, use the following code:

```
for line in range(0, (SIZE+1)*2, 2):
    mc.setBlocks(MAZE_X+line, GROUND+1, MAZE_Z,↵
    MAZE_X+line, GROUND+HEIGHT, MAZE_Z+(SIZE*2), MAZE_MATERIAL)
    mc.setBlocks(MAZE_X, GROUND+1, MAZE_Z+line, ↵
    MAZE_X+(SIZE*2), GROUND+HEIGHT, MAZE_Z+line, MAZE_MATERIAL)
```

The for loop gives the variable line the values of even numbers starting at 0 and finishing at SIZE*2, in turn. You have to add 1 to SIZE before doubling it because the range function doesn't include the last number in the sequence. If you use range(1, 10), for example, you get the numbers 1 to 9. The number 2 at the end of the range function is the step size, so it adds 2 each time it goes around the loop, and only gives you the even numbers. That means you leave a gap for the cell between each wall. Each time around the loop, it uses cuboids to draw two walls that stretch across the maze from edge to edge in the x and z dimensions. It doesn't matter that the same block is set twice where those lines intersect. You build the wall starting at GROUND+1, so the grass is still underneath when you knock down the walls to make paths.

Don't forget the colon at the end of the for statement, and that the next two lines should each be indented by four spaces to tell Python that they belong to the loop.

You should now have a grid that looks like Figure 13-3.

Understanding the maze algorithm

Before you dig into the code that turns your waffle into a maze, let us tell you how it works. You're going to make what's known as a "perfect maze" (that's a technical term, not us bragging). That means there are no loops in it, and no parts of the maze you can't get into. There is only one path between any two points in the maze.

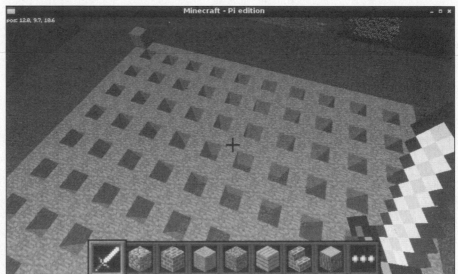

Figure 13-3:
Your grid in
Minecraft.

Here's how the program works:

1. You start with the "waffle" you've built, with every cell having all four walls.

2. You pick a random cell in the maze to start at.

3. You look at your current cell's neighbors, and make a list of all those that have all four walls intact. These are the cells that have not yet been visited.

4. If you found some unvisited neighbors, you pick one at random, knock down the wall between it and your current cell, and then move into that cell, making it your current cell.

5. If your current cell has no unvisited neighbors, you go back one cell in the path you've taken, and make that your current cell.

6. Repeat Steps 3 to 5 until you've visited every cell.

Setting up the variables and lists

To implement this algorithm, you'll use the following variables:

- numberOfCells: This is the total number of cells in the maze, which will be SIZE*SIZE. (Remember, * is the symbol for multiplication.)

- numberOfVisitedCells: This keeps track of how many cells you've visited so far. When this is the same as the numberOfCells, every cell has been visited and had a wall demolished, and is therefore reachable. The maze is finished.

- xposition: This remembers your x position as you move through the maze generating it. It's measured in cells, and starts as a random number between 1 and the maze SIZE.

- zposition: This remembers your z position as you move through the maze generating it, also measured in cells, and also starting as a random number.

- cellsVisitedList[]: This is a list that stores the path you've taken, so the program can retrace its steps. When you set it up, you put your starting position into it using the append() list method.

- playerx and playerz: These are used to remember the starting position, so you can put the player there when the maze has been built.

When an algorithm like this is implemented (it's called a *depth-first maze generation algorithm*), it often requires a list or similar data structure to be used to store the locations of walls. You don't need that because you have actual walls in Minecraft you can look at. The game world stores your maze, if you like.

The following code lines set up your starting variables:

```
numberOfCells = SIZE * SIZE
numberOfVisitedCells = 1 # 1 for the one you start in
cellsVisitedList = []

xposition = random.randint(1, SIZE)
zposition = random.randint(1, SIZE)
playerx = xposition
playerz = zposition
showMaker(xposition, zposition)
# see the next section, "Creating the functions"
cellsVisitedList.append((xposition, zposition))
```

Creating the functions

There are a number of basic functions you will need for your program:

- ✔ `realx(x)` and `realz(z)`: These convert coordinates in the maze (measured in cells) into coordinates in the Minecraft world (measured in blocks, and offset from the maze's starting position).

- ✔ `showMaker(x,z)` and `hideMaker(x,z)`: These functions use a gold block to show which cell the program has reached as it builds the maze. It's fun to watch from above, and is useful while building and debugging the program.

- ✔ `demolish(realx, realz)`: This knocks down a wall in the maze, and takes a real coordinate in the Minecraft world as its parameters.

- ✔ `testAllWalls(cellx, cellz)`: This checks whether the four walls on a cell are intact. If all of them are, it returns `True`. Otherwise, it returns `False`. It uses the command `mc.getBlock(x, y, z)`, which tells you the `blockTypeId` at a particular location. You use two equals signs, as usual, to test whether a block in a wall position is the same as the `MAZE_MATERIAL`, which means that there's a wall there.

Add these function definitions at the start of your program, after where you set up the Minecraft module:

```
def realx(x):
    return MAZE_X + (x*2) - 1

def realz(z):
    return MAZE_Z + (z*2) - 1

def showMaker(x, z):
    mc.setBlock(realx(x), GROUND+1, realz(z), 41)  # 41=gold

def hideMaker(x, z):
    mc.setBlock(realx(x), GROUND+1, realz(z), 0)

def demolish(realx, realz):
    mc.setBlocks(realx, GROUND+1, realz, realx, ↩
    HEIGHT+GROUND, realz, 0)

def testAllWalls(cellx, cellz):
    if mc.getBlock(realx(cellx)+1, GROUND+1,↩
    realz(cellz))==MAZE_MATERIAL and mc.getBlock↩
    (realx(cellx)-1, GROUND+1, realz(cellz))==MAZE_MATERIAL ↩
    and mc.getBlock(realx(cellx), GROUND+1, realz(cellz)+1)== ↩
    MAZE_MATERIAL and mc.getBlock(realx(cellx), GROUND+1,↩
    realz(cellz)-1)==MAZE_MATERIAL:
        return True
    else:
        return False
```

If you have an error, check for missing colons at the end of your `def` and `if` statements.

Creating the main loop

Your maze algorithm runs until you've visited every cell, so it starts with the following statement:

```
while numberOfVisitedCells < numberOfCells:
```

You need to test whether your current cell's neighbor cells have all their walls intact. To do that, you check each direction in turn, using the `testAllWalls(x, z)` function. When you find a cell with all the walls intact, you add its direction to the list `possibleDirections[]` using the `append()` list method. This implements step 3 in the algorithm, and remember it's all indented underneath the `while` statement:

```
possibleDirections = []

if testAllWalls(xposition - 1, zposition):
    possibleDirections.append("left")

if testAllWalls(xposition + 1, zposition):
    possibleDirections.append("right")

if testAllWalls(xposition, zposition - 1):
    possibleDirections.append("up")

if testAllWalls(xposition, zposition + 1):
    possibleDirections.append("down")
```

The values of `up`, `down`, `left`, and `right` are somewhat arbitrary in 3D space, but we've used them because they're easy to understand. If you fly into the air and look down on the maze as it's being generated and you have the block identifying the starting corner of the maze (`MAZE_X`, `MAZE_Z`) in the top left, these directions will look correct to you.

Incidentally, you might have noticed that there's no check for whether these cell positions are inside the maze borders. What happens if you look for a cell off the left edge of the maze, or off the bottom edge? No problem. The program implementation automatically respects the borders of the maze because when it looks at "cells" outside the borders, they don't have all four walls (their only wall is the maze's border), so they are never visited.

Step 4 in the algorithm is to pick a random direction if you found any unvisited neighbors, knock down the wall in that direction and move into that cell. To decide whether you found any possible directions, you check the length of the `possibleDirections` list and act if it is not equal to 0 (`!=0`). All of this should be indented under the `while` loop. If you get lost in the indenting, consult the full code in Listing 13-1 near the end of this chapter.

Before you start moving your position, you hide the gold brick that shows where you are in the maze:

```
hideMaker(xposition, zposition)
if len(possibleDirections) != 0:
    directionChosen=random.choice(possibleDirections)

    if directionChosen == "left":
        demolish(realx(xposition) - 1, realz(zposition))
        xposition -= 1

    if directionChosen == "right":
        demolish(realx(xposition) + 1, realz(zposition))
        xposition += 1

    if directionChosen == "up":
        demolish(realx(xposition), realz(zposition) - 1)
        zposition -= 1

    if directionChosen == "down":
        demolish(realx(xposition), realz(zposition) + 1)
        zposition += 1
```

After you've moved into a new cell, you need to increase your tally of cells visited by one, and add the new cell to the list that stores the path taken. This is also a good time to show the gold block in the cell to highlight how the maze is being built:

```
numberOfVisitedCells += 1
cellsVisitedList.append((xposition, zposition))
showMaker(xposition, zposition)
```

The way you've stored the list of cells visited deserves some explanation. You've put the `xposition` and `zposition` in parentheses, which are used to indicate a tuple. A *tuple* is a data sequence, a bit like a list, with a key difference being that you can't change its values. (It's immutable.) So `cellsVisitedList` is a list that contains tuples, which in turn contain pairs of x and z coordinates. You can use the Python shell to take a look inside this list. Here's an example from one run of the program, showing a path taken through the maze:

```
>>> print cellsVisitedList
[(6, 6,), (6, 7), (6, 8), (5, 8), (4, 8), (3, 8), (3, 7)]
```

For step 5 in the algorithm, you go back to the previous position in the path if your cell has no unvisited neighbors. This involves taking the last position out of the list. There's a list method called `pop()` you can use to do that. It takes the last item from a list and deletes it from that list. In your program, you put it into a variable called `retrace`, which then stores a tuple for the x and z positions in the maze. As with a list, you can use index numbers to access the individual elements in a tuple. The index numbers start at 0, so `retrace[0]` will hold your previous x position, and `retrace[1]` will hold your previous z position. Here's the code, including a line to show the gold block in its new position:

```
else: # do this when there are no unvisited neighbors
    retrace = cellsVisitedList.pop()
    xposition = retrace[0]
    zposition = retrace[1]
    showMaker(xposition, zposition)
```

Note that your `else` statement should be in line with the `if` statement it's paired with, in this case the one that tests whether you found any possible directions to move in.

Step 6 in the algorithm has already been implemented because the `while` loop will keep repeating the indented code underneath it until every cell has been visited.

Adding a ceiling

Personally, we think it's more fun to leave the ceiling open and be free to fly up and marvel at your maze, and drop into it at any point. If you want to build a game around your maze, though, and stop people from cheating, you can add a ceiling using the following code. Just change the variable `CEILING` to `True` at the start of the program. We've made the ceiling out of glass bricks, so it doesn't get too dark in there:

```
if CEILING == True:
    mc.setBlocks(MAZE_X, GROUND+HEIGHT+1, MAZE_Z, ↵
MAZE_X+(SIZE*2), GROUND+HEIGHT+1, MAZE_Z+(SIZE*2), 20)
```

Positioning the player

Finally, let's place the player at the random position where you started generating the maze. You could put the player anywhere, but this seems as good a place as any, and it uses random numbers you have already generated:

```
mc.player.setTilePos(realx(playerx), GROUND+1, ↵
    realz(playerz))
```

Now you're ready to play! Figure 13-4 shows the maze from the inside.

Figure 13-4:
Finding your
way around
the maze.

The final code

Listing 13-1 shows the final and complete code:

Listing 13-1: The Minecraft Maze Maker

```
import sys, random
from mcpi import minecraft
mc = minecraft.Minecraft.create()

mc.postToChat("Welcome to Minecraft Maze!")

def realx(x):
    return MAZE_X + (x*2) - 1

def realz(z):
    return MAZE_Z + (z*2) - 1

def showMaker(x, z):
    mc.setBlock(realx(x), GROUND+1, realz(z), 41) # 41=gold

def hideMaker(x, z):
    mc.setBlock(realx(x), GROUND+1, realz(z), 0)

def demolish(realx, realz):
    mc.setBlocks(realx, GROUND+1, realz, realx,↩
    HEIGHT+GROUND, realz, 0)
```

```
def testAllWalls(cellx, cellz):
    if mc.getBlock(realx(cellx)+1, GROUND+1, ↵
    realz(cellz))==MAZE_MATERIAL and mc.getBlock↵
    (realx(cellx)-1, GROUND+1, realz(cellz))==MAZE_MATERIAL ↵
    and mc.getBlock(realx(cellx), GROUND+1, realz(cellz)+1)==↵
    MAZE_MATERIAL and mc.getBlock(realx(cellx), GROUND+1, ↵
    realz(cellz)-1)==MAZE_MATERIAL:
        return True
    else:
        return False

mc.setting("world_immutable", True)

# Configure your maze here
SIZE = 10
HEIGHT = 2
MAZE_X = 0
GROUND = 0
MAZE_Z = 0
MAZE_MATERIAL = 1 # 1=stone
GROUND_MATERIAL = 2 # 2=grass
CEILING = False

# clear area
mc.setBlocks(MAZE_X-10, GROUND, MAZE_Z-10, MAZE_X+↵
(SIZE*2)+10, GROUND+150, MAZE_Z+(SIZE*2)+10, 0) # air

# lay the ground
    mc.setBlocks(MAZE_X-10, GROUND, MAZE_Z-10, MAZE_X+↵
    (SIZE*2)+10, GROUND, MAZE_Z+(SIZE*2)+10, GROUND_MATERIAL)

# origin marker
mc.setBlock(MAZE_X, GROUND+HEIGHT+1, MAZE_Z, MAZE_MATERIAL)

# move player above middle of maze
mc.player.setTilePos(MAZE_X+SIZE, GROUND+25, MAZE_Z+SIZE)

mc.postToChat("Now building your maze...")

# build grid of walls
for line in range(0, (SIZE+1)*2, 2):
    mc.setBlocks(MAZE_X+line, GROUND+1, MAZE_Z, ↵
    MAZE_X+line, GROUND+HEIGHT, MAZE_Z+(SIZE*2), MAZE_MATERIAL)
    mc.setBlocks(MAZE_X, GROUND+1, MAZE_Z+line, MAZE_X+↵
    (SIZE*2), GROUND+HEIGHT, MAZE_Z+line, MAZE_MATERIAL)

# setup of variables for creating maze
numberOfCells = SIZE * SIZE
numberOfVisitedCells = 1 # 1 for the one you start in
cellsVisitedList = []
```

(continued)

Listing 13-1 *(continued)*

```
xposition = random.randint(1, SIZE)
zposition = random.randint(1, SIZE)
playerx = xposition
playerz = zposition
showMaker(xposition, zposition)
cellsVisitedList.append((xposition, zposition))

while numberOfVisitedCells < numberOfCells:
    possibleDirections = []

    if testAllWalls(xposition - 1, zposition):
        possibleDirections.append("left")

    if testAllWalls(xposition + 1, zposition):
        possibleDirections.append("right")

    if testAllWalls(xposition, zposition - 1):
        possibleDirections.append("up")

    if testAllWalls(xposition, zposition + 1):
        possibleDirections.append("down")

    hideMaker(xposition, zposition)

    if len(possibleDirections) != 0:
        directionChosen=random.choice(possibleDirections)

        #knock down wall between cell in direction chosen
        if directionChosen == "left":
            demolish(realx(xposition) - 1, realz(zposition))
            xposition -= 1

        if directionChosen == "right":
            demolish(realx(xposition) + 1, realz(zposition))
            xposition += 1

        if directionChosen == "up":
            demolish(realx(xposition), realz(zposition) - 1)
            zposition -= 1

        if directionChosen == "down":
            demolish(realx(xposition), realz(zposition) + 1)
            zposition += 1

        numberOfVisitedCells += 1
# after the move, increase number of visited cells
        cellsVisitedList.append((xposition, zposition))
        showMaker(xposition, zposition)
```

```
    else: # do this when there are no unvisited neighbors
        retrace = cellsVisitedList.pop()
        xposition = retrace[0]
        zposition = retrace[1]
        showMaker(xposition, zposition)

if CEILING == True:
    mc.setBlocks(MAZE_X, GROUND+HEIGHT+1, MAZE_Z, ↵
MAZE_X+(SIZE*2), GROUND+HEIGHT+1, MAZE_Z+(SIZE*2), 20)

mc.postToChat("Your maze is ready!")
mc.postToChat("Happy exploring!")
mc.player.setTilePos(realx(playerx), GROUND+1, ↵
                     realz(playerz))
```

Adapting the Program

When the maze is built, the gold brick is left showing, so you could try to solve the maze to find the brick. You could also plant other objectives in the maze, and time how long it takes the player to find them. The `mc.player.getTilePos()` command checks where the player is in the Minecraft world, and gives you a result in the form `x`, `y`, `z`.

You could add an entrance and exit in a random position in the border of the maze, so the goal is to travel from one side to the other. You could make huge mazes more playable by adding landmarks. (Try using different wall materials, or putting blocks on top of some walls.) After the maze has been generated, you could knock out random walls, so there are some shortcuts through the maze. Or maybe just replace them with glass blocks, to provide a tantalizing glimpse into another corridor. What about a multistory maze, with stairs between the levels? The possibilities are . . . ahem! . . . amazing.

Chapter 14

Making Music with Sonic Pi

In This Chapter

▶ Playing notes and melodies using Sonic Pi

▶ Creating random computer-generated music

▶ Adding samples to your compositions

▶ Synchronizing your tunes with drumbeats and samples

*F*or much of the music we hear today, computers are at least as important in the studio as microphones are, and they have been for many years. Using Sonic Pi, you can start composing your own computer music by programming your Raspberry Pi. It enables you to put together simple programs that play synthesizer melodies and sampled sounds, generating your own distinctive instrumental music.

Sonic Pi is based on the Ruby programming language, so it works differently than the Python code you've become familiar with in the last couple of chapters. It uses some of the same ideas you saw there and in Scratch, however, including loops and lists (here in the form of arrays). We don't have space in this book to teach you the Ruby programming language, but we can give you some examples that you can experiment with and modify to make your own musical programs. If you've completed the chapters on Python, the syntax might look strange, but what it's doing should feel intuitive.

Sonic Pi runs from the desktop environment (see Chapter 4) and is preinstalled in Raspbian.

You run Sonic Pi by clicking the Programs Menu button in the bottom-left of the screen, clicking Programming, and then clicking the entry for Sonic Pi. There is also a large icon on the desktop you can double-click.

Understanding the Sonic Pi Screen Layout

Figure 14-1 shows the screen layout for Sonic Pi. You might see some differences between your screen layout and ours, but the fundamentals should be the same. Click to enlarge the window if necessary (see *Resizing and closing your program windows* in Chapter 4). On the left is the Programming panel, where you type in your code. On the right is the Output panel, where Sonic Pi tells you what it's doing as it plays your music. At the bottom is the Help panel, which is opened and closed by clicking the Help button in the top right.

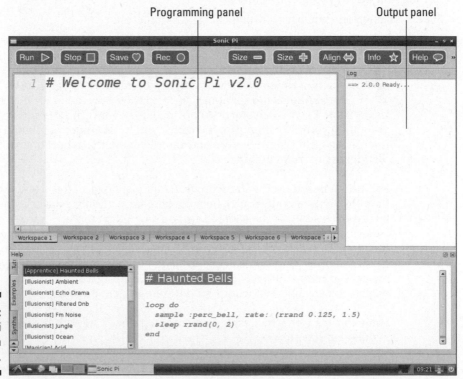

Figure 14-1:
The Sonic Pi screen layout.

Sonic Pi uses eight different workspaces, which you access by clicking the tabs at the bottom of the Programming panel. You can think of each workspace as being like having a different file open for editing, but you can play music from different workspaces at the same time. This can be particularly useful for live performance: You might set up a loop in one workspace and then experiment with code to add notes on top in another workspace. When you exit Sonic Pi, the content of your workspaces is saved for you, and it's loaded when you come back again.

At the top of the screen are buttons to run your program (play your music) and stop it. They use symbols similar to any audio player: a triangle to play and a square to stop. There are also buttons to adjust the text size, fix the alignment in your code, show the info screen, and show the help panel at the bottom of the screen.

There is also a Preferences button to the right of the Help button. It doesn't fit on our screen, so we have to press the double-arrow symbol beside the Help button to find it. The Preferences panel provides a volume control and enables you to force the audio output to go through headphones or through the HDMI cable.

Playing Your First Notes

Click in the Programming panel and type the following:

```
play 60
```

Nothing happens because you've entered your program but haven't run it yet. Click the Run button and you will hear a middle C note sound. At the same time, you'll see the Output panel update.

The note numbers used are standard MIDI note numbers, widely used in electronic instruments. You've already seen them in Scratch. Higher-sounding notes use higher numbers, and lower-sounding notes use lower numbers.

Try adding some more notes to your program:

```
play 60
play 64
play 67
```

When you click the Run button, you still hear just one sound, but three different notes are playing at the same time. It's actually a C chord you hear, which uses the notes C (60), E (64), and G (67). If you want to play the notes separately, you can add a pause between them using the sleep command:

```
play 60
sleep 0.5
play 64
sleep 0.5
play 67
sleep 0.5
play 72
```

We added an extra higher C note on the end of that sequence to make it sound like a fanfare. You can experiment with writing your own tunes. Just put together a sequence of notes.

Table 14-1 shows the standard MIDI notes, which run from 0 to 127. In practice, they sound extremely tinkly at the high end and descend into indistinct soft thuds at the low end. For best results, we recommend you keep your numbers between 48 and 96, but feel free to experiment to find out what sounds good to you.

Table 14-1						MIDI Notes					
Note		0	1	2	3	4	5	6	7	8	9
C	0	12	24	36	48	60	72	84	96	108	120
C#	1	13	25	37	49	61	73	85	97	109	121
D	2	14	26	38	50	62	74	86	98	110	122
D#	3	15	27	39	51	63	75	87	99	111	123
E	4	16	28	40	52	64	76	88	100	112	124
F	5	17	29	41	53	65	77	89	101	113	125
F#	6	18	30	42	54	66	78	90	102	114	126
G	7	19	31	43	55	67	79	91	103	115	127
G#	8	20	32	44	56	68	80	92	104	116	
A	9	21	33	45	57	69	81	93	105	117	
A#	10	22	34	46	58	70	82	94	106	118	
B	11	23	35	47	59	71	83	95	107	119	

As you can see, the numbers in the table go from top to bottom, and from left to right. Notes get higher as you go down the table and as you move from left to right across the columns. The next highest note after B (at the bottom of the table) is the C at the top of the next column to the right. It's like a piano, where the same key layout (running from C to G, then A to B, and then starting from C again) repeats all the way along it.

If you don't know much about music, stick to the notes that don't have a # on them and avoid too many huge leaps. Try moving a few notes up or down a column and dip into a neighboring column when you're near the top or bottom of your column. By following those simple guidelines, you should end up with a jolly little ditty.

Writing Shorter Programs

There is a more efficient way you can play a sequence of notes and specify the time, in seconds, between each one: Use the `play_pattern_timed` command. Click a tab to go to a new workspace and try this:

```
play_pattern_timed [60, 64, 67, 72], [0.5, 0.5, 1]
```

Pay careful attention to the brackets and commas here. This command takes two different sets of information, and each set is between square brackets. The first set is the notes you want to play, and they are the same notes as we used in our fanfare earlier. The second set of information is separated from the first set by a comma, and it is the length of the pause between the notes. There are four notes but just three gaps between them, so the second set of brackets has fewer items in it. The numbers we've used here put a half a second pause between the first and second notes, and the second and third notes, but double that to build up the suspense (such as it is) before the final note sounds.

Composing Random Tunes Using Shuffle

The bracketed sections are Ruby arrays, similar to lists in Python. You can add different methods to the arrays to change the order of the items in them. For example, try this, using the reverse method:

```
play_pattern_timed [60, 64, 67, 72], [0.5, 0.5, 1]
play_pattern_timed [60, 64, 67, 72].reverse, [0.5, 0.5, 1]
```

You'll hear the notes of the fanfare played forward and then backward, but with the same timing each time. You can use the `shuffle` method to hear a random tune. Try this:

```
play_pattern_timed [60, 62, 64, 65, 67, 69, 72].shuffle, ↵
        [0.5, 0.5, 1, 0.5, 0.5, 1]
```

We've used a simple rhythm there, two short notes and then a long note. You might have noticed that we added a pause after the final note too. It's a cheery melody, but it's a bit short, so get Sonic Pi to repeat it. Here's how:

```
4.times do
  play_pattern_timed [60, 62, 64, 65, 67, 69, 72].shuffle, ↵
        [0.5, 0.5, 1, 0.5, 0.5, 1, 2]
end
play 60
```

We've wrapped our tune playing code in a loop that repeats it four times. The start of the loop is 4.times do and the end of the repeating section is marked, appropriately enough, with the word end. We indent our musical code by two spaces to show it's the part that is to be repeated. If you want to repeat more or less than four times, change the number 4 at the start.

We made two other changes here too: First, we added a timing value for the last note in the sequence. It's the 2 that has sneaked inside the last square bracket. We've also added a final note, C. Whatever randomness happens in the rest of the tune, this sequence of notes always sounds good when it ends on a C because all the notes in the sequence are from the C major scale.

Using Array Names in Your Programs

The arrays of notes and values can make your program look cluttered, but you can tidy it up by giving the arrays names. That makes it easier to reuse them too. You can streamline your previous program like this:

```
note_pitches = [60, 62, 64, 65, 67, 69, 72]
note_timings = [0.5, 0.5, 1, 0.5, 0.5, 1, 2]
4.times do
  play_pattern_timed note_pitches.shuffle, note_timings
end
play 60
```

Using Threads to Play Accompaniments

Threads are different bits of program that run at the same time. We can write two different pieces of code to play music, and have them play together, if they are in different threads. We can use different synthesizer sounds too, to create a richer accompaniment. Try it out with this program:

```
note_pitches = [60, 62, 64, 65, 67, 69, 72]
note_timings = [0.5, 0.5, 1, 0.5, 0.5, 1, 2]

in_thread do
  use_synth :zawa
  4.times do
    play_pattern_timed note_pitches.shuffle, note_timings
  end
  play 60
end

in_thread do
  use_synth :saw
  2.times do
    play_pattern_timed note_pitches.reverse, note_timings
    play_pattern_timed note_pitches, note_timings
  end
  play 48
end
```

That program uses two threads. The first thread is the same as your previous program, and plays the notes in a random sequence four times. The second thread takes those same notes, but plays them first in reverse order (going from high to low), and then in their real order (from low to high), and then repeats that. The final note in that thread is a lower C.

We've used two different synth sounds here, so it's easier to hear the different parts of the music: zawa and saw. To get a full list of the synths available, click the Help button at the upper right of the screen and then click the Synths tab in the bottom left. If it's not shown, use the arrows next to the help tabs to show it first.

Playing Random Notes

You can play random notes, like this:

```
lowest_note = 60
note_range = 24
play lowest_note + Random.rand(note_range)
```

In that program, lowest_note and note_range are variables. You can change the numbers after them to change the random note chosen. For example, if you want to pick one of three notes starting with F, change the lowest_note to 65 and the note_range to 3. Each time you run the program, you get a different note. This uses the Ruby language to produce a random number.

Sonic Pi also offers a way to get random numbers in a repeatable fashion. That is, you let the computer pick the notes to play, but each time you run the program, it generates the same random numbers, so the music sounds the same. This example invents a melody for you, but always plays the same tune:

```
lowest_note = 60
highest_note = 84
6.times do
  play rrandi_i(lowest_note, highest_note)
  sleep 0.5
end
```

The problem with generating totally random numbers is that not all notes sound good together. In this chapter, we've been using the notes from the white keys on the piano (the scale of C major) and none of the sharp notes. When you start throwing in sharp notes randomly, it can start to sound too chaotic. An alternative way to pick a random note is to create an array of the notes you like (the scale of C major we've been using so far) and then use the Ruby sample array method to pick a random note from it. Here's an example:

```
note_pitches = [60, 62, 64, 65, 67, 69, 72]
loop do
  play note_pitches.sample
  sleep 0.2
end
```

That program uses a loop that repeats forever, so it'll keep improvising until you click the Stop button. Each time you run that program, you get a different sequence of notes.

Sonic Pi has an approach you can use to randomly pick numbers from the array in a repeatable fashion too, similar to the way `rrand_i()` works for picking random numbers. To use it, replace the `play` line in the code above with:

```
play choose(note_pitches)
```

The Output panel shows you the note numbers that are played, so you can use this to see which notes are being chosen and check to make sure that your program is behaving as you expect.

Later in this chapter, we talk about snippets of music called *samples*. Don't get confused by the sample array method we're using here in Ruby, which picks a random item from your array.

Turning Names into Music

Ever heard a song on the radio and thought it was written just for you? Well, it wasn't, but thanks to Sonic Pi, you can have a piece of music personalized for you, or at least lay claim to your very own jingle.

This short program takes a name and turns it into music. In the software, letters are represented by numbers, called *ASCII numbers*. You can get the ASCII number for each letter in a word, and then play it as if it were a MIDI number, effectively turning letters into notes and words into tunes.

The program actually plays two notes: One is the note from your name, and the other is the same note plus 12, which is an octave higher. This shows how you can use mathematics to generate a richer sound:

```
name = "Karen"
name.each_byte do |note|
  play note
  play note + 12
  sleep 0.25
end
```

Using Note Names

MIDI notes are great because you can use sums to generate music with them, but if you're more musically inclined, you might prefer to use the proper note names. Sonic Pi enables you to do that by using the name of the note (a letter from A to G), plus the number of the octave it's in. You can see those numbers labeling the columns in Table 14-1.

For example, to play a middle C, you can use

```
play :c4
```

To play the B one note before it, which is in the next lowest octave, you would use

```
play :b3
```

The Output panel shows that Sonic Pi plays notes 60 and 59 respectively. You can check the note names and numbers in Table 14-1 to confirm that this is what you expected.

You can also use names to play chords. You tell Sonic Pi the lowest note in the chord and can optionally add if you want the chord to be a minor chord. Try this:

```
play chord(:a3)
sleep 0.25
play chord (:a3, :minor)
```

In each case, it plays three notes at the same time. If you look at the note numbers in the Output panel, you can see that the middle note was one pitch lower in the second chord because it's a minor chord. Again, you can use Table 14-1 to check the note numbers Sonic Pi displays against the musical note names.

Using Samples

The programs you've made so far are an interesting way to explore computer music, especially when the computer starts surprising you with its random compositions.

It doesn't sound like proper recorded music, though. Sonic Pi also has the capability to use samples, which are short snippets of music that you can manipulate, such as by changing their speed or adding effects to them. Sonic Pi includes more than 70 samples, and you can see a list of them by clicking the Help button and then using the tabs in the bottom left to see the samples. Use the arrow to scroll the tabs if the one you need isn't showing.

Here's one of our favorites:

```
sample :loop_industrial
```

You can speed it up or slow it down by changing its rate. Here's how you make it play at half its normal speed:

```
sample :loop_industrial, rate: 0.5
```

Take care with where you put spaces around colons. The program won't work if you put a space between the colon and the sample name.

We can repeat that sample to make a continuous rhythm. Like we did when we were playing notes, we use the sleep command to put a pause between each repetition. Samples can be different lengths, however, so Sonic Pi provides a feature in the language to find out how long a particular sample is, called sample_duration. You can use it like this:

```
loop do
  sample :loop_industrial
  sleep sample_duration :loop_industrial
end
```

If you change the rate of your sample, remember that your sleep duration needs to change too. If you play your sample at half speed (0.5), it's going to take twice as long as usual to finish playing. That means you need to sleep for twice as long as the sample duration. To perform calculations like this, use a variable to store how long Sonic Pi should sleep for between each sample playback.

```
drum_rate = sample_duration :loop_industrial
drum_rate = drum_rate * 2
loop do
  sample :loop_industrial, rate:0.5
  sleep drum_rate
end
```

In that program, we set the variable drum_rate to be equal to the length of the sample, and then double it because we're playing the sample at half speed.

Adding Special Effects

You can play a sample and add effects to it, including distortion, echo, and reverb. There is a full list of effects (also known as Fx) in the Help pane. This is how you add distortion to one of the guitar samples:

```
with_fx :distortion do
  sample:guit_e_fifths
end
```

Synchronizing with Your Drumbeat

You now know how to play a repeating rhythm, and you can use threads to play other samples and synth melodies on top of it. One of the tricky things is to synchronize all the threads so they play to the same rhythm. Sonic Pi provides two commands you can use for this, cue and sync. They work a bit like broadcasts in Scratch (see Chapter 10).

The cue command sends a message to all the threads, and the sync command pauses a thread until it receives a particular message. We can use these commands to synchronize threads with a drumbeat. Here's an example:

```
in_thread do
  drum_rate = sample_duration :loop_industrial
  drum_rate = drum_rate * 2
  loop_number = 0
  loop do
    loop_number = loop_number + 1
    puts "Loop number " + loop_number.to_s #Displays ↩
        loop number
    cue :cymbals_begin if loop_number == 3
    cue :loop_start
    sample :loop_industrial, rate: 0.5
    sleep drum_rate
  end
end

in_thread do
  sync :cymbals_begin
  4.times do
    sync :loop_start
    sample :elec_cymbal
  end
end
```

In that program, the first thread plays the loop_industrial sample forever. Just before each playback, it sends the message loop_start to all the other threads. Threads can choose to wait until they get that message, and you can use a different message name if you prefer.

It also uses the variable loop_number to keep track of how many times it has repeated its loop. If this is the third repetition, it sends the message cymbals_begin, which is used to cue in the cymbals.

The second thread waits to receive the cymbals_begin message before it does anything else. That means it doesn't play anything until loop_industrial has played two times. Then it plays the elec_cymbal sample four times, synchronized with the start of the loop_industrial sample. The effect is of the drums starting first, and then a cymbal comes in on the first beat in the bar.

You can use this technique to synchronize different samples and synth patterns and build up a piece of music. The following program uses a sample for the drums, two guitar samples, and a synth melody, all in separate threads. They're synchronized with the drumbeat using the cue and sync commands.

```
# Showroom Dummies (minimal)
# Music example from Raspberry Pi For Dummies, 2nd Edition

in_thread do
  drum_rate = sample_duration :loop_industrial
  drum_rate = drum_rate * 2
  loop_number = 0
  loop do
    loop_number = loop_number + 1
    puts "Loop number " + loop_number.to_s #Displays ↵
        loop number
    cue :guit_e_begin if loop_number == 5
    cue :melody_begin if loop_number == 9
    cue :slide_begin if loop_number == 19
    cue :loop_start
    sample :loop_industrial, rate: 0.5
    sleep drum_rate
  end
end

in_thread do
  sync :guit_e_begin
  loop do
    with_fx :distortion do
      sample :guit_e_fifths
    end
    2.times do
      sync :loop_start #Gap before repeating this part
    end
  end
end

in_thread do
  sync :melody_begin
  loop do
    note_pitches = [67, 62, 64, 64, 67, 62, 64, 67, 62]
    note_pitches.each do |note|
      use_synth :saw
      with_fx :wobble do
        play note
        play note-12
      end
      sync :loop_start
    end
    7.times do
      sync :loop_start #Gap before repeating this part
    end
  end
```

```
end

in_thread do
  sync :slide_begin
  loop do
    with_fx :echo do
      sample :guit_e_slide
    end
    4.times do
      sync :loop_start #Gap before repeating this part
    end
  end
end
```

Anything after a # symbol on the same line is a comment, to help you see what the different bits of program do. The guitar samples don't start immediately: The `guit_e_fifths` sample waits until the drum loop has played four times before coming in at the start of the fifth drum loop, and the `guit_e_slide` sample waits until after the synth melody has played before coming in. The effect is of the music gradually building up, but each part of the music starts in sync with the drumbeat because they're all taking their timings from its `cue` command. For an extended version of this music, visit Sean's website at www.sean.co.uk.

This program also introduces a new technique you can use for playing music in Sonic Pi. The notes for the synth to play are stored in an array called `note_pitches`, and a loop plays each note in turn. The following line sets up a loop that goes through the array and takes each item in it in turn and puts it into the variable note:

```
note_pitches.each do |note|
```

If you have a particular melody you want to play and you want to synchronize with a rhythm or do other fancy things with the notes, this code enables you to do that.

We hope that this chapter has inspired you to experiment with making music on the Raspberry Pi. You've learned how to play melodies using different synths. You've also discovered several different ways to create improvised music, using random note numbers, random notes picked from an array, or by converting words into music. We've shown you how to bring it all together, too, combining effects and synth melodies and synchronizing them to a drumbeat. Using the code in this chapter, and the rich range of samples and tools that Sonic Pi provides, you can compose your own music. Whether you like dance, prog, pop, or rock, Sonic Pi deserves to be in your band.

Part V

Exploring Electronics with the Raspberry Pi

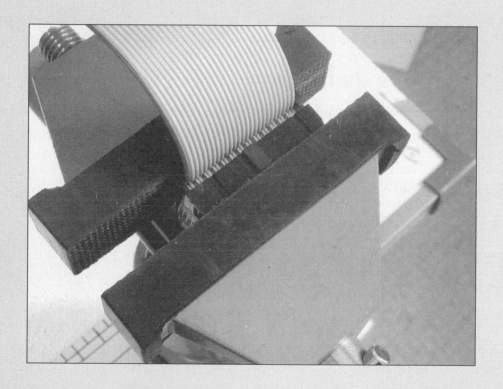

Visit www.dummies.com/extras/raspberrypi to learn about hexadecimal notation on the Raspberry Pi.

In this part . . .

- ✔ Discover the fundamentals of electricity, how to calculate current, and how to solder.

- ✔ Find out how the Raspberry Pi can reach out through its GPIO pins.

- ✔ Use Python and the Raspberry Pi's input pins to build a ball position-sensing maze game.

- ✔ Create the Copycat game by reading inputs and controlling lights.

- ✔ Build the Raspberry Ripple to allow the Raspberry Pi to read and write analog values.

- ✔ Use the Raspberry Ripple to make a curve tracer, drawing generator, music maker, and digital thermometer

Chapter 15

Understanding Circuits and Soldering

*P*art V of this book deals with what is known as *physical computing*, making your program reach out beyond the confines of keyboard and screen, and into the physical world. You discover how to use your Python programming skills to sense what is happening in the outside world and to control lights, motors, and in fact anything else that uses electricity. However, before you can do this safely, without risking damage to you or your Pi, you need to look at a little bit of background electrical theory, so you have a foundation to build on.

In this chapter, we show you the relevant concepts that allow you to understand why the projects look like they do and what you should avoid doing. Next we introduce you to the concept of GPIO connections, explain what they are, and look at why they are included in the Raspberry Pi computer. We also discuss how you can use them.

Although you can make the first project in Chapter 16 without soldering, in order to make most things in electronics, you have to be able to use a soldering iron. We show you how to go about this and discuss safety concerns. Finally, although all the projects in this book can be made without them, we introduce you to the concept of ready-made add-on boards because they make building stuff simpler.

Discovering What a Circuit Is

The first thing you have to understand is that a circuit is something where electricity can flow; it is a path, or a conduit. It is continuous; that is, it's a loop with no dead ends. If you have a dead end, you don't have a circuit. Electricity has to be able to flow. So let's be more specific in what we mean by electricity. There are two aspects of electricity: current and voltage.

Current is what actually flows. *Voltage* is what forces the current round a circuit. Voltage can't flow and current doesn't exist in the absence of a voltage. However, voltage can exist in the absence of current. You've no doubt felt the effects of static electricity, which is the build-up of voltage that occurs when insulators (materials that don't normally conduct electricity) are rubbed together.

It's kind of like how rubbing a balloon on wool can make the hairs on the back of your hand stand up. You can feel it, but only because you feel your hairs being lifted. You aren't feeling the electricity itself. You only feel static electricity when it stops being static and a current flows. At a very high voltage, a little current can hurt a lot. You've probably felt the static discharge shock of touching a metal object after walking over a nylon carpet.

Understanding the nature of electricity

So what is electric current? It is a flow of electrons past a point, just like a flow of cars past a motorway sign. With electric circuits, we measure current in amps. One amp of current is about 6.24×10^{18} electrons per second passing a point, or 624 followed by 16 zeros. That's a big number and fortunately we don't have to count all of those zeroes. The bigger the voltage, the more current is forced through a circuit, but circuits have a property that resists the flow of current. We call this the *resistance* of a circuit. This resistance depends on the materials the circuit is made from and is measured in a unit called *ohms*. So because we know how to define an amp in terms of electron flow, we can define these other two properties in terms of an amp:

One volt is the voltage you need to drive one amp through a circuit with a resistance of one ohm.

You can get a long way in electronics by just knowing that single fact. In fact, that definition is contained in what is known as *Ohm's law*:

```
Volts = Amps × Ohms
```

However, it would be too easy to just use that as a formula. People would understand it straight off and that would never do! You have to build up a mystique. Imagine how you would feel about a doctor if he actually told you in plain English what was wrong with you? No, it needs to be dressed up so not everyone can understand it. Ohm's law becomes

```
E = I x R
```

where E is the electromotive force measured in Volts, I is the current measured in amps, and R is the resistance measured in ohms.

This is the formula you see in books and all over the Internet, but remember — it's just

```
voltage = current x resistance
```

Connecting things to the Raspberry Pi involves juggling voltage and current, and often you need to use a resistor to limit the current a voltage pushes through a device in a circuit. Using Ohm's law is the simple way to work out what you need. In Chapter 17, we show you how to use this to make sure you drive light-emitting diodes (LEDs) correctly.

Resistance is not the only thing we can calculate. If we know two of the quantities in a circuit, we can calculate the other one. We do this by rearranging this simple formula to find any one of the quantities if we know the other two. We like the Ohm's law triangle, which gives the three formulas in one go:

```
E = I x R
I = E / R
R = E / I
```

When scientists were first discovering electricity, they knew that it flowed from one terminal to the other. They said the flow was from the positive to the negative, but which was which? Experiments with making a current flow through a solution of water and copper sulphate showed that copper was dissolved from one wire and deposited on the other. So they quite reasonably assumed that the metal was flowing with the flow of electricity and named the dissolving wire an *anode* or *positive* and the wire receiving the metal the *cathode* or *negative*. They were wrong: The electrons that constitute the current actually flow the other way. However, this notion became so entrenched that today we still use it. We call it *conventional current* and it flows from the positive to the negative.

In a way, it doesn't matter which direction we think of it as flowing. It's the fact that it *is* flowing that is important, and we use the terms *positive* and *negative* so we know what way round it is flowing. Power sources, like batteries and power supplies, are all marked with a positive and negative symbol so you can connect them the correct way. This is known as *direct current (DC)* because the current only flows in one direction.

The other sort of power supply you can get drives the current round in one direction for a short length of time and then reverses the direction for a short time. This is known as *alternating current (AC)*. A favorite trick that electricians play on their apprentices is to send them to the store to fetch the non-existent AC battery.

Switches are used to make or break circuits, so an early name for a switch was a *breaker*.

Putting theory into practice

To see how this works, consider a simple circuit. To make things a bit clearer and easy to draw, we use symbols to represent components and lines to represent wires that connect the components together, as shown in Figure 15-1.

Figure 15-1:
Two circuit symbols representing a switch.

Single-throw switch   Double-throw switch

Take a switch. Its symbol is simple (shown in Figure 15-1). There are two types of switches: single throw and double throw. In the single throw, a connection is made or not made through the switch, depending on the switch position. In the double throw switch, a common connector is connected to one or the other switch contact, depending on the switch's position. That is, when the switch is one way, there is a connection through the switch from one connection to the common connection. When the switch is the other way, the connection is between the other connection and the common connection.

This is called a *double-throw switch*, or sometimes a *changeover switch*, because the switch changes over which terminal is connected to the common one. The figures in this section help explain this. However, the important thing to note is that we use the same symbol for a switch, no matter what the physical switch looks like. Figure 15-2 shows just some of the many physical forms a switch can take.

Figure 15-2:
Just a few
of the many
different
physical
forms a
switch can
take.

Figure 15-3 shows the symbols for a battery, a small flashlight or torch bulb, and a resistor. Note that there are two symbols for a resistor: one for the U.S and one for Europe. In the U.K., we used to use the U.S. symbol until the late 1960s. Today, both are understood.

The world's simplest circuit is shown in Figure 15-4. While the switch is open, there is no complete circuit, and so there is no current flow and no lighting of the bulb.

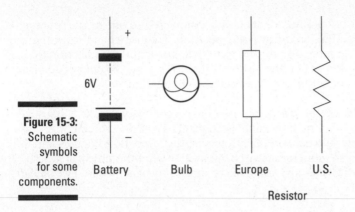

Figure 15-3:
Schematic
symbols
for some
components.

Battery   Bulb   Europe   U.S.

Resistor

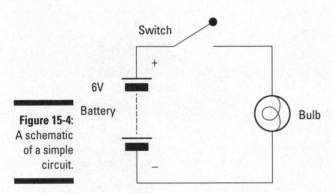

Figure 15-4:
A schematic
of a simple
circuit.

However, when the switch is closed as in Figure 15-5, a path for the current to flow along is created and the bulb lights. Note that this diagram has a different symbol for a closed switch than the one used in Figure 15-4. This is so you can more easily see what is going on. Normally, you have to imagine the switch in the open and closed position and visualize the resulting circuit or break in the circuit. We call this a *series circuit* because all the circuit elements are in a line one after the other, and the same current flows through all elements of the circuit.

So for a circuit like this, there is only one value of current. When the switch is closed, current flows from the positive end of the battery through the switch, through the bulb lighting it up, and finally back into the battery's negative terminal. Note here the actual electrons are returned to the battery. The battery loses energy because it has to push them round the circuit. The positive and negative terminals of a battery show the direction it will push the current, from the positive to the negative. In this circuit with an incandescent light bulb, the direction of the current doesn't matter; however, this is rare in electronics. In most circuits, the current must be sent round the circuit in the right direction.

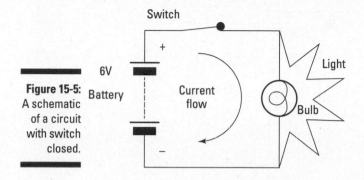

Figure 15-5:
A schematic of a circuit with switch closed.

Communicating a circuit to others

You should use circuit symbols in schematics because they're a universal language and make it easy to see what is going on. Many people waste their time using diagrams that show the physical appearance of components, wires, and their interconnection. Although this might appear at first to be attractive, especially to a beginner, physical layout diagrams like this are almost impossible to follow in all but the most trivial circuits. Despite the initial small hurdle of learning to read the symbols, a schematic is a very much simpler way of defining a circuit. Physical layout diagrams are a dead end for anything more than a trivial circuit and should be avoided.

Some time ago, Mike was visiting Russia and bought his son an electronic construction set. Even though the words were in Russian and incomprehensible to both of them, the diagrams were in the language of schematic and perfectly understandable.

To show the units of resistance, we can use various symbols. We can say 18 ohms, 18 Ω, or, as we use in this book, 18 R.

Although the units for calculation are volts, amps, and ohms, in practice, 1 amp (A) is a lot of current and it's more common to talk of *milliamps* or *mA*. There are 1,000 mA in 1A. Similarly, 1,000 R is one kilohm or 1 K.

Calculating circuit values

Although the circuit shown in Figure 15-5 is all very well because it describes what's actually wired up, it's not useful for calculating anything using Ohm's law because it shows no resistances. However, each real component has associated with it a resistance. We say it has an *equivalent circuit*. These are shown in Figure 15-6. All components, even the wires, have some *series resistance*. In other words, it behaves like it has a resistor in line with the component. Sometimes this is important, and sometimes it is not. The trick is in knowing when to ignore them.

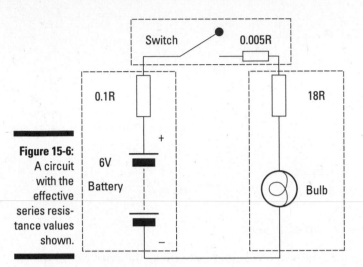

Figure 15-6:
A circuit
with the
effective
series resis-
tance values
shown.

When resistors are placed in series, or in line with each other, you can find the resistance simply by adding up all the individual resistance values. Figure 15-6 shows our circuit with the series resistance values shown. If we add up all the values around the circuit, you get 18R105 (that's 18.105 ohms). Note that virtually all the resistance in the circuit comes from the bulb. The series resistance of the switch is negligible, as is the series resistance of the battery. This is not always the case, as you shall see in Chapter 17. So with 18R resistance and 6V, we can calculate that the current through the circuit should be

```
I = E/R -->
Current = 6/18 = 0.333 Amps or 333mA
```

Determining how a component needs to be treated

So how do we know the series resistance of a component? Well, it is normally in that component's *data sheet,* the document that the manufacturers of all components produce to exactly define the component and its properties. However, it's not always given as a straightforward value. Take a bulb, for instance. This is normally "rated" as a voltage and a current; that is, we would say that the bulb is 6V at 0.33 amps. If we need to know the equivalent resistance, we use Ohm's law. Other bulbs, especially big ones, are given a power rating in watts. Current multiplied by voltage is equal to the power in watts.

The other point is that a bulb doesn't have a constant resistance. We say it's a *nonlinear device*; that is, the resistance changes depending on what current is going through it. This is because a bulb is just a coil of wire. As current passes through it, the wire heats up. This causes the resistance to increase, thus limiting the current. An equilibrium point is reached where the temperature reaches a point where the resistance is such that the current is limited to the design value at the design voltage. We use this concept of a nonlinear resistance in Chapter 17 when we come to calculate what resistor we need to use with an LED.

When dealing with units like volts and ohms that include a decimal point, often the point is missed out and the letter of the unit is substituted, so 3.3 volts becomes 3V3, or 4.7K becomes 4K7. This is done to make it clear there is a decimal point that otherwise might be lost in small print.

The series resistance of a battery, or any power supply for that matter, is an important concept in that it limits the current that the battery can deliver. This is all wrapped up in the chemistry of the battery, but its effects can be summed up by a theoretical series resistance. A battery that can deliver a lot of current has a low series resistance. This is sometimes known as the *output impedance* of the battery.

Now these concepts may seem like they are nothing to do with the Raspberry Pi, but as you shall see in later chapters, these concepts are the ones you need to get the Pi to interact to the world outside the keyboard and screen.

Testing circuits with simulators

Nowadays there are circuit simulators that allow you to test a circuit before you build it. This is a great idea to make sure you are not doing anything silly. However, some simulators have a steep learning curve and others use ideal components instead of real ones. This can give some misleading results with simple circuits, but on the whole they are a very good idea. One simulator written especially for the Raspberry Pi is free. Find out more at www. raspberrypi.org/archives/1917.

Getting Familiar with the GPIO

The Raspberry Pi was made from a BCM2835 system on a chip. Unlike traditional microprocessors, these are designed to be used in an embedded system. An *embedded system* has a computer inside it, but you don't use it as a computer — things like mobile phones, media players, and set-top boxes.

These chips have a number of connections to them in order for the software in them to control things like push buttons, displays, and getting sound in and out. The BCM2835 has 54 such signals. They are called General Purpose Input/Output pins (GPIO) and they can be controlled by software. Some of these signals are used to build and control the peripheral devices that turn the BCM2835 into a computer, like the SD card reader, the USB, and the Ethernet. The rest are free — that is, not needed to make the Pi — so they are surplus to requirements.

Rather than just ignore them, the designers of the Raspberry Pi have routed some of these surplus GPIO lines out of the chip and to the connector called P1 on the board for us to play with. It's a bonus. This sets the Pi apart from mainstream computers in this respect. However, they have not routed all the spare pins out to this connector. Some go to other connectors like the camera socket and some are not even connected to anything at all. This is because the BCM2835 is in a ball grid array (BGA) package with connections less than a millimeter apart. So close are they that you can only have enough room for one trace (PCB wire) between the connectors.

This means that to get some of the inner connections out to other components, you have to use a printed circuit board (PCB) that has a number of extra layers of wiring inside the board. You might think the Pi's board has just a top side and underside, but in fact it is made from several boards sandwiched together to create six layers of wiring.

Even with this many layers, there is not enough room to route out all 54 GPIO signals. Adding more layers would significantly increase the price of the PCB and make our bonus cost something instead of being free. You are no doubt aware that the price point of the Pi is one of its major features. However, over successive hardware revisions, an increasing number of these pins have been brought out to use. There were 17 on the original board, revision 2 saw some rearrangement and another socket bring the total to 21. Finally the Model B+, being revision 3, saw this increase to 28, all on one 40-pin header. This still leaves 8 GPIO pins not routed out or used internally on the board. The Raspberry Pi foundation has announced that the Model B+ represents the last revision of this product. You see exactly where these signals are brought out physically in the next chapter.

Putting the general purpose in GPIO

GPIO pins are called *general purpose* because we can use them for anything we want under the control of a program. They're called *input/output* pins because the software can configure them to be either an input or an output. When a pin is an input, the program can read whether this has a high voltage or a low voltage put on the pin. When the pin is an output, the program can control whether a high voltage or low voltage appears on that pin. In addition, many pins have one or more superpowers, or alternative functions as a secret identity, like so many comic book heroes. These powers are not shared by all pins, but are specialist functions able to do things without software intervention. They are ways to tap directly deep into the computer's inner workings. When we switch to these functions, they stop being general-purpose pins and do a specific job. For example, one pin can be used to output a continuous stream of high and low voltage levels, that, after they get going, continue without any further intervention from the program. So if you connect that pin to a speaker or amplifier, you can generate a tone that keeps on sounding until you command it to stop.

However, for the moment, just take a look at the GPIO function of these pins.

Understanding what GPIOs do

GPIOs are the gateway to interaction with the outside world and in essence are quite simple.

Figure 15-7 shows the equivalent circuit of a Raspberry Pi GPIO pin when it is configured as an output. You can see it is simply a double throw switch that can be connected between the computer's power supply of 3V3 or ground (that's 0V). This is sometimes called the *common point* or *reference*, and is the basis of all measurements in a circuit. Basically, it's the other end of the battery — the negative terminal, if you will. Between this switch and the output is in effect a series resistor, one that is in line with the voltage coming from the Pi. It limits the current you can get through the output pin.

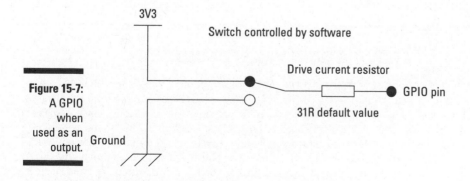

Figure 15-7:
A GPIO when used as an output.

On the Pi, the value of this resistor can be changed over a limited range. The default value is 31R, but note that this resistor, by itself, is insufficient to protect the Pi from giving too much current if you connect it to too low a resistance load. So an output pin can switch between only two voltages — 0V and 3V3. These are known as *logic levels* and they have a number of names: *high and low, true and false, zero and one,* and even *up and down.*

Although the logic voltages levels on the Pi are simple, the current that these outputs can supply is more complex, with a current limit of about 16mA. This limit is how much current the Pi *should* supply into a load, not how much it can supply or *will* supply. That depends on the resistance of the load connected to the pin. Now I say the limit is about 16mA, but this is a bit of a gray area. This value is considered safe for the Pi to supply, but that is not to say a value of 17mA would be considered dangerous or excessive.

Putting an output pin to practical use

So what can you do with a switched output? Well, you can drive a small current through a load, or you can control another device that can control a bigger current through a load. Put like that, it doesn't sound exciting, but it's what physical computing is all about. The load can be a light, a motor, a solenoid (an electromagnetic plunger used to prod or strike things), or anything that uses electricity. As that includes most everything in the modern world, it is safe to say that if it uses electricity, it can be controlled.

Take a look at controlling a light, not the current-heavy light bulb we looked at earlier, but a component known as a light-emitting diode (LED). These can light up from just a tiny bit of current and the 16mA we have available is more than enough. In fact, you're going to limit the current to less than 10mA by adding a 330R series resistor. Why this value? Well, you see exactly how to calculate this value in Chapter 17.

Finding a safe value of current

There *is* a value of current that would instantly destroy at least the output circuitry of the pin, if not the whole Pi itself. But, there is *also* a value of current that would not instantly kill the Pi but would damage the circuitry and lead it to fail prematurely. Lower that current, and the damage is lowered, until you get to a point where no damage occurs. However, these values are not known for the chip used on the Pi. In fact, they are not known for the vast majority of chips. It's best to stick to the "safe" value or lower.

Beware of people who say that they have a circuit that takes 30mA or more from a pin and it's still working. They tend to be naive people who confuse whether a pin is dead yet with whether a pin is safe. It's just like smoking: You can do it and it doesn't kill you immediately, but it does do harm and eventually it can kill, if nothing else gets you first. No one would pretend that it's safe.

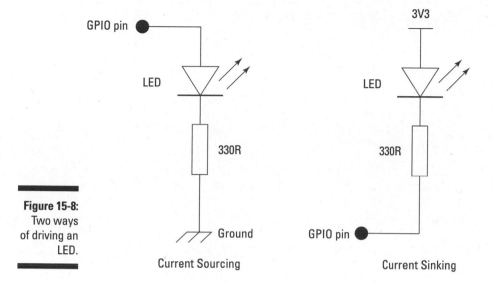

Figure 15-8:
Two ways
of driving an
LED.

For the moment, just look at the circuit in Figure 15-8. This shows two ways to wire up an LED, or any other load, directly to a GPIO pin. Here we just show the GPIO pin and not the equivalent series resistance of the power source as discussed earlier — in the context of a 330R resistor, 31R is negligible.

The first way to wire it is called *current sourcing* and is perhaps the way a beginner might think of as natural. When the GPIO pin is set by the program to produce a high voltage (that is, set the switch to connect the 3V3 line to the output pin), current flows from the pin through the LED, through the resistor and to ground, thus completing the circuit, causing current to flow and so lighting up the LED. When the GPIO pin is set by the program to produce a low voltage (that is, set the switch to connect the 0V or ground line to the output pin), no current flows and the LED is not lit. This method is known as *current sourcing* because the source of the current, the positive connection of the power, is the GPIO pin.

The second way of wiring, also shown in Figure 15-8, is known as *current sinking*. When the GPIO pin is set by the program to produce a low voltage, the current flows through the LED, through the resistor, and to ground, through the GPIO pin. To turn the LED off, set the output to a high voltage. There's no way current can flow round the circuit because both ends of the load (LED and resistor) are connected to 3V3, so there is no voltage difference to push the current through the components.

Note in both circuits the position of the resistor and LED can be interchanged — it makes no difference. You might like to think of these two approaches as switching the plus and switching the ground. More of this when you do some real projects in Chapters 17 and 18.

Using GPIOs as inputs

The other basic mode of operation for a GPIO pin is as an input. In this case, you don't have to worry about the current because when the pin is an input, it has a very high input impedance, or a high value of series resistance. A *resistance* is a special form of impedance, which, as its name implies, impedes the flow of electricity. There is a bit more to impedance than simple resistance, but at this stage, you can think of them as the same sort of thing. They are both measured in ohms.

Resistance is the property of a material, whereas impedance is the property of a circuit and includes how it behaves with AC as well as DC. So an input pin has a very high impedance. It hardly allows any current to flow through it, so much so that we can connect it directly to either 0V or 3V3 directly without any extra resistors at all. In fact, an input is so high-impedance that if you just leave it unconnected, it picks up very tiny radio waves and other forms of interference and gives random values when you try to read it.

In fact, the human body can act as an antenna when close to or touching a high-impedance input, causing any readings to go wild. This often amazes beginners, who think that they have discovered something mysterious. They haven't. In fact, the tiny amounts of energy in the radio waves that are all around us are not absorbed by the high-impedance circuits as they would be by low-impedance circuits. A low impedance would cause current to flow, but it would easily absorb all the power, leaving minuscule amounts of voltage. Just the fact that you have a wire carrying AC power (mains) close by is enough for that wire to radiate radio wave interference.

To explain why this is, consider that interference of, say, 2V is enough to override the signal from a chip and cause it to malfunction. With a low resistance, say 1K, in order to develop 2V across, it needs to have a current of 2mA (Ohm's law) flowing through it. This represents a power (volts×current) of I×V=4mW of interference. However, with a resistance of 1M, you can get 2V across it by only having 2uA flowing through it. This represents a power of 4uW. So a high resistance is much more sensitive to interference because it requires less power from the interfering source to develop the same voltage. Therefore weaker fields produce enough interfering voltage to disrupt a circuit.

This underlines an important thing with inputs: They can't just be left alone. They must be driven to one voltage state or the other; that is, either 3V3 known as high, or 0V known as low. If you connect an input to the output from some other chip, that's fine, but if you want to detect whether a switch is made or broken, you have to give the input pin some help. This is normally done with a resistor connected from the input to either the 3V3 or the ground.

When a resistor is used in this way, it's called a *pull-up* or *pull-down* resistor, as shown in Figure 15-9. Of the two arrangements, a pull-up is preferable, mainly because switches are normally on the end of long runs of wire and it is safer to have a ground than a 3V3 voltage on a wire. This is because it tends to cause less damage if you accidentally connect a ground wire to the wrong place rather than to a power wire. This arrangement of pull-up or pull-down resistors is so common that the computer processor in the Pi has them built-in, and there is a software method for connecting or enabling internal pull-up or pull-down resistors. We show you in Chapter 16 how to control this from software.

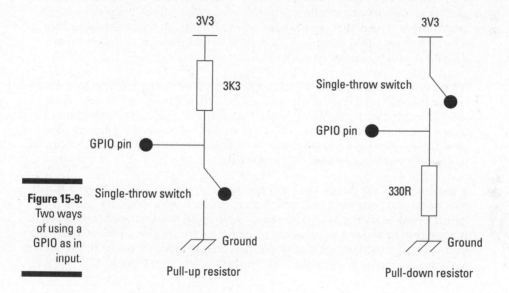

Figure 15-9: Two ways of using a GPIO as in input.

Learning which end is hot: Coming to grips with a soldering iron

Although you can do some interfacing without resorting to the soldering iron to join components together, to get serious, you'll have to do some soldering at some stage or the other. This often induces fear and panic in the newcomer, but even a child can solder successfully. In fact, Mike had his first soldering iron at the age of nine and by and large taught himself. Soldering involves two parts, the *solder*, which is an alloy of two or more metals, and the *flux*, a chemical cleaning agent. If you are soldering something like a gas pipe, you would apply the flux round the joint, heat the joint up with a blow torch, and apply the rod of solder to the hot joint. The job of the flux when it is heated is to clean the surface and make the solder flow. It does this by breaking down the surface tension on the molten solder. Without it, the solder would clump together in round globs held by the tight surface tension.

Water has surface tension as well, and to reduce that we use soap, which allows the water to wet things. You can't use soap with solder because it wouldn't stand the heat, so you need something else. Most fluxes for heavy jobs are made from nasty chemicals like hydrochloric acid, or phosphoric acid. These are too corrosive to be used with electronics, so what is normally used is some sort of rosin flux. Although you can get this in a pot, by far the best thing is to use Multicore solder, where the flux is built into the solder wire as five very thin strands. That way, the right amount of flux is always delivered with whatever amount of solder you use.

We recommend using a good quality 60/40 tin/lead solder alloy, with a diameter of 0.7mm and a built-in rosin-based flux core. Anything else is making life difficult for yourself. We've found that solders with self-cleaning fluxes or non-fuming fluxes are harder to work with, as well as being more expensive. Couple the right kind of solder with a good soldering iron, preferably a temperature-controlled one with a fine tip.

It is often said that you can use any old tool to learn on, and then get a good tool when you get good at using it. This is rubbish. As a beginner, you are fighting how to do the job, so you don't want to be fighting your tools as well. A good iron includes a stand and a place for a sponge. Use a proper soldering iron sponge, a natural one that won't melt on contact with the iron. Do not use a plastic foam sponge because your iron will go straight through it.

Making a soldered joint

The first thing you should do when making a soldered joint is to make a mechanical joint. For example, if you're joining two wires together, bend each end into a hook and squeeze together lightly with your pliers.

Wipe the tip of the iron on a damp sponge and melt just a spot of solder on the tip. This wets the tip and allows good thermal contact to take place between the tip and the work. Then apply the iron, solder, and wires all together. The secret is then to look at the joint and the solder closely and how it sits. Remove the solder, but keep the iron on the joint until you see the solder flow around the joint and see it seep into the cracks. Only then is the joint hot enough for you to withdraw your iron. It is a quick process and needs a bit of practice.

Complying with environmental regulations

There is a further complication nowadays with the advent of the Reduction of Hazardous Substances (RoHS), which bans the use of certain metals and plasticizers in certain classes of electrical equipment in the E.U., the most prominent of which is lead. In fact, some people think RoHS is entirely about being lead-free, but it's not. You can get lead-free solders, but they are expensive because they have a large amount of silver in them, and they are difficult to work with. Also, they tend to produce a product with a shorter lifetime. They require a hotter iron and so are potentially more harmful to the components.

They also don't wet as well, which means they don't flow around the joint as well. Tin whiskers often grow out of the joints, causing shorts years later. Home-built electronics are not required to be lead free in the U.S. or Europe and there is no measurable health effect in using solder that contains lead. RoHS was mainly brought in to stop lead accumulating in landfill sites from mass consumer electronics and potentially polluting the water supply, although there is no evidence that this happens. In Europe, you are under no legal or health requirements to use lead-free solder. If you start making stuff to sell in the E.U., however, you're legally required to make sure it's RoHS-compliant. This is like home brewing: You can brew as much as you like, but you can't sell any. It's always sensible to wash your hands after soldering and avoid putting solder in your mouth. The same goes for the soldering iron when it is on.

Many beginners make the mistake of putting too much solder on a joint. Try to use as little solder as possible. A joint is rarely bad because of too little solder, but it's often bad because of too much. When you are done, you see a small amount of black flux residue around the iron tip. Wipe that away on a damp sponge before returning the iron to its stand. Do not move the joint as the solder sets. A good quality iron is ready immediately for the next joint. A poor iron needs a few seconds to come up to temperature.

Using some sort of fume extractor when soldering is a good idea. A simple fan works to guide the curl of smoke from the iron away from your face. Air currents from the warmth of your body tend to attract the flux. Try not to breathe it in. This is more important as you spend a long time (hours at a time) with a soldering iron in your hand. The fumes are from the flux in the solder; they are not lead fumes.

Although Chapter 16 contains a project that can be made without the use of a soldering iron, such projects are few and far between. The last two chapters of this Part contain projects for which you definitely need to be able to solder.

Looking at Ready-Made Add-On Boards

Many ready-made interface boards are available for the Raspberry Pi. These are designed to make things easier for you to do by building part of the circuits for you. They range from simply providing easier access to the GPIO pins, to including small sub circuits, to giving the Pi more inputs and outputs, or to performing special functions not available on the Pi directly, like being able to control the brightness of many LEDs. You can always incorporate these sub-circuits into your projects when you need them, but these boards provide a shortcut to some projects by building them for you.

However, note that they are not essential and can be an expensive way of doing a project, mainly because they often contain more capabilities than you actually need for any one project. If you want to break up your project after you have finished it, you get value from these boards, but if you want to keep your projects and plug them in at any time to show others, you're better off just building what you need. Dedicating a board to a project is an expensive way of doing things. All the projects in later chapters of this book are self-contained and do not require any third-party boards. However, some offer convenience that might be attractive to some people. New boards are constantly being developed and produced. In the next sections, we look at a few.

The Gert board

The Gert board is the granddaddy of expansion boards. It is the closest thing there is to an official Raspberry Pi interface because it's designed by Gert van Loo, one of the Pi's design team. It is not a Pi Foundation product. It is a compressive collection of interfaces, including an Arduino-like processor. The Arduino is a standalone controller very popular with artists and engineers alike, it is superficially like a Raspberry Pi but is fundamentally a very different beast. It's better than the Pi at doing things that require very quick responses and accurate timing, but it has no display and can only be programmed in C++. The Pi and the Arduino can work quite well together and so Gert has included one of these processors on his board. The board is designed for education, to give a flavor of different types of interfacing techniques. Basically, it's a ready-built board you simply plug into the Pi. Its features are

- Twelve I/O ports buffered through 74HC244, each with an LED
- Three push buttons
- MCP4802: Two channel 8-bit D/A converter
- ULN2803A: Six open collector channels up to 50V ~80ma/channel

⮑ ATmega328P: Atmel®AVR® 8-bit microcontroller (Arduino)

⮑ L6203: 48V 4A motor controller

⮑ 780xx 3V3 low drop-out voltage regulator

It also contains the printed circuit board and the headers, jumpers, straps, flat cable, and sockets to connect to the Pi. It would take a whole book to describe what all these features are and how to use them.

It's very improbable that any one project would need all these features and it's probably too advanced for the average beginner. But as you begin to explore this subject beyond what we can cover in this book, you might want to look at it.

The best thing about the Gert is that the manuals are downloadable, so you can see in advance what you are letting yourself in for. You can read all about it and find the manuals' download links at `www.raspberrypi.org/archives/1734`.

Pi Face

The Pi Face board is designed by a team at the School of Computing Science at the University of Manchester (U.K.) and is aimed at the education market. It is roughly the same price as the Gert board, but comes ready-assembled. It is much less ambitious in scope but contains a good mix of things you would actually need for many simple projects. These include onboard LEDs and push-button switches for simple interaction along with two relays (physical switches moved by an electromagnet) for switching large currents. There are eight protected inputs and eight buffered outputs and the whole thing has screw connection access to connect it to the outside world. You can download a comprehensive list of documents and examples from Google Documents at `https://github.com/piface` and follow some of the new projects using the board from `www.raspberrypi.org/archives/tag/pi-face`. If you're curious about doing projects using Pi Face, check out the book *Raspberry Pi Projects* by Dr. Andrew Robinson (published by Wiley).

Other boards

There are many other boards from small start-up manufacturers as well as web-based projects for you to build. You can find a good starting point for information on many of these at `http://elinux.org/RPi_Expansion_Boards`.

Tipping your HAT

There is a standard way of attaching boards to the Raspberry Pi known as a HAT board. HAT stands for Hardware Attached on Top, and is applicable only to the model B+ of the Raspberry Pi. This board has to meet certian criteria to qualify it as being a HAT. One of which is that it has to have a small read-only memory chip on it to allow the Raspberry Pi to know what GPIO pins are being used so that they are configured during boot-up, load any required drivers, and prevent any possible pin usage conflicts. Read more about HATs at www.raspberrypi.org/introducing-raspberry-pi-hats/.

Chapter 16

Making Your First Project with the Raspberry Pi

In This Chapter

▶ Discovering how to get at the GPIO pins

▶ Making a breakout board

▶ Figuring out how to read inputs in software

▶ Creating your first physical computing project: the Blastoff game

▶ Customizing your Blastoff game

*I*n Chapter 15, we cover the GPIO (General Purpose Input/Output) signals on the Raspberry Pi and show you the sorts of things they could do. In this chapter, we help you use that knowledge to create your own unique game, all without needing to use a soldering iron. We talk about how you can define the rules of your game and control exactly how it operates. Along the way, we show you how to build a solder-less breakout board so you can access the GPIO pins for the project in this chapter and the others in this book.

Bringing a project to life through software is an important part of physical computing. In this chapter, you see how the software and hardware are intimately connected.

Getting Started with the Blastoff Project

For your first project, we show you how to make a Blastoff game. This is a marble maze game where you have to visit six locations in the correct order to blast off the rocket. Each location is one stage in the countdown, and the Raspberry Pi shouts out the countdown number as you progress. If you do not visit the locations in the correct order or if you hit the end stops, the countdown aborts and you have to start again.

The game is played with a metallic marble or ball bearing in a sealed box, and you move the marble about by tilting the box. At various locations or traps in the box, the marble electrically connects two contacts together. This allows the Raspberry Pi to sense the location of the marble through the GPIO pins we look at in Chapter 15. It is a game of dexterity and manual skill, with the Raspberry Pi keeping track of the countdown progress.

It is a blend of the old and the new with youngsters, oldsters, and game-savvy kids all having an equal chance of success.

You need to connect this game to the P1 connector of the Raspberry Pi. There are two ways you can do this, as a 28-way connector (this is suitable to use on all Raspberry Pi revisions), and a 40-way connector (this will only work with the model B+). You can make a 26-way version for the B+, but to do this, you will need to use a 40-way socket even if you don't use the extra connections. For this first project, we've devised a way to do this (and in fact, build the whole game) without a soldering iron. Typical workshop hand tools are required to build the game and you have plenty of scope for making your own unique variations, which allows you to produce a one-of-a-kind product.

If you want to flip ahead and see our take on the game, look at Figure 16-26 later in this chapter. We're sure you will be able to put your own ideas into this.

Here is a list of the parts you'll need for the breakout board 26-pin version:

- 1 26-way 0.05" (1.27mm) pitch IDC (insulation displacement connector) socket — use a 40-way connector if you have a B+

- 2 13-way screw terminal blocks

- 1 4 1/2" (110mm) by 3" (80mm) 1/4" (6mm) plywood

- 8 6BA (M2.5) – 5/8" (15mm) long countersunk machine screws

- 8 6BA (M2.5) hexagonal nuts

- 2' 26-way ribbon cable

Here is a list of the parts you'll need for the breakout board 40-pin B+ only version:

- 1 40-way 0.05" (1.27mm) pitch IDC (insulation displacement connector) socket

- 4 13-way screw terminal blocks

- 1 4 1/2" (110mm) by 5" (80mm) 1/4" (6mm) plywood

- 8 6BA (M2.5) – 5/8" (15mm) long countersunk machine screws

- 8 6BA (M2.5) hexagonal nuts

- 2' 40-way ribbon cable

Here are the parts you'll need for the Blastoff game:

- 1 3/4" or 15mm ball bearing
- 2' of self-adhesive copper foil
- 2 8" (200mm) squares 1/4" (6mm) plywood
- 1 8" (200mm) square 3/16" (4mm) acrylic sheet (Plexiglas or Perspex)
- 1 8" (200mm) square 3/32" (2mm) black foam plastic sheet
- 3' (900mm) of 13/32" (10mm) by 3/16" (5mm) strip pine
- 3' (900mm) of 11/16" (17mm) by 3/16" (5mm) strip pine
- 4 3/4" (20mm) 4BA (M3) tapped brass hexagonal pillars or spacers
- 4 3/8" (10mm) 4BA (M3) tapped brass hexagonal pillars or spacers
- 4 1/2" (6mm) 4BA (M3) studding
- 22 6BA (M2.5) – 3/4" (20mm) long countersunk machine screws
- 44 6BA (M2.5) hexagonal nuts
- 22 6BA (M2.5) washers
- 2' 26-way ribbon cable
- 1 packet of space-themed stickers

Getting at the GPIO Pins

GPIO connections are the way for the outside world to get into your Raspberry Pi. In this chapter, we concentrate on using them for inputs only. In Chapter 17, we cover using them for outputs as well. Most of the GPIO lines on the Raspberry Pi power up as floating inputs. That means inputs not connected to anything else; in other words, they are high-impedance inputs. The exceptions are GPIO pins 14 and 15. These are used on boot-up for outputting data to a serial terminal. Notwithstanding this, these pins can simply be changed back into an input. Also the I2C bus lines have strong external pull-up resistors fitted to the board.

The bulk of the free GPIO pins appear on one connector — the double row connector along the top-left edge of the board (assuming you hold it so the writing is the right way up). It's called P1, which stands for *plug one*. It's a plug because it has male connections. Female connections are called *sockets* and there are a few of those on the board as well. In the Model B+, this has two rows of 20 pins. On the other revisions, this has two rows of 13 pins.

A word about the cost of parts

Modern consumer electronics and even the Raspberry Pi itself have left people with an unrealistic expectation of how much components cost. Electronic components and tools can seem expensive when you buy then in very small quantities. Manufacturers regard 10,000 units of something as a small quantity, so to get what you need, you will have to buy stuff through distributors and small suppliers. The economies of scale matter. You can buy an iPad much cheaper than you could buy the individual parts to make one, for example. When dealing with small numbers, postage is often a large fraction of the cost, so when you do buy parts and have them shipped to you, always get a spare or two and build up your own stock. Some parts only come in reels, giving you much more that you would ever need. Those are great opportunities for group purchasing, or for entrepreneurs to sell buyers only the quantity they need.

Two ways exist of numbering the pins on a component in electronics. One way is to start at one corner and number the pins in an anti-clockwise (counterclockwise) direction all the way round. This is universally done with integrated circuits (ICs). The other way of numbering pins is to have them alternating from side to side, so that one side has all the odd number pins and the other all the even numbers. This is done mainly with plugs and sockets, especially those with two rows. This is the case with P1 on the Raspberry Pi: It has a row of odd-numbered pins and row of even-numbered ones. To refer to a physical pin on this plug, you give it the plug name followed by the number. For example, pin 6 on this plug would be described as P1-06. (Numbers less than ten have a leading zero.)

Being aware of Raspberry Pi board revisions

There are three board revisions of the Pi, with the GPIO signals going to different pins on P1. The GPIO signals on pins P1-03, P1-05, and P1-13 are different on the first two board revisions. The Model B+, the third revision, has the first 26 pins on P1 identical to the revision 2. In addition, there are another 14 pins carrying some extra GPIO signals. All the projects in this book can be done with any of the board revisions. Any pins that were different in the revision 1 board are shown in brackets.

Figure 16-1 shows the signals on P1 for all revision of the Raspberry Pi. It shows a 5V and 3V3 power connection, along with a GND or ground connection. The other pins are labeled with the names of the GPIO signals they are attached to. Note that pin 2 is the pin closest to the corner of the printed circuit board. Figure 16-2 shows a photograph of a Model B+ board with the pins labeled.

Issue 1

	3V3	1	○ ○	2	5V	
GPIO 0	GPIO 2	3	○ ○	4	5V	
GPIO 1	GPIO 3	5	○ ○	6	Gnd	
	GPIO 4	7	○ ○	8	GPIO 14	
	Gnd	9	○ ○	10	GPIO 15	
	GPIO 17	11	○ ○	12	GPIO 18	
GPIO 21	GPIO 27	13	○ ○	14	Gnd	
	GPIO 22	15	○ ○	16	GPIO 23	
	3V3	17	○ ○	18	GPIO 24	
	GPIO 10	19	○ ○	20	Gnd	
	GPIO 9	21	○ ○	22	GPIO 25	
	GPIO 11	23	○ ○	24	GPIO 8	
	Gnd	25	○ ○	26	GPIO 7	
	ID_SD	27	○ ○	28	ID_SC	
	GPIO 5	29	○ ○	30	Gnd	
	GPIO 6	31	○ ○	32	GPIO 12	
	GPIO 13	33	○ ○	34	Gnd	
	GPIO 19	35	○ ○	36	GPIO 16	
	GPIO 26	37	○ ○	38	GPIO 20	
	Gnd	39	○ ○	40	GPIO 21	

Issue 1 and 2

Model B+

Figure 16-1: Connector P1 on all revisions of Raspberry Pi.

ID_SD = GPIO 0

ID_SC = GPIO 1   But only use for identification EEPROM

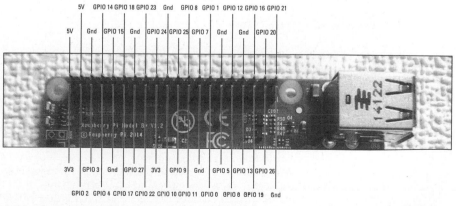

Figure 16-2: Connector P1 on a Model B+ board.

5V   GPIO 14 GPIO 18 GPIO 23   Gnd   GPIO 8 GPIO 1   GPIO 12 GPIO 16 GPIO 21

5V   Gnd   GPIO 15   Gnd   GPIO 24 GPIO 25 GPIO 7   Gnd   Gnd   GPIO 20

3V3   GPIO 3   Gnd   GPIO 27   3V3   GPIO 9   Gnd   GPIO 5 GPIO 13 GPIO 26

GPIO 2   GPIO 4   GPIO 17 GPIO 22 GPIO 10 GPIO 11   GPIO 0   GPIO 8   GPIO 19   Gnd

The Model B+ has 40 pins and many 26-way connectors will simply fit on the first 26 pins of this. Make sure, however, that the connector is aligned to the first row of pins and is not shifted over. A good way to check is to count the number of free pins over at the end — this should be seven. You should not connect anything to the Raspberry Pi when the system is powered up. Unfortunately, the solderless type of connector we are going to use for this project requires a bit of extra space at each side of the plug. This is fine for a 26-way connector fitting on the 26-way plug or the 40-way plug fitting on the B+, but a 26-way connector of the type we are going to use will not fit on the 40-way socket unless you cut off pins 27 and 28 from the P1 connector. Although this is possible, it's not recommended as you lose access to the auto configure pins that are used on HAT (Hardware Attached to Top) standard boards, and we suggest you use a 40-way connector if you are making this project with the B+, even if you only use 26-way cable.

Making the connection

The two main ways of making a connection to P1 is to use either individual *patch wires* or a multi-way connector. Patch wires, or *jumper wires*, come in two types, male and female. What you want here is a female-to-male wire: They have a crimped socket on one end, a single plug on the other, and are covered in heat-shrink sleeving (tubing). If you want to solder them to a board, get the female-to-female sort and cut them in half, giving you two for the price of one. However, these are a bit fiddly to get into the right place, especially if you are using more than four or five connections, so using a multi-way socket is usually best.

Two types of multi-way sockets fit the sort of connector used in P1 — these have solder connections or insulation displacement connections (IDC). Although IDC sockets are slightly more expensive, they are extremely easy to use and very quick to make up. The trick is that an IDC uses a ribbon cable, named not after the World War I German flying ace Baron von Ribbon Cable, but after the fact that it is cable, but it looks like a ribbon.

Ribbon cable is a number of wires molded together in a flat strip. It comes in various widths, and wide ribbon cable is easily split down into the exact size you need. However, you can get the exact size needed for this project: 26-way or 40-way ribbon of 0.05" (1.27mm) pitch. This pitch is the most common type. It comes in two types, multicolored rainbow or gray. With the multicolored cable, or hippie cable as it is sometimes called, each strand is one of ten colors corresponding to the number/color matching of the resistor color code. The gray cable is quite a bit cheaper than the multicolored and has just one end wire colored red for reference. The electricity does not care what color wire it flows down, so we recommend using the gray.

Making a Breakout Board

A *breakout board* is a device that allows you to easily make connections to an electrical component. It is necessary because sometimes connections to modern electronic devices are small or difficult to access. Here we want to access the GPIO signals of the Raspberry Pi, but the multiway connector makes this a bit tricky. In order to make connections to it more easily, we are going to construct a breakout board that will allow us to connect circuits to the Raspberry Pi using just screw connectors, no soldering involved. You can then use this board to simply attach your projects. The one we show you how to make now has its connections in exactly the same pattern as the P1 connector. You are going to make a breakout board based on an IDC connector and some connection block strips. There are two versions you could make, one with a 26-way connector suitable for all versions of the Raspberry Pi, and one with a 40-way version suitable for the Model B+ only. Figures 16-4 and 16-5 and Figures 16-7 to 16-10, along with Figure 16-12, show the 26-way version. Figures 16-6 and 16-11 show the changes you need for the 40-way version as well. Note that if you are making a 26-way version for the Model B+, you will still need to use a 40-way connector but only put 26-way ribbon cable into it.

Connection block, or *chock block* as it is sometimes called, is normally used for connecting domestic AC wiring and comes in various sizes. You want the smallest you can get, which is normally the 3 amp sort. You can buy it in a thrift shop (or a pound shop in the U.K.) very cheaply. They come in strips of 12 connections, which is a pity because we need two strips of 13. However, you can easily cut them with a hobby knife. Cut your connection blocks into two strips of 9 and two strips of 4 for the 26-way version, or four strips of 10 for the 40-way version. This is to ensure you have sufficient mounting holes to attach it to a board.

Get a piece of plywood 80×110mm (3"×4 1/2") or (5"×4 1/2") for the 40-way version and mark the position of two mounting holes in each strip so that the strips are approximately 5mm (1/4") apart. Then drill two 2.5mm (1/8") holes and countersink the back. (If you want to make a proper job of this, give the board three layers of medium oak staining varnish and lightly rub it down between coats.)

Now attach two sections of the connector blocks in a line on the board with some 15mm M2.5 countersunk screw and nuts (5/8" 6BA). The nuts just fit between the soft plastic connections. Next, you need to make the cable to attach the board to the Raspberry Pi.

Creating the cable

The way insulation displacement ribbon cable works is that sharp forks in the socket cut through the insulation and make contact with the wire inside. The connector and cable are held together by clips in the plug. Mounting a socket on a piece of ribbon cable is a one-time event. It's not easy to remove the cable and make the joint again, so you need to make sure you have the right length of cable and that the socket is the right way around the first time.

On one end of the socket is a small triangular mark, as shown in Figure 16-3. This shows the location of pin 1 — you usually connect this to the red end of the wire. Feed the ribbon cable into the socket with the polarizing bump or key (if any) pointing toward you. Put it in a vise, as shown in Figure 16-4, but don't tighten it yet. Make sure the cable is at right angles to the socket, and then slowly tighten the vise until you can see you are not squashing it up any more. Then remove it from the vise, fold the cable over the socket, and clip in the strain relief clip to make the cable end look like it is shown in Figure 16-5.

Pin 1

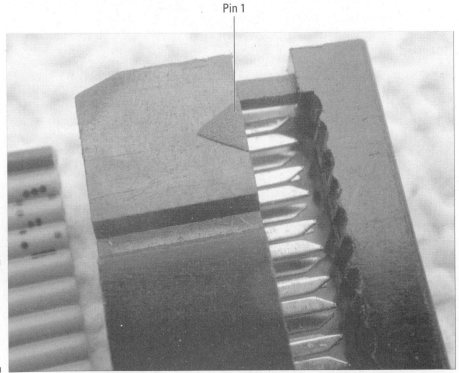

Figure 16-3:
An IDC connector with a triangle marking pin 1.

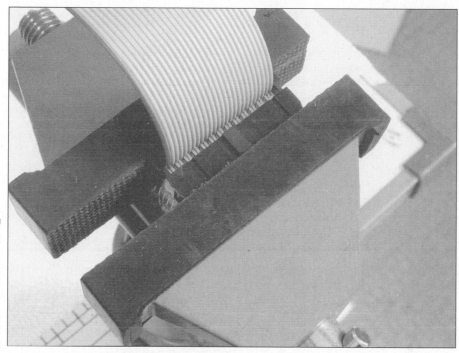

Figure 16-4:
An IDC con-
nector and
ribbon cable
in a vise
ready to be
squeezed.

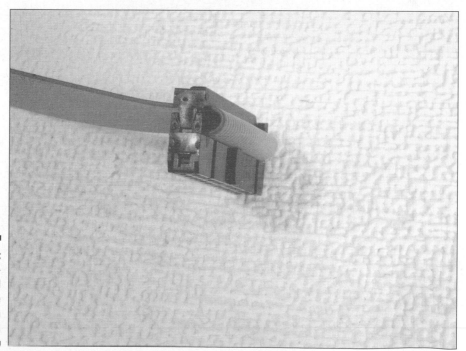

Figure 16-5:
An IDC con-
nector and
ribbon cable
with a strain
relief clip.

Wiring the cable

The connections you've made to P1 are shown in Figure 16-6. Now to prepare the cable, nick the insulation between the wires with a sharp knife, and separate the strands by pulling them back, as shown in Figure 16-7. Next, strip the insulation off of the last 10mm (1/2") or so of the wire, and then take the strands of wire between finger and thumb and twist the strands together, leaving no free whiskers.

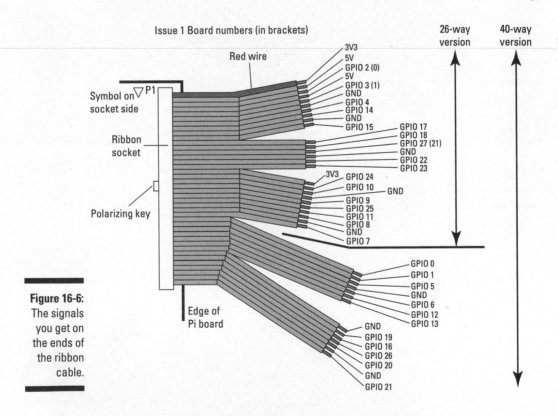

Figure 16-6:
The signals you get on the ends of the ribbon cable.

Bend the exposed wire back on itself about halfway to give the connection block screw something to bite on. You are going to wire up every other wire to one of the rows of connecting blocks. Start at the end of the red wire and connect it to the right connecting block and then proceed connecting every other wire. At this stage, it should look like Figure 16-8.

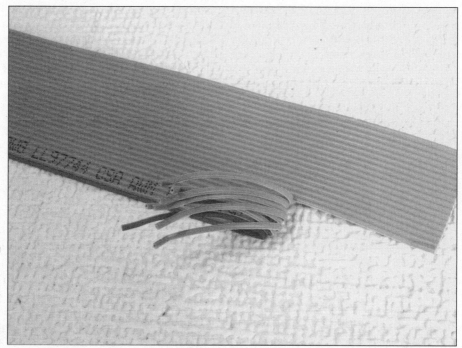

Figure 16-7:
Separating the strands of a ribbon cable.

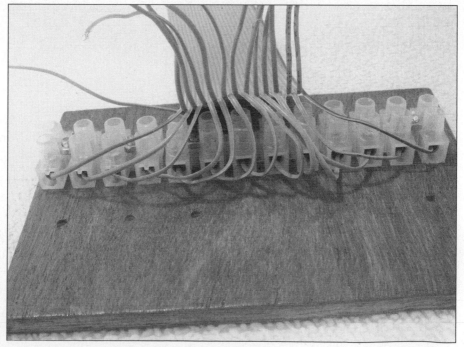

Figure 16-8:
The first stage in wiring the cable to the connectors.

Next, you need to connect the second row of connectors. Because there is only a small gap between the two rows of connection block, you have to do this before fixing the two blocks to the board. Again, every other wire is to be connected. Check as you go to make sure there are no mistakes in the first row. When you're done, it should look like Figure 16-9. You can now mount the second row of connection blocks on the base, as shown in Figure 16-10.

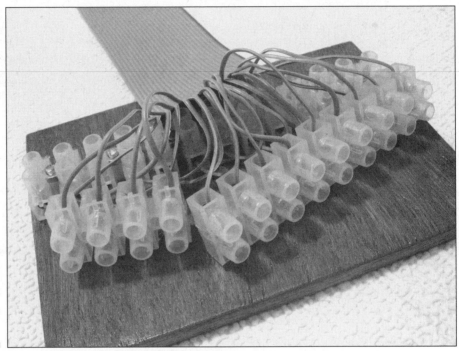

Figure 16-9:
Wiring the
second
row of
connectors.

Here is the opportunity to use that label maker you bought but never use: to label each connection block. Alternatively, you can print labels out on the computer and attach each with double-sided sticky tape or use adhesive labels and write on them with a good black pen. Figure 16-11 shows you what the labels should be for both the 26-way and 40-way version. The dotted line shows the extension you need for the 40-way version. You can label yours for just the revision board you have or you put the changed pin numbers in brackets (parentheses) like we've done. When you're finished, it should look like Figure 16-12. Note that on the 40-way version, GPIO 0 and 1 are reserved for an I2C EEPROM that is read on boot up; thereafter, you are free to use them. But on boot-up, there will be some activity on these lines. This activity involves the operating system probing these lines for a device: There will be burst of zero and one outputs on the clock line. The data line will be pulled low and then released, and then it will be monitored to see if it being pulled low by the external device. If the devices you connect to these two lines can stand this activity and not interfere with it, fine. If you have any doubts about this, choose some other lines to use.

Figure 16-10:
Fixing the
second row
of connec-
tors to the
board.

Testing the breakout board

Your next step is to test the breakout board. To do this, you need a *multime-ter*, a device for measuring current, voltage, and resistance. You can obtain a cheap one from a thrift shop for less than $10. First, select resistance or continuity on the switch on the front of the meter and make sure that there are no shorts between adjacent wires in the ribbon cable. You will know it is a short when the continuity indicator bleeps or the resistance measurement shows zero or a very low ohm reading (less than 10 ohms). Next, plug the cable into your Raspberry Pi with the ribbon running away from the board and the polarizing bump pointing into the board. Do not power up your Raspberry Pi yet.

Check that you have continuity between the five ground connections. Now power up your Pi. If there is no light immediately upon power up, remove the power right away because this indicates you have shorted the supply somewhere. Set your meter to measure voltage and put the black or negative meter wire on a ground connector and the red or positive meter wire on a 5V block. You should see close to 5V (4.8 to 5.2V). Next measure the voltage between the ground and the two 3V3 connections in turn. Again, you should see a value very close to 3V3. If these checks fail, shut down the Raspberry Pi, disconnect the cable, and check all the wiring.

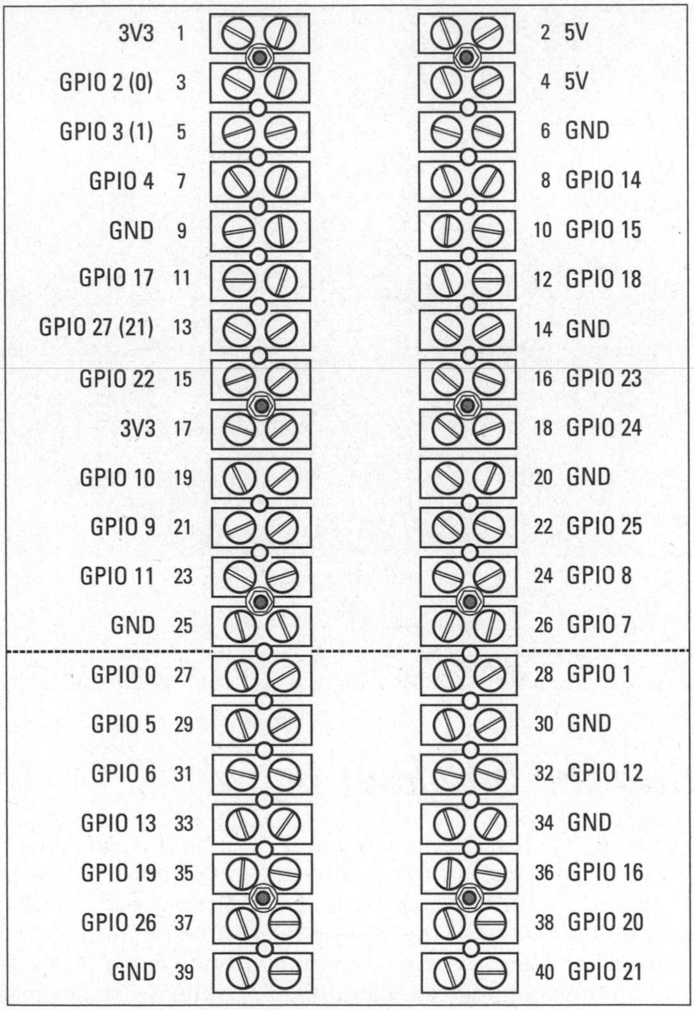

3V3	1	2	5V
GPIO 2 (0)	3	4	5V
GPIO 3 (1)	5	6	GND
GPIO 4	7	8	GPIO 14
GND	9	10	GPIO 15
GPIO 17	11	12	GPIO 18
GPIO 27 (21)	13	14	GND
GPIO 22	15	16	GPIO 23
3V3	17	18	GPIO 24
GPIO 10	19	20	GND
GPIO 9	21	22	GPIO 25
GPIO 11	23	24	GPIO 8
GND	25	26	GPIO 7
GPIO 0	27	28	GPIO 1
GPIO 5	29	30	GND
GPIO 6	31	32	GPIO 12
GPIO 13	33	34	GND
GPIO 19	35	36	GPIO 16
GPIO 26	37	38	GPIO 20
GND	39	40	GPIO 21

Figure 16-11: Labels for the breakout board.

Issue 1 board numbers in brackets

Controlling the GPIO pins

In order to have the Raspberry Pi gain access to the GPIO pins, you must install a Python module that acts as an interface between the language and the pins. This allows a program to read in what is happening to the signals on the GPIO lines. A few different choices exist, but perhaps the most used is RPi.GPIO. It comes already installed on your system, but just to make sure you have the latest version, you can type this command in a terminal window:

```
sudo apt-get install python-rpi.gpio
```

To use Python, we like to use the IDLE shell, but when accessing the GPIO pins, Linux likes to be running as root. Therefore to start up IDLE as root, don't double-click the desktop icon, but open up a terminal window and type

```
gksudo idle
```

Any Python program that needs to access the GPIO pins must do the following operations:

1. **Import the module to talk to the pins.**

2. **Set up how you want to refer to the pins.**

3. **Initialize the GPIO pins you want to use.**

4. **Read or write to the pins.**

This sequence is neatly encapsulated in the program in Listing 16-1. This simply sets all the GPIO pins to be inputs and then constantly reads them back into the Raspberry Pi. It prints out the new state when any of the inputs change.

Listing 16-1:   Monitoring the GPIO Pins as Inputs

```
#!/usr/bin/env python
#GPIO input state monitor on the Raspberry Pi
#GPIO state - show the state of all the GPIO inputs on P1
#non GPIO pins shown as x

import RPi.GPIO as GPIO

print "Display the GPIO input pin states"
print "Ctrl C to stop"

boardRevision =  GPIO.RPI_REVISION
ways = 26
 #define the pins to use
if boardRevision == 1:
    pinout = [-1,-1,0,-1,1,-1,4,14,-1,15,17,18,21,-1,22,23,-1,24,↵
              10,-1,9,25,11,8,-1,7]
if boardRevision == 2:
    pinout = [-1,-1,2,-1,3,-1,4,14,-1,15,17,18,27,-1,22,23,-1,24,↵
              10,-1,9,25,11,8,-1,7]
if boardRevision == 3:
    pinout = [-1,-1,2,-1,3,-1,4,14,-1,15,17,18,27,-1,22,23,-1,24,↵
              10,-1,9,25,11,8,-1,7,0,1,5,-1,6,12,13,-1,19,16,26,20,-1,21]
    ways = 40

GPIO.setmode(GPIO.BCM) # use real GPIO numbering
inputState = [ 5 for temp in range (0,ways)] # blank list for input levels

for pin in range(0,ways): # set all pins to inputs
  if pinout[pin] != -1:
    GPIO.setup(pinout[pin],GPIO.IN, pull_up_down=GPIO.PUD_UP)
    # replace line above with the line below to see the effect of ↵
      floating inputs
    # GPIO.setup(pinout[pin],GPIO.IN, pull_up_down=GPIO.PUD_OFF)

while True: # do forever
   needUpdate = False
   for check in range(0,ways): # look at each input in turn
     if pinout[check] != -1:
       if GPIO.input(pinout[check]) :
         latestState = 1
       else:
         latestState = 0
       if(latestState != inputState[check]):
           needUpdate = True
           print "GPIO ",pinout[check], "changed to a logic", latestState
           inputState[check] = latestState
   if needUpdate: # display all pin states
     print "Current state"
     for row in range(1,-1, -1):
        for show in range(row,ways,2) :
          if inputState[show] != 5:
            print inputState[show],
```

```
        else:
            print "x",
      print " "

#end of main loop
```

Take a look at the code and see what is happening. After importing the RPi. GPIO module, the code finds the board revision and initializes a list based on what the board revision is. The list has a value of -1 in the pin positions where there is no GPIO pin (that is, where there is a power or ground pin). Otherwise, it has the GPIO number in the corresponding pin position of the list. Then the code creates a list that holds the input values for each pin.

When we wrote this code, we filled this in with an arbitrary value of 5, knowing that any real input value will be only a zero or one. Later on, we use this default value to see how to display each pin. Next, all the pins are set to be inputs with the internal pull-up resistors enabled. We talked about pull-up resistors in the previous chapter (see Figure 15-9). That ends the setup portion of the program.

The rest of the code is a loop that runs forever. It checks each input in turn by looking at the `pinout` list and calling the `GPIOinput(pin)` to return the value of each input. Then this is compared with the value we got last time. If it's different, it prints out the current state of that input along with all the values of input arranged in the same order as the P1 connector's pins.

To test this out, choose Run Module from the Run menu and then simply connect one end of a wire to one of the ground connections. Then go around, in turn, connecting the other end of the wire to each input. All the inputs initially show as logic ones on the screen and change to logic zeros when you ground the input.

Be careful not to connect this ground wire to any of the power outputs: This will short out your Raspberry Pi's power. To prevent this, we put a small piece of plasticine (Play-Doh, modeling clay, or blue tack) in the screw tops of the power connectors.

Floating GPIO pins

Here's an interesting experiment to do. Change the line that defines the pins to be inputs with a pull-up enabled to one with no pull-ups. Remove one hash and add another so that section of the code now reads

```
#GPIO.setup(pinout[pin],GPIO.IN, pull_up_down=GPIO.PUD_UP)
# replace line above with the line below to see the effect of ↵
        floating inputs
GPIO.setup(pinout[pin],GPIO.IN, pull_up_down=GPIO.PUD_OFF)
```

Now when you run the program again, some of the pins that aren't connected to anything change all the time. We say they are *floating*, and they are being affected by tiny airborne electrical interference signals. As you can see, this is not a stable situation and should be avoided.

Getting a better display

The output of this program is a bit crude because it depends on printing to the console. On the website for this book, you can find another program called GPIOmon.py that displays the state of the input pins in a window superimposed over an image of the Raspberry Pi's P1 connector. This image will automatically change to reflect if you have a B+ or an earlier model. (See this book's Introduction for more on accessing the website.) The logic ones are shown in red, and the zeros in blue, with the fixed level pins in black. A screenshot of this program is shown in Figure 16-13. This program can be closed by pressing Esc or simply by closing down the window.

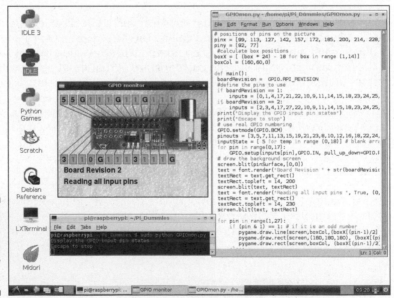

Figure 16-13: A screenshot of the GPIOmon.py program.

Creating the Blastoff Game

Blastoff is a marble maze/puzzle type game that can sense the presence of the marble at various parts of the board. The idea is to visit each one of a series of traps or positions in the correct order without running into the sides. The best thing is that you know all you need to know about electronics to make this now.

To build this game, you use a 15mm (3/8") ball bearing in a box, using copper foil strips to sense the position of the ball. The copper foil strips are connected to the GPIO inputs and ground and the ball bearing simply shorts two strips together, thus grounding the pin and allowing the computer to read it. When each numbered trap is visited, the Raspberry Pi plays a sound file enunciating that number in the countdown. If the ball bearing touches the side abort strips or if traps are visited out of order, however, the computer resets the game and you have to start the countdown again. This is great fun, especially at a party or with a group of friends.

Making the box

We used metric nuts and bolts to make this game, specifically M2.5 and M3 nuts and bolts. In imperial measure, these correspond to BA sizes, with M2.5 being roughly 6BA and M3 corresponding to 4BA. Fortunately, absolute sizes do not matter in making this project, so feel free to use whatever system is available to you.

To start off, you need a playing surface. We built most of this from 6mm (1/4") plywood finished in varnish, a sheet of acrylic, and some pine wood strips. The box basically consists of a number of layers shown in Figure 16-14. This can be any size you like, but we made ours 200mm (8") square. We started off by cutting out two squares of plywood and one of 4mm (1/4") acrylic sheet. Then we marked four holes 10mm (3/8") in from each corner and clamped all the pieces together. Then we drilled one of the holes at 3mm (1/8"), put an M3 bolt through it, and tightened it up, as shown in Figure 16-15. We then drilled and bolted the other corners in turn. This ensured all the holes lined up. It's worthwhile to mark one edge so you can assemble all the pieces back in the same way when putting it back together.

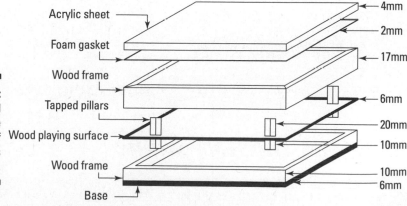

Figure 16-14: An exploded view of the Blastoff game's construction.

- Acrylic sheet — 4mm
- — 2mm
- Foam gasket — 17mm
- Wood frame — 6mm
- Tapped pillars — 20mm
- Wood playing surface — 10mm
- Wood frame — 10mm
- — 6mm
- Base

Figure 16-15:
Bolting all three large boards together to make sure the holes line up.

To make the bottom tray, cut four pieces of 10mm (3/8") strip pine and chamfer the ends at 45 degrees with a disc sander. Now use a Stanley Bailey band clamp, or a similar device meant for clamping objects, to secure all four pieces while you glue them together to form a frame. Finally, glue and clamp the frame to the base. This completes the underside tray.

To make the top frame, do exactly the same thing that you did to create the bottom tray, except using 17mm (11/16") strip pine. When this is set, glue it into a piece of 2mm (3/32") foam from a hobby or card-making shop or office-supply store. You can then cut the foam to size on the inside and outside of the frame using a sharp knife. In that way, you get a neat gasket that looks good through the acrylic and helps bed things down.

The playing surface is held between the tray and the acrylic by using two tapped pillars at each corner. We used those with an M3 thread (4BA) and had a 20mm (3/4") long one for the top and a 10mm (3/8") long one for the bottom. We used a small length of M3 studding to fix them both to the board. If you don't have any studding, you can just cut the head off an M3 bolt. See Figure 16-16.

Figure 16-16:
Attaching
the two
pillars to
the playing
surface.

Making the ball traps

The next step is to enable the ball bearing to make an electrical contact between two points. This is a bit harder than you might think. The ball is a sphere and only makes contact with a surface at one point. If you want it to bridge two conductors, they have to be very close. The solution is to use a raised wall for one contact and a conducting strip for the other. For this task, we need self-adhesive copper strip (foil). It is sold by the reel in hobby shops for making Tiffany-style stained glass and also by electronics suppliers for radio frequency (RF) screening. You can get it in various widths; we used a 5mm (1/4") wide strip. Figure 16-17 shows how this foil can be used to make a detector or trap for the ball.

See how the ball is forced against the corner of the wall and at the same time makes point contact with the foil on the playing surface? On the playing surface, first drill and countersink a 2.5mm (1/8") hole, and then lay the foil over the top and smooth it down. You will see the indentation of the countersink hole. Take a sharp pencil and make a hole in the foil. Gradually make it larger and then put the countersunk bolt into the hole and tighten up a nut on the other side. This pulls the foil into the countersink and makes a good electrical contact. It's a good idea to make the countersink slightly deeper than flush so that the ball can nestle in it. This is shown in Figure 16-18. We made the wall from 5mm (1/4") square strip pine. The foil only needs to wrap round the corner and cover only half the countersink hole.

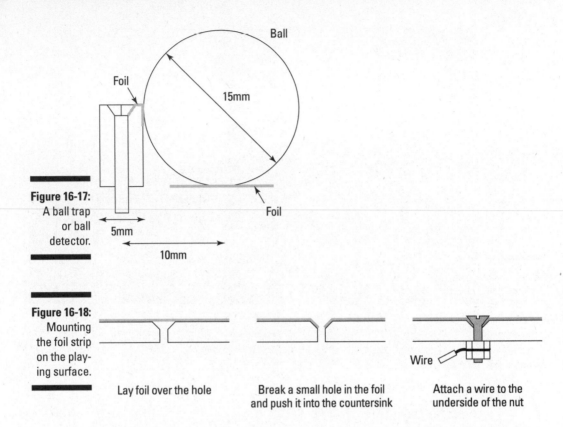

Figure 16-17:
A ball trap
or ball
detector.

Figure 16-18:
Mounting
the foil strip
on the play-
ing surface.

Lay foil over the hole

Break a small hole in the foil
and push it into the countersink

Attach a wire to the
underside of the nut

Figure 16-19 shows how we arranged the ball traps. Down each side is an abort trap. They are wired together because you don't need to differentiate between the two sides. The other six traps, the ones we want to hit, are distributed on alternate sides of the playing surface. Figure 16-20 illustrates how this looks.

Wiring up the Blastoff game

Figure 16-21 shows the schematic of the Blastoff game's wiring. We've used a push-button symbol, the T shape with the two triangles, to represent the traps. You can see this as a plunger shorting out two contacts, which is very much the same as what the ball does. You can see the two abort traps wired together or, as we say, *in parallel*. One side of all the traps goes to the same line, the ground. The ground is denoted by the symbol with three diagonal lines. All points connected to this symbol are always connected together. In this circuit, there are just two ground points. We could have drawn the connection in, but this is how you will see it on other schematics. The important thing to remember is that all grounds must be connected together on all circuits if they use the same symbol.

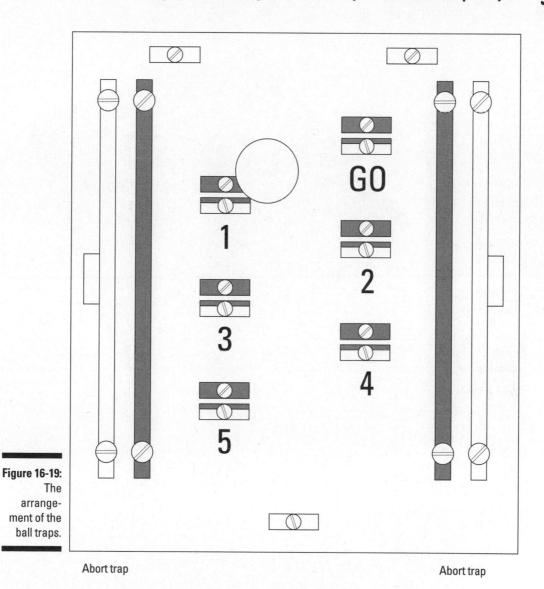

Figure 16-19:
The
arrange-
ment of the
ball traps.

Abort trap   Abort trap

The schematic is a simple way of showing what needs to be connected to
what. Contrast that with Figure 16-22, which is a physical wiring diagram
of how to connect things up. It's not terribly clear what's going on, but this
is still clearer than Figure 16-23, which is a photograph of the real wires.
Learning to read a schematic pays great dividends; it should be your top
learning priority.

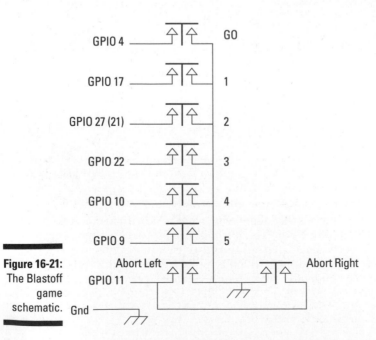

Figure 16-21:
The Blastoff
game
schematic.

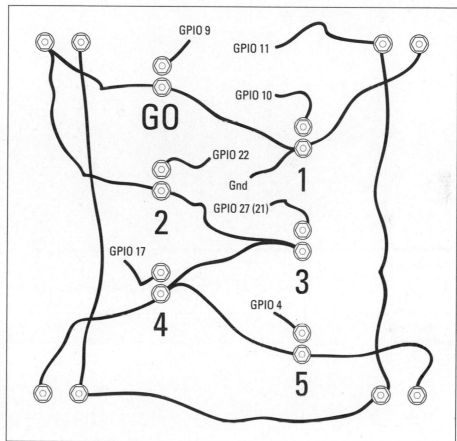

Figure 16-22:
A physical
wiring
diagram
of the ball
traps.

You can wire up the traps by just wrapping wire around the bolt, placing a washer over it, and tightening up another bolt. However, if you don't mind a tiny bit of soldering, you can bend the wires round a bolt, remove the bolt, and just apply a little solder to form an eyelet like the one shown in Figure 16-24. We used a piece of 8-way ribbon cable, stripped down from the 26-way cable we used to make the breakout board, to wire up the game. We used a file to cut a recess in the top of the tray to let the wires out, as shown in Figure 16-25. We used hot melt glue to fix the ribbon cable to the base (refer to Figure 16-23). We then connected the other end of the wires to the breakout board.

Finally, in order to dress it up a little, we found some space-themed stickers in a local toy store along with some number stickers and added just a few to give it the finishing touch, as shown in Figure 16-26. Try not to go overboard on the number of stickers you use: Less is more. They can also affect the path of the ball and so become subtle obstacles in the game.

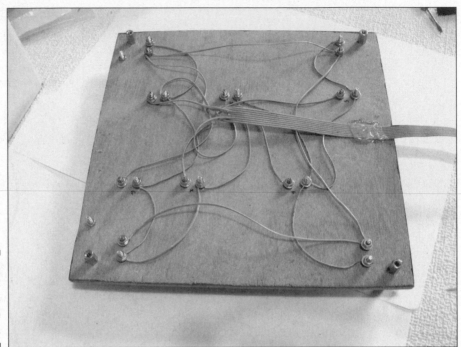

Figure 16-23:
A photo-
graph of the
wiring of the
ball traps.

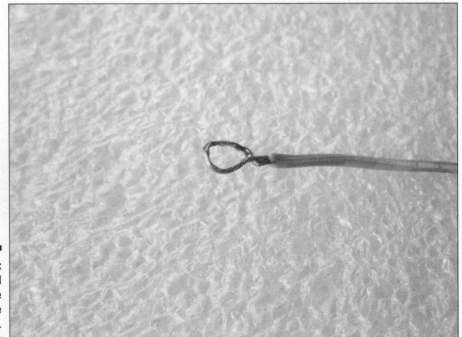

Figure 16-24:
A soldered
loop on the
end of the
wire.

Figure 16-25:
A recess cut
with a file
to allow the
ribbon cable
into the tray.

Figure 16-26:
The finished
Blastoff
game with
stickers.

Testing the hardware

With the hardware built, it's time to test it. Fire up one of the two input monitoring programs mentioned earlier in this chapter and place the ball in turn on each of the trap positions. You should see a logic zero appear on the appropriate GPIO pin. Don't worry if this shows up as a rapidly changing zero and one on the pin, or if you sometimes touch a trap and nothing appears to happen. As long as you can make the ball produce a logic zero on the right pin some of the time, it's fine. If you're using old copper foil, you might have to wipe the surface clean with some solvent to remove any fingerprint oils and improve the contact. (The same goes for the ball bearing.) In stubborn cases, you can lightly rub the foil with an ink eraser (an eraser with grit embedded in it) to get a better surface.

Writing the software

The next step is to write the software that brings the game to life. This is shown in Listing 16-2. We want to play a sound file and print on the screen the state of the countdown. You have to go from five to zero (blastoff) without touching any of the side traps. If you do, the countdown has to start again.

Listing 16-2:   The Blastoff Game

```python
#!/usr/bin/env python
# Blastoff marble game - python 2
# with sound effects
# run with - sudo python BlastOff.py

import RPi.GPIO as GPIO
import pygame
from pygame.locals import *
pygame.init()
pygame.mixer.quit()
pygame.mixer.init()

def checkContacts(pins):
    made = -1 # number of the contact made
    for test in range (0,7):
        if(GPIO.input(pins[test]) == False): # if contact is made
            made = test
    return made

print "Loading sound files"
```

```
effect = [ pygame.mixer.Sound("sounds/"+str(s)+".ogg") for s in range(0,6)]
abortSound = pygame.mixer.Sound("sounds/abort.ogg")
countWords = ["BLASTOFF", "ONE", "TWO", "THREE", "FOUR", "FIVE"]

print "Hi from Python :- Blastoff game"
print "start the count from five"
print "control-C to quit"
GPIO.setmode(GPIO.BCM)  # use real GPIO numbering
boardRevision = GPIO.RPI_REVISION
if boardRevision == 1:
    inputs = [9, 10, 22, 21, 17, 4, 11]
if boardRevision > 1:
    inputs = [9, 10, 22, 27, 17, 4, 11]
# set up GPIO input pins with pull ups enabled
for pin in inputs:
    GPIO.setup(pin, GPIO.IN, pull_up_down=GPIO.PUD_UP)

nextCount = 5 # the next trigger to hit
while True: # run the game forever
    newState = checkContacts(inputs)
    # check if something is making contact and it is not the last pad
    if newState != -1 and newState != nextCount +1:
        if newState == 6 and nextCount !=5: # the abort bar touched ↵
                                            during countdown
            print "Technical difficulty -- countdown aborted"
            print "Recommence at five"
            abortSound.play()
            nextCount = 5

        if newState == nextCount:  # the next pad is reached
            print countWords[nextCount]
            effect[nextCount].play()
            nextCount = nextCount -1
            counting = True
        else:
            if nextCount != 5:  # the wrong pad is reached
                print "Countdown out of sequence -- countdown aborted"
                print "Start again at 5"
                abortSound.play()
                nextCount = 5
    if nextCount == -1: # successfully finished Countdown so reset game
        nextCount = 5
# end of main loop
```

The program uses the Pygame module that comes preinstalled for Python 2 on the Raspberry Pi. It is a very useful module that allows you to easily create applications in a desktop window and to easily handle sound files. We used it in the GPIOmon.py program mentioned earlier in this chapter. The program starts with the definition of a function for reading in all the input pins to the game. Ignore that for a moment and take a look at the loading of the sound files. We want the sounds to be in a list, with their position in the list corresponding to the count. The files are called 0.ogg, 1.ogg, and so on up to 5.ogg. This filename is made by turning the loop counter into a string and adding a string on either side of that to create the filename. These sound filenames are initialized into a list called effect. The abort sound is initialized in a more conventional way with the filename in quotes.

Next, the inputs list is initialized depending on what revision of board it is running on. If you want to change any of the wiring or in fact if you wired it from back to front, you can correct for this by simply changing the numbers in this list. This list is used to initialize the GPIO pins as inputs and to turn on the pull-up resistors. The variable nextCount is initialized to 5. This variable drives the game, and all the rules about what happens when a trap switch is closed depend on it.

When the variable is 5, the countdown hasn't started, so we don't want any of the abort strips to trigger anything. If it its value is less than 5, the countdown is under way, the abort strips are active, and the next trap triggered must be the value of this variable. If the next trap triggered is not the correct one, the countdown is aborted because of an out-of-sequence count. In fact, we still allow a trap to be visited at one less than the next count variable because that removes any consequences from what we call *contact bounce*. Contact bounce is the effect of a contact being made and broken very rapidly and looking like multiple contacts. However, this is faster than could be physically made, so sometimes we have to add delays to stop the computer from seeing multiple triggers. Fortunately in this program, because of the way we want it to work, we simply sidestep any contact bounce issue. This is because after we have reached any trap, we are looking for either the next trap to be triggered, for correct progress, or a trap that is not the next one or the current one for an error. Therefore, any contact bounce on the current trap is neatly ignored.

Finally the checkContacts() function sets a variable called made to be -1. It then goes through each input in turn and, if it finds a logic zero, makes the made variable equal to the position in the list of the logic zero input. This is exactly what we want. For example, if there was a logic zero on GPIO 17, this is the fourth entry in the list and corresponds to ball trap 4. Note the abort trap is returned as 6 by the software and if the ball is not bridging anything, a -1 is returned. Also we only have one ball, so only one contact trap is closed at any one time.

The game logic

So after reading the inputs, if we have a value not equal to -1 and not equal to the last number in the countdown, we have a new contact and the game needs to move on. An if statement tests whether the abort trap was triggered when the countdown was active; that is, the next count is not equal to 5. If it is, the abort sound is played, a statement is printed, and the next count is set to 5, which starts off the game again.

If the new state is the value we are looking for, we play the sound, print out the count, and reduce the next count by one. Otherwise, we have an out-of-sequence count, the countdown is aborted, and the game is reset as before. Finally, if the next count has reached -1, blastoff has occurred and we reset the game, ready for the next countdown. That's a lot of logic in a few lines, so look at the code and read this paragraph again. Make sure you understand it.

In computing terms, the variable nextCount is known as a *state variable* and it drives what the program does next. This is a technique often used in computing.

Creating the sounds

The only thing that remains to do is to create the sound files. You can download our efforts from the book's website along with the code, but it's even greater fun to make your own countdown samples. (See this book's Introduction for more on how to access the website if you prefer.) The sound files should be put in a directory called sounds in the same directory as the program. These files should be in the .ogg sound format. Pygame can cope with .wav formats, but it's a bit fussy about the specific type of .wav file, so you are better off sticking to the .ogg format.

Fortunately, a great free application can run on your laptop or desktop computer to record the sound and save it in the .ogg format. It is called Audacity and can be downloaded from http://audacity.sourceforge.net/. Transfer the sound files you create to your Raspberry Pi using a memory stick. We used the GarageBand application, free with all Macs, to record both voice and an accompanying chord. Save the sample as an MP3 and then use Audacity to convert it into an .ogg file. A customized sound version of the project can be seen at https://vimeo.com/65274719.

Customizing the Blastoff Game

In addition to using your own sound files, you can customize this game in lots of ways to make it unique. You can have more ball traps required to complete the sequence. You can have abort strips at the top and bottom of the frame as well, and you can add strips of wood on the board to act as obstacles. You can fashion the game like a traditional maze with places to visit and places to avoid. Going one step further, you can retheme the game as a treasure hunt, lock-picking game, or rally game. You could even make the playing surface out of thin translucent acrylic sheet and have concealed lights, flashing or guiding you to the next trap, beneath. However, before you do that, you need to learn how to control lights from the Raspberry Pi, which is the subject of the next chapter.

Chapter 17

Putting the Raspberry Pi in Control

. . . .

In This Chapter

▶ Discovering how to output logic signals

▶ Learning how to drive an LED

▶ Creating the Copycat game

▶ Customizing the Copycat game

▶ Creating the deluxe Copycat game

. . . .

*I*n Chapter 16, we cover GPIO signals on the Raspberry Pi and show how they could be used as inputs. We used those inputs to sense the position of a steel ball in our Blastoff game. In this chapter, we show you how to make these GPIO lines turn things on and off, to exercise control using the power of your computer and its program.

We do this first by showing you how to light up a light, specifically a light-emitting diode (LED). Then we show you how to combine this knowledge with the input techniques you learned in the last chapter to create a Copycat game. (If you just can't wait to see what the final game will look like, flip to Figure 17-15 at the end of this chapter.)

The GPIO lines are limited in the power that they can output, so to control things that require more power, you must give the tiny signals a boost. The simplest way of doing this is with a transistor. We show you how to do this to control much brighter lights, allowing you to make a deluxe version of the Copycat game. We show you how to handle surface-mount components as well.

Using GPIO Pins as Outputs

We show in Chapter 15 how the GPIO lines could be made to act like a switch between the 3V3 power rail and the ground. Now it's time to put that into action and use that switch to control something. The first thing you should control is a simple LED. We say they're simple because they are ubiquitous nowadays, but they still require a little explanation. The letters *LED* stand for *light-emitting diode.*

You probably understand the first two words, but the last one might need explaining. A *diode* is an electrical component that lets current pass in one direction but not in the other direction, a bit like a non-return valve. The symbol tells a little story about this because the current arrives on the long side of the triangle, called an *anode,* and gets squashed down to a point and out through the barrier at the other end, the *cathode.* Current flowing in the other direction towards the cathode hits the barrier and can't flow through the device. In a diode, the current flows from the anode to the cathode, as shown in the following image.

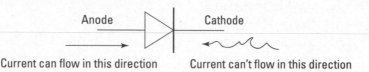

Anode   Cathode

Current can flow in this direction   Current can't flow in this direction

In an LED, the current does exactly the same thing, but as it flows, it also generates light. In a normal incandescent bulb, light is generated because the filament gets hot and glows white-hot. In an LED and fluorescent light tube, the light creation mechanism is different. Light is produced by exciting the atoms in it and then as these atoms decay to their normal state, they emit a small packet of light, a *photon.* The difference is that in a fluorescent light, this happens in a gas, whereas in an LED, this happens in a solid crystal. The light's color depends on the material the crystal is made from and several alloys can be used to make an LED.

You need a voltage to overcome the initial resistance of the LED, but after the voltage has been reached, you get a big change in current for a very small change in voltage. This is a device that does not obey Ohm's law where the current is simply proportional to the voltage. You can think of an LED as having a voltage-dependent resistance. For low voltages, the resistance is high, but for higher voltages, the resistance drops to a very low value. We say this is a *non-linear* device. This means we can't just simply connect it up to a voltage and expect it to work. So whenever you use an LED, you always need some form of current-limiting device, and a resistor is the simplest.

Beware: On the Internet, many people tell you that you do not need anything else when driving an LED. They connect an LED directly to a pin.

They might even have fancy-sounding technical descriptions justifying their assertions. They may say it is being rapidly turned on and off. This is known as *multiplexing,* which stops current from building up. However, they're wrong, most through ignorance or misunderstanding, and a few are trying to be funny or malicious. Listening to such advice can end up damaging your computer.

A resistor is simple to add. You need one resistor per LED. The resistor value is not too critical. If you can't be bothered calculating the exact value you need, take heart: You won't go wrong with anything between 220 R and 470 R. That being said, we explain in the next section how to calculate exactly what you need.

This method is sufficient for all low-powered LEDs; that is, LEDs that require a current of 100 mA (milliamperes) or less. The most popular form of LED has a maximum current rating of 20 mA.

Preparing to Build the Copycat Game

The idea behind the game is that four different-colored LEDs come on in a random sequence. Beside each LED is a small push-button switch. You have to mimic the sequence by pushing the switches next to the appropriate LED. If you get it right, an extra light is added to the sequence and you try to mimic it again. As the sequence becomes longer, the game gets more difficult. If you want to skip ahead and look at the simple version of the game, see Figure 17-4. However, we also describe a more sophisticated way of constructing the game with illuminated push buttons. This version, shown in Figure 17-15, looks a lot less like a circuit board and more like a game.

Here are the parts you'll need to build the simplest version of Copycat:

- 1 3.3" × 3.3" copper strip prototype board.
- 4 tack push-button switches.
- 1 3mm red LED – red diffuse encapsulation.
- 1 3mm green LED – green diffuse encapsulation.
- 1 3mm yellow LED – yellow diffuse encapsulation.
- 1 3mm blue LED – blue diffuse encapsulation or clear if you can't get blue. Note, the forward drop should be 3V2 or less.
- 4 270 R wire-ended resistors.

If you want to build the deluxe version of Copycat, you'll need these materials:

- 4 1.6" × 1.6" copper strip prototype board
- 4 1.6" × 1.6" 3/16" (4mm) acrylic sheet (Plexiglas or Perspex)
- 2 6" (150mm) square 1/4" (6mm) plywood
- 2' (600mm) of 13/32" (10mm) × 3/16" (5mm) strip pine
- 4 3/8" (10mm) 4BA (M3) countersunk machine screws

- ✔ 4 3/8" (10mm) 4BA (M3) flat-head machine screws
- ✔ 4 3/8" (10mm) 4BA (M3) tapped brass hexagonal pillar or spacer
- ✔ 4 tack push-button switches
- ✔ 2 table tennis balls
- ✔ 1 surface-mount red LED – clear encapsulation
- ✔ 1 3mm green LED – clear encapsulation
- ✔ 1 3mm yellow LED – clear encapsulation
- ✔ 1 3mm blue LED – clear encapsulation
- ✔ 4 4K7 wire-ended resistors
- ✔ 4 BC237BG NPN transistors or any other NPN general-purpose small signal transistor
- ✔ 3 150R wire-ended resistors
- ✔ 1 82R wire-ended resistor
- ✔ 32 1/4" (6mm) foam pads

Choosing an LED

A totally bewildering number of different types of LEDs are available in all sorts of shapes and sizes. For this project, you require LEDs with leads known as the *through-hole mounting* type. The two main sizes are 5mm or 3mm. The size is not too important here. LEDs also come in two main types of plastic covering, colored or clear, and also two surface treatments, diffused or water clear. For the project you are about to make, you need the colored cover and preferably the diffused type.

One thing you have to look out for when looking for LEDs to be driven directly from the Raspberry Pi is the forward voltage. You have only 3V3 coming out of the GPIO pins, so you want an LED with a forward voltage of no more than 3V. Some older types of blue LEDs are a bit above this and won't work.

The other thing to look at is how bright the LED is when a certain amount of current is flowing through it. This is normally quoted in the data sheets in the units of *candelas* or more, usually mille- or microcandela. Knowing the LED's brightness is useful here because Copycat gameplay requires the player to look directly at an LED and you don't want it to be too bright. However, you can always cut down on the brightness by reducing the current through the LED. For this project, go for those of about 1 millecandela (mCd).

The websites of big distributors such as Farnell in the U.K., known as Newark in the U.S., have a selection filter to help you cut down on the overwhelming choices. From more than 3,000 offerings, you can whittle your selection down at `http://uk.farnell.com/jsp/search/browse.jsp?N=2031+204192&Ntk =gensearch&Ntt=led`. The alternative approach is buying a mixed bag of LEDs from eBay. You don't know what you are getting, but you can easily measure the forward voltage drop.

To light up an LED, you put it in series with a resistor and apply some power, as shown in Figure 17-1. You need to control the current through it by picking the correct value of resistor. You can't use Ohm's law on the LED itself, but you can use it on the resistor. When the LED is on, it has an almost fixed voltage across it, independent of the current. The resistor has a voltage across it that is proportional to the current, which is Ohm's law. So in order to find the right value of resistor and so set the current to what you want, you have to first work out what voltage you want across the resistor. This is easy: It's simply the voltage of the power source minus the forward volt drop of the LED. Then if you know the voltage across a resistor and you want a certain current, Ohm's law tells you what resistor value that has to be.

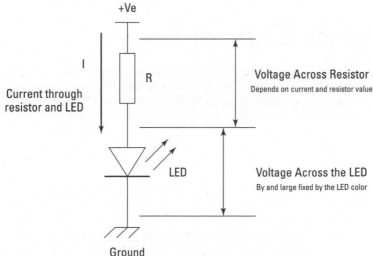

Figure 17-1: Lighting an LED.

Suppose we have a red LED with a forward voltage drop of 1V18 and we are powering it from a GPIO pin giving out 3V3. The voltage across our resistor is going to be

```
3.3-1.18 = 2.12
```

Now suppose we want to run this at a current of 7mA. In that case, Ohm's law gives us a resistor value of

```
2.12/0.007 = 302R
```

However, this is not quite the value to use. Remember in Chapter 15, we saw there was a drive impedance to a GPIO output of 31R, so you need to subtract that from the total resistance value to get

```
302-31 = 271R
```

Be aware that you can't buy that exact value. This is because resistors come in standard values. The closest one to the value we want is 270R, so that is the one to go for. You do calculations to get you in the right area, but the exact value is not normally important. Here, by using a slightly lower value, we are putting a very tiny bit of extra current through the LED. Because we are operating nowhere near its maximum value, it doesn't matter that a tiny bit more current is flowing. In fact, for everyday applications, you can use a 270R resistor for lighting up any LED direct from a Raspberry Pi's GPIO output pin. Armed with that knowledge, you're ready to make the next project, Copycat.

Creating the Copycat Game

Copycat is a simple game of remembering a sequence of colors and entering them in again. The computer plays a sequence of color flashes and you have to repeat it by pressing buttons. If you are successful, an extra step is added to the sequence and you try to enter that. If you are not successful, you get to have another go. However, three failures in a row ends the game and your score is the length of sequence you managed to get right. You can create a game with lots of different variations on this theme (as you see later in this chapter), some of which make it fiendishly difficult. You can make two versions of this game, the simple or the deluxe. We're going to start off with the simple one.

Figure 17-2 shows the schematic of the Copycat game. It's simply a switch and LED circuit repeated four times. The only differences in each of the circuits are the GPIO to which the switch and LED is attached to and the color of the LED. Notice that the LED resistor is the same value for all the LEDs, as we discuss in the previous section.

The only component we have not mentioned previously is the push-button switch. Switches can be quite expensive, but one small type of switch is very cheap and is in most sorts of equipment, normally lurking behind plastic molding. This is called a *tack* switch. It's square, but the four pins are not on a square grid. There is a long side and short side as far as the pin spacing goes. The two pins on the long side are electrically joined together. When the button is pressed, the two long sides are electrically joined. You have to be careful not to mix up the two sides; otherwise, it will appear that the switch is permanently being pressed.

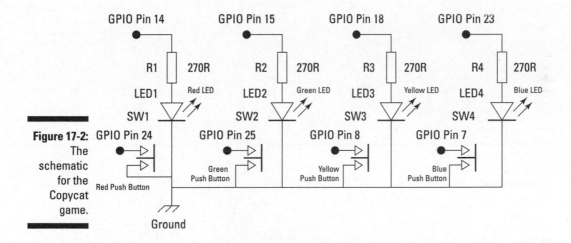

Figure 17-2: The schematic for the Copycat game.

You are going to make this game on a piece of prototype strip board, sometimes known by the trade name Veroboard. It's very useful and flexible for making small electronic circuits. It has a matrix of holes at a 0.1" (2.54mm) pitch, which is very common for electronic components. On the underside of the board run horizontal lines of copper. By soldering components onto the board, you can make some of the connections with this copper. Sometimes, however, the copper joins up the components in the wrong way. When this happens, it's a simple matter to cut the copper track with a twist drill bit (not attached to the drill) or a specially made tool called a *spot face cutter*. Personally, we prefer to remove the copper from each side of a hole with a sharp knife.

We've heard that it's hard to get strip board in the U.S., but it is stocked by all the major suppliers under various names such as *BusBoard Prototype System*, *Vectorbord Circbord*, or *breadboard*. You don't want any fancy substrate like fiberglass — just the cheapest saturated resin bonded paper (SPBP). Look for the circuit pattern type of common bus to make sure you get the strips. The game is made on a piece of 3.4"×3.4" strip board and the layout is shown in Figure 17-3. Compare that with the photograph shown in Figure 17-4. In the layout, the strips of copper on the underside are shown by using dotted lines. This is a conventional way of showing hidden details on a drawing.

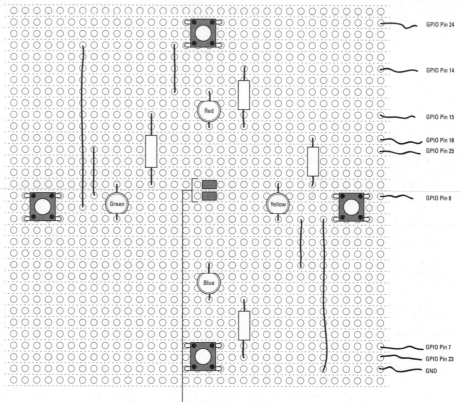

GPIO Pin 24

GPIO Pin 14

GPIO Pin 15

GPIO Pin 18
GPIO Pin 25

GPIO Pin 8

GPIO Pin 7
GPIO Pin 23
GND

Figure 17-3:
The physical
layout of
the Copycat
game.

Make two breaks here.

The five vertical black lines represent tinned copper links. This is simply solid copper wire. You can get reels of it or just replace it with regular wires between the relevant holes. We think the tinned copper looks neater here. You only need to make two breaks on the back of the board. These are shown in Figure 17-3 as dotted shading or on the back of the board, Figure 17-5, as black marks. Either way, the breaks prevent the yellow and green LEDs from joining together. The track next to it prevents the yellow and green switches from joining together. All the other connections the strips make are supposed to be made.

Strip board works well here because the grid acts as its own measuring stick. The board should be 33 holes by 33 holes to match the diagram. Cutting the strip board to the right size is quite easy. All you need to do is to score heavily down a row of holes with a sharp knife, and then turn the board over and score the other side of the same row. Then place the scored line along the edge of a table, hold the board flat to the table with one palm, and snap the board by using your other palm to bend it. If you are being particularly neat, you can sand the edges flat with a disc sander or file.

Figure 17-4:
A photo-
graph of
the Copycat
game.

Figure 17-5:
The strip
side of the
Copycat
game.

With such a small board, the construction order is not important, but normally you would start with the lowest height component first, so put the copper links on. Make sure they are in exactly the right holes, solder them up, and then trim the surplus wire from the back with side cutters. Then add the resistors and the LEDs. The LEDs have to be put in the correct way or they will not work. Many LEDs have a small flat by one wire. This marks the cathode or negative connection. However, all LEDs have the anode wire (positive connection) the longer of the two, so make sure the long wire is opposite the position of the flat on the diagram. Finally, fit and solder the switches. As mentioned earlier, make sure you get the rotation correct, with the long side going along the copper strip.

If you can't tell what color your LEDs are when they're off, apply a small spot of the appropriate color paint or a sticker to the switch or close to the LED.

Now all you need to do is to wire the circuit board up to the GPIO connection board you made in Chapter 16. We've assigned the pins for this game to be different from Chapter 16's Blastoff game, so you can have both of them wired up at the same time if you want.

Whenever you do physical computing like this, make sure that the hardware is working before you try to make it do something complex. That way, you have confidence that when you look at the inputs or change the outputs, it will work like you expect it to. To that end, here's a little program, Listing 17-1, that tests out the hardware you have made.

Listing 17-1: Copycat Hardware Test Program

```
#!/usr/bin/python
# run by sudo python copyCatTest.py
# or from IDLE launched by typing gksudo idle

import RPi.GPIO as GPIO

leds = [14, 15, 18, 23]
buttons = [24, 25, 8, 7]

print"hi from pi - Copycat Hardware test"
print"press the buttons to turn the LEDs off"
GPIO.setmode(GPIO.BCM)  # use real GPIO numbering
GPIO.setwarnings(False) # to remove spurious warnings on re running ↵
   code for pin in leds:
   GPIO.setup(pin, GPIO.OUT)
for pin in buttons:
   GPIO.setup(pin, GPIO.IN, pull_up_down=GPIO.PUD_UP)

while True: # loop forever
   for position in range(0,4): # look at each button in turn
      if GPIO.input(buttons[position]) == 0 : # if button pressed
         GPIO.output(leds[position], 0) # turn off LED
      else:
         GPIO.output(leds[position], 1) # turn on LED
```

It is quite simple: First, all the LEDs are turned on and the buttons are scanned. When a button is found to be pressed, it turns off its corresponding LED. Run this and press each button in turn. The LED next to the button should turn off. If it doesn't, there is a wiring mistake somewhere on the board. If you can't find it, just check out your breakout connector again by running the test code in the previous chapter (Listing 16-1).

The way we tackled the program for the game was to first generate a sequence of random numbers from 0 to 3 in a list, each number representing a color. Then a variable called `far` indicates how far in the sequence you have got, with functions to say the sequence, get a button press, and to check if the button is the right one. The code is shown in Listing 17-2. Take a look.

Listing 17-2:   Copycat Game

```
#!/usr/bin/python
# run by sudo python copyCat.py
# or from IDLE launched by typing gksudo idle

import RPi.GPIO as GPIO
from time import sleep
import random
import pygame
from pygame.locals import *

pygame.init()
pygame.mixer.quit()
pygame.mixer.init()

def getPress():
    pressed = False
    while pressed == False:
      for test in range(0,4):
        if GPIO.input(buttons[test]) == False: # button held down
            GPIO.output(leds[test],1)
            effect[test].play()
            pressed = True
            sleep(0.05) # debounce delay
            while GPIO.input(buttons[test]) == False: # hold until ↵
                                    button released
               sleep(0.05)
            GPIO.output(leds[test],0)
            return test

def saySeq(length):
    for number in range(0,length):
        effect[sequence[number]].play()
        GPIO.output(leds[sequence[number]],1) # turn LED on
        sleep(1.2)
        GPIO.output(leds[sequence[number]],0) # turn LED off
        sleep(0.5)
```

(continued)

Listing 17-2 *(continued)*

```
def getSeq(length):
    goSound.play()
    print"Now you try"
    for press in range(0,length):
        attempt = getPress()
        # uncomment next line to show what you are pressing
        #print"key press ", colours[attempt], "looking for", ↵
                          colours[sequence[press]]
        #note the game is too easy with the above line
        if attempt != sequence[press]:
            sleep(0.8)
            return -1
    return 1

colours = ["red", "green", "yellow", "blue" ]
print "Loading sound files"
effect = [ pygame.mixer.Sound("sounds/"+colours[c]+".ogg") for ↵
                       c in range(0,4)]
goSound = pygame.mixer.Sound("sounds/go.ogg")
dohSound = pygame.mixer.Sound("sounds/doh.ogg")
maxLength = 35
sequence = [ random.randint(0,3) for c in range(0,maxLength)]

leds = [14, 15, 18, 23]
buttons = [24, 25, 8, 7]

print"hi from Pi - Copycat, you copy the sequence"
print"Ctrl C to quit"
GPIO.setmode(GPIO.BCM)  # use real GPIO numbering
GPIO.setwarnings(False) # to remove spurious warnings on ↵
                       re running code for pin in leds:
    GPIO.setup(pin, GPIO.OUT)
    GPIO.output(pin, 0) # turn LEDs off
for pin in buttons:
    GPIO.setup(pin, GPIO.IN, pull_up_down=GPIO.PUD_UP)
maxFails = 3

while True: # repeat forever
    fail = 0  # number of fails
    # generate new sequence
    for c in range(0,maxLength):
        sequence[c] = random.randint(0,3)
    far = 2
    while fail < maxFails: # number of fail attempts before reset
        print"a sequence of",far
        saySeq(far)
        if getSeq(far) != -1:
            far = far + 1
            print"Yes - now try a longer one"
            fail = 0 # reset number of fails
        else:
            fail = fail +1
            print"Wrong",fail,"fail"
```

```
        if fail < maxFails:
            dohSound.play()
            print"try that one again"

    sleep(1.5)
    if far > maxLength:
        print"Well done Master Mind"
        exit() # suspect a cheat
dohSound.play()
print"Game over - Your score is",far-1
print"Try again"
sleep(2.0)
```

What does this code do? First it imports a new module, `random` — as you might guess, this is for generating random numbers. Skip over the function definitions for the moment and come back to them later. Next the sound files are loaded in, as well as the files for the colors. There are also two other sounds: a go sound, which is an invitation for you to enter your guess, and a sound to indicate an error, which is `dohSound`.

Next a list of the whole sequence is generated, the length set by the `maxLength` variable. This value is more than the human brain can remember. Unless someone is cheating by writing down the sequence or a non-human is playing, it should be long enough. The initial sequence length is set to a value of 2. You can change this if you want to start off with a longer sequence. Finally, before entering the main loop, the `maxFails` variable is set to control how many times you can get it wrong before ending your turn.

The program then sets up the variables to play one round of the game. That round continues until the number of fails you have on any one turn is equal to the maximum. A running commentary on the state of the game prints out on the screen, but you play the game by looking at the buttons and lights. The sequence is output and then your attempt at copying it is checked by the `getSeq` function. This function returns a value of `-1` if you make an error so that the program can either increase the sequence length or increase the error count, depending on how you got on. Finally, if the sequence length is equal to the maximum length, the game suspects the player is cheating, so it prints out an ironic message and quits the program.

Now take a look at the functions that interact with the hardware. The `saySeq` function takes in a length value and produces the sound associated with each number. It also turns the appropriate LED on and then off. The sleep delays ensure that the sound has time to finish playing and that you have long enough to see the LED. The GPIO pin to use for any number/color is stored in the list called `leds`. The current number to use is stored in the list called `sequence` and the current position in that list is given by the `number` variable. So the line

```
GPIO.output(leds[sequence[number]],1) # turn LED on
```

is what is known as a *double look-up* because the GPIO pin number you want is looked up from the index of the sequence list, which in turn uses the number variable to find the right value.

The getPress function returns the number of buttons currently being pressed. However, the function won't return until the button is released. This prevents the program from thinking it's your next guess. It does this because compared to human reactions, this program works very fast. So when a button is detected as being pressed, the appropriate LED is turned on and then an appropriate sound produced. A small delay known as a *de-bounce delay* occurs. This is because buttons sometimes don't make or break cleanly, but physically bounce and look like they have been pressed many times. This delay prevents the program from looking at the button again until it has settled down. Then a loop repeats a delay until the button is released. The function then returns the number of the button pressed.

Finally the getSeq function plays the goSound (we used a small bleep here) and then repeatedly calls the getPress function, checking that the returned value is correct. It does this until either an error is detected or the end of the sequence thus far is reached.

If you want to make the game easier, uncomment the print line in the getSeq and it prints out the sequence as the player goes on. It's great for testing, but because it prints out the sequence so far, all you have to remember is the last color.

The sounds can be produced in exactly the same way you did for the Blastoff game. Mike recorded himself saying the names of the colors and saved them as an .ogg file.

Customizing the Game

You can customize this game and make many different variations. We made a version that substituted the names of the colors for different cat sounds, in keeping with the name of the game. We got the sound of a domestic cat along with several big cats like lions and tigers. This made it harder to play because players didn't get the reinforcement of hearing the sounds named.

However, if you want to really blow the minds of your players, change the line

```
colours = ["red", "green", "yellow", "blue" ]
```

to

```
colours = ["blue", "red", "green", "yellow" ]
```

This means that the game says the wrong color. The player has to ignore the sound and go off the color of the LED alone. This makes the game very hard.

You can also remove the line where the `fail` variable is set back to zero on a successful guess. That way, the player can only make a total number of failed guesses in any one round and not on any one guess.

The random number generator can throw up the same numbers several times in a sequence. Although this is truly random, it sometimes feels like it's not. You can change the bit of the program that generated the sequence to choose another number if it's the same as the previous number. This tends to reduce the length of the sequence the player can remember.

One other variation you might like to try is to have another set of sounds with the announcement of the color preceded by a cat meow. These are the ones used in the correct sequence. However, keep the original sounds and throw a few in at random, along with the LED lighting, in the routine that says the sequence. In other words, these extra colors, if not preceded by a cat meow, are not part of the sequence and should not be entered.

Making a Better Game

The Copycat game is good, but it doesn't have a very good user interface. That is, you just have a bare piece of strip board, which looks very unfinished. You can do something about this, but first you have to learn how to control something a bit more powerful with the GPIO lines of the Raspberry Pi. The maximum current from any one GPIO pin is 16mA. Although this is good enough to light an LED, anything more and it's just a bit feeble. The solution is to use the GPIO lines to control something that can switch more power, and the simplest thing that can achieve that is a transistor.

A *transistor* is a simple device for switching current. It has three terminals called the emitter, base, and collector. Their symbol is shown in Figure 17-6. It works by making a current flow through the base to the emitter: This is called the *base current*. When a base current flows, it causes another current to flow from the collector to the emitter. The trick is that this collector-to-emitter current you cause to flow in this way is the size of the base current multiplied by a gain factor, which can be as much as a few hundred times.

If you have a transistor with a gain of 200, and you put 15mA in the base, are you going to get a current of 15×200=000mA or 3A flowing? Not normally: The current you actually get depends on the power supply feeding the collector and the resistance of the load R1 in the collector. Also, the transistor probably can't stand that much current anyway. So what's the point? The transistor is said to be fully turned on or *saturated,* as we say. That is, it's acting like a switch and allowing as much current to flow as Ohm's law says it should, just from a small current into the base.

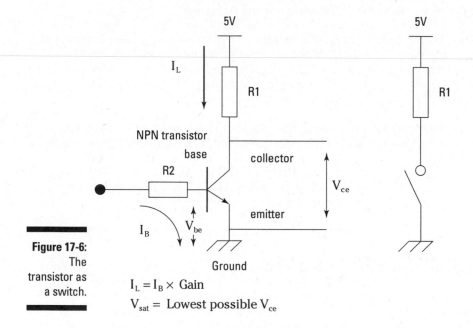

Figure 17-6: The transistor as a switch.

$I_L = I_B \times \text{Gain}$

$V_{sat} = \text{Lowest possible } V_{ce}$

Figure 17-7 shows an LED connected to a transistor being driven from a GPIO pin. Note that there is a resistor in line with the base. This is needed to limit the current into the base and out of the GPIO pin to the small amount we need. The transistor's collector/emitter is sinking current from the power supply through the resistor and LED, so a small amount of current from the GPIO controls the large amount of current through the LED.

The voltage of the LED's power supply can be anything, so you are not restricted to the 3V3 maximum voltage of the GPIO pin. Using a transistor, you can control a large current at a large voltage from a small current at a low voltage. It need not be an LED and resistor in the load — it can be anything, even a motor, an electromagnet, or another piece of electronic equipment. It's like a lever, amplifying the force from your GPIO pin to control anything.

To make this game better, you need to make better set of buttons for the game: buttons that are larger and illuminated, but still use the same tack switches as before. The idea is to use half a table-tennis ball as the button cover mounted on the copper side of the board and have the tack switch on the plane side of the board pointing down.

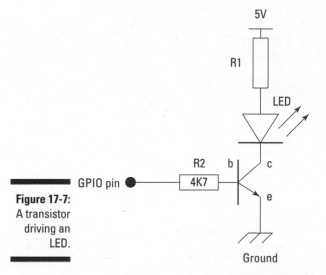

Figure 17-7:
A transistor
driving an
LED.

We'll place four pieces of 6mm (1/4") thick foam in the corners of the board to give the button a nice tactile feel. You can always glue several layers of thinner foam together if you can't get any that thick. On the copper strip side illuminating the half ball will be an LED of the appropriate color. This means that the LED needs to be bright so that you can see it shine through skin of the ball. This means two things: You need to push more current through it than a GPIO output can supply and you need to use a surface-mount LED to ensure even illumination.

This involves putting a transistor on the board along with the tack switch. The schematic is shown in Figure 17-8 and the physical layout for one switch is shown in Figure 17-9. You need to make this circuit four times. Note that there is a cut in the copper track between each of the tack switch leads. This is marked as a shaded area. You can see it more clearly on Figure 17-10, which is a diagram of the back of the switch board. As to the circuit, it turns out that you can use the same value of current-limiting resistor for all the LEDs except the blue one, which needs to be a bit smaller.

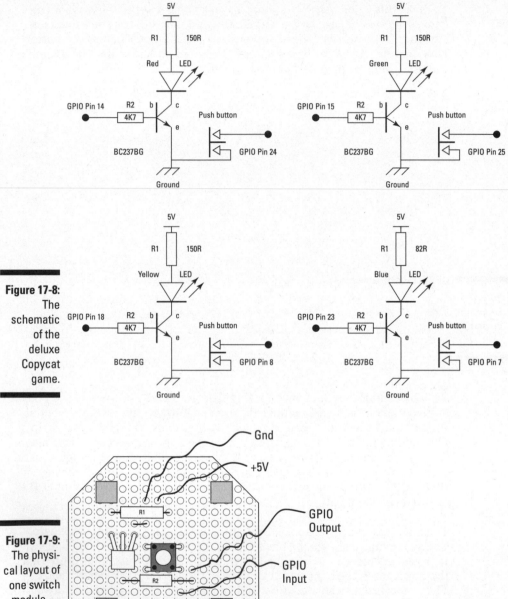

Figure 17-8:
The
schematic
of the
deluxe
Copycat
game.

Figure 17-9:
The physi-
cal layout of
one switch
module —
component
side.

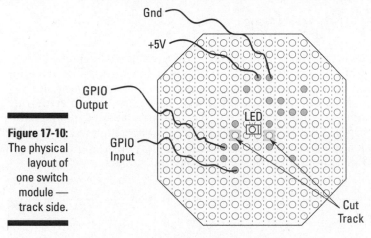

Gnd
+5V
GPIO
Output
GPIO
Input
LED
Cut
Track

Figure 17-10:
The physical
layout of
one switch
module —
track side.

Illuminated push button, track side

Choosing the LEDs can be tricky because a very wide variety of types is available. You want one with at least a 20 mA current rating to produce about 500 mCd of illumination. Many different types of surface-mount LED exist, and the only one not suitable is the type with a bubble lens molded in. This type won't evenly illuminate the half ball. You are going to solder the LED between two tracks of the strip board, so packages like PLCC (plastic leaded chip carrier) and SMD (surface-mount devices) are fine. Most major electronic component distributors have a filter function at their websites, so you can narrow down the choice of parts to just the suitable ones.

The transistor we chose to use was the BC237BG, mainly because of the price. At less than five cents each, they are good value. You're looking for a general-purpose NPN transistor with a modest current rating of 100 mA or so. Any one of literally thousands of types will do here.

The *NPN* in the description describes how the transistor is made up of three layers of silicon. There are two types of silicon: N type, where the current is carried by electrons, and P type, where it is carried by holes or lack of electrons. Don't worry too much about that: Just don't get the other type of transistor, the PNP type. These two types are distinguished in the schematic symbol by having the arrow on the emitter pointing in a different direction.

The pin out (that is, where the pins are physically located on a transistor) can be anything. The transistor we used has the pin out (shown in Figure 17-9) when the flat of the transistor is placed against the board. Notice we've marked these pins c, e, and b, although no such markings appear on the transistor itself. If you use a different transistor, make sure it either has the same pin out or adjust the physical layout to suit.

Putting It All Together

To put the game together, make four of the boards, as shown in Figure 17-11, solder up the parts, and attach the LED on the copper strip side. You have to get the LED the right way round. On surface-mount LEDs, the cathode or negative end is normally marked by a thin green line or has a green arrow on the underside pointing to the cathode end. The cathode must be connected to the copper strip that has the current limiting resistor connected to it. You need a fine pair of tweezers to hold the LED in place when soldering it. Figure 17-12 shows a photograph of the LED soldered in place.

Figure 17-11:
Four switch module boards.

After you have made the board, solder four wires up and test it. Wire the +5V and ground up to a power supply or the appropriate points on the breakout board, and then take the control wire (the one connected to the base resistor) and touch it on the +5V line. The LED should light up. Do not worry if the LED glows dimly when this wire is not connected to anything. Just make sure that the LED is off when it is touched to the ground. Check the continuity of the switch to the ground when pressed either by using a meter or by using the GPIO port monitor program (refer to Listing 16-1) or the GPIOmon.py on the website.

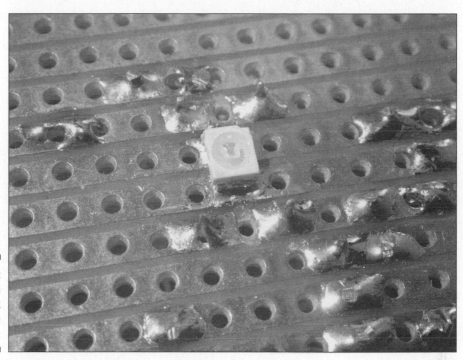

Figure 17-12:
The LED on
the track
side of the
board.

Next, make a tray similar to the project in the last chapter, cut two 15mm (6") squares of plywood, and drill a hole in each corner. Then glue a 10mm frame of strip pine to the base. Cut four 40mm (1 9/16") holes using a saw drill in the top. Join the top and base together using pillars in the corner holes. Paint the four quadrants of the tray in colors to match the LEDs.

In order for the strip board to be flush with the top of the tray, we glued a 50mm (2") square of 4mm (5/32") thick styrene to the foam pads of each push assembly with impact adhesive. Then we wired the four switch assemblies to a piece of strip board to act as a distribution point, and then wired a piece of 10-way ribbon cable to this strip (Figure 17-13). We filed a small recess in the side of the tray to accommodate the ribbon cable so that the lid will fit on.

Only when the board checks out should you glue the table tennis ball halves over the LED. You can slice a table tennis ball in half in a number of ways. Using a scalpel or knife is a bit tricky. Avoid cutting yourself (obviously) and try to get a smooth edge. If your edge is rough, you can always sand the edge smooth after. A better method is to use a small bench circular saw and rotate the ball against the blade.

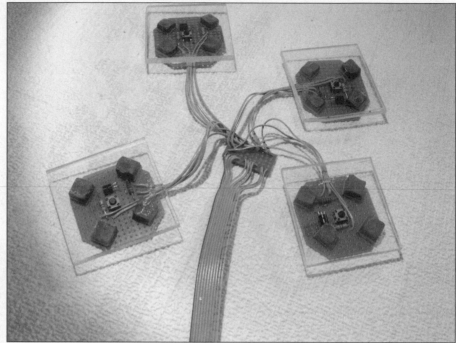

Figure 17-13:
The four
switch
modules
wired
together.

However, the best way is to use a hot wire cutter of the type sold in hobby shops for cutting sheets of expanded polystyrene. Clamp the wire cutter and move the ball through the wire, avoiding burning your fingers. You can find many videos on YouTube showing you how to cut a table tennis ball in half. At this point, mark the component side of the strip board with the color of the LED so you can fit it in the right place. Use a few spots of impact adhesive — it doesn't have to be a continuous line of glue.

Finally, use hot melt glue to fix the switch assemblies in place directly under each hole in the lid. Do this by fixing the lid on with one screw and aligning the other holes. Then by holding onto the top of the table tennis ball, remove the lid without moving the switch so that the switch assembly can be fixed in place with a fillet of glue (see Figure 17-14). Do this now without moving the switch. When the glue has cooled, repeat separately for each of the remaining three switches to ensure that they are all in exactly the right place.

All that remains is to wire up the 10-way ribbon cable to the breakout board and to run the test software again, as shown in Figure 17-15. The final appearance and the way it works surpasses our expectations!

Figure 17-14:
The switch modules glued in place.

Figure 17-15:
The final game.

Chapter 18

The Raspberry Pi in an Analog World

*I*n the previous two chapters, we show how the Raspberry Pi could sense logic levels on the GPIO pins when they were configured to be inputs. We also show how you could switch LEDs on and off when GPIO pins were configured to be outputs. We also show how, by using a transistor, you can use the Pi to control much larger currents than you can get directly from the GPIO pins.

In this chapter, we show you how to use the GPIO to talk to other integrated circuits. There are many ways to do this, called *protocols*. This chapter concentrates on one called the I2C protocol. Many integrated circuits use this protocol to allow you to do many things. However, one very different sort of thing is how to input and output, not in the strict on/off way of the digital world you have seen so far, but in an analog or proportional way.

In this chapter, we show you how to make the Raspberry Ripple, a board to allow you to input and output analog signals. Then we explore some of the interesting things that you can do in this new analog world.

Exploring the Difference: Analog versus Digital

With a digital signal, everything is either on or off, no half measures. Indeed, many things work in this manner; for example, your radio is either on or off. It makes no sense for it to be anything else. However, this is not true of everything. For example, a light can be half on or dimmed. A volume control can be full on, full off, or somewhere in between. These are proportional controls.

Taking small steps

So how does a computer handle a proportional control? In a program, variables can take on any value you assign them. You can do the same with a voltage. However, the voltage is not continuously variable, but split up into small steps, or *quantized*. The number of small steps used is given by the resolution of the circuit. By combining several on/off signals, with each one contributing an unequal small voltage, you can produce very close to whatever voltage you want. The circuit to do this is called a *digital-to-analog (D/A) converter*, and there are several different designs. Figure 18-1 shows one such method using four digital outputs, or as we say, four bits. Each switch is a digital output from the computer and can send current through a resistor or not, depending on whether the switch is open or closed. The important thing is the relative resistor values, not the absolute values.

The resistor R is any value and 2R is twice that value, 4R four times, and 8R eight times. The voltage that is switched is called a *reference voltage* or *Vref* and is in effect the maximum voltage that will be output. The current from each of these switched resistors is fed into a current summing circuit. The output of the summing circuit is driven through a resistor with a value of R, shown in Figure 18-1 as Rs.

To see how this works, suppose only switch 3 is made. Current I3 flows into the current summing circuit, and, as no more switches are made, that is the current that flows out of the current summing circuit. This flows through Rs and thus develops a voltage across the summing resistor. As the resistor on Sw3 has a value of R and the summing resistor has a value of R, the voltage developed across the summing resistor is equal to half the reference voltage. If only switch 2 is made, the output voltage is a quarter of Vref; similarly, switch 1 produces an eighth and switch 0 a sixteenth. When more than one switch is made, the current from each switch is added together and produces an output voltage, Vout, which is the sum of these fractional voltages of Vref.

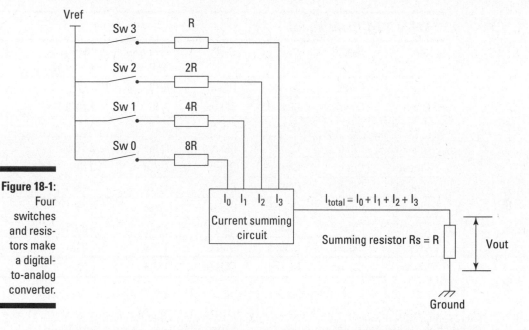

Figure 18-1:
Four switches and resistors make a digital-to-analog converter.

With four switches, you can have a number of combinations of switches made and unmade. The total number of combinations is given by two (the number of states) raised to the power of four (the number of switches). So we can have 16 different combinations and so 16 different voltages out of Vout. Table 18-1 shows each one of these. Note that the voltages are not "nice" round values and that the maximum voltage is just short of the reference voltage, or Vref. In fact, it is short by one increment; that is, by one sixteenth of the reference voltage.

Table 18-1   Output Voltage for All Combinations of Switch States

Sw3	Sw2	Sw1	Sw0	Fraction of Vref	Voltage if Vref = 5V
Open	Open	Open	Open	0/16	0
Open	Open	Open	Closed	1/16	0.3125
Open	Open	Closed	Open	2/16	0.625
Open	Open	Closed	Closed	3/16	0.9375
Open	Closed	Open	Open	4/16	1.25
Open	Closed	Open	Closed	5/16	1.5625

(continued)

Table 18-1 *(continued)*

Sw3	Sw2	Sw1	Sw0	Fraction of Vref	Voltage if Vref = 5V
Open	Closed	Closed	Open	6/16	1.875
Open	Closed	Closed	Closed	7/16	2.1875
Closed	Open	Open	Open	8/16	2.5
Closed	Open	Open	Closed	9/16	2.8125
Closed	Open	Closed	Open	10/16	3.125
Closed	Open	Closed	Closed	11/16	3.4375
Closed	Closed	Open	Open	12/16	3.75
Closed	Closed	Open	Closed	13/16	4.0625
Closed	Closed	Closed	Open	14/16	4.375
Closed	Closed	Closed	Closed	15/16	4.6875

As there are four switches, we say that this D/A has a resolution of four bits. If you replace the open and closed in the switches columns with logic 0 and 1s, the whole thing starts to look like a *binary number,* which is exactly how a computer stores an integer variable. Four bits is rather coarse, and a typical D/A converter can normally have anything from 8 to 16 bits, with even 24 bits being possible. With a 16-bit converter and a 5V reference voltage, each voltage step will be

```
5V/(2¹⁶) = 5/65536 = 0.00007629395 V or 76.29395 uV
```

Those still aren't nice round numbers, but it's very fine control indeed. In fact, this is a much smaller step that any interference or noise likely to be in most digital circuits. We cover this interference in Chapter 15. So the step size is small compared to circuit noise. For all intents and purposes, the voltage output can be thought of as continuously variable.

Reading small steps

You can see how, by combining lots of outputs, you can make a voltage that is adjustable in small steps. But what if you want to read how big a voltage is — that is, perform the opposite task of an analog-to-digital conversion (A/D)? You have to have a D/A along with a circuit known as a comparator. A *comparator* is simply an amplifier with a very high gain. It has two inputs marked: + (plus sign) and – (minus sign). Its output is high if the + input has a higher voltage on it than the – input. If the – input is higher, however, the output is low. So a comparator simply produces a signal that tells you which input is higher. Team that up with a D/A and you have an A/D, as shown in Figure 18-2.

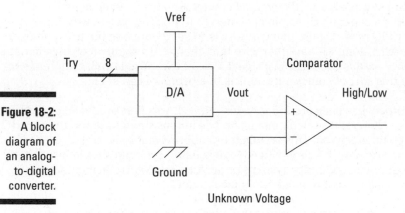

Figure 18-2:
A block diagram of an analog-to-digital converter.

This is a block diagram, which means it only shows how a thing works, not the wiring you need to make it work. A new symbol here is the thick line with a slash across it and the number eight above. This means that there are really eight wires here, each one going into the D/A. Into these go a number, denoted by a combination of high and low lines, which is a guess as to what our unknown voltage will be. If the guess is too high, the comparator output is high; if the guess is too low, the output is low. To find the exact value of our unknown voltage, you must find a number that results in a low output of the comparator, yet with only an addition of one to the number results in that output being high.

This means that in order to get the A/D to function it has to be driven; that is, something must implement an algorithm of guesses and responses to the guess. This can be done with dedicated logic circuits or it can be driven from a computer. The simplest algorithm is called a *single ramp*. The guess is incremented by one repeatedly until it reaches the value of the unknown voltage. This is simple but not very efficient. A much more efficient way is to use successive approximation.

Suppose you are asked to guess a number between 0 and 256 and the only information you could get is whether your guess is too high or too low. The best strategy is to guess at half the range and keep on halving. So your first guess should be 128. If that's too low, your next guess should be between 128 and 256, so halve that and guess 192. It that's too high, you know the number is between 128 and 192, so halve the difference and guess 160. Keep repeating that, and in only eight guesses, you will have honed in on the correct number.

Investigating Converter Chips

Special chips have all the circuitry and can do all of these processes for you. Your computer can connect to these chips in a wide variety of ways. One of the simplest ways is called a *parallel* connection, where each signal in the circuit has a separate GPIO pin allocated to it. It is the fastest way, but it uses a lot of GPIO pins. A more efficient way is to send data one bit at a time over a single wire along with another wire that changes to signify a change in data. This other wire is called a *clock* signal. One of the more popular implementations of this sort of communications is to a protocol called I2C.

This protocol has been around for a long time. It was first produced in 1982 by Philips to allow its ICs to communicate. The initials stand for Inter-Integrated Circuit communication. This is sometimes abbreviated to IIC or I2C, otherwise known as *twin wire*. It's pronounced "eye squared cee" and should be written as I^2C, but not all computer systems or languages have the facility for superscript capability, so it remains I2C in most places.

The idea is that communication takes place over two wires: One carries the data and the other the clock. As there is only one line for the data, and that can only be high or low, transmitting numbers or *bytes* (a collection of 8 logic levels defining a number) happens serially; that is, one bit at a time. The rising edge of the clock line tells the receiver when to sample the data signal, and each message to and from a device consists of one or more bytes.

In its simplest form, there is one master device, which in our case is the Raspberry Pi, and up to 128 different slave devices. In practice, there are very rarely this many, and it is normal just to have one or two. Each slave device has to have its own unique address, and this is, in the main, built into the chip you are using. The first thing in any message from the master is the address of the slave it wants to communicate with. If a slave sees something that is not its own address, it ignores the message.

Building the Raspberry Ripple

What you are going to make next is the Raspberry Ripple, an analog input/output board. In electronics, the word *ripple* is used to denote small, often rapid, changes in a voltage. This board is going to look at changing voltages, hence the name. After you've made it, you can make a whole range of projects with analog signals. We show you some examples at the end of the chapter.

Here are the parts you'll need to build the Raspberry Ripple:

- ✔ 1 2.8"×1.7" copper strip prototype board.
- ✔ 1 16-way DIL IC socket.

- ✔ 1 PCF8591P 8-bit A/D and D/A converter.
- ✔ 1 2N2222 NPN transistor.
- ✔ 1 1N4001 diode (or any other diode).
- ✔ 2 47uF capacitor 6V8 or greater working voltage.
- ✔ 1 1K wire-ended resistors.
- ✔ 5 3-way PCB mounting terminal block with screw connectors.
- ✔ Note the Phoenix contact–PT1,5/6-5.0-V–terminal block, PCB, screw, 5.0mm, 6-way can be split in half by sliding the components apart.
- ✔ 2' 24 SWG (or similar) tinned copper wire.

Note: A 10K potentiometer might be required for testing.

The chip at the heart of the Ripple

At the heart of the Raspberry Ripple is the PCF8591 chip, a venerable design that has stood the test of time. It is widely available, but the price can vary dramatically depending on where you buy it. It contains a four-input, 8-bit A/D converter and a single output 8-bit D/A converter. In fact, it only has one A/D converter, and the four inputs are achieved by electronically switching from one of the four inputs into the A/D converter. It has three external address lines, which means that part of the address of this chip can be determined by how these lines are wired up. This means that up to eight of these chips can coexist on the I2C bus and all have their own unique address. The other 4 bits of the address are fixed. When you know what bits need to be set, you can find the address by adding up the value of each bit with a one in it, as shown in Figure 18-3.

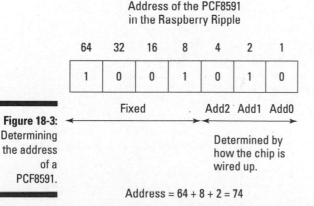

Address of the PCF8591
in the Raspberry Ripple

64	32	16	8	4	2	1
1	0	0	1	0	1	0

Fixed   Add2 Add1 Add0

Figure 18-3: Determining the address of a PCF8591.

Determined by how the chip is wired up.

Address = 64 + 8 + 2 = 74

Putting the chip into a circuit

The schematic of the Raspberry Ripple is shown in Figure 18-4. There isn't much to it apart from the chip. However, one component we have not met before is the capacitor. There are two here, C1 and C2. Their job is to smooth out any variations, or noise, on the power supply to the chip and the reference voltage. The reference voltage needs to be stable because if it changes, the voltage reading changes, even if there is no real change in the input voltage. Adding a resistor and having another capacitor on the voltage reference pin gives a more stable reference than just connecting it to the supply. The capacitors have a working voltage associated with them. As long as it's more than 5V, it doesn't matter what it is. However, the higher the voltage, the bigger the capacitor will be.

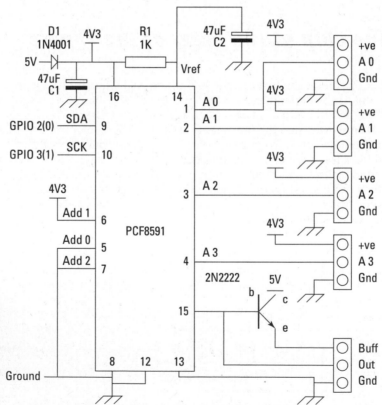

Figure 18-4:
The schematic of the Raspberry Ripple.

The diode D1 is there to drop the supply voltage by a tad. Although a diode is used to restrict current flow in one direction, when current is flowing through, it drops a constant voltage across it of about 0.7V independent of the current flow. Strictly speaking, you need this because the Raspberry Pi can only deliver a 3V3 signal, and the lowest signal the data sheet says can be seen by this chip as a logic one is 0.7 of the supply voltage. If the supply voltage is 5V, the signal must be 3V5 to be recognized. In practice, we've found it works quite happily without the diode, but going against the information in the data sheet is a very bad idea because you have no guarantees of anything.

We have wired address line 1 to the supply to make it a logic one, and the other two address lines to ground or logic zero, to give the address 74. You can have up to eight of these circuits running at the same time. You just have to ensure that each circuit has a different combination of logic levels wired to these address lines.

The four analog inputs are wired to their own three-way screw terminal block with both a ground and a supply voltage on them. We used Phoenix contact–PT1,5/6-5.0-V–terminal block, PCB, screw, 5.0mm, six-way. They are in fact two three-way blocks and it is easy to just slide them apart. It is actually cheaper to buy a six-way block and split it than it is to buy three-way blocks. These screw terminal blocks have a blank area next to the contact that is ideal for putting a label on. Using a screw block makes wiring up the later projects to this a lot easier. The analog output of this chip is fed directly to a screw terminal and through a transistor to act as a current buffer if you need to get more drive from the output.

Wiring it up

Figure 18-5 shows the layout of the Raspberry Ripple on strip board. Note the hidden detail showing where the tracks are cut between the adjacent pins of the IC as well as in four other places. Figure 18-6 shows a photograph of the same thing. The capacitors must be placed the right way round. The positive end is marked by a depression in the can and the negative end by a black line in the type (the marking might be different on other types). The diode has a line marking the cathode or pointy end of the symbol. All the diodes we've seen are marked like this. Finally, the chip has to be fitted the right way round as well. It has a small circular indent marking the top.

Note the link next to the +ve connection on the A1 connection block. Here two wires go into the same hole, denoted by the gray hole. Put both wires through before soldering them up. We also used an IC socket for the chip so it could be replaced in case of accidents. The board is wired up to GPIO pins

2 and 3 (or 0 and 1 if you have an issue 1 board). These two different GPIO signals are physically on the same pins for the two board issues. Unlike the other projects in this book, you have no choice in pin assignment because we are going to use these pins' special hidden powers to talk to the chip.

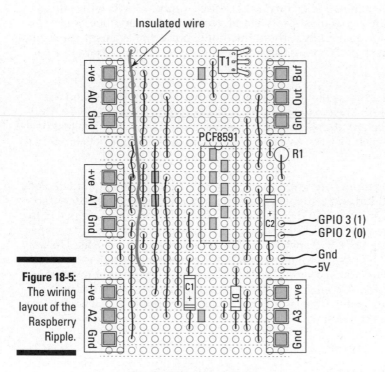

Insulated wire

Figure 18-5:
The wiring
layout of the
Raspberry
Ripple.

27 strips high, 16 holes wide

Installing the drivers

Before you can use the Raspberry Ripple board, you have to install an I2C driver to allow the GPIO pins to become a specialist I2C bus driver. This means that the Raspberry Pi's hardware will handle the transfer of data along these two wires. A few drivers are available, but the SMBus driver is by far the easiest to install and the commands are quite easy to use. In fact, many distributions already have it installed as standard, but by default it is disabled. To enable it, you have to change two files. Type the following into the command line:

```
sudo nano /etc/modprobe.d/raspi-blacklist.conf
```

Figure 18-6:
A photo-
graph of the
Raspberry
Ripple.

Add a # at the start of the line `blacklist i2c-bcm2708` and then press
Ctrl+X. Press Y to save and exit. Next, you need to edit the modules file,
so type

```
sudo nano /etc/modules
```

Add a new line to this file that says `i2c-dev`. Again, press Ctrl+X and then
press Y to save and exit. Install a handy little utility for checking what is on
the I2C bus by typing two lines:

```
sudo apt-get update
sudo apt-get install i2c-tools
```

Finally, you need to tell the system you can use it. Assuming you still have the
default user name of *pi*, type

```
sudo adduser pi i2c
```

Then reboot the machine with

```
sudo shutdown -h now
```

Remove the power, plug in the Raspberry Ripple board, and power it up again. After you have logged in, type

```
sudo i2cdetect -y 0
```

You should see a table with all blank entries except one saying 4a, which is the address, in hexadecimal, of the Raspberry Ripple board. Remember, this is the same as the decimal value of 74 you calculated earlier in the chapter. If you do not see this address, check the wiring again for any errors. One big advantage of installing the drivers in this way is that you can now run your Python programs direct from the IDE. You don't need to run them with root privileges with a sudo prefix.

Using the Raspberry Ripple

Now we are ready use the Raspberry Ripple board. The first thing you need to do is to learn how to talk to the board and test it out. The PCF8591P has one control register: This is a single 8-bit (one *byte*) memory location in the chip that controls how it operates. So when you talk to the chip, you first send it an address, then the control byte, and then the data you want to send. The control byte is shown in Figure 18-7 and is a simplified version of that shown in the data sheet. We encourage you to download the data sheet and read it. It contains far more than you need to know and like any data sheet, it can be a bit intimidating when you first see it. However, it will describe the alternative input configuration modes that we're not using here. You will just be using the straightforward four channels of analog input in this book.

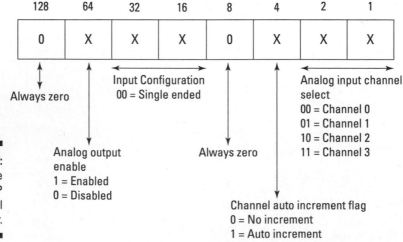

Figure 18-7:
The
PCF8591P
control
register.

You will see that the control byte has one bit, bit 6, that controls whether the analog output is enabled. It also has two bits that select what analog channel to read, and there is also a bit that enables the auto-incrementing of the channel select. This is useful because it means that you can look at all four input channels just by doing four successive reads. You don't need to set up the channel first.

Just a word of caution — when you read an analog channel, you do two things. You get back the last reading and you trigger the next one. Sometimes this is not a problem, but at other times, you have to bear in mind that's what is happening.

Testing the analog inputs

If an input channel is not being used, you should wire it to ground; otherwise, you get wildly fluctuating results from it. Therefore you need to put a wire between the A1, A2, and A3 input and the respective ground for this first test. Next you need to wire a variable voltage source to A0. The simplest and best way of doing this is to use a new component: a *potentiometer* or *pot*, sometimes also called a *variable resistor*. Basically, it's a knob. It has three terminals and is shown in Figure 18-8. They come in a variety of values. You're better off using a 10K one for this experiment, but any value between 1K and 47K will do. If you wire the middle terminal or *wiper* to A0, wire the bottom end connections to ground and the top end to +ve. Now you're ready to run the program in Listing 18-1. Note that the only thing that will happen if you swap the top end and the bottom end around is that it will produce the maximum voltage when it is turned fully anti-clockwise (counterclockwise).

A Potentiometer

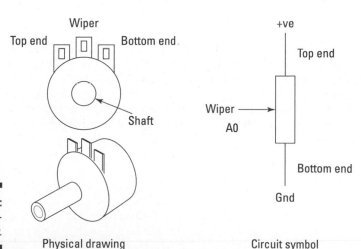

Figure 18-8:
A potentio-
meter.

Physical drawing

Circuit symbol

Listing 18-1:   Analog Input A0 Reading

```
# Read a value from analog input 0
# in A/D in the PCF8591P @ address 74
from smbus import SMBus

# comment out the one that does not apply to your board
#bus = SMBus(0) # for revision 1 boards
bus = SMBus(1) # for revision 2 or 3 boards
address = 74
Vref = 4.3
convert = Vref / 256

print("Read the A/D channel 0")
print("print reading when it changes")
print("Ctrl C to stop")
bus.write_byte(address, 0) # set control register to read channel 0
last_reading =-1

while True: # do forever
   reading = bus.read_byte(address) # read A/D 0
   if(abs(last_reading - reading) > 1): # only print on a change
      print"A/D reading",reading,"meaning",round(convert * reading,2),"V"
      last_reading = reading
```

This simply reads the voltage value on analog input channel 0 and prints it out if it has changed. The program prints out two values: The first is the raw A/D converter reading and the second is what this means in terms of volts. The values the program prints is restricted to two decimal places because 8 bits resolution does not justify any more significant digits. In calculating the voltage from the reading, the variable Vref is used to hold the reference voltage. This is right only if your Raspberry Pi is running off exactly 5V, something that is a bit unusual. To make this voltage value more accurate, use a volt meter and measure the voltage across C2; that is, place each of the two volt meter leads to each end of the capacitor.

If you get a negative reading, swap them. Take the value you measure and put it in as the value for Vref in the program. This applies to all the listings with a Vref variable. However, many programs you write using an A/D are not interested in the actual voltage but just use the raw reading. You can modify the listing to read any of the input channels by simply changing the value in the bus.write_byte instruction to change the control register so it selects another channel.

Testing the analog output

To check out the analog output, you need an LED and resistor wired up as shown in Figure 18-9. The wire to A1 is for the next experiment, so you can leave it out for now. Enter and run the program in Listing 18-2.

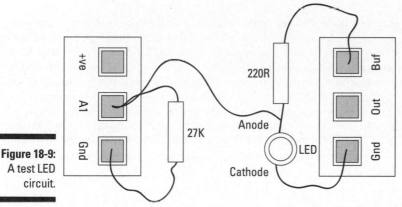

Figure 18-9:
A test LED
circuit.

Listing 18-2: D/A Output Ramp

```
# Output a count to the D/A in the PCF8591P @ address 74
from smbus import SMBus
from time import sleep

# comment out the one that does not apply to your board
# bus = SMBus(0) # for revision 1 boards
bus = SMBus(1) # for revision 2 & 3 boards
address = 74
control = 1<<6 # enable analog output

print("Output a ramp on the D/A")
print("Ctrl C to stop")
while True:
  for a in range(0,256):
     bus.write_byte_data(address, control, a) # output to D/A
     sleep(0.01)
```

You see the LED blink on and off, but on closer inspection, you see it rapidly fade up and then blink out. What is happening here is that the voltage output is gradually increasing as the `for` loop outputs successively bigger voltages. At some point, the LED comes on and gets brighter as more current flows through it. Note how it appears to stay the same brightness for a time even though the current through it is rising. This is due to the logarithmic light response of the human eye.

Making a Curve Tracer

You are going to make a *curve tracer*; that is, a device that outputs a varying voltage, applies it to a simple circuit, and reads back a measurement. When using the analog output, the analog input A0 is not functional and must be left unconnected. The analog input A1 has a high-value pull-down resistor to stabilize the readings when no voltage is applied. This resistor doesn't affect the measurements. In Listing 18-3, the voltage across the LED is measured by analog channel A1 and printed out along with the analog output voltage. Look at how the voltage "sticks" at close to the LED's turn-on voltage. When the LED is on, the voltage across it does not rise by much despite the voltage applied to the whole thing increasing. This sticking voltage depends on the LED's color and type.

Listing 18-3: LED Curve Tracer

```
# LED_trace1 - Buf --resistor -- A1 -- LED -- Gnd
# Print the voltage across an LED a voltage applied to LED and resistor
from smbus import SMBus
from time import sleep

# comment out the one that does not apply to your board
bus = SMBus(0) # for revision 1 boards
# bus = SMBus(1) # for revision 2 boards
address = 74
control = 1<<6 | 1 # enable analogue output and set to read A1
Vref = 4.44
convert = Vref / 256

print("Output a ramp on the D/A")
print("Ctrl C to stop")
while(True): # do forever
  for v in range(28,256): # start close to 0.7V
     bus.write_byte_data(address, control, v) # trigger last value to D/A
     bus.write_byte_data(address, control, v) # trigger this value to D/A
     reading = bus.read_byte(address) # read to kick off conversion
     reading = bus.read_byte(address) # read value
     Vbuf = (convert * v) - 0.7 # compensate for 0.7V lost ↵
                   in the buffered output
     if Vbuf < 0:
        Vbuf = 0
```

```
Vin = convert * reading
if Vin > Vbuf:
    Vbuf = Vin
Vout = convert * v # raw output voltage
print "Out",round(Vout,2),"V Buffered",round(Vbuf,2) , ↩
                "V --> Measured input 1 ", round(Vin,2),"V"
sleep(0.01)
```

The circuit is being driven from the buffered output of the Raspberry Ripple. The normal output of the Raspberry Ripple goes through a transistor in a configuration known as an *emitter follower*. This transistor allows the Ripple to drive much more current into a circuit than the PCF8591P alone; however, it does slightly complicate things. The voltage on the emitter follows the voltage on the base, with an offset of 0.7V. For example, if you output 2.7V from the D/A, you get 2V on the buffered output. This means that if you are ramping up the voltage to a circuit, there will be nothing out of the buffer until there is 0.7V going out.

To compensate for this, an offset is subtracted from the output value in the program. However, if the output value is below 0.7V, subtracting this offset results in a negative output value, which of course is absurd. Therefore, the program zeros the calculated buffered output if it's negative.

You can get the list of reading produced by this program plotted out as a graph of applied voltage against voltage across the LED. See if you can write a program to do this. If not, there is one on the website for this book called LEDtrace2. (See this book's Introduction for more on how to access the website.) A more normal sort of curve for an LED is the voltage against current. You can plot this by just taking the difference between the voltage across the LED and the voltage being output, giving you, in effect, the voltage across the LED's resistor. This voltage is directly proportional to the current and can be used as a current reading.

In fact, because you have three working analog channels, you can measure three curves at once. Figure 18-10 shows the circuit to plot the curve from a variable resistor and two different colors of LED, red and blue. Note the top end of the pot is not connected to anything. All three are plotted at once as shown in Figure 18-11. Again, you can find the program to do this on the website for this book. It's called LEDtrace4. The resistor is a simple straight line whose slope is determined by the resistor value. Because there is a pot acting as a resistor in the A1 input, altering the pot's value changes the slope of the curve. Any coarseness in the plotted graph is simply the inevitable noise or dither on the least significant bit you get with any A/D conversion.

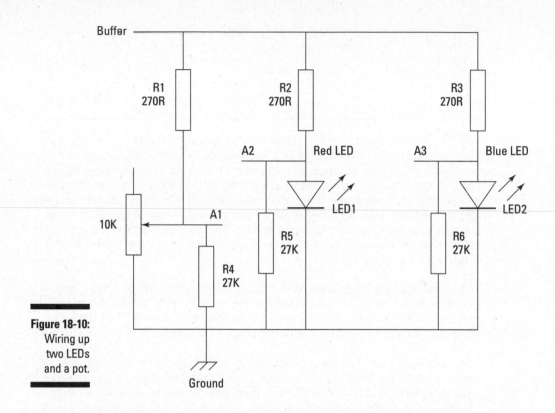

Figure 18-10:
Wiring up
two LEDs
and a pot.

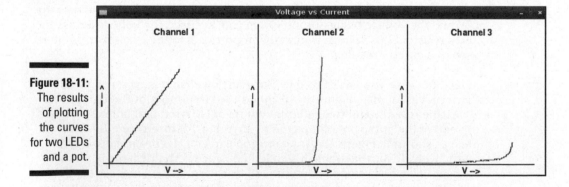

Figure 18-11:
The results
of plotting
the curves
for two LEDs
and a pot.

Making a Pot-a-Sketch

You are now well on your way to exploring what the Raspberry Ripple board can do for you. Next up you can make "pot-a-sketch," or a pot box drawing tool. This is simply four potentiometers in a box. Figure 18-12 shows the schematic and Figure 18-13 shows a photograph of the finished product. We used a small plastic box and push-on knobs with red, green, blue, and yellow push-on tops. For this program, you have one pot for the X movement and one pot for the Y movement, with the other two defining the color in terms of hue and saturation. The Delete key or spacebar is used to wipe the screen clean. Figure 18-14 shows a screen dump of it in action. Fire up the program pot-a-sketch.py and twiddle the knobs to make your drawing. Again, the code to drive this is on the website. (See this book's Introduction for more on how to access the website.)

A Potentiometer Box

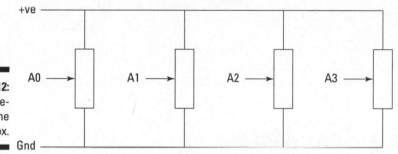

All pots any value between 1K and 50K

Figure 18-12: The schematic of the pot box.

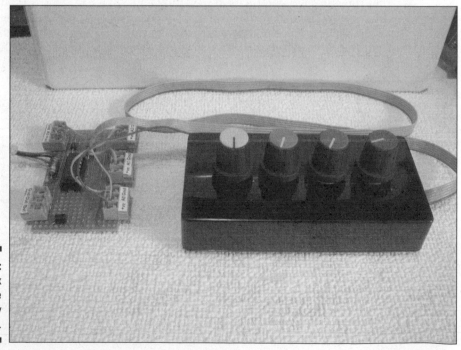

Figure 18-13: The pot box wired to the Raspberry Ripple.

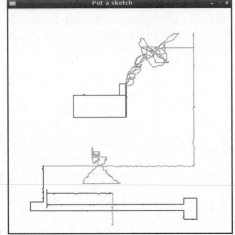

Figure 18-14:
A scribble
produced
by Pot-a-
Sketch.

Making Real Meters

Do you want to have the readings from the pots displayed like a real meter?
Figure 18-15 shows a program that does this. Basically all that is happening is
that the analog reading is used to set the angle of a line. This is plotted over
the top of an image of a meter we created in Photoshop on a desktop computer. You can find the program to do this called PotMeter4.py on the website
that accompanies this book and use it as a basic analog input check or incorporate it into you own program.

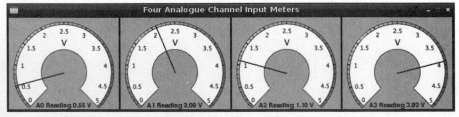

Figure 18-15:
Displaying
real meters.

Making a Steve Reich Machine

Without changing the hardware, you can use these four pots to control
your very own Steve Reich machine. Steve Reich is a well-known modern
composer whose signature sound is one of slow development of a repetitive

motif, often played on one or many marimbas. This program has eight sound samples of a scale played on a marimba, and it plays them back in a sequence of eight notes. After a number of repetitions, the sequence is mutated by replacing some of the original notes with new ones. Using the pot box, you can control the speed of the notes, the number of repeats before mutation occurs, and the number of notes that are changed in a mutation. You can also control whether the notes are playing. An interesting effect can be achieved by disconnecting the A0 input channel — controlling the speed. This then reads wildly fluctuating values and gives the output a bit of a random rhythm. The program is called Pot_Reich.py and can be found on the website that accompanies this book.

However, the magic of this program literally comes to light when you replace the pots with light-dependent resistors (LDRs). As the name implies, these devices change their resistance depending on the strength of light falling upon them. Although the Raspberry Ripple can't measure resistance directly, it's easy to make the LDR produce a voltage by simply putting it in series with a resistor, putting a voltage across it, and measuring the voltage across the LDR with the Raspberry Ripple.

Figure 18-16 shows how this is wired up for one channel. You can replace as many pots as you like with your hand control. We used a cheap LED reading light to shine on the LDRs and then moved our hands over them to change the readings. The code needs a bit of a tweak to adjust for the reduction in range the light controls have compared to the pots. The 27K resistor also affects the range. You might have to change the value of the resistor a little if you get another type of LDR. A program with these code tweaks called Light_Reich.py is on the website that accompanies this book.

Another program on the website that accompanies this book is called Light_Play.py uses four LDR sensors to trigger the notes themselves, like a four-note instrument played by waving your hands over the sensors. You can see a video of this in action at `https://vimeo.com/62776651`.

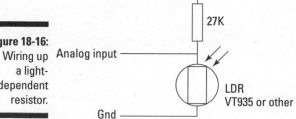

Figure 18-16:
Wiring up a light-dependent resistor.

Taking the Temperature

Finally, here is a quick way to measure temperature. The LM335 is a cheap temperature sensor. In its cheapest form, it's in a plastic package and looks just like a transistor. However, with the simple addition of a 1K resistor, it can produce a voltage across it that is proportional to the absolute temperature in degrees Kelvin. The connection to the Raspberry Ripple is shown in Figure 18-17. The resistor goes from the +ve to the analog input, along with the center pin of the LM335, and the right pin goes into the ground. The LM335 can be clamped to a surface to measure its temperature, or if you seal the wires with silicone rubber, you can measure the temperature of liquids.

Note that the left pin is not connected to anything. For each degree Kelvin increase in temperature, the output increases by 10mV or 0.01 of a volt. Because the Raspberry Ripple can detect a change of about 15mV, we can use this chip to measure to the nearest two degrees. For a more accurate reading with this sensor, you need to use an A/D converter that has more resolution; that is, more bits. To calibrate this temperature measuring system, you need to take the difference between the reading and the real temperature. A simple addition or subtraction of a constant is all that you need to do. The code, called Read_temp.py, is on this book's website. For more on accessing the website, see the Introduction to this book.

Figure 18-17:
Attaching
an LM335
temperature
sensor.

Part VI
The Part of Tens

Visit www.dummies.com/extras/raspberrypi to find out about top ten languages ported to the Raspberry Pi.

In this part . . .

- ✔ Download and install ten great software packages for your Raspberry Pi, including games, art packages, and productivity tools.

- ✔ Be inspired by ten innovative projects for the Raspberry Pi, including a weather station, a jukebox, and remote-controlled cars.

- ✔ Troubleshoot common problems on the Raspberry Pi, change more advanced settings, and connect external storage devices using the Linux shell.

- ✔ Consult our table of the GPIO as you connect your own electronics projects to the Raspberry Pi.

- ✔ Get to know RISC OS.

Chapter 19

Ten Great Software Packages for the Raspberry Pi

In This Chapter

▶ Downloading and playing games

▶ Discovering educational software

▶ Using e-mail, accounts systems, and other productivity tools

*O*ne of the best things about the Raspberry Pi is that you can easily download so many software packages over the Internet and install them. In this chapter, we give you some pointers to ten software packages to get you started.

Before you start, issue the following command in the shell to make sure your software cache is up-to-date:

```
sudo apt-get update
```

The software you run on your computer is as much a matter of taste as the music you play on your stereo, so we hope you use this list as a starting point and then make your own software discoveries. For a full explanation of finding and installing software on your Raspberry Pi, see Chapter 5.

Penguins Puzzle

Penguins Puzzle, shown in Figure 19-1, is a 3D puzzle game where you are tasked with safely escorting a penguin to the exit without letting him fall off the iceberg into the freezing water. You use the arrow keys to move around, press Z to zoom out for a wider angle view, and press R to reset the level. The game has 50 levels to test your mettle. When you've finished playing, press Escape to exit.

Figure 19-1:
Penguins
Puzzle
is a cute
3D puzzle
game.

The game is preinstalled with Raspbian. If you need to install or update it, use

```
sudo apt-get install penguinspuzzle
```

You start the game from the shell by typing

```
penguinspuzzle
```

The software is charityware, which means you are invited to make a donation to charity if you enjoy it. For more information on Penguins Puzzle, see the website at http://penguinspuzzle.appspot.com/.

FocusWriter

Whether you're writing the next blockbuster from your bedroom, or you just need to get your work done without distraction, FocusWriter might be the application for you. It's a word processor that is designed to be distraction-free. Most of the time when you're using it, the only thing onscreen is your writing.

When you move the mouse to the top of the screen, the menus for changing the settings and saving your files appear. To keep your motivation up, you can set a daily goal in the Preferences settings for time spent writing or (better still) words written per day. When you move the mouse to the bottom of the screen, you can see the word count and how much progress you have made toward your daily goal.

To install FocusWriter, use

```
sudo apt-get install focuswriter
```

To start FocusWriter, go into your desktop environment and click its entry in the Office category of your Programs menu.

You can find out more about the application at http://gottcode.org/focuswriter/.

Mathematica

Mathematica is what is known as a symbolic package, or a CAS (Computer Algebra System), and it's preinstalled in Raspbian. It is one of the best systems there is for exploring anything to do with numbers, from mathematics, to complex multidimensional graphics and music.

To get started, go to the desktop and double-click on the Mathematica icon. There is a splash screen and then two windows open: a blank notebook, and in front of that, an invitation to visit three websites. Wait until the CPU usage box in the bottom right is no longer solid green, and then click the notebook to bring it to the front. Type

```
2^8
```

and then hit Return. This means two to the power of eight, but you don't see an answer. You've input the expression into Mathematica, but to tell the program to evaluate it (and give you the answer), use Shift+Return. Your input is shown in bold, and Mathematica's answers are non-bold under it.

Mathematica can expand equations for you:

```
Expand[(1+x)^6]
1 + 6x + 15x² + 20x³ + 15x⁴ + 6x⁵ + x⁶
```

It can plot graphs, such as these parametric plots:

```
For[n=1, n<4, n++,
ParametricPlot[ {Sin[n t], Sin[(n+1) t]}, {t, 0, 2Pi}] // ↵
          Print]
```

Graphical output might take a moment to render, so be patient if necessary. It even plots 3D graphics (see the bottom of Figure 19-2):

```
SphericalPlot3D[Sin[t] Cos[t] Sin[f], {t, 0, Pi}, {f, 0,
          2 Pi}]
```

One of Mike's favorite shapes is generated with the following code:

```
Plot3D[Sin[Sqrt[x^2 + y^2]]/Sqrt[x^2 + y^2],
{x, -6 Pi, 6 Pi}, {y, -6 Pi, 6 Pi},
Boxed -> False, Mesh -> False, PlotPoints -> 60,
PlotRange -> All, Axes -> False]
```

Try it out to see what it looks like! This book's Introduction explains how to access the online materials on the companion website.

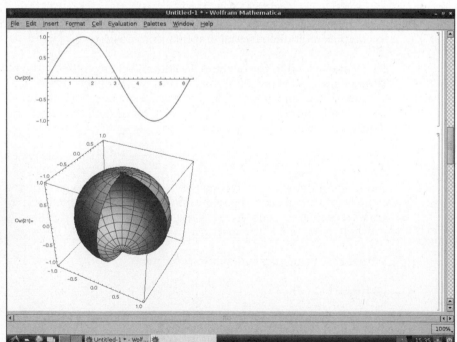

Figure 19-2:
Two example plots from Mathematica.

XInvaders 3D

If you're a fan of classic arcade cabinets from the 1970s and 1980s, you'll have a blast with XInvaders 3D. The game uses line graphics (like the classic game Asteroids), and puts a fresh spin on Space Invaders. The 3D rendering makes the aliens move progressively closer to you, and you move in four directions to line up your shots. It's good, clean, retro fun. Move using the cursor keys and fire by pressing the spacebar.

To install XInvaders 3D, use

```
sudo apt-get install xinv3d
```

XInvaders 3D installs into the Other category in your Programs menu.

Fraqtive

Fractals are patterns generated using mathematical formulae that are self-similar. That means that if you zoom in on the Mandlebrot set (shown on the left in Figure 19-3), for example, you'll find the same shape repeats in its nooks and crannies, and you can zoom in again and again and again. Fraqtive is a program for exploring fractals and generating images. You can save the images and use them as wallpaper on your Raspberry Pi (see Chapter 4). The software has a tutorial to get you started.

To install Fraqtive, use

```
sudo apt-get install fraqtive
```

After installation, you can find Fraqtive in the Education category of your Programs menu.

For more information on Fraqtive, visit the creator's website at http:// fraqtive.mimec.org/.

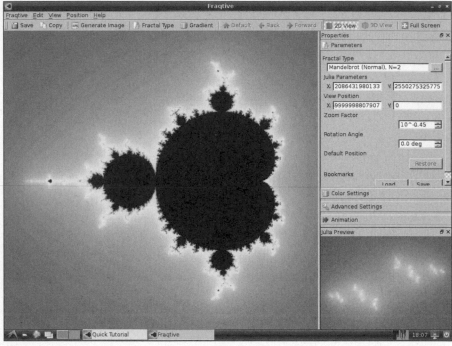

Figure 19-3: Generate colorful fractal images easily using Fraqtive.

Tux Paint

Tux Paint, shown in Figure 19-4, is a simple drawing program for children, with tools that help them to quickly create art on the Raspberry Pi. As well as enabling freehand drawing and the placement of shapes and lines in common with most art packages, it also has a Magic tool. This can be used to create effects such as brick walls, flowers, snow balls, rainbows, waves, and various creative image distortions. The Stamp tool is used to stamp clip art onto the screen, including animals, penguins, hats, food, and musical instruments.

Tux Paint is named in tribute to Tux, the penguin who is the official mascot of the Linux kernel. The application has been created with the help of more than 300 contributors worldwide and has been downloaded tens of millions of times.

To install Tux Paint, use

```
sudo apt-get install tuxpaint
```

Figure 19-4:
Tux Paint
turns every
child into an
artist. And
us too.

The Tuxpaint Project (www.tuxpaint.org)

After you've installed it, you can start Tux Paint from the Education category of your Programs menu.

The official website for Tux Paint can be found at www.tuxpaint.org.

Grisbi

If you want to manage your home accounts on your Raspberry Pi, Grisbi is a free application you can use to keep track of your regular and one-off payments. Although other programs are also available, Grisbi is the easiest one we've tried, both to set up and keep updated. Many banks enable you to download your bank statement in a format that can be used in Grisbi, so you might be able to analyze your financial situation without too much rekeying.

To install Grisbi, use

```
sudo apt-get install grisbi
```

You can find it in the Office category of your Programs menu.

Beneath a Steel Sky

Beneath a Steel Sky is a game that tells a science fiction story about Robert Foster, a boy who survived a helicopter crash and was raised by indigenous Australians in a wasteland called The Gap. Many years later, when Robert has grown up, armed forces arrive in another helicopter, kidnap him, and fly him back to the city. He escapes, and you pick up the controls to guide him on his journey of discovery. Why is he here? Who is in charge?

It's a point-and-click adventure game, shown in Figure 19-5, which means you solve puzzles and interact with the environment using your mouse cursor and clicking objects and people. The left mouse button is used to examine things and the right mouse button is used to take an action (such as opening or closing a door, picking up an object, or looking through a window). You can talk to characters in the game by clicking them and choosing from the provided phrases. When you move the cursor to the top of the screen, the inventory of items you are carrying appears so you can use things you are carrying. To walk through an exit, click it.

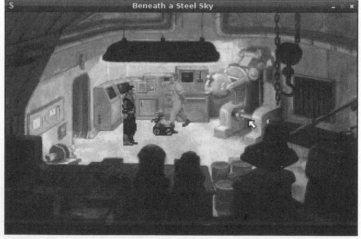

Figure 19-5: Beneath a Steel Sky, an interactive science fiction story.

Revolution Software Ltd

The game's fantastic opening sequence and witty dialogue draw you in, and the solution is available online if you'd like to experience the full story but get stuck on one of the puzzles.

This hit game from 1994 was officially released as freeware in 2003, and is available for you to install on your Raspberry Pi, like this:

```
sudo apt-get install beneath-a-steel-sky
```

It installs into the Games category of your Programs menu.

The Little Crane That Could

If you're a fan of those grabber games at the fair, you're in for a treat here. The Little Crane That Could by Abraham Stolk (Figure 19-6) is a charming game in which you control a crane, solving puzzles such as loading up trailers, picking up basketballs and dropping them in the hoop, and unlocking gates. You'll need patience and precision as you move the crane and its arm to solve the puzzles. If a level proves too tough, you can skip it or restart it, using the menu. Just tap the Escape key to access it.

This game is available for free download in the Pi Store. To get it, double-click the Pi Store icon on your desktop and then search for *crane*. Click the Free Download button to get the game. To see the software you've downloaded from the Pi Store, click My Library. To start a game, click it in your library and then click the Launch button.

Figure 19-6:
The Little Crane That Could: a 3D physics puzzle.

Abraham Stolk

PXDrum

If you're a fan of electronic music, as Sean is, another free app in the Pi Store will bring back memories of 1980s classics. PXDrum is a simple drum machine that emulates the sound of the Roland CR-78 (as heard on Ultravox's "Vienna") and Linn LM-1 (used on Genesis's "Mama") among others. A grid lists drum sounds down the screen and timings across it. To play a specific drum at a particular point in the looping sequence, fill in the appropriate box in the grid. You can download this application from the Pi Store, and start it using the Launch button in your library in the store.

Chapter 20

Ten Inspiring Projects for the Raspberry Pi

....

In This Chapter

▶ Finding the inspiration to get started

▶ Understanding what the Pi can do

▶ Discovering sources of more project information

....

*I*f you've read the rest of the book and worked through the projects, you now know how to program and how to create your own electronics projects with the Raspberry Pi. What you learn next, and what you create with that knowledge, is up to you.

It's amazing to see what people of all ages are doing with their Raspberry Pis. In this chapter, we've collected some of the most interesting and inspiring projects we've come across. Each one has a link so you can find out more and perhaps follow instructions to replicate the project, or get some advice for similar projects of your own.

One-Button Audiobook Player

Michael Clemens has used the Raspberry Pi to create an audiobook player for his wife's grandmother, who is visually impaired and finds digital audio players difficult to use.

This project requires some electronics work, adding transistors, an LED, a pair of speakers, and a large button into a plastic case and linking the button and LED to the Raspberry Pi's GPIO pins.

A Python script enables the button to control the media player software: Pressing the button pauses or plays the audiobook, and holding it down for four seconds sends it back one track.

To change the audiobook, you just plug in a USB drive with the new audiobook on it. It is automatically copied across to the Raspberry Pi, replacing the old audiobook.

Instructions, Python code, and photos are on Michael's blog: `http://blogs.fsfe.org/clemens/2012/10/30/the-one-button-audiobook-player/`.

Raspberry Pi Synthesizer

Music aficionado Phil Atkin has decided that the best use for the Raspberry Pi is to create a synthesizer. He has compared his synth to a Moog instrument, which costs £600 ($963) and only plays one note at a time. His Pi-based synth, on the other hand, can play eight notes simultaneously and costs about £30 ($48). He's working on a MIDI interface so he can connect other instruments to it.

He demonstrated the synth at a Raspberry Jam session in Bristol, U.K., one of many community events that bring Raspberry Pi fans together worldwide (see `http://raspberryjam.org.uk/`).

The Raspberry Synthesizer blog details the complete development of the synth from its start to present day, together with a discussion of some of the issues Phil faced with audio-related elements of the Pi. You can also watch videos of the synth in action. Find out more at `http://raspberrypisynthesizer.blogspot.co.uk`.

Ping-Pong Ball-Collecting Robot

Will Jessop built a remote controlled robot that can pick up ping-pong balls from the floor (Figure 20-1). It has a large fork on the front of it, which you can trigger to scoop a ball into a cage mounted on the robot. It has caterpillar tracks down the sides for movement, and a camera mounted on the top so the person controlling it can have a scoop's eye view of the terrain.

The robot was based on MotorPiTX, a board that sits on top of the Raspberry Pi and combines a motor controller and power supply. The board was developed by Jason Barnett and can be ordered through the shop link at `www.boeeerb.co.uk/motorpitx/`.

To find out more about Will's robot and see videos of it in action, visit Will's website at http://blog.willj.net/category/ping-pong-robot/.

Figure 20-1:
The robot
with the
MotorPiTX
board
mounted on
the right.

Weather Station

When Steve Wardell heard about the development of the Raspberry Pi, he decided that it could be the ideal computer to connect to his WS2350 weather station, replacing his Windows PC. One of the challenges he had to overcome was to find an adapter that would enable the weather station, which has a serial port, to connect to the Raspberry Pi's USB port. He tried a couple that didn't work before finding one with an FT232RL chip that did.

The Raspberry Pi gathers information from the weather station using Open2300, a package of tools for reading data from the weather station. Steve's written a Python script that converts this data into a tweet and posts it on Twitter, and is now looking at using the Raspberry Pi to post weather updates on his website.

On Steve's blog, you can find a couple of articles explaining what he's done, and how he overcame some of the technical hurdles of integrating all the different systems: http://stevewardell.wordpress.com/tag/raspberrypi/.

Jukebox

A wireless jukebox was the first project that Tarek Ziadé decided to undertake with his first Raspberry Pi. The idea is that people can add songs to the jukebox's queue over the local network. It's a relatively simple project that doesn't require any electrical skills.

Tarek's first steps were to add a USB stick to create more storage for the music library and to buy a USB battery to power the Raspberry Pi. All the components he chose were small, so that the jukebox would be portable. Tarek used the default Debian image for the Raspberry Pi, and after some updates to the operating system, including enabling sound (which was at that time turned off by default), he was ready to start creating the jukebox.

His original plan had been to write his own jukebox program in Python, but Tarek then found an existing application called Jukebox that met all his requirements. Jukebox enables anyone to search for a song (by artist, title, album, year, or genre) in the music library on the USB storage device and then add it to a queue for playing.

Since completing his Raspberry Pi jukebox, Tarek has added a miniature speaker, created a Lego case, and made the Raspberry Pi jukebox truly portable. Find out more at `http://raspberry.io/projects/view/a-rapsberry-pi-juke-box-1/` and `http://blog.ziade.org/2012/07/01/a-raspberry-pi-juke-box-how-to/`.

T-Shirt Cannon

David Bryan and Lucas Saugen turned to the Raspberry Pi when they were asked to repair the T-shirt cannon used at the Minnesota RollerGirls' roller derby games. The cannon is used to fire T-shirts into the audience during the timeouts, which last for up to about a minute and a half. They wanted a design that would enable more than one T-shirt to be fired in that period, and that would also enable the cannon to tweet a photo when a T-shirt was fired.

The resulting design uses four clear PVC tubes for the barrels, and compressed air to fire the T-shirts. There are three buttons: one to choose which barrel to fire from, and the other two that are pressed together to fire a shirt. As an additional safety measure, there's a key to disarm the cannon. The Raspberry Pi is used to control the device, with software written in Python that uses the GPIO Python libraries.

To find out more about how the cannon was built, watch videos and download the code, visit David's website at `http://drstrangelove.net/2014/01/raspberry-pi-powered-t-shirt-cannon/`.

Remote-Controlled Cars

Everyone loves remote-controlled cars, which is the reason one family thought it would be interesting to use the Raspberry Pi to resurrect some of their old toys. They've hacked the controllers and connected them to the Raspberry Pi. It's been a useful introduction to programming for their 5- and 6-year-old boys, who now enjoy setting the cars to skid from within Scratch. This project requires some technical skill because the radio controller unit needs to be opened up and connected via a suitable cable to the GPIO pins on the Pi.

You must take two steps to enable the car to be controlled from Scratch. First, you need to have a script running on the Raspberry Pi to listen for Scratch commands and send them on to the GPIO pins. The result is that setting different pins on the Pi exercises different functions on the car.

Second, within Scratch, you need to enable remote sensing and create variables for each action that's supported by the car's remote control — for example, left, right, forward, backward, turbo boost, and so on — matching the variable names to those used in the listening script. These variables are given values of 1 or 0 to turn the GPIO pins on or off.

After this is done, it's easy to use the Scratch interface to create a sequence of commands and set them running. You can see more information and videos about creating a pi-car, as well as racing results, at `www.pi-cars.com`.

Home Automation

One Raspberry Pi programmer, Will Q., has used the Pi to create a web app for controlling lights, using a wireless remote control and switch set to turn the lights on and off. The great thing about this project is that you can control anything that's plugged into a power socket, not just lights.

The most complicated part is using the Raspberry Pi GPIOs to emulate pressing the buttons on the remote control: You'll have to take apart your remote control unit and do some additional wiring and soldering. Will uses a ribbon cable as an interface between the unit and the Pi in his solution.

For software, Will installed a web server called Web2py and a Python GPIO module to run the outputs on the Raspberry Pi. The finished project enables you to turn your lights off using any web browser to send a signal to the Raspberry Pi, so you could use an iPhone or a PC to remotely control your house.

You can find detailed instructions about how Will achieved this project, including the home_lights program code, at www.instructables.com/id/ Raspberry-Pi-GPIO-home-automation/.

If this inspires you, look around on the web for more ideas: Home automation is a growing trend. Projects range from the simple to the incredible. For example, you could turn your house into a Halloween attraction with a spooky light and music display, triggered by a PIR (passive infrared) motion detector: www.instructables.com/id/Raspberry-Pi-Halloween-Lights-and-Music-Show/.

Magic Mirror

For London Fashion Week, Photobot.Co created a photobooth for The Body Shop that's guaranteed to capture your best side. They built three vertical panels that each has five Raspberry Pis and Raspberry Pi cameras in it. Together, they make a Magic Mirror (see Figure 20-2) that compiles full-body portraits of subjects, angled from the left, the right, and face on.

The photobooth was triggered when somebody tweeted the booth to say what color she was wearing. The composite photo, a single image that showed all three angles, was tweeted back to her. The tweet also included a response that was appropriate for the color she said she was wearing if it was one of the hundred recognized color names.

The system used a Mac Mini as the central controller (although the developers say they later found a Raspberry Pi could have done this job too). The controller ran software in Python that listened for tweets, told the Raspberry Pis to capture images and send them to it, and then created the composite image. The controller connected to the Raspberry Pis using Secure Shell (SSH), so it could control them remotely, and access their image data.

To find out more, see www.raspberrypi.org/archives/5275.

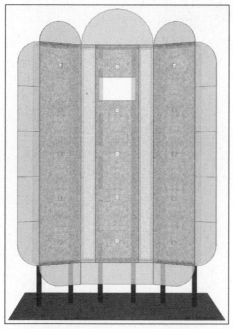

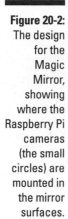

Figure 20-2:
The design for the Magic Mirror, showing where the Raspberry Pi cameras (the small circles) are mounted in the mirror surfaces.

Panflute Hero

At the 2013 Way Out West Hackathon in Gothenberg, Sweden, a team created a game in which you are challenged to play some panpipes in time with the music. They made the fake panpipes by sticking together some short bamboo canes and added Arduino sound sensors to them to detect when the player blows each pipe. Those sensors were connected to the Raspberry Pi's GPIO, and read using the Python package RPi.GPIO. The Raspberry Pi was mounted on the back of the panpipes.

The game runs on a desktop PC and pulls in panpipe music from Spotify, challenging players to blow on the pipes at the right time to simulate playing the music.

You can find out more about this inspired and eccentric project at `www.pixelfolders.se/2014/WOWHack-2013.html` and `www.raspberrypi.org/archives/5924`.

Appendix A

Troubleshooting and Configuring the Raspberry Pi

. . . .

In This Chapter

▶ Troubleshooting and fixing common problems

▶ Adjusting the settings on your Raspberry Pi

▶ Mounting external storage devices in the Linux shell

▶ Fixing software installation issues

▶ Troubleshooting your network connection

. . . .

Many people find that they can just connect up their Raspberry Pi, and everything works fine the first time. Fingers crossed, that will hopefully apply to you!

Sometimes people experience problems, however, or want to make more advanced changes to their computer's settings (also known as *configuring* it).

In this chapter, we show you how to resolve some common complaints and how to change some of the settings. Hopefully you won't need to consult this chapter much, but it might prove valuable if you experience undesirable behavior when you first set up the Pi, or if you have an unusual setup.

 Whatever you're doing on the Raspberry Pi (or any computer, come to that), it's a good idea to save your work regularly. If it does crash, you'll be able to pick things up from your last saved version, which will hopefully prevent you from losing too much work.

Troubleshooting the Raspberry Pi

When Sean first started using his Raspberry Pi, he couldn't connect to the Internet in the desktop environment, although it was working fine in the Linux command line. The problem, it turned out, was an incompatible keyboard. That's something he never would normally have suspected from the symptom he was seeing. For that reason, we recommend you work your way through this entire 12-point checklist, whatever the problem is and how-ever unlikely it might seem that these steps will fix things. Humor us, and you might be pleasantly surprised!

These steps are listed in a rough order of priority, with the quickest tests and simplest solutions first. You can try any of these solutions at any time, but if you respect this order (more or less), you can minimize any expense and hassle.

1. **Be patient.**

   When your Raspberry Pi is busy, it can appear to be unresponsive, so you might think it's crashed. Often, if you wait, it recovers when it fin-ishes its tasks. If it's not doing anything you particularly care about, you can always just restart the machine, but that loses any data in memory and it's not a good idea to reset during operations like software installa-tions (if you can avoid it) because it leaves them half-finished. Note that the Raspberry Pi has a screensaver built in, so you can recover the Pi from a blank screen by wiggling the mouse (when in the desktop envi-ronment) or pressing any key (in the command line). You can use the Shift key, so that nothing appears onscreen.

2. **Restart your Raspberry Pi.**

   Very occasionally, the machine has crashed in a way that we haven't been able to replicate, so a simple reset can sometimes do the trick. To reset, remove the power, pause a moment, and then reconnect it.

3. **Check your connections.**

   Switch off your Raspberry Pi and make sure that all your cables are firmly fixed in the right sockets. Chapter 3 is a guide to setting up your Raspberry Pi, including connecting its peripherals and cables.

4. **Check that your SD or MicroSD card is inserted correctly.**

   If your Raspberry Pi's red PWR light comes on, but the green OK light does not flicker or light, the Raspberry Pi is having difficulty using the SD or MicroSD card. In the first instance, check that the card is correctly inserted (see Chapter 3).

5. **Try a new SD or MicroSD card.** If the red light comes on but the green one still won't, try a new card. We've occasionally had problems with SD cards or MicroSD cards, and with adapters that convert a MicroSD card to fit an SD card slot. You can find a list of SD cards at `http://elinux.org/RPi_SD_cards` that have been reported as compatible with the Raspberry Pi.

6. Disconnect peripherals.

Try disconnecting the USB hub, keyboard, and mouse and then restart. Obviously, this won't help much if the problem you're experiencing requires input devices for you to replicate it, but it can help to identify any device incompatibilities that might stop the Pi starting up correctly. If you need to use a keyboard to test whether the problem reoccurs, try connecting it directly to the Raspberry Pi. You could try disconnecting it again after you've entered the password or started whatever programs you need to test. If the Pi works fine without anything connected, use a process of elimination (connecting devices one at a time and restarting) to identify which one is causing problems.

7. Try new peripherals.

If possible, try a new keyboard, mouse, and USB hub, ideally chosen from the list of devices at `http://elinux.org/RPi_VerifiedPeripherals` that are known to work. Many of the problems people experience are the result of using incompatible devices with the Raspberry Pi, so replacing the keyboard, mouse, and USB hub can resolve a wide range of apparently different problems (including the strange experience Sean had with his Internet connection, mentioned earlier). The previous step can help you to identify which peripherals might be causing problems.

8. Try new cables.

Especially if you're having problems with the network connection and audio or visual output, try using new cables to rule out faulty cables as the cause of the problem.

9. Try a new screen.

If you can't see anything on the screen, but the Raspberry Pi appears to be powering up (the red light comes on and the green light flickers), try connecting to a different monitor or TV. See Chapter 3 for advice on this.

10. Update your software.

Assuming your Internet connection is working, you can update the operating system and other software on your Raspberry Pi (without overwriting any of your work files) using the Linux command

```
sudo apt-get update && sudo apt-get upgrade
```

11. Try a new power supply.

We've put this near the end because it's probably hardest to do, although dodgy power has been reported to cause a wide range of different problems. If you have a friend with a Raspberry Pi and hers works fine, try using her power supply to see whether it fixes the issues you're seeing on yours. Alternatively, you might need to buy a new power supply. See Chapter 1 for advice on that.

12. **Check online for a solution.**

    It's not possible to cover every eventuality here, so if you're still experiencing difficulties, check the rest of this appendix and then see the troubleshooting guide at `http://elinux.org/R-Pi_Troubleshooting`, search the forums at `www.raspberrypi.org`, or search the web with Google for a solution. You're highly likely to find that someone else has already overcome any difficulties you encounter.

Adjusting the Settings on Your Raspberry Pi

The settings that your Raspberry Pi uses are stored in files on the SD card, and many of them are in a file called config.txt that's in the /boot directory. You can edit this file directly to change your computer's settings using a simple text editor called Nano that is pre-installed on your Raspberry Pi.

You might not need to adjust the settings manually. Try running the Raspi-config program, which gives you a simple menu for changing some of the most frequently used options (see Chapter 3). You can run the program at any time using the following command in the shell:

```
sudo raspi-config
```

Raspi-config can help with problems such as

- ✔ **Keyboard configuration problems:** Under Internationalisation Options, you can select your keyboard type.

- ✔ **Camera problems:** Ensure the camera is enabled here.

- ✔ **Audio problems:** In Advanced Options, you can force the audio to use the headphone jack or HDMI output.

The shell is covered in Chapter 5, but in brief it is the first prompt you see after logging in to your Raspberry Pi. You can also open it by double-clicking the LXTerminal icon in the desktop environment (see Chapter 5).

Raspi-config can make changes for you without you having to edit any configuration files, so it's more convenient than editing config.txt yourself, and there is less risk of error too. If the option you need isn't covered in the Raspi-config menu, you need to edit the configuration file manually.

Before you start tampering with the config.txt file, make sure you've backed up any important data on your Raspberry Pi (see "Mounting External Storage Devices" in this Appendix). There is a risk that you could, for example, render the screen display unreadable, which would make it difficult to use the Raspberry Pi to access your files. In that event, you might be able to edit the config.txt file back again using another computer. If you delete the config.txt file on the SD card using another computer and then restart the Raspberry Pi with that card inserted, the default settings are used. This is a useful recovery plan if the Raspberry Pi is useable with those defaults.

Using Nano to edit config.txt

To open the config.txt file in the Nano editor, enter the following command in the shell, all in lowercase:

```
sudo nano /boot/config.txt
```

The Nano text editor, with config.txt open, looks like Figure A-1.

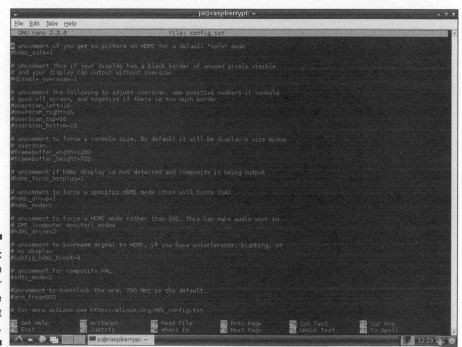

Figure A-1:
The Nano text editor with the config.txt file open.

Use the cursor keys to move around the document. At the bottom of the window is a menu explaining Nano's controls, where the upward arrow represents the Control key. The shortcuts here are different to what you might be used to, but the main ones you should know about are

- **Ctrl+W:** Search for a word or phrase. This option (short for Where Is?) enables you to jump straight to the configuration option you want to edit.

- **Ctrl+V:** Next page.

- **Ctrl+Y:** Previous page.

- **Ctrl+K:** Cut the current row of text.

- **Ctrl+U:** Uncut text, which means paste the text you previously cut at the cursor's location.

- **Ctrl+G:** Get help, which provides more detailed instructions.

- **Ctrl+O:** Write out, or save, the current file.

- **Ctrl+X:** Exit Nano and return to the shell.

The first thing you'll notice about config.txt is that the # (hash mark) symbol is used at the start of most lines. This symbol has a special meaning to the computer, which is "ignore the rest of this line." You might wonder why anyone would enter information into a computer that he wants it to ignore, but this concept is often used (not often enough, some would say) to help the human users of a particular program or file. Any line with a # symbol at the start of it isn't actually doing anything at all, but it's there to guide you as you edit config.txt. Lines like this are called *comments*.

The first two lines in config.txt say

```
# uncomment if you get no picture on HDMI for a default ↵
        "safe" mode
#hdmi_safe=1
```

The first line is obviously intended for you to read, but the second line shows the settings you need to use to turn the HDMI safe mode on. This takes the form that all settings in config.txt do, namely

```
setting_name=value
```

Each setting needs a line of its own. If you wanted to turn the HDMI safe mode on, you would remove the comment symbol (the hash mark) before the second line, or "uncomment" that line, so that the first two lines now read

```
# uncomment if you get no picture on HDMI for a default ↵
        "safe" mode
hdmi_safe=1
```

Don't remove the # symbol from the line of instructions. That remains a comment that's only intelligible to human readers. You should only remove the # symbol from lines you want the computer to do something with.

Just taking out that single hash mark makes all the difference! Save the file (Ctrl+O) and reboot the computer, and the safe mode is activated. You can reboot the Raspberry Pi with the following command:

```
sudo reboot
```

If you need to disable a setting, you can just put a # symbol in front of it again to turn its line into a comment that the computer will ignore.

You can add your own comments too. It's a good idea to add a line starting with a # symbol to remind yourself what you changed and when, in case you need to change the settings back later.

Troubleshooting screen display issues

The Raspberry Pi can be used with a wide variety of TVs and monitors, but that wide compatibility means you might need to tinker with the settings to get your Pi working with your choice of display. The computer should automatically adjust its output to the screen in use, but there might be times when you want to fine-tune its settings, override its defaults, or force your own preference.

If you're experiencing difficulties getting a consistent and clear image, try adjusting one or more of the settings in Table A-1.

Table A-1   Troubleshooting Screen Display Issues

Symptom or Issue	Setting to Change	Values to Use
Image spills off left of screen.	overscan_left	The overscan settings are all set using pixels, the smallest dots the display recognizes. For example, overscan_left=50
Image spills off right of screen.	overscan_right	The overscan is set using pixels. For example, overscan_right=50

(continued)

Table A-1 *(continued)*

Symptom or Issue	Setting to Change	Values to Use
Image spills off top of screen.	overscan_top	The overscan is set using pixels. For example, overscan_top=50
Image spills off bottom of screen.	overscan_bottom	The overscan is set using pixels. For example, overscan_bottom=50
Image has a black border around it.	disable_overscan	Use a value of 1 to disable overscan, like this: disable_overscan=1
Text or other content is too small.	framebuffer_width-framebuffer_height	See "Adjusting the screen display" in this Appendix.
Text or other content is too big.	framebuffer_width-framebuffer_height	See "Adjusting the screen display" in this Appendix.
Picture fails when using an analog TV.	sdtv_mode	The composite video output is NTSC by default, which is used in North America. You may need to change this setting for use in other regions. Valid values are 0 for NTSC, 1 for NTSC-J for Japan, 2 for PAL (used in the UK and most of Europe), or 3 for PAL-M (used in Brazil). For example, sdtv_mode=2
Picture is stretched or squashed on TV. Aspect ratio looks wrong.	sdtv_aspect	The aspect ratio of the image is the ratio between the width and height of the image. There are three valid values for this setting: 1 (for the aspect ratio 4:3), 2 (for the aspect ratio 14:9), and 3 (for the aspect ratio of 16:9). Example usage: sdtv_aspect=2
HDMI screen is blank.	hdmi_force_hotplug	If the Raspberry Pi can't detect a HDMI monitor, you can force it to output through the HDMI connector anyway by setting this value to 1, like this: hdmi_force_hotplug=1

Symptom or Issue	Setting to Change	Values to Use
DVI monitor image is snowy or blown out.	hdmi_drive	This setting adjusts the voltage output by the HDMI port. If you're using a DVI monitor, try a value of 1. If you're using a HDMI monitor, try a value of 2. Example usage: hdmi_drive=1
No audio through computer monitor.	hdmi_drive	Use a value of 2 to force HDMI mode and send the audio down the HDMI cable, like this: hdmi_drive=2
Picture blanks, has interference, or is missing.	config_hdmi_boost	Valid values range from 1 to 7 and define how much power is output through the HDMI port. Try increasing this value progressively. The HDMI safe mode uses a value of 4 for this setting. Example usage: config_hdmi_boost=4
Any problems using HDMI monitor	hdmi_safe	If you experience any problems using an HDMI monitor, try using the safe mode. This sets hdmi_force_hotplug to 1 to force output on the HDMI port, sets config_hdmi_boost to 4 to boost the power, disables overscan, and sets the additional hdmi_mode and hdmi_group settings to a generally safe combination. Those settings are used to override the HDMI screen resolution. For more details on those settings, see `http://elinux.org/ RPi_config.txt`. To use the HDMI safe mode, use hdmi_safe=1

You can change multiple settings at the same time, but each setting must be on its own line. Most of these settings have text you can edit in config.txt already, but don't forget to remove the # symbol.

We're assuming here that the screen display is plugged in, switched on, and tuned in correctly. Before changing configuration settings, it's always a good idea to double-check that.

Adjusting the screen display

You can adjust the width and height of the screen display, measured in pixels. When the width and height values are smaller, the onscreen content appears bigger. The screen display is adjusted using the settings `framebuffer_width` and `framebuffer_height`. To change the screen display size to 1024×768, for example, use

```
framebuffer_width=1024
framebuffer_height=768
```

There is a comment for these settings in the config.txt file, so you can edit the lines that are already there. As well as changing the values to your chosen width and height, don't forget to remove the # symbol at the start of both lines to activate these settings.

Exploring more advanced settings

There are many more settings you can control on the Raspberry Pi through the config.txt file but we don't have space to document them all here. You can find a more detailed list at `http://elinux.org/RPi_config.txt`.

Mounting External Storage Devices

When you plug in an external storage device such as a USB key or flash drive, the desktop environment recognizes it automatically and opens it in File Manager for you. Not so when using the shell. You need to mount the device yourself, which means you need to connect the device to a folder in the directory tree where you want to browse its contents.

If your only goal is to back up your data to an external storage device, it's probably easier to use File Manager in the desktop environment (see Chapter 4).

To use external storage in the shell, we first need to create a directory that will be the mount point for the USB key, which means when we look in that directory, we are actually looking at the contents of the external storage device. You can reuse this directory, but the first time you mount a device, you need to create the directory. You can create this directory anywhere (including inside your home directory), but it's conventional to mount temporary devices in the /mnt directory:

```
sudo mkdir /mnt/usbdrive
```

Next, we need to investigate the device we're connecting. To do that, connect your storage device and then enter this command:

```
sudo fdisk -l
```

The last character of this command is a letter l (lowercase L), and not a number 1. The output looks like this:

```
Disk /dev/mmcblk0: 4025 MB, 4025483264 bytes
4 heads, 16 sectors/track, 122848 cylinders, total 7862272 sectors
Units = sectors of 1 * 512 = 512 bytes
Sector size (logical/physical): 512 bytes / 512 bytes
I/O size (minimum/optimal): 512 bytes / 512 bytes
Disk identifier: 0x000714e9


        Device Boot      Start         End      Blocks   Id  System
/dev/mmcblk0p1            8192      122879       57344    c  W95 FAT32 (LBA)
/dev/mmcblk0p2          122880     7862271     3869696   83  Linux

Disk /dev/sda: 16.0 GB, 16037969920 bytes
32 heads, 63 sectors/track, 15537 cylinders, total 31324160 sectors
Units = sectors of 1 * 512 = 512 bytes
Sector size (logical/physical): 512 bytes / 512 bytes
I/O size (minimum/optimal): 512 bytes / 512 bytes
Disk identifier: 0x1707001e

   Device Boot      Start         End      Blocks   Id  System
/dev/sda1   *           63    31322591    15661264+   c  W95 FAT32 (LBA)
```

This lists the different storage devices that are connected to the Pi. In the preceding example, you can see the first disk (Disk /dev/mmcblk0) is 4025 MB, which is a 4GB SD card, and the second one (Disk /dev/sda) is 16GB, which is a USB key we've connected. The important information we need from this is the device name and the partition number, which is shown at the bottom of the output and is sda1.

To mount the drive for the user pi (uid=pi) and the group pi (gid=pi), we then use

```
sudo mount -o uid=pi,gid=pi /dev/sda1 /mnt/usbdrive
```

To view the contents of the USB key, you can then use

```
ls /mnt/usbdrive
```

To back up your home directory to the USB key, use

```
cp -R ~/* /mnt/usbdrive
```

Fixing Software Installation Issues

The apt package manager should enable you to cleanly install and remove software. If software isn't working, try removing it and then reinstalling it as described in Chapter 5.

Packages often require other packages (called *dependencies*) to work. The package manager looks after these dependencies for you, but in the event they get broken, you can fix dependencies using

```
sudo apt-get -f install
```

Troubleshooting Your Network Connection

In the desktop environment (see Chapter 4), you can easily test whether your network is working by using the web browser. In the Linux shell, you can test whether it's working with the ping command:

```
ping -c 5 www.google.com
```

This makes five attempts to connect with Google and reports on its success. You should see that five packets were transmitted and five were received if the network is working perfectly. If this fails, try substituting another website address to rule out the possibility that the problem is on Google's end. Firewalls can sometimes interfere with the ping command, but this is rare. If the command works, it's a guarantee that the Pi is connected to the Internet.

You can query the network devices on your Raspberry Pi using

```
ifconfig
```

This shows you the information for eth0 (your Ethernet connection on a Model B or B+), wlan0 (your Wi-Fi connection if available), and the local loopback, which is how the Raspberry Pi refers to itself, and which you can safely ignore. If there is an inet addr entry for eth0 or wlan0, it means your Raspberry Pi has connected to the router and been assigned an IP address successfully.

The Ethernet connection should be automatically activated, but in the event it isn't, you can manually activate it like this:

```
sudo ifup eth0
```

You can deactivate the Ethernet connection using

```
sudo ifdown eth0
```

Your Raspberry Pi should automatically connect to home routers using Dynamic Host Configuration Protocol (DHCP), but these tips can help you to identify where the problem lies if you experience difficulties.

If you experience network problems, try a new cable to rule out problems with the physical connection, and make sure your power supply is strong enough for the Raspberry Pi (see Chapter 1).

See Chapter 3 for advice on configuring your Wi-Fi connection.

Appendix B

The GPIO on the Raspberry Pi

*T*able B-1 is a handy reference on how the GPIO pins from the processor for the three hardware revisions of the Raspberry Pi are used. For a detailed explanation of what this means and for more information on how to use the GPIO to connect your Raspberry Pi to your own electronics projects, refer to Chapters 15 to 18.

The Raspberry Pi Foundation has announced that the model B+ represents the final revision of the Raspberry Pi. In this revision, GPIO pins 0 to 27 are all made available to the user. Earlier revisions just have a subset of these available.

Table B-1			GPIO Usage			
	Issue 1			*Issue 2*		*Issue 3*
GPIO	*Access*	*Use*	*Access*	*Use*	*Access*	*Use*
0	P1-03	I2C Bus 1 Data 1K8 pull-up	S5	General use	P1-27	Boot I2C Bus 0 Data no pull-up
1	P1-05	I2C Bus 1 Clock 1K8 pull-up	S5	General use	P1-28	Boot I2C Bus 0 Clock no pull-up
2	S5	General use	P1-03	I2C Data Bus 1 1K8 pull-up	P1-03	I2C Bus 1 Data 1K8 pull-up
3	S5	General use	P1-05	I2C Data Bus 1 1K8 pull-up	P1-05	I2C Bus 1 Clock 1K8 pull-up
4	P1-07	General use	P1-07	General use	P1-07	General use
5	S5-12	Camera clock	S5-12	Camera clock	P1-29	General use
6		LAN RUN-reset		LAN RUN-reset	P1-31	General use
7	P1-26	General use	P1-26	General use	P1-26	General use

(continued)

Table B-1 *(continued)*

GPIO	Issue 1 Access	Use	Issue 2 Access	Use	Issue 3 Access	Use
8	P1-24	General use	P1-24	General use	P1-24	General use
9	P1-21	General use	P1-21	General use	P1-21	General use
10	P1-19	General use	P1-19	General use	P1-19	General use
11	P1-23	General use	P1-23	General use	P1-23	General use
12		Not tracked		Not tracked	P1-32	General use
13		Not tracked		Not tracked	P1-33	General use
14	P1-08	TXD0	P1-08	TXD0	P1-08	TXD0
15	P1-10	RXD0	P1-10	RXD0	P1-10	RXD0
16		Status LED output		ACK LED output	P1-16	General use
17	P1-11	General use	P1-11	General use	P1-11	General use
18	P1-12	General use	P1-12	General use	P1-12	General use
19		Not tracked		Not tracked	P1-35	General use
20		Not tracked		Not tracked	P1-38	General use
21	P1-13	General use	S5-11	Camera GPIO	P1-40	General use
22	P1-15	General use	P1-15	General use	P1-15	General use
23	P1-16	General use	P1-16	General use	P1-16	General use
24	P1-17	General use	P1-17	General use	P1-17	General use
25	P1-18	General use	P1-18	General use	P1-18	General use
26		Not tracked		Not tracked	P1-37	General use
27	S5-11	Camera GPIO	P1-13	General use	P1-13	General use
28		Configuration resistor	P5-3	General use		*Boot I2C Bus 0 Data 1K8 pull-up
29		Configuration resistor	P5-4	General use		*Boot I2C Bus 0 Clock 1K8 pull-up
30		Configuration resistor	P5-5	General use		Not tracked

	Issue 1		Issue 2		Issue 3	
GPIO	Access	Use	Access	Use	Access	Use
31		Configuration resistor	P5-6	General use		LAN-Run output
32		Not tracked		Not tracked		CAM_GPIO1 Camera output
33		Not tracked		Not tracked		Not tracked
34		Not tracked		Not tracked		Not tracked
35		Not tracked		Not tracked		PWR_LOW_N input signal
36		Not tracked		Not tracked		Not tracked
37		Not tracked		Not tracked		Not tracked
38		Not tracked		Not tracked		USB_Limit_1A2 output
39		Not tracked		Not tracked		Not tracked
40		PWM0 Right audio to jack		PWM0 Right audio to jack		PWM0 Right audio to jack
41		Not tracked		Not tracked		CAM_GPIO0 Camera output
42		Not tracked		Not tracked		Not tracked
43		Not tracked		Not tracked		Not tracked
44		Not tracked		Not tracked		Ethernet Clock output
45		PWM1 Left audio to jack		PWM1 Left audio to jack		PWM1 Left audio to jack
46		Input from HDMI		Input from HDMI		Input from HDMI
47		Card Detect input		Card Detect input		Status LED

(continued)

Table B-1 *(continued)*

| GPIO | Issue 1 | | Issue 2 | | Issue 3 | |
	Access	Use	Access	Use	Access	Use
48		SD_CLK_R		SD_CLK_R		SD_CLK_R
49		SD_CMD		SD_CMD		SD_CMD
50		SD_DAT0		SD_DAT0		SD_DAT0
51		SD_DAT1		SD_DAT1		SD_DAT1
52		SD_DAT2		SD_DAT2		SD_DAT2
53		SD_DAT3		SD_DAT3		SD_DAT3

** **Note:** GPIO 28 & 29 use the same alternate function as GPIO 0 & 1, only they are used internally on the board and have pull-ups fitted.*

Appendix C

RISC OS

*I*n the 1980s in Cambridge, there was a little start-up company called Acorn. As you might expect from its name, it grew into something big, in part because it won a contract from the British Broadcasting Corporation (BBC) to provide a computer for a TV computer literacy program.

Over time, this company invented the ARM processor, which initially stood for Acorn RISC Machine (although the company now says the A stands for Advanced). In order to use this processor, Acorn also invented a desktop operating system to go with the ARM chip, called RISC OS.

RISC OS is one of the operating systems you can install on your Raspberry Pi using the NOOBS software (see Chapter 2). In this Appendix, we provide a short introduction to RISC OS to help you start exploring it.

What Is RISC OS?

The RISC (Reduced Instruction Set Computer) processor was a reaction to the CIS (Complex Instruction Set) processors of the 1980s. Processors were being made with increasingly convoluted instruction sets, and the code used to implement them was slowing down the overall speed of the processor. Acorn, and others, looked at lots of real programs and analyzed which processor instructions programmers actually used. Then they made a processor that implemented them. This meant that in terms of the silicon chip, the processor was much smaller, easier to implement, cheaper to make, and ran on very low power. The downside was that the complex instructions had to be done in several steps, but this did not matter because they were used so rarely, and the instructions that were implemented ran a lot faster. Because the chip was smaller, it also meant that there was room for ultra-fast buffer memory built into the processor.

The instruction set of the RISC processors, unlike CIS processors, was orthogonal. *Orthogonal* means you can perform all the instructions using any of the registers (internal memory locations) as opposed to having special registers that only work with some of the instructions.

Thus the ARM chip was born, and this is the processor at the heart of the Raspberry Pi today. But along the way, a complete desktop operating system was developed for the processor, called RISC OS. It had the unique capability to be able to be stored completely in ROM (read-only memory), making the computer turn on almost immediately because little booting was needed. Today RISC OS must run from RAM, but transferring it from the SD card is very fast and the whole boot time is only about 30 seconds. The majority of this time is spent looking for the Internet connection.

RISC OS is available for installation in the Raspberry Pi, instead of or alongside Linux on your SD card. For years, people have been running RISC OS on the PC and Mac using emulators. Now, RISC OS is coming home.

Seven Things We Like about RISC OS

RISC OS has introduced features that have been adopted by other operating systems over the years, but there are still some great things about it that are unique or rare.

Figure C-1 shows the RISC OS desktop with some directories open.

Respectful windows

When you click any part of a window on most desktops, it springs to the front, obscuring everything underneath it. Rather like an eager-to-please puppy, it says, "You want me! Yes, yes, here I am! Out of the way everybody else, they want *me*." With RISC OS, this only happens when you click the title bar of the window. If you click the body of the window, it will get the keyboard focus. That is, you can type into it, but the window does not barge its way to the front. You can even drag a window behind another window. If you right-click a window's title bar, you can move that window without bringing it to the front.

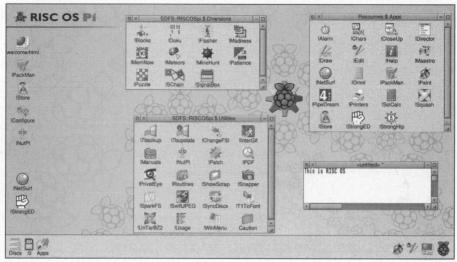

Figure C-1:
The RISC OS
desktop.

Contextual drop-down menus

The RISC OS mouse has three buttons. The center one is reserved for bringing up a menu. The menu it brings up depends on where on the screen the pointer is. This removes the need for a menu bar, thus freeing up more screen real estate.

Automatically resizing menus

All menus automatically expand to the maximum size of the screen, automatically adding scroll bars if there are too many items to display. This is in marked contrast with some other systems that have tiny menu windows with lots of options to scroll through.

Closing the last window does not quit

When you close the last window of an application on some other systems, the application automatically quits. This is often not what you want to do, and you are forced to keep a window open just to stop an application from quitting.

True drag-and-drop

Although RISC OS did not invent drag-and-drop, it pushed the idea to a total philosophy of desktop operation. Although other systems can use drag-and-drop for copying files, when it comes down to saving and loading, you have to go through a menu system to find the file to load or a place to save it. With RISC OS, all saving is done by dragging the save icon to an open directory window, or by simply clicking if you want to use the same directory path. (You'll need to use the middle mouse button to open the menu to find the Save option first.) But more than this, you can actually save data into the open window of another application.

Applications and files can be kept where you want them

There is no special place for applications. They don't spread files all over the storage system: They run where you put them. This also means there are no lengthy install procedures to run. The result is that you can simply delete them as well, and you know all the files associated with that application are gone. There is no wastebasket, so you're not asked whether it's okay to move something to the wastebasket and you're not asked whether it's all right to empty the wastebasket. Just delete and it's gone.

It's easy to see inside applications

All applications are stored in a directory. What makes them look like applications on the desktop is that the name starts with pling (!). This tells the operating system to treat them like an application when you double-click them. However, if you hold down the Shift key as you double-click, the directory opens up and you can see all the files inside. You can look at the source code, you can simply change what the icon looks like, or you can add or amend a help file. Also, you can simply build up your own double-clickable applications.

What to Do Next

The first thing to do is to make an SD with RISC OS installed (see Chapter 2).

To use RISC OS easily, you will need a mouse with a scroll knob. The scroll knob also doubles as a switch when you press it and this is the central or menu button. The left button is called Select and is used like any other select button. The right button is called Adjust and is used for editing or dragging a window while maintaining its position in the order of windows.

When you run RISC OS for the first time, a browser window will open up and you can read a number of pages about getting started on RISC OS. You can read these at any time, with or without an Internet connection, by clicking the Welcome icon on the desktop. This presentation takes you through the fundamentals of how to drive the desktop and is a must if you are a newcomer to RISC OS. Figure C-2 shows part of a page from this welcome presentation.

When you double-click an application to run it, the application's icon appears in the next space on the lower right of the icon bar. To bring up a window or create a new one, left-click or menu-click this icon.

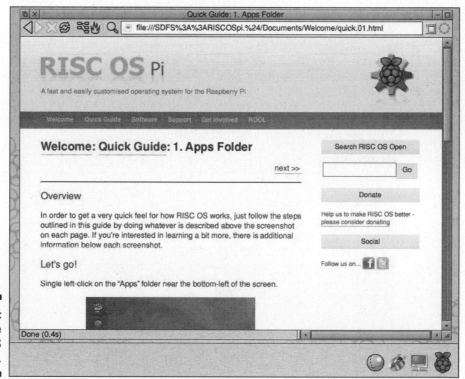

Figure C-2:
Welcome to RISC OS tutorial.

Next play with some of the standard applications. First make yourself a directory to play in. Click the SD :0 icon at the bottom left of the screen (see Figure C-1) to bring up the top-level or $ directory. To make the directory, use the middle button to menu click inside the $ window and move the pointer to New Directory, and then move to the right of that to get a Save window. The small white rectangle in that window is a text entry field. Type **test** and click the OK button. Now a directory called test appears. Double-click that to open up the blank window.

Now to run an application, click on the Apps icon in the bottom left and, from the resulting window, double-click the !Draw icon. This icon will now appear at the bottom right of the screen to show it is running. Click that to bring up a blank window. Now you can play with the drawing tools in the toolbar to the left of the blank window. The second tool down will allow you to construct a polygon by clicking and dragging each line in turn. A double-click completes the figure. Click the pointer tool, at the bottom, and click your polygon. You get a rectangular outline with two small boxes on its edge. Dragging the bottom one resizes the polygon and dragging the other rotates it.

Now move your pointer into the large dotted rectangle and click the middle menu button. Move down to the Select entry and then across and click Edit. The object will be drawn with each vertex highlighted. You can adjust each of the sides if you right-click and drag each highlighted vertex. Next, to save your drawing, use the middle button to menu-click in the !Draw window and choose Save⇨File to get to the Save As window. Now drag the file icon into the empty test directory to save it. This is shown in Figure C-3, with multiple pointers showing your drag path.

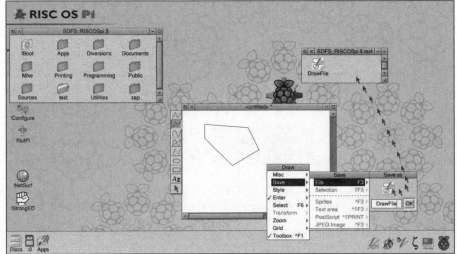

Figure C-3:
!Draw
saving.

You can save files not only into directories, but also into other open windows. To see this, double-click the !Edit icon in the Apps directory and click the icon bar version in the bottom right to open up a blank window. Type in something like **my test text** and press Return. Now, use menu-click to open the menu, move over the Save option to open the Save box, and then drag and drop the save icon directly into the draw window. The text is inserted in the drawing. If you can't see the text, move the scroll bars to locate it.

There is no need to drag and drop to do a subsequent save on this drawing. Just menu click, move to Save⇨File, click File, and the changes are saved.

Further exploration

We suggest that you take a look around the desktop and rummage in the folders. There are lots of goodies, although you might not understand them all at first. Here is a good tip: Point at any icon and press the middle menu mouse button. The second option is a menu concerning the file or application you clicked. Move to this and, if it is an application, choose the Help option. This normally brings up a page describing what that application does. There are plenty of applications and utilities to get your teeth into, allowing you to get an idea of how things work. In particular, we would draw your attention to PipeDream. This aims to offer the same features you would find in word processor, database, and spreadsheet applications.

Also included is a bitmapped drawing application called !Paint, the complement to !Draw. You can add a painting to a !Draw file by directly saving it into !Draw's open window, just like you did with the words from !Edit. There are several much more powerful editors than !Edit with features useful to programmers. !StrongEdit and !Zap are the two leading free applications. The former is included, whereas the latter can be downloaded using the !Store application.

When it comes to shutting down, menu-click the Raspberry icon in the bottom right of the screen and choose Shut Down from the menu that appears. Almost instantly you get a screen inviting you to restart. You can then safely remove the power.

What RISC OS is not good at

Even the most ardent RISC OS fan will have to admit that there are areas where RISC OS does not shine. These flaws are mainly as a result of developments in the last ten years that RISC OS has not kept pace with. Things like a lack of support for Flash and the absence of an up-to-date JavaScript interpreter make web browsing a bit hit-and-miss.

Support for hardware such as scanners and printers is sketchy, and video editing is not possible. Displaying large JPEG images is slow, and handling music files, although possible, is not very flexible.

You don't find many mega applications on RISC OS; instead, the applications concentrate on doing one simple thing and doing it well. The strength lies in the fact that most applications work well together.

Taking it further

If you want to know more about using RISC OS, plenty of material is available online. RISC OS has been ported to various platforms, including emulators for PC and Mac as well as open-source platforms such as the Beagle Board platforms. You can still buy native RISC OS machines in a variety of configurations. A lot of one-time commercial software and books have been released into the public domain over the last 15 years. Despite this, there is still a market for commercial software sales.

However, for a good introduction to programming and hardware interfacing specifically with the Raspberry Pi implementation in mind, take a look at Mike's book *Raspberry Pi Projects For Dummies* (Wiley). It has five chapters covering programming and interfacing under RISC OS.

Index

• C •

• D •

• U •

• V •

About the Authors

Sean McManus is an expert technology and business author. His other books include *Scratch Programming in Easy Steps, Microsoft Office for the Older and Wiser, Web Design in Easy Steps,* and *iPad for the Older and Wiser.* His tutorials and articles have appeared in magazines including *Internet Magazine, Internet Works, Business 2.0, Making Music,* and *Personal Computer World.* He is also a Code Club volunteer, helping children at a local school to learn computer programming. Visit his website at www.sean.co.uk for bonus content from his books.

Mike Cook has been making electronic things since he was at school. A former lecturer in physics at Manchester Metropolitan University, he wrote more than 300 computing and electronics articles in the pages of computer magazines for 20 years starting in the 1980s. Leaving the University after 21 years when the physics department closed down, he got a series of proper jobs where he designed digital TV set-top boxes and access control systems. Now retired and freelancing, he spends his days surrounded by wires, patrolling the forums as Grumpy Mike.

Dedication

Thank you to my wife, Karen, for all her support throughout this project. —Sean

To my wife, Wendy, who always acts delighted whenever I show her yet another blinking LED. And also to the late Leicester Taylor, World War II radar researcher and inspirational supervisor of my post-graduate research at the University of Salford. —Mike

Author's Acknowledgments

Thank you to my co-author, Mike, for bringing his electronics expertise and fantastic project ideas. Thank you to Craig Smith for commissioning us to write the first edition of this book; Katie Mohr, our acquisitions editor on this second edition; to Linda Morris for her editing support on both editions; and to Paul Hallett, our technical editor on the first edition, and Ryan Walmsley, the technical editor on the second edition. Olivier Engler, who translated the first edition into French, provided much-appreciated feedback. Thanks also to Lorna Mein and Natasha Lee in marketing, and to the . . . *For Dummies* team for making it all happen.

Many people helped with research or permissions requests, including Karen McManus, Liz and Eben Upton, Leo McHugh, Mark Turner, Peter Sayer, John Hartnup, Bill Kendrick, Simon Cox, Jon Williamson, Paul Beech, Peter de Rivaz, Michał Męciński, Ruairi Glynn, Stephen Revill, Lawrence James, Bram Stolk, Adam Kemeny, Will Jessop, and David Bryan. We wouldn't have a book to write if it weren't for the wonderful work of the Raspberry Pi Foundation, the manufacturers who took a gamble on it, and the many thousands of people who have contributed to the Raspberry Pi's software. —Sean

I would like to thank Sean McManus for inviting me to contribute to this book and the staff at Wiley for making the process of producing this book as painless as possible. —Mike

Publisher's Acknowledgments

Senior Acquisitions Editor: Katie Mohr

Project Editor: Linda Morris

Copy Editor: Linda Morris

Technical Editor: Ryan Walmsley

Editorial Assistant: Claire Johnson

Sr. Editorial Assistant: Cherie Case

Project Coordinator: Melissa Cossell

Cover Image: © Mike Cook

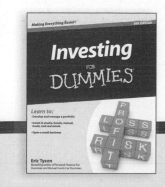
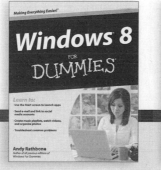

Math & Science

Algebra I For Dummies,
2nd Edition
978-0-470-55964-2

Anatomy and Physiology
For Dummies, 2nd Edition
978-0-470-92326-9

Astronomy For Dummies,
3rd Edition
978-1-118-37697-3

Biology For Dummies,
2nd Edition
978-0-470-59875-7

Chemistry For Dummies,
2nd Edition
978-1-118-00730-3

1001 Algebra II Practice
Problems For Dummies
978-1-118-44662-1

Microsoft Office

Excel 2013 For Dummies
978-1-118-51012-4

Office 2013 All-in-One
For Dummies
978-1-118-51636-2

PowerPoint 2013
For Dummies
978-1-118-50253-2

Word 2013 For Dummies
978-1-118-49123-2

Music

Blues Harmonica
For Dummies
978-1-118-25269-7

Guitar For Dummies,
3rd Edition
978-1-118-11554-1

iPod & iTunes
For Dummies, 10th Edition
978-1-118-50864-0

Programming

Beginning Programming
with C For Dummies
978-1-118-73763-7

Excel VBA Programming
For Dummies, 3rd Edition
978-1-118-49037-2

Java For Dummies,
6th Edition
978-1-118-40780-6

Religion & Inspiration

The Bible For Dummies
978-0-7645-5296-0

Buddhism For Dummies,
2nd Edition
978-1-118-02379-2

Catholicism For Dummies,
2nd Edition
978-1-118-07778-8

Self-Help & Relationships

Beating Sugar Addiction
For Dummies
978-1-118-54645-1

Meditation For Dummies,
3rd Edition
978-1-118-29144-3

Seniors

Laptops For Seniors
For Dummies, 3rd Edition
978-1-118-71105-7

Computers For Seniors
For Dummies, 3rd Edition
978-1-118-11553-4

iPad For Seniors
For Dummies, 6th Edition
978-1-118-72826-0

Social Security
For Dummies
978-1-118-20573-0

Smartphones & Tablets

Android Phones
For Dummies, 2nd Edition
978-1-118-72030-1

Nexus Tablets
For Dummies
978-1-118-77243-0

Samsung Galaxy S 4
For Dummies
978-1-118-64222-1

Samsung Galaxy Tabs
For Dummies
978-1-118-77294-2

Test Prep

ACT For Dummies,
5th Edition
978-1-118-01259-8

ASVAB For Dummies,
3rd Edition
978-0-470-63760-9

GRE For Dummies,
7th Edition
978-0-470-88921-3

Officer Candidate Tests
For Dummies
978-0-470-59876-4

Physician's Assistant Exam
For Dummies
978-1-118-11556-5

Series 7 Exam For Dummies
978-0-470-09932-2

Windows 8

Windows 8.1 All-in-One
For Dummies
978-1-118-82087-2

Windows 8.1 For Dummies
978-1-118-82121-3

Windows 8.1 For Dummies
Book + DVD Bundle
978-1-118-82107-7

Available in print and e-book formats.

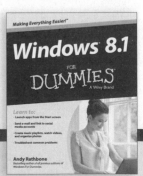